MW01627953

PEOPLE V. THE COURT

The Constitution divides power between the government and We the People. It grants We the People an affirmative, collective right to exercise control over the government through our elected representatives. The Supreme Court has abused its power of judicial review and subverted popular control of the government. The Court's doctrine divides constitutional law into rights issues and structural issues. Structural constitutional doctrine ignores the Constitution's division of power between the government and We the People. The Court's rights doctrines fail to recognize that the Constitution grants the People an affirmative, collective right to exercise control over our government. *People v. The Court* presents an indictment of the Supreme Court's constitutional doctrine. It also provides a set of proposals for revolutionary changes in the practice of judicial review that are designed to enable We the People to reclaim our rightful place as sovereigns in a democratic, constitutional order.

David L. Sloss is the John A. and Elizabeth H. Sutro Professor of Law at Santa Clara University.

People v. The Court

THE NEXT REVOLUTION IN CONSTITUTIONAL LAW

DAVID L. SLOSS
Santa Clara University

Shaftesbury Road, Cambridge CB2 8EA, United Kingdom

One Liberty Plaza, 20th Floor, New York, NY 10006, USA

477 Williamstown Road, Port Melbourne, VIC 3207, Australia

314–321, 3rd Floor, Plot 3, Splendor Forum, Jasola District Centre, New Delhi – 110025, India

103 Penang Road, #05–06/07, Visioncrest Commercial, Singapore 238467

Cambridge University Press is part of Cambridge University Press & Assessment, a department of the University of Cambridge.

We share the University's mission to contribute to society through the pursuit of education, learning and research at the highest international levels of excellence.

www.cambridge.org
Information on this title: www.cambridge.org/9781009651233

DOI: 10.1017/9781009651226

When citing this work, please include a reference to the DOI 10.1017/9781009651226

First published 2025

A catalogue record for this publication is available from the British Library

Library of Congress Cataloging-in-Publication Data
NAMES: Sloss, David L. author
TITLE: People v. the court : the next revolution in constitutional law / David L. Sloss.
OTHER TITLES: People v. the court
DESCRIPTION: Cambridge, United Kingdom ; New York, NY : Cambridge University Press, 2025.
IDENTIFIERS: LCCN 2025006323 | ISBN 9781009651233 hardback | ISBN 9781009651257 paperback | ISBN 9781009651226 ebook
SUBJECTS: LCSH: Constitutional law – United States | People (Constitutional law) – United States | United States. Supreme Court | Judicial review – United States | Constituent power – United States | Democracy – United State | Political questions and judicial power – United States
CLASSIFICATION: LCC KF4880.5 .S56 2025 | DDC 342.73–dc23/eng/20250306
LC record available at https://lccn.loc.gov/2025006323

ISBN 978-1-009-65123-3 Hardback
ISBN 978-1-009-65125-7 Paperback

This book is dedicated to the next generation of Supreme Court Justices. May they have the humility to exercise judicial restraint in the vast majority of cases involving constitutional claims, the courage to engage in aggressive judicial review to correct flaws in the electoral process, and the wisdom to understand when judicial restraint is appropriate and when judicial activism is necessary.

Contents

Figures

Tables

Foreword: Nine Principles for Judicial Review

1 The Constitution divides power between the government and We the People. We the People are the ultimate sovereign. The government is our servant.

2 We the People exercise control over the government through our elected representatives in Congress and in state legislatures. The purpose of the electoral process is to ensure that laws enacted by legislatures express the will of the people.

3 If the electoral process works properly, then almost all laws enacted by Congress are constitutionally valid. In that case, the Supreme Court has a constitutional duty to enforce federal statutes because those laws express the will of the people.

4 Except as provided in 4a and 4b, the Supreme Court violates constitutional limits on its own judicial power when it declares that a law enacted by Congress is unconstitutional.

  a If Congress enacts a law that conflicts directly with unambiguous constitutional text, then the Supreme Court must declare that the law is unconstitutional because the Constitution is higher law. (In modern constitutional litigation, the constitutional text is rarely unambiguous.)

  b If the electoral process malfunctions so that our elected representatives in Congress, or in state legislatures, fail properly to represent the People, then the Supreme Court must act to correct flaws in the electoral process. Such action is necessary to preserve the People's affirmative, collective right to exercise control over the government.

5 In our current system of judicial review, courts rely primarily on the Bill of Rights and the Fourteenth Amendment to protect individual rights from government infringement. Excessive judicial reliance on the Bill of Rights and the Fourteenth Amendment is antithetical to the Constitution's division of power between the government and the People because it concentrates too much power in unelected, unaccountable judges.

6 In the nineteenth century, the Supreme Court relied primarily on international law, not constitutional law, as the primary source of law to protect individual rights from government infringement.
7 The United States is a party to the International Covenant on Civil and Political Rights (ICCPR) and the Convention on Racial Discrimination (CERD). Both treaties are the Supreme Law of the Land under Article VI of the Constitution.
8 State and federal courts can protect individual rights from government infringement by enforcing the ICCPR and CERD. Judicial application of these two human rights treaties would provide an (almost) complete substitute for judicial enforcement of the Bill of Rights and the Fourteenth Amendment.
9 Judicial reliance on human rights treaties enables our elected representatives in Congress to provide a democratic check on judicial power because Congress has the power to override judicial decisions based on treaties. Therefore, compared to our current system of judicial review, a treaty-based approach to protecting individual rights would be more compatible with the Constitution's division of power between the government and We the People.

Acknowledgments

Many people have contributed to this book in a variety of ways. I presented early drafts of some chapters during faculty workshops at Santa Clara University. I benefited greatly from feedback I received from my wonderful colleagues at Santa Clara, including Michael Asimow, Colleen Chien, Taylor Dalton, Adriana Duffy, Eric Goldman, Deep Gulasekaram, Caitlin Jachimowicz, Brad Joondeph, Michelle Oberman, Tyler Ochoa, Britton Schwartz, Nick Serafin, Steven Smith, Tseming Yang, and David Yosifon. Special thanks to Marina Hsieh, who read the entire manuscript and provided valuable comments.

I was very fortunate to receive feedback on drafts of several chapters, both orally and in writing, from leading legal scholars around the country. I benefited greatly from comments I received from the following individuals: Nate Atkinson, Ash Bhagwat, Barry Cushman, John Dehn, Bill Dodge, Paul Finkelman, Ned Foley, Mark Graber, Jonathan Green, Stephen Griffin, Rick Hasen, Kyle Langvardt, Earl Maltz, Neil Netanel, Terri Peretti, Rick Pildes, Harry Pohlman, Ed Purcell, Josh Sarnoff, Miguel Schor, Howard Schweber, Eric Segall, Tim Sellers, and Larry Solum.

Dean Michael Kaufmann has been a constant source of support for my scholarship, financially and otherwise, during his tenure as Dean at Santa Clara. I am indebted to him for his support and leadership. Ellen Platt, one of our research librarians, provided stellar research assistance. Four student research assistants helped me along the way, including Trixia Buscagan, Barbara Chung, Marisa Hawley, and Kyle Vogel. The book is undoubtedly better as a result of their efforts.

I am fortunate to be working with the great editorial staff at Cambridge University Press, including Matt Gallaway, Jadyn Fauconier-Herry, and Laura Blake, as well as Ramya Selvaraj and Megha Sharma from Lumina Datamatics. I thank all of them for helping me turn the manuscript into a finished product.

Finally, I want to express my heartfelt gratitude to my wife Heidi, my son Dakin, and my grandson Bodhi for filling my life with joy.

Introduction

The Problem of Democratic Decay

In his farewell address to the nation, on his last day as President, Ronald Reagan said: "Ours was the first revolution in the history of mankind that truly reversed the course of government, and with three little words: 'We the People.' 'We the People' tell the government what to do; it doesn't tell us. 'We the People' are the driver; the government is the car."[1] This quotation nicely captures a central theory of our Constitution, a theory known as "popular sovereignty." We the People are sovereign because we govern ourselves through our elected representatives. We the People are sovereign because we control the government; it does not control us. (The term "popular sovereignty" means different things to different people. Chapter 1 presents a more detailed explanation of that concept.)

Unfortunately, the reality of government in the United States today is at odds with the principle of popular sovereignty. Today, the U.S. Supreme Court is the driver and We the People are mere passengers. Our elected representatives in Congress and in state legislatures have very little power to accomplish major legislative reforms because the Supreme Court has constructed an intricate web of constitutional rules that severely constrains the power of elected legislatures. Moreover, the powerlessness of average citizens is exacerbated by the fact that we have very little power to elect our legislators. According to Cook Political Report, only 43 out of 435 seats in the House of Representatives are considered "competitive" in the 2024 elections. Only twenty-one of those forty-three seats are genuine "toss ups," where neither party has a clear advantage.[2] Thus, to return to President Reagan's analogy, the Supreme Court is the driver, Congress and state legislatures are passengers who can occasionally wrest the steering wheel away from the Court, and We the People are like babies in car seats who have no control over the speed or direction of travel.

Two examples illustrate the point that the Supreme Court has restricted the power of legislatures by fabricating new constitutional rules that have no basis in the Constitution's text. In 2010, the Supreme Court decided in *McDonald v. City of Chicago* that the Second Amendment imposes binding constitutional limitations on the power of state and local government to enact gun control regulations.[3] For more than two centuries before *McDonald*, the question of what gun control regulations to enact at the state and local levels was a public policy question decided by democratically elected legislatures. *McDonald* converted that public policy question into a question of constitutional law to be decided by the Supreme Court. In 2015, in *Obergefell v. Hodges*, the Supreme Court decided that the Fourteenth Amendment creates a constitutional right to gay marriage.[4] Before *Obergefell*, state legislatures had the power to decide, as a matter of public policy, whether to recognize gay marriage. *Obergefell* converted that public policy question into a question of constitutional law to be decided by the Supreme Court.

The Court's decisions in *McDonald* and *Obergefell* are byproducts of the historical processes of "constitutionalization" and "federalization." Federalization transferred decision-making authority from state legislatures to federal courts. Constitutionalization transformed public policy questions into questions of constitutional law, which are subject to the control of unelected, unaccountable judges. Both constitutionalization and federalization have contributed to democratic decay in the United States; they have weakened representative democracy and undermined popular sovereignty. (See Chapter 2 for additional analysis of constitutionalization and federalization.) In the words of Abraham Lincoln: "[I]f the policy of the government, upon vital questions affecting the whole people, is to be irrevocably fixed by the decisions of the Supreme Court ... the people will have ceased to be their own rulers."[5]

In a prescient article written in 1893, Professor James Bradley Thayer warned that the process of constitutionalization (my term) – which was just beginning at that time – would weaken American democracy.[6] For far too long, the judicial branch has accumulated more and more power at the expense of state and federal legislators. The capacity of our elected representatives to enact meaningful legislation to promote the common good has diminished, in part because the judiciary has constructed an intricate web of constitutional rules that create tremendous uncertainty as to which statutes might survive the Court's exacting constitutional scrutiny. In response, many legislators make a seemingly rational decision to spend their time on fundraising and political posturing,[7] rather than legislating, because any attempt to pass meaningful legislation is fraught with constitutional difficulties.

Data from numerous sources confirms that the quality of democratic governance in the United States has been declining for more than a decade. The Varieties of Democracy Institute (V-Dem) provides several indices for measuring the quality of democratic governance. The U.S. score on the "liberal democracy" index declined from .856 in 2010 to .723 in 2020; our ranking dropped from number seven to number thirty. The U.S. score on the "participatory democracy" index declined from .661 in 2010 to .537 in 2020; our ranking dropped from number ten to number thirty-two.[8] According to Freedom House, "the United States' aggregate Freedom in the World score declined by 11 points," from 94 to 83, between 2010 and 2020.[9] *The Economist* downgraded the United States from a "full democracy" to a "flawed democracy" in 2016.[10]

Democratic decay in the United States is related to two other trends: declining trust in government and increasing polarization. The Pew Research Center has collected polling data to measure trust in government since 1958.[11] The polls measure the percentage of people who say that they "trust the government in Washington to do what is right 'just about always' or 'most of the time.'" In 1964, 77 percent of Americans trusted the federal government "to do what is right" all or most of the time. By June 2023, that figure had declined to just 16 percent.[12] The figure has not topped 40 percent since 2004.

Measuring polarization is trickier than measuring trust in government because there are different types of polarization. For example, one could measure polarization in the media, or in the general population, or in members of Congress. Here, let us focus on polarization in Congress. Political scientists use "DW-Nominate" scores to measure polarization in Congress.[13] The database scores each Member of Congress on a scale from most liberal to most conservative. Higher positive scores are more conservative. Higher negative scores are more liberal. Table 0.1 presents the median score for both major parties in both Houses of Congress for the 93rd Congress, the 103rd Congress, and the 118th Congress.[14]

TABLE 0.1 *Polarization in Congress*

	House Republicans (median)	Gap	House Democrats (median)	Senate Republicans (median)	Gap	Senate Democrats (median)
93rd Congress (1973–74)	+.25	.600	−.3505	+.278	.597	−.319
103rd Congress (1993–94)	+.377	.715	−.3385	+.346	.655	−.309
118th Congress (2023–24)	+.5045	.893	−.389	+.537	.885	−.348

The data shows that, in both the House and the Senate, the ideological gap between the median Republican and the median Democrat increased substantially between 1974 and 2024. During that fifty-year period, Democrats in both the House and the Senate became slightly more liberal, while Republicans in both chambers became much more conservative. The Democrats have been a center-left party for the past fifty years, but the Republicans changed from a center-right party to a far-right party. Consequently, the ideological gap between the median House Democrat and the median House Republican increased from .60 in 1973–74 to .893 in 2023–24. Similarly, the ideological gap between the median Senate Democrat and the median Senate Republican increased from .597 to .885. The growing ideological gap between Democrats and Republicans has made it increasingly difficult to strike the types of bipartisan deals that are necessary for Congress to enact legislation to promote the public interest.[15] Congress's inability to enact legislation to promote the public interest contributes to both declining trust in government and democratic decay.

This book advances two central claims. First, the Supreme Court is partially responsible for the twin problems of increasing polarization and democratic decay. The Court may not be the primary cause of either problem, but its constitutional doctrine has exacerbated both problems. The Court has implemented a set of revolutionary changes in constitutional doctrine since the 1990s. At least some of those changes demonstrate that the Justices, like the public at large, have lost faith in the capacity (or the will) of the political branches of government to "do what is right" most of the time. Consequently, the Court has developed a body of constitutional law that is rooted in a deep-seated mistrust of the People's elected representatives. That body of constitutional law is one of several factors contributing to the problem of democratic decay.

My second main claim is that the Supreme Court could become part of the solution, instead of being part of the problem. However, to become part of the solution, the Court will need to repudiate much of the constitutional doctrine developed since World War II. In short, we need a Copernican revolution in constitutional law to reverse the process of democratic decay and revitalize popular control of the government. This will require a fundamental change in the way that the Supreme Court thinks about constitutional law. For at least the past thirty years, and arguably for the past seventy years, the Court has placed itself at the center of our constitutional universe.[16] Other actors in the system – Congress, the President, the states, and We the People – revolve around the Court, like planets revolving around the sun. To restore popular sovereignty and reverse the process of democratic decay, the Court must place We the People at the center of our constitutional universe, with the other actors (including the Court) revolving around us.

The Constitution creates a system of representative democracy in which We the People govern ourselves through our elected representatives. If the electoral system works properly, so that all citizens "have an equally effective voice"[17] in choosing our elected representatives, then laws enacted by democratically elected legislatures represent the will of the people. In that case, the courts' only function is to apply the laws enacted by our elected representatives, unless a particular law violates a clear, unambiguous constitutional rule. If the electoral system functions properly, then it is an abuse of judicial power to apply vague, ambiguous constitutional text – or vague, general constitutional principles – to invalidate laws enacted by democratically elected legislatures. If, on the other hand, the electoral system is not working properly – in particular, if all citizens do not have an equally effective voice – then the Supreme Court should use its judicial power to correct malfunctions in the electoral process to help ensure that democratic legislatures fairly represent the will of the people.

Chapter 1 sketches the contours of a theory of judicial review. The theory divides constitutional law issues into three "baskets": democratic self-government (popular sovereignty), individual rights, and structural issues (federalism and separation of powers). We the People adopted the Constitution to create a system of democratic self-government based on the principle of popular sovereignty.[18] Current constitutional doctrine is divided between "rights" issues and "structural" issues. Structural constitutional law focuses on the division of power among government actors. That framing ignores a key structural feature of the Constitution: the division of power between the government and We the People. Constitutional rights doctrine focuses on negative, individual rights, not affirmative, collective rights. By ignoring affirmative rights, constitutional doctrine ignores the collective right of We the People to exercise control over our government. The Supreme Court's constitutional doctrine has erased We the People from the Constitution. If one views the Constitution through the lens of the Court's constitutional doctrine, We the People are invisible. We do not appear in the Court's structural constitutional doctrine because that doctrine focuses exclusively on government actors. And we do not appear in the Court's rights doctrine because it focuses on negative, individual rights, not affirmative, collective rights.

This book presents a critique of the Court's constitutional doctrine, but it also charts a path forward. The path forward begins by recognizing that constitutional law, properly conceived, consists of three baskets: structure, rights, and democratic self-government (or popular sovereignty). Chapter 1 distinguishes between "strong" and "weak" judicial review. In a system of strong judicial review, the Supreme Court gets the last word on contested issues. In a system of weak review, Congress has the power to override the Court's decisions by changing the governing rule for future cases. The theory of judicial review that I present and defend in this book can be summarized briefly as follows:

- The Court should apply strong judicial review in election cases to enhance the quality of representative democracy and strengthen the power of We the People to maintain control over the government through our elected representatives. For example, courts should apply strong judicial review to ban partisan gerrymandering.
- The Court should apply weak judicial review for most individual rights claims. Courts can protect individual rights by applying international human rights treaties – instead of applying the Constitution – as the primary source of protection for individual rights. In this way, courts can provide robust protection for rights while still preserving an option for legislative override if Congress disagrees with the Court's resolution of a particular issue.
- The Court should apply deferential review for claims involving federalism-based limits on Congress's legislative powers.[19] The Court's modern federalism jurisprudence does not actually promote the ostensible goal of protecting state autonomy. Instead, the Court's federalism doctrine transfers federal lawmaking authority from Congress to the Supreme Court, in violation of separation-of-powers principles.

The overall plan of the book is as follows. Chapter 1 presents the basic theory of judicial review. Chapter 2 presents a historical account of four previous revolutions in constitutional law. Chapter 3 discusses elections and Chapter 4 analyzes the problem of misinformation (which is a key factor contributing to democratic decay). Chapters 5 and 6 address judicial application of international law to protect individual rights. Chapter 7 addresses federalism. Finally, Chapter 8 provides a roadmap for revolutionary change. It addresses the question: "How do we get from here to there?"

Before concluding this Introduction, it may be helpful to say a few words about global trends related to democratic decay. The V-Dem annual report from 2022 noted that "dictatorships are on the rise and harbor 70% of the world population." Additionally, "the level of democracy enjoyed by the average global citizen in 2021 is down to 1989 levels. The last 30 years of democratic advances are now eradicated."[20] Thus, democratic decay in the United States is not an isolated phenomenon; it is one element of the worldwide trends of creeping authoritarianism and democratic erosion. It is impossible to prove that developments in the United States are causing democratic erosion elsewhere, but there is no question that the United States, as the most powerful nation in the world, has a significant influence on global trends.

In the same farewell address quoted previously, Ronald Reagan referred to one of his favorite metaphors – the United States as "a shining city on a hill." He explained that the United States is "still a beacon, still a magnet for all who must have freedom, for all the pilgrims from all the lost places who are hurtling through the darkness, toward home." He added that, in his vision of that shining city, "the walls had doors and the doors were open to anyone with the will and the heart to get here."[21] The contrast between Presidents Reagan and Trump is striking. President Trump wants to build a wall to keep people out. President Reagan wanted to open the doors "for all the pilgrims from all the lost places."

Like President Reagan, I firmly believe that the United States has the capacity to serve a higher mission: to help spread freedom, democracy, and human rights to other countries throughout the world. To fulfill that mission, though, we must reverse the process of democratic decay at home. We cannot effectively combat democratic erosion in other countries until we get our own house in order. Moreover, without U.S. leadership, the global process of democratic decay will continue, and may even accelerate. It may sound odd to modern sensibilities to suggest that the Supreme Court has an important role to play in promoting democracy and human rights around the world. However, that is precisely what the Truman Administration told the Supreme Court in its brief in *Brown v. Board of Education*:

> It is in the context of the present world struggle between freedom and tyranny that the problem of racial discrimination must be viewed. The United States is trying to prove to the people of the world, of every nationality, race, and color, that a free democracy is the most civilized and most secure form of government yet devised by man. We must set an example for others by showing firm determination to remove existing flaws in our democracy.... The continuance of racial discrimination in the United States remains a source of constant embarrassment to this

> Government in the day-to-day conduct of its foreign relations; and it jeopardizes the effective maintenance of our moral leadership of the free and democratic nations of the world.[22]

The message was not lost on the Justices: nothing less than the United States' leadership of the free world was at stake. Justices Burton and Minton, in particular, were probably swayed by "the Cold War imperative for racial change."[23]

Today, we are once again engaged in a global struggle between the forces of democracy and autocracy.[24] For the past few decades, the Supreme Court has been on the wrong side of that battle. The Court has strengthened the domestic political forces that are undermining democracy; it has nurtured creeping authoritarianism in the United States. It is long past time for the Court to get on the right side of history by aligning itself with the forces that are fighting to enhance the quality of democratic self-government in the United States. It is not hyperbole to suggest that the future of freedom in the world is at stake.

1

A Political Process Theory for the Twenty-First Century

Chapter 1 presents a theory of judicial review that builds on the work of John Hart Ely. In his seminal book, *Democracy and Distrust*,[1] Ely presented a theory of judicial review known as representation-reinforcement or political process theory. Ely's theory built on footnote 4 in *U.S. v. Carolene Products*.[2] In that case, Justice Stone announced a general presumption in favor of a deferential standard of review (rational basis review) for most cases where litigants challenge the constitutional validity of federal legislation. Footnote 4 identified three categories of cases where a less deferential approach might be appropriate.[3]

Ely agreed that a deferential approach to judicial review is appropriate in most cases because he rejected "the claim that appointed and life-tenured judges are better reflectors of conventional values than elected representatives."[4] He reserved some of his sharpest criticism for scholars and judges who advocated an aggressive approach to judicial review to defend or enforce "fundamental values."[5] In his view, under a correct reading of the Constitution, "the selection and accommodation of substantive values is left almost entirely to the political process."[6] However, heightened judicial scrutiny is appropriate when "the political market is systematically malfunctioning."[7] In particular, Ely focused on two types of malfunctions in the political marketplace, which correspond to two of the three categories identified by Justice Stone. First, political malfunction occurs, and heightened judicial scrutiny is therefore warranted, when "the ins are choking off the channels of political change to ensure that they will stay in and the outs will stay out."[8] Second, heightened scrutiny – or what I will call strong judicial review – is necessary when "representatives beholden to an effective majority are systematically disadvantaging some minority" due to hostility or prejudice.[9]

Justice Stone's third category calling for less deferential judicial review involved "legislation [that] appears on its face to be within a specific prohibition of the Constitution, such as those of the first ten Amendments."[10] In contrast, Ely rejected what he called "clause-bound interpretivism" because the Constitution "contains several provisions whose invitation to look beyond their four corners … cannot be construed away."[11] In short, Ely was skeptical of a textualist/originalist approach to the Bill of Rights because he recognized that interpretation of the Constitution's broadly worded rights provisions necessarily involves policy judgments. Moreover, in his view, the Constitution confers authority on elected legislatures, not judges, to make those kinds of policy judgments. Therefore, even when applying what Justice Stone called "specific prohibitions" in the Bill of Rights, judges should generally defer to legislatures unless "the political market is systematically malfunctioning."[12] Ely's theory can be summarized as shown in Table 1.1.

TABLE 1.1 *Ely's Theory*

Malfunction in democratic process	Harm to minority rights	Threats to fundamental values	Everything else
Strong judicial review	Strong judicial review	Deference to legislature	Deference to legislature

Ely developed his theory in part as a response to the scholarship of Alexander Bickel. Bickel's book, *The Least Dangerous Branch*,[13] identified the "counter-majoritarian difficulty" as the central problem of constitutional theory.[14] In his view: "The root difficulty is that judicial review is a counter-majoritarian force in our system.... [W]hen the Supreme Court declares unconstitutional a legislative act or the action of an elected executive, it thwarts the will of representatives of the actual people of the here and now; it exercises control, not in behalf of the prevailing majority, but against it."[15] Writing a few decades after Bickel, Professor Barry Friedman argued "that the classic complaint about judicial review – that it interferes with the will of the people to govern themselves – is radically overstated."[16] Friedman acknowledged that the "Justices today unequivocally exercise more authority than they did at the founding."[17] However, in his view: "We have the Court we do because the American people have willed it to be so."[18] In short, constitutional scholars should stop worrying about the counter-majoritarian difficulty because the Court's counter-majoritarian function is itself a product of the popular will. With due respect, I find Professor Friedman's thesis unpersuasive. The fact that public confidence in the Supreme Court is currently at an all-time low[19] suggests that We the People have not agreed to relinquish our right to democratic self-governance or consented to be governed by unelected, unaccountable Supreme Court Justices.

Unlike Professor Friedman, Ely agreed with Bickel that the counter-majoritarian difficulty is a significant problem, but he rejected Bickel's proposal for judicial passivity as an across-the-board solution. Instead, Ely advocated for strong judicial review to address "those situations where representative government cannot be trusted" and deferential review for "those where we know it can."[20] Although Ely wrote *Democracy and Distrust* more than forty years ago, he was right about three key points that remain relevant today. First, it is essential for constitutional theory to distinguish between the types of cases where judicial deference to the legislature is warranted and the types of cases where more aggressive judicial review is needed. Second, a baseline presumption of deferential review is the only presumption consistent with the Constitution's commitment to popular sovereignty because legislators, not judges, are elected to represent We the People.[21] Third, strong judicial review is necessary to remedy malfunctions in the political marketplace, especially those that undermine popular sovereignty by eroding the power of We the People to govern ourselves through our elected representatives. In light of these points, one of the primary goals of this book is to update Ely's theory for the twenty-first century. An updated theory must account for several important developments over the past forty years, including changes in both constitutional doctrine and constitutional theory, as well as changes in society, information technology, and government.

POPULAR SOVEREIGNTY, REPRESENTATION, AND LEGISLATIVE PRIMACY

The Constitution expresses the idea of popular sovereignty in several ways. The Preamble affirms that "We the People … do ordain and establish this Constitution." The Ninth Amendment refers to rights "retained by the people." The Tenth Amendment refers to powers "reserved … to the people." Even so, popular sovereignty is a contested concept. It does not have a single, fixed meaning. I suggested in the Introduction that "popular sovereignty" means that We the People control our government; it does not control us. This formulation begs the question: How do we control the government? One potential form of control is through mob rule. The Framers feared mob rule, and they feared that democracy might degenerate into mob rule. They created a system of checks and balances that was designed, in part, to help ensure that democracy would not degenerate into mob rule.[22]

Another potential mechanism for We the People to control our government is through direct democracy. Many states in the United States allow citizens to make laws by means of referenda,[23] which are a form of direct democracy. However, the Constitution does not include any mechanism for lawmaking through referenda at the national level. Instead, the Constitution establishes a system of representative democracy that, at least in theory, enables We the People to exercise control over our national government indirectly through our elected representatives. More specifically, the Constitution provides that we elect members of the House of Representatives every two years;[24] we elect the President and Vice President every four years;[25] and we elect Senators every six years.[26] Thus, the U.S. Constitution establishes a system of representative democracy that enables We the People to exercise control over the government indirectly through the mechanism of periodic elections.

We the People also exercise control over our government through the mechanism of social movements.[27] Social movements constitute a distinct form of popular control that is different from mob rule, direct democracy, or representative democracy. First Amendment protections for freedom of speech, freedom of the press, and freedom of assembly facilitate the use of social movements as a mechanism for popular control over the government.[28] Without discounting the importance of social movements, it is fair to say that periodic elections and representative democracy are the primary mechanisms codified in the Constitution's text to help ensure that We the People maintain effective control over our government.

In the late eighteenth century, when We the People adopted the Constitution, the Framers did not agree on a single concept of representation.[29] Broadly speaking, the Framers were torn between what I will call "democratic" and "republican" concepts of representation. The democratic ideal of representation emphasized responsiveness to the electorate. Proponents of the democratic ideal emphasized that "a representative assembly should be in miniature an exact portrait of the people at large. It should think, feel, reason and act like them."[30] In contrast, the republican ideal emphasized that representatives should serve the common good. They should "possess an independence of mind and a breadth of experience or knowledge that would provide a capacity for deliberation that ordinary citizens lacked" so that our representatives would make laws "that would contribute to the prosperity of society and the happiness of its citizens."[31] In short, the democratic ideal emphasizes that representative democracy is government "by the people," whereas the republican ideal emphasizes that representative democracy is government "for the people."

Chapter 3 argues that, in practice, the best way to realize both democratic and republican ideals of representation is to design a competitive electoral process that incentivizes candidates to compete for the vote of the median voter. If electoral rules encourage candidates to compete for the vote of the median voter, then elections should produce a legislative body that conforms with democratic ideals of representation. Moreover, if elections are truly competitive, and legislators fail to serve the common good, then We the People can vote the rascals out and replace them with better legislators. In short, from an institutional design perspective, electoral rules that enhance democratic representation should also help promote republican ideals.

In sum, this book contends that the Constitution relies primarily on a system of representative democracy to give effect to the ideal of popular sovereignty at the national level. The Constitution's Framers began with an assumption of "legislative primacy."[32] Legislative primacy means that – of the three branches of the federal government – Congress is first among equals because Congress represents the people. The norm of legislative primacy is manifested in the Constitution's structure: The text begins in Article I with the legislative branch because the legislature comes first. Thus, Woodrow Wilson said that Congress is "unquestionably, the predominant and controlling force, the centre and source of all motive and of all regulative power" in the federal government.[33] In Justice Scalia's words: "The reason for insistence on legislative primacy is obvious and fundamental: In a democratic society legislatures, not courts, are constituted to respond to the will and consequently the moral values of the people."[34] The principle of legislative primacy means that legislatures, not courts, have the primary responsibility for protecting fundamental rights. As the Supreme Court said in *Hurtado v. California*, the greatest security for "those fundamental principles of liberty and justice which lie at the base of all our civil and political institutions … resides in the right of the people to make their own laws [through their elected representatives], and alter them at their pleasure [through periodic elections]."[35]

Scholars who favor the republican ideal of representation contend that – even though Congress is more representative in a democratic sense (i.e., more responsive to the will of the people) – the judicial and executive branches are better equipped to promote a republican vision of the common good. For example, Professor Bickel argued that legislators "act on expediency," whereas courts apply "a coherent body of principled rules."[36] At this point in the argument, I will simply note that "legislative primacy" is not "legislative supremacy." The theory of judicial review developed later in this chapter gives ample room for the judiciary to serve as a check on legislative power to promote the common good.

INTERPRETATION, CONSTRUCTION, AND JUDICIAL LAWMAKING

Although I am not an originalist, I believe originalist scholars have made a valuable contribution to constitutional theory by highlighting the critical distinction between interpretation and construction. Professor Randy Barnett says: "Interpretation is the activity of identifying the semantic meaning of a particular use of language in context. Construction is the activity of applying that meaning to particular factual circumstances."[37] Professor Lawrence Solum contends – correctly, in my view – that constitutional construction is unavoidable. Judges cannot decide constitutional claims without engaging in both interpretation and construction.[38]

The language in Article II, Section 1, clause 5, illustrates the point. It says: "No person except a *natural born Citizen* … shall be eligible to the Office of the President."[39] In 2016, Ted Cruz sought to appear on the primary election ballot for the Republican Presidential primary in Pennsylvania. Senator Cruz was born in Canada; his mother was a U.S. citizen. Carmon Elliott, a registered Republican who lived in Pennsylvania, challenged Cruz's eligibility on the ground that he was not a "natural-born citizen."[40] The court surveyed a variety of authorities, concluding that "an individual born to a U.S. citizen parent – whether in California or Canada or the Canal Zone – is a U.S. citizen from birth and is fully eligible to serve as President."[41] The Court reached that conclusion as a matter of *constitutional interpretation* by examining the semantic meaning of that particular clause. Having reached that conclusion by engaging in the activity of interpretation, the process of construction (applying that meaning to the facts) was very straightforward because the parties stipulated that Senator Cruz's mother was a U.S. citizen when he was born.

The activity of constitutional construction is not always so easy. "Irreducible ambiguity, vagueness, contradictions, and gaps create constitutional questions that cannot be resolved simply by giving direct effect to the rule of constitutional law that directly corresponds to the communicative content of the constitutional text. Such cases are underdetermined by the meaning of the text."[42] In Professor Solum's terms, cases where the text is under-determinative are "in the construction zone." For cases in the construction zone, the activity of constitutional construction "is essentially driven by normative concerns."[43] When construction is driven by normative concerns, judges necessarily engage in judicial lawmaking. Some originalists resist use of the term "judicial lawmaking" because they think it is pejorative. In contrast, I do not attach a negative connotation to the term. Judicial lawmaking is a necessary feature of judicial activity in the construction zone. I will argue later that it is important to constrain judicial lawmaking, but it is impossible to eliminate judicial lawmaking.

Professor Jack Balkin contends that the Constitution contains three kinds of provisions: rules, standards, and principles.[44] The requirement that the President must be a natural-born citizen is a rule. Some interpretation is required, but application of that rule to a particular factual situation does not require courts to weigh competing normative principles. Professor Balkin says that the Fourth Amendment prohibition on "unreasonable searches and seizures" is a standard, whereas the First Amendment protection for freedom of speech is a principle.[45] For present purposes, the similarity between standards and principles is more important than the differences between them.[46] When courts and other decision-makers apply standards or principles, the text is usually under-determinative. Thus, application of standards and principles typically occurs in the construction zone, where normative judgment is necessary.

Professor Balkin argues that constitutional drafters use the "abstract and general language" of standards and principles "to paper over disagreements that would emerge if more specific language were chosen."[47] I learned this lesson early in my career as a treaty negotiator. In 1990, I was a member of a U.S. government delegation that was negotiating an agreement on treaty language among twenty-three countries. As an eager junior officer, I wanted to nail down specific language to avoid future disagreements. More experienced members of the U.S. delegation explained to me that vague, general language was actually quite useful because it could help us finalize the text of an agreement more quickly, without having to argue about too many controversial details. The same lesson applies to both legislative drafting and constitutional drafting. When the Constitution's drafters chose to frame particular constitutional provisions as standards or principles, they made a conscious choice "to channel politics through certain key concepts but delegate the details to future generations."[48] Thus, whereas rules are designed to limit the discretion of future decision-makers, standards and principles grant discretion to future decision-makers.

Most contemporary originalist scholars agree on two ideas, which Professor Solum calls the "fixation thesis" and the "constraint principle." The fixation thesis holds that "the linguistic meaning of the constitutional text is fixed for each provision at the time that provision was framed and ratified."[49] The constraint principle holds that "constitutional construction should be constrained by the original meaning of the constitutional text."[50] The fixation thesis and the constraint principle make sense when applied to constitutional provisions that are framed as rules. Scholars who embrace living constitutionalism are not being faithful to the text when they resist application of the fixation thesis and the constraint principle to constitutional rules.[51] Conversely, when originalists try to apply the fixation thesis and the constraint principle to standards and principles, they are not being faithful to the framers' deliberate choice to delegate the details to future generations.

The Supreme Court's decision in *District of Columbia v. Heller*[52] illustrates the problems associated with applying the fixation thesis and the constraint principle to constitutional standards. *Heller* involved application of the Second Amendment to a law that prohibited DC residents from possessing handguns in their homes. The Second Amendment states: "A well regulated militia, being necessary to the security of a free state, the right of the people to keep and bear arms, shall not be infringed." The Second Amendment is a standard, not a rule. Like all standards, it requires "people to engage in considerable practical reasoning (which includes moral reasoning) in order to apply the legal norm to specific circumstances."[53]

The Court in *Heller* divided 5-4 along ideological lines. Justice Scalia wrote the majority opinion for the Court's five conservative Justices. Justices Stevens and Breyer wrote separate dissents. Both Justices Scalia and Stevens engaged in detailed historical analysis in an effort to determine the original meaning of the Second Amendment, but they reached diametrically opposite conclusions. Justice Scalia's historical analysis led him to conclude that the right of self-defense "was the central component" of the right to keep and bear arms.[54] In contrast, Justice Stevens concluded that "there is no indication that the Framers of the Amendment intended to enshrine the common-law right of self-defense in the Constitution."[55] Justices Stevens and Scalia were able to employ originalist analysis to support opposite conclusions because the text is under-determinative.

The competing historical arguments in *Heller* support only one definite conclusion: The text is indeterminate with respect to the key question of whether the Second Amendment constitutionalized the right of self-defense. Originalism, as a method of interpretation, is supposed to determine how "the text [was] received and understood by the people" at the time of its adoption.[56] As a thought experiment, imagine that you conducted a survey in 1789 and asked people a single question: "Does the Second Amendment protect the right of self-defense?" Respondents must choose among three options: yes, no, or "I don't know." I suspect that the vast majority would have said "I don't know." That is the original public meaning of the text.

Insofar as originalists want to apply the fixation thesis to the Second Amendment, they are making a category mistake. Language that is deliberately intended to be vague and indeterminate does not have a fixed semantic meaning. The fact that the Second Amendment is framed as a standard, not a rule, means that the Framers deliberately delegated to future decision-makers the task of determining what types of gun control regulations are consistent with "the right of the people to keep and bear arms."[57]

In his majority opinion in *Heller*, Justice Scalia treated the Second Amendment as a rule, not a standard. He said that "the enshrinement of constitutional rights necessarily takes certain policy choices off the table." The Second Amendment, in his view, bars governments from making the policy choice to prohibit possession of "handguns held and used for self-defense in the home."[58] Justice Scalia's analysis is conceptually confused because – driven by his originalist commitment to the fixation thesis and the constraint principle – he construed the Second Amendment as a rule that limits the discretion of policymakers, even though the text is framed as a standard that grants future policymakers discretion to flesh out the details of the Amendment's indeterminate language.

The preceding analysis raises a question: Which future policymakers are responsible for fleshing out the details? In particular, how is that policymaking authority divided between legislatures and courts? As a general matter, the principle of legislative primacy means that legislatures, not courts, have the primary responsibility to flesh out the details of constitutional provisions that are framed as indeterminate standards. However, constitutional standards that address individual rights also implicate the principle of individual liberty. In our constitutional system, courts have a special role to play in protecting individual liberty.[59] The normative issues at stake in *Heller* required the Justices to strike a balance (implicitly, if not explicitly) between the competing principles of legislative primacy and individual liberty. The majority gave greater weight to the principle of individual liberty. The dissent gave greater weight to the principle of legislative primacy. Weighing these competing principles necessarily involves judicial lawmaking. Courts can choose to be transparent by stating explicitly how they are weighing those competing principles, or they can be intellectually dishonest by pretending that they are simply applying a fixed, determinate rule that ties their hands.[60] Either way, they cannot avoid judicial lawmaking when they apply under-determinative standards to concrete, factual situations.

Professor Solum contends that there are three, and only three, "fundamental and feasible options" for constitutional design, which he calls "judicial supremacy," "legislative supremacy," and "constitutional supremacy."[61] The preceding discussion suggests that constitutional supremacy is the correct approach for all constitutional text that is framed as rules. If the semantic meaning of the text is clear, the Constitution controls because the Constitution is the supreme law. However, most constitutional litigation involves standards and principles. For such cases, constitutional supremacy is not a feasible option because we are in the construction zone, where judicial lawmaking is necessary. In the construction zone, are courts forced to choose between judicial supremacy and legislative supremacy?

I suggested in the Introduction that we should divide constitutional law into three baskets: rights, structure, and democratic self-government. I will argue later in this chapter that each of these three baskets involves a different trade-off between judicial and legislative supremacy and that the rights basket, in particular, requires an intermediate option that involves neither judicial nor legislative supremacy. First, though, it is necessary to discuss judicial review.

DIFFERENT TYPES OF JUDICIAL REVIEW

The term "judicial review" can be defined broadly or narrowly. Under the narrowest definition, the Supreme Court engages in judicial review when it invalidates statutes enacted by Congress. Under this definition, the Supreme Court engaged in judicial review in 1803 in *Marbury v. Madison*.[62] This book adopts a broader definition: Courts engage in judicial review when they adjudicate claims challenging the legality of legislative or executive actions by federal, state, or local government actors. Under this definition, the Supreme Court engaged in judicial review in 1796 in *Ware v. Hylton*, a case where the Court invalidated a Virginia statute that conflicted with a federal treaty.[63] The broader definition includes: challenges to federal legislation (type I), challenges to federal executive action (type II), and challenges to state or local government action (type III).

Weak vs. Strong Judicial Review

Ely's theory distinguished between deferential review and strong judicial review. Since Ely developed his theory, scholars have identified a third type of judicial review, often called "weak judicial review," which offers an intermediate option between deference and strong judicial review.[64] In contemporary constitutional theory, the concept of weak judicial review has been developed primarily by comparative law scholars.[65] In a system of weak judicial review, "although courts have powers of constitutional review, they do not necessarily or automatically have final authority on what the law of the land is." In contrast to strong judicial review, "their decisions are not unreviewable by ordinary legislative majority."[66] (Weak judicial review is sometimes called "dialogic judicial review" because it encourages dialogue between the legislative and judicial branches regarding the constitutionality of legislation.) The practice of strong judicial review exacerbates the counter-majoritarian difficulty because it permits unelected judges to override the will of the people, as embodied in statutes enacted by our elected legislators.[67] In contrast, weak judicial review is more compatible with the principle of legislative primacy because judicial decisions are reviewable by democratically elected legislatures. However, as explained more fully in Chapters 5 and 6, weak judicial review can still provide strong protection for individual rights.

When federal courts adjudicate type III claims, they do not need to apply the Constitution as a rule of decision. Instead, they have the option of applying federal statutes or treaties to invalidate state or local government action because statutes and treaties are "the supreme Law of the Land" under the Supremacy Clause.[68] Judicial review based on statutes and treaties is a form of weak judicial review because Congress retains the power to amend the relevant federal statute, or to enact legislation that overrides the relevant treaty.[69] *Ware v. Hylton* is a paradigmatic example of weak judicial review.[70] In *Ware*, the Court invalidated a state law that conflicted with a treaty. As discussed in more detail in Chapter 5, federal courts in the nineteenth century were much more likely to apply weak judicial review, rather than strong judicial review, when they adjudicated type III claims. The process of constitutionalization that began in the 1890s shifted the path of judicial decision-making away from a practice of weak judicial review based on the Supremacy Clause toward a practice of strong judicial review based on the Fourteenth Amendment. Federal courts today could enhance popular control over the government by reducing reliance on the Fourteenth Amendment and reviving a practice of weak judicial review, in which courts apply federal statutes and treaties (especially human rights treaties) in conjunction with the Supremacy Clause.

Similarly, when federal courts adjudicate type II claims, they do not need to apply the Constitution as a rule of decision. Instead, they have the option of applying federal statutes and treaties to review federal executive action because the President and all subordinate executive officers have a constitutional duty to "take Care that the Laws be faithfully executed."[71] The laws that federal officers must faithfully execute include federal treaties.[72] In the modern era, the Supreme Court frequently applies federal statutes to constrain federal executive action. In the nineteenth century, the Court routinely applied both treaties and customary international law to constrain federal executive action.[73] For example, in *United States v. Schooner Peggy*, the Supreme Court ordered the commander of a U.S. naval vessel to return a captured French merchant ship to its owners to comply with the terms of a treaty between the U.S. and France.[74] The practice of applying international law to constrain federal executive action waned in the twentieth century, but it never completely disappeared.[75] Judicial application of statutes and treaties to constrain federal executive action is a form of weak judicial review. When the Court engages in this type of judicial review, Congress retains the power to change the governing law if it does not approve the results of judicial action.

When federal courts adjudicate type I claims, the options for weak judicial review are more limited because the U.S. Constitution is the only source of law that courts can apply to invalidate a federal statute. However, weak judicial review remains an option even for type I claims. The most common strategy here involves the canon of constitutional avoidance.[76] Justice Brandeis's concurring opinion in *Ashwander v.*

Tennessee Valley Authority provides the classic statement of the canon: "When the validity of an act of the Congress is drawn in question, and even if a serious doubt of constitutionality is raised, it is a cardinal principle that this Court will first ascertain whether a construction of the statute is fairly possible by which the [constitutional] question may be avoided."[77] From the perspective of democratic theory, a judicial decision based on statutory interpretation is preferable to a decision based on constitutional law because Congress remains free to amend the statute, or draft a new statute, if it does not approve the result of the Court's decision.

In sum, scholarly debates about constitutional law and constitutional theory in the United States are often based on an unstated assumption that courts must choose between deferential review and strong judicial review. That assumption is false. Courts have a variety of options for engaging in weak judicial review. Weak judicial review is generally preferable to strong judicial review – other things being equal – because weak judicial review is more compatible with the constitutional principle of legislative primacy. By engaging in weak judicial review, the Court can provide robust protection for individual rights, while still ensuring "that the channels of political participation and communication are kept open" for subsequent action by democratically elected legislators.[78]

Antidemocratic Judicial Review

Professors David Landau and Rosalind Dixon coined the term "abusive judicial review" to refer to cases where courts engage in "intentional attacks on the core of electoral democracy."[79] Elsewhere, they say that "a judicial decision is an act of abusive judicial review if it has a significant negative impact on the minimum core of electoral democracy."[80] Landau and Dixon's work is comparative. They examine several countries where courts are arguably engaged in intentional attacks on electoral democracy.[81] I prefer the term "antidemocratic judicial review" because I do not wish to suggest that the U.S. Supreme Court is intentionally undermining democracy in the United States. Even so, the Court has issued numerous decisions that, in the aggregate, have had a significant negative impact on the power of We the People to exercise control over our government. For example, in *Rucho v. Common Cause*, the Supreme Court allowed state legislatures in Maryland and North Carolina to engage in extreme partisan gerrymandering to skew their electoral maps heavily in favor of the Democratic Party (in Maryland) and the Republican Party (in North Carolina).[82] *Rucho* is an example of "passive" antidemocratic review. In *Rucho*, the Court refused to intervene to remedy what was generally agreed to be a constitutional violation by state legislatures.[83]

At times, the Court has also engaged in "active" antidemocratic judicial review. This occurs when "courts themselves are the ones actively undertaking antidemocratic changes."[84] The Supreme Court's decisions in *Buckley v. Valeo*[85] and *Shelby County v. Holder*[86] are examples of active antidemocratic judicial review.

In both cases, the Court invalidated portions of federal statutes that were designed to enhance the quality of electoral democracy in the United States. In *Shelby*, the statute at issue (the 1965 Voting Rights Act) had been operative for almost fifty years before the Court's decision; there was strong empirical evidence that the Voting Rights Act had the intended effect of enhancing democratic governance before the Court held that a key provision was unconstitutional.[87] In *Buckley*, the campaign finance rules that the Court invalidated did not operate for long enough to enable us to reach a definitive conclusion as to whether they would have enhanced the quality of electoral democracy. However, several scholars have conducted studies indicating that *Buckley* had a significant negative impact on democratic governance in the United States.[88]

Chapter 3 analyzes *Rucho*, *Buckley*, and *Shelby County* in more detail. For present purposes, the key point is that the Supreme Court sometimes uses its judicial power to do precisely the opposite of what Ely recommended. Instead of correcting malfunctions in the political marketplace, the Court sometimes engages in antidemocratic judicial review that exacerbates malfunctions in the political marketplace.[89]

JUDICIAL SUPREMACY VS. JUDICIAL IMPERIALISM

Professor Solum says: "The contemporary constitutional order in the United States is currently best understood as a system of judicial supremacy; the Supreme Court has final and ultimate authority to determine the content of constitutional law and does not consider itself bound by the constitutional text."[90] Professor Solum is correct. However, it is important to distinguish between judicial supremacy and "judicial imperialism." The term "imperialism" is adapted from Professor Mark Lemley's essay on "the imperial Supreme Court."[91] As used in this book, judicial supremacy means that the Supreme Court's pronouncements about the meaning of the Constitution are binding on all state and local government actors. In contrast, judicial imperialism means that the Court's construction of the Constitution is binding on Congress, the President, and all executive and administrative agencies. This section contends that we currently have a system of judicial imperialism in the United States, and that judicial imperialism is fundamentally at odds with the Constitution's division of power between Congress and the Supreme Court. However, I defend a qualified version of judicial supremacy. My theory differs, in this respect, from the leading proponents of popular constitutionalism, who generally reject judicial supremacy without distinguishing between supremacy and imperialism.[92]

In his widely acclaimed study of the historical origins of judicial supremacy,[93] Professor Larry Kramer demonstrates that judicial supremacy did not gain broad acceptance as a feature of our constitutional system until after the Supreme Court's 1958 decision in *Cooper v. Aaron*.[94] *Cooper* arose in the context of Southern resistance to the Supreme Court's decision in *Brown v. Board of Education*. State officials in Arkansas declared that they had no duty "to obey federal court orders resting on this Court's considered interpretation of the United States Constitution" in *Brown*.[95] The lawyers representing Arkansas could have cited James Madison as authority,[96] but the Supreme Court was determined to assert its own authority. After citing the Supremacy Clause, which makes clear that the Constitution is binding on state governments, the Court said: "It follows that the interpretation of the Fourteenth Amendment enunciated by this Court in the *Brown* case is the supreme law of the land, and Article VI of the Constitution makes it of binding effect on the States."[97]

With due respect, the Court's assertion in *Cooper* finds no support in the text of the Constitution. Article VI provides that three specific categories of federal law are the "supreme law of the land": the Constitution, statutes, and treaties.[98] Article VI does not say that the Supreme Court's construction of the Constitution is the supreme law of the land. From a purely textual standpoint, the fact that Article VI does not mention Supreme Court decisions strongly implies that such decisions are not the supreme law of the land under the Supremacy Clause. Nevertheless, as Professor Kramer notes, the idea that Supreme Court pronouncements about the meaning of the Constitution are the supreme law of the land gained broad acceptance in the years after *Cooper v. Aaron*.[99] Even so, it bears emphasis that *Cooper* did not establish judicial supremacy over Congress (judicial imperialism); it merely established judicial supremacy over the states.

Chapter 2 analyzes four revolutions in constitutional law. The Court decided *Cooper* during the Warren Court revolution (the third revolution). The fourth revolution, which I call the "Federalist Society revolution," began in the 1990s.[100] The Warren Court gave us judicial supremacy; the Federalist Society ("Fed Soc") Court has given us judicial imperialism. Professor Lemley argues that the Court has exploited its power of judicial review to accumulate more and more power for itself, at the expense of all other actors in the system. In his words, "the Court has begun to implement the policy preferences of its conservative majority in a new and troubling way: by simultaneously stripping power from every political entity *except* the Supreme Court itself."[101] The Court's 1997 decision in *City of Boerne v. Flores*[102] was the key move from judicial supremacy to judicial imperialism.

In *Boerne*, the Court invalidated key provisions of the Religious Freedom Restoration Act (RFRA). Congress enacted RFRA in response to the Court's 1990 decision in *Employment Division v. Smith*.[103] In *Smith*, Native Americans challenged the application of an Oregon state drug law, insofar as the law penalized them for religious use of peyote. Under the Supreme Court's precedents construing the Free Exercise Clause – in particular, *Sherbert v. Verner*[104] and *Wisconsin v. Yoder*[105] – the Native Americans arguably should have won because Oregon could not demonstrate that it had a compelling interest in imposing a substantial burden on their free exercise of religion.[106] However, *Smith* held that facially neutral laws of general applicability, like Oregon's drug law, do not violate the Free Exercise Clause.[107] Although the majority in *Smith* claimed that it was not changing the law, four Justices agreed that the Court's rationale was flatly inconsistent with leading precedents construing the Free Exercise Clause.[108] Congress agreed with the minority in *Smith*. Accordingly, in RFRA, Congress attempted to overrule *Smith* by directing courts to reinstate the compelling interest test from *Sherbert v. Verner* and *Wisconsin v. Yoder*.

Then, in *Boerne*, the Court reacted to RFRA by, in effect, telling Congress to "keep your hands off our Constitution." The central question in *Boerne* was whether Section 5 of the Fourteenth Amendment empowers Congress to enact a statute that strengthens protection for freedom of religion, beyond the narrow protection provided by *Smith*. The leading precedent on that question was *Katzenbach v. Morgan*,[109] where the Warren Court upheld a provision of the 1965 Voting Rights Act that enhanced protection for minority voting rights, beyond the protection provided by the Court's own precedents under the Equal Protection Clause. In *Katzenbach*, the Court said that the proper standard for evaluating Section 5 legislation was the standard articulated by Chief Justice Marshall in *McCulloch v. Maryland*:[110] "Let the end be legitimate, let it be within the scope of the constitution, and all means which are appropriate, which are plainly adapted to that end, which are not prohibited, but are consistent with the letter and spirit of the constitution, are constitutional."[111]

If the *Boerne* Court had applied the *Katzenbach/McCulloch* test, then RFRA clearly would have been constitutional, because that test requires the Court to defer to Congress when Congress exercises its Section 5 power.[112] However, the Court in *Boerne* rejected application of that deferential standard, without directly overruling *Katzenbach*, and replaced it with a newly minted "congruence and proportionality" test that is much less deferential.[113] In *Katzenbach*, the Warren Court viewed Congress as a partner in the promotion of human rights;[114] the Court gave Congress broad leeway to enact legislation that strengthened protection for human rights.[115] In *Boerne*, the Rehnquist Court viewed Congress as its adversary in a dispute over who would exercise ultimate decision-making authority. Whereas the *Katzenbach* Court recognized that the power to interpret the Constitution is shared among the three branches of the federal government,[116] the *Boerne* Court claimed for itself the exclusive authority to interpret the Constitution.[117]

With respect to Section 5, in particular, that claim of exclusive authority is directly contrary to the text of the Fourteenth Amendment, which vests power in Congress, not the Court. Section 5 says: "The Congress shall have power to enforce, by appropriate legislation, the provisions of this article."[118] Nowhere does the Constitution say that the Supreme Court has the power to enforce the Fourteenth Amendment by engaging in judicial lawmaking. Nevertheless, the Court in *Boerne* claimed that power for itself.

The Court's decision in *Boerne* is also contrary to the original understanding of the Fourteenth Amendment, which was designed to "enlarg[e] the powers of the Congress, not those of the federal judiciary."[119] Professor Michael McConnell says: "Section Five of the Fourteenth Amendment was born of the fear that the judiciary would frustrate Reconstruction by a narrow interpretation of congressional power."[120] He adds that "the remedy for the violation of the fourteenth and fifteenth amendments was expressly not left to the courts. The remedy was legislative, because in each the amendment itself provided that it shall be enforced by legislation on the part of Congress."[121]

Here is a key passage from the Court's opinion in *Boerne*:

> If *Congress* could define its own powers by altering the Fourteenth Amendment's meaning, no longer would the Constitution be superior, paramount law, unchangeable by ordinary means. It would be on a level with ordinary *legislative* acts, and, like other acts ... alterable when the *legislature* shall please to alter it. Under this approach, it is difficult to conceive of a principle that would limit *congressional* power. Shifting *legislative* majorities could change the Constitution and effectively circumvent the difficult and detailed amendment process contained in Article V.[122]

I have italicized the words "Congress," "legislative," "legislature," and "congressional" in this passage. If one substitutes, respectively, the words "Supreme Court," "judicial," "judiciary," and "judicial," then the problem with the Court's analysis in *Boerne* is evident. In both *Smith* and *Boerne*, the Supreme Court altered the Fourteenth Amendment's meaning, treating its own precedents as "alterable when the *judiciary* shall please to alter" them. (*Smith* overruled the Court's Free Exercise precedents, *sub silentio*, and *Boerne* overruled *Katzenbach, sub silentio*.) The net result is that, under *Boerne*, shifting *judicial* majorities have the power to "change the Constitution and effectively circumvent the difficult and detailed amendment process contained in Article V."[123] Of course, *Boerne* was not the first case to hold that the Supreme Court can overrule its own precedents. However, *Katzenbach* held that Congress can use its Section 5 power to exercise a check on judicial power when Congress thinks that the Court has provided insufficient protection for fundamental rights. *Boerne* removed that legislative check on judicial power. *Boerne* thereby distorted the constitutional balance of power between Congress and the Supreme Court, leaving no meaningful legislative check on judicial power, and giving rise to judicial imperialism.

Here, I want to emphasize four points about *Boerne* and the rise of judicial imperialism. First, whereas *Cooper v. Aaron* involved an interpretive dispute between the Supreme Court and the Arkansas state government, *Boerne* involved an interpretive dispute between Congress and the Supreme Court. The Court in *Boerne* insisted that its construction of the Free Exercise Clause must prevail over Congress's preferred construction, even though Congress's construction was consistent with the construction that the Court itself applied for almost three decades.

Second, "departmentalism" is the view that each of the three branches of the federal government interprets the Constitution for itself.[124] The *Cooper* doctrine of judicial supremacy, like *Marbury v. Madison*, was entirely consistent with a departmentalist approach to constitutional construction.[125] In contrast, the Court in *Boerne* emphatically rejected departmentalism in favor of judicial imperialism. Under the modern system of judicial imperialism that arose from *Boerne*, the Court insists that Supreme Court decisions creating new constitutional rules are automatically binding on Congress, even if Congress prefers a different constitutional rule that is equally consistent with the text and original public meaning of the Constitution.

Third, in accordance with *Carolene Products* and Ely's theory, one of the core goals of judicial review is to protect discrete and insular minorities. The Court's decision in *Cooper* is defensible on the grounds that strong judicial review was necessary in that case to protect minority rights. In contrast, the Court in *Boerne* used its judicial power to weaken legislative protection for the rights of religious minorities.[126]

Finally, the *Cooper* doctrine of judicial supremacy is defensible as a prophylactic rule that is necessary to give effect to the constitutional principle of federal supremacy. Moreover, there is no dispute that federal supremacy is a core constitutional value. Indeed, one of the main reasons for adopting a new Constitution to replace the Articles of Confederation was to entrench the supremacy of federal law over state law.[127] In contrast, the *Boerne* doctrine of judicial imperialism does not promote any core constitutional values.[128] *Boerne* was a naked power grab by the Supreme Court; judicial imperialism serves no purpose other than judicial self-aggrandizement.[129] The *Boerne* doctrine is antithetical to the constitutional principle of legislative primacy because judicial imperialism transfers lawmaking power from elected legislators to unelected judges.

Larry Alexander and Frederick Schauer have presented the leading defense of judicial supremacy.[130] They argue that judicial supremacy is desirable because the rule of law requires a single, authoritative decision-maker, without which we would have "interpretive anarchy." However, as Mark Tushnet has shown (using different terminology), assuming that Alexander and Schauer present a persuasive case for the *Cooper* doctrine of judicial supremacy, their argument fails to make a normative case for the *Boerne* doctrine of judicial imperialism.[131] Assuming that we need a single, authoritative decision-maker to avoid interpretive anarchy, Congress could perform that function just as well as the Supreme Court. Indeed, recent vicissitudes in Supreme Court doctrine due to shifting judicial majorities suggest that a system of weak judicial review, which would give Congress the last word, might produce greater stability and predictability than our current system of judicial imperialism.

FOUR REVOLUTIONS IN CONSTITUTIONAL LAW

This book presents a normative argument in favor of the "next revolution" in constitutional law. Chapter 2 presents a brief history of judicial review that focuses on four prior revolutions in constitutional law. Table 1.2 summarizes those four revolutions. Chapter 2 presents a narrative account that fleshes out the content of Table 1.2 in more detail. The bottom row of Table 1.2 presents a concise summary of the

TABLE 1.2 *Four Revolutions in Constitutional Law*

	Democratic Self-Government	Individual Rights	Federalism (Congress vs. States)	Court vs. Congress	Court vs. States
Before 1890	n.a.	Weak review (Chapter 5)	Deference to Congress	Legislative primacy	State autonomy
Lochner Revolution (1890–1936)	Deference	Strong review	Strong review	Judicial primacy	Rising judicial power
New Deal Revolution (1937–1953)	Deference	Deference to Cong., strong review for states	Deference to Congress	Legislative primacy	Rising judicial power
Warren Court Revolution (1954–1971)	Strong review	Strong review	Deference to Congress	Partnership	Judicial supremacy
Transition Period (1972–1994)	The seeds of antidemocratic review	Strong review	Deference to congress	Struggle	Judicial supremacy
Federalist Society Revolution (1995–2023)	Antidemocratic review	Strong review	Strong review	Judicial imperialism	Judicial supremacy
My Proposals (The Next Revolution)	Strong review for election law (Chapter 3)	Weak review (Chapters 5 & 6)	Deference to Congress (Chapter 7)	Partnership with legislative primacy	Judicial supremacy w/ congressional override (Chapters 6 & 7)

revolutionary changes that I propose. The final section of this chapter unpacks those proposals in greater detail. Here, I want to explain the division of Table 1.2 into historical periods (the separate rows) and subject areas (the separate columns).

Table 1.2 divides U.S. constitutional history into six historical periods; it draws bright lines to separate discrete historical periods. Of course, the reality is more complicated. For example, Table 1.2 suggests that the transition from the *Lochner* era to the New Deal era occurred between 1936 and 1937. In contrast, a leading historical account of the New Deal revolution argues that the transition occurred more gradually, between 1934 and 1942.[132] No constitutional revolution happens instantaneously; all such revolutions are the product of changes that build over time. Nevertheless, the use of bright lines to separate discrete historical periods can be useful because it enables the historian to draw quantitative comparisons between different periods. Chapter 2 makes use of quantitative analysis to highlight differences between distinct historical periods. Drawing bright lines to separate those periods necessarily involves some arbitrary line-drawing, but the analytical benefits of quantification (hopefully) justify the artificial division of time into discrete periods.

Table 1.2 suggests that the *Lochner* revolution began in 1890 with the Supreme Court's decision in *Hans v. Louisiana*.[133] *Hans* created a doctrine of state sovereign immunity that went beyond the text of the Eleventh Amendment. The table indicates that the *Lochner* period ended in 1936 with the Court's decisions in *Carter v. Carter Coal Co.*[134] and *Morehead v. Tipaldo*.[135] The New Deal period, characterized by a liberal reaction to the conservative jurisprudence of the *Lochner* era, began in 1937 with decisions in *West Coast Hotel v. Parrish*[136] and *NLRB v. Jones & Laughlin Steel Corp.*[137] Table 1.2 marks the end of the New Deal era in 1953 – the year that President Eisenhower appointed Earl Warren as Chief Justice.

The Warren Court revolution began in 1954 with the Court's decision in *Brown v. Board of Education*.[138] Table 1.2 links the end of the Warren Court to the retirement of Justices Black and Harlan in 1971, even though Warren Burger replaced Earl Warren as Chief Justice in 1969. Table 1.2 identifies the period from 1972 to 1994 as a transition period. The period begins with the appointments of Justices Powell and Rehnquist in 1972, which created a conservative majority on the Court for the first time since 1936. Although constitutional doctrine changed substantially during this period – relative to the Warren Court era – those changes did not amount to a constitutional revolution. Reasonable people may disagree about the appropriate point to mark the beginning of the Federalist Society revolution. (See Chapter 2, pp. 51–52 for an explanation of that terminology.) Table 1.2 dates the most recent revolution to the Court's 1995 decision in *United States v. Lopez*,[139] which revived strong judicial review to enforce federalism-based limits on the Commerce Power for the first time since the *Lochner* era.[140] The Federalist Society revolution is continuing as I write this book; Table 1.2 marks the endpoint in 2023 solely for the purpose of quantitative analysis.

I suggested in the Introduction that constitutional doctrine should be divided into three baskets: individual rights, structural issues, and democratic self-government (or popular sovereignty). The first three columns in Table 1.2 correspond to those three baskets, except that this book's analysis of structural issues focuses primarily on federalism.[141] In accordance with the preceding analysis of the distinction between judicial imperialism and judicial supremacy, the two right-hand columns in Table 1.2 distinguish between the Court's relationship with Congress and the Court's relationship with state governments.

Chapter 2 presents a more detailed analysis of the history of judicial review, including a defense of the historical claims summarized in Table 1.2. Here, I want to emphasize three key takeaways from that table. First, although this book proposes a revolution in constitutional doctrine, the proposed revolution is not as "revolutionary" as it might initially appear, because there have been four major revolutions in constitutional doctrine over the past 140 years: in the 1890s, in the 1930s, in the 1950s, and in the 1990s. In light of that history, a future constitutional revolution seems almost inevitable.

Second, a careful look at Table 1.2 shows that there is historical precedent for this book's recommended approach in each of the subject areas corresponding to the five columns. Strong judicial review for election law cases finds support in the Warren Court era. Weak judicial review for individual rights claims was the dominant approach in the nineteenth century. Deference to Congress on federalism issues has been the dominant approach for most of U.S. history. Constitutional doctrine was broadly consistent with the norm of legislative primacy in the nineteenth century and during the New Deal era. In the right-hand column, my proposal for judicial supremacy with the option for congressional override may appear to be novel based on the summary information in Table 1.2, but the more detailed analysis in later chapters shows that there is also historical precedent for this approach.

Finally, the revolution that I advocate is actually more radical, in one respect, than any of the previous constitutional revolutions summarized in Table 1.2. Most of the prior revolutions involved changes from the immediately preceding period in only three or four subject areas. In contrast, this book advocates a modified approach to judicial review in all five subject areas, compared to the Federalist Society period. Although my proposal is revolutionary in that respect, this book contends that radical change is necessary to rescue the American body politic from the current pathology of democratic decay.

POLITICAL PROCESS THEORY FOR AN AGE OF DEMOCRATIC DECAY

It is now possible to present a concise summary of the book's core theory, which consists of three main claims. First, courts should apply strong judicial review in at least some election law cases to help preserve the power of We the People to exercise control over our government. Second, courts should apply weak judicial review for most individual rights claims. Third, courts should apply deferential review for all claims that seek to impose federalism-based limits on Congress's legislative powers. Table 1.3 summarizes the theory and compares it to Ely's theory and to current Supreme Court doctrine.

TABLE 1.3 *An Updated Political Process Theory*

	Democratic Self-Government	Individual Rights	Federalism
Ely's Theory	Strong judicial review to remedy political malfunctions	Strong review for minority rights; deference for fundamental rights	Deference to legislature
Current Doctrine	Deference to legislature; some antidemocratic review	Strong judicial review	Strong judicial review
An Updated Theory	Strong judicial review to remedy political malfunctions	Weak judicial review	Deference to legislature

Preserving Popular Control over the Government

As shown in the left-hand column in Table 1.3, I fully endorse Ely's view that strong judicial review is necessary to correct malfunctions in the political marketplace. More precisely, strong judicial review of election-related laws is necessary in some cases to preserve the Constitution's division of power between citizens and the government, and to help ensure that We the People exercise effective control over the government.

Here, it is important to highlight two key points. First, democratic political theory supports democracy-enhancing judicial review. As Thomas Jefferson wrote in the Declaration of Independence, it is "self-evident" that governments "deriv[e] their just powers from the consent of the governed."[142] I noted in the Introduction that only about 10 percent of the seats in the House of Representatives are considered "competitive" in the 2024 congressional elections.[143] If We the People do not have an effective voice in choosing our elected representatives, because the vast majority of legislative elections are not competitive, then our consent to be governed by the laws enacted by the legislature is purely illusory. Strong judicial review of election-related laws is necessary to help ensure that We the People have an effective voice in choosing our elected representatives.

Second, at this particular moment in history – when the United States is undergoing a period of rapid democratic decay[144] – it is vitally important for the Supreme Court to exercise its judicial power for the purpose of combatting the process of democratic decay, rather than accelerating it. One way for the Court to combat democratic decay is to apply strong judicial review to election-related laws to help ensure that We the People exercise effective control over the government. This will require reconceptualizing structural constitutional law to focus on the division of power between the government and The People, rather than focusing exclusively on the division of power among various government actors. Textual support for this approach can be found, *inter alia*, in the Ninth Amendment (which refers to rights "retained by the people"),[145] the Tenth Amendment (which refers to rights "reserved to … the people"),[146] and in Article IV, Section 4, which provides that "the United States shall guarantee to every State in this Union a Republican form of government."[147]

Current Supreme Court doctrine tends to undermine popular control over the government, rather than bolstering that control. Two distinct doctrinal areas are especially important here: doctrines related to the conduct of elections and First Amendment doctrine related to the information ecosystem. I have already suggested that the Court's decisions in *Buckley v. Valeo*[148] (campaign finance), *Shelby County v. Holder*[149] (Voting Rights Act), and *Rucho v. Common Cause*[150] (partisan gerrymandering) are examples of antidemocratic judicial review. All three decisions undermine the Constitution's division of power between the people and the government by impairing the power of We the People to exercise control over our government. Chapter 3 develops this argument in greater detail. Chapter 3 also explains how the Court can exercise strong judicial review, modeled on decisions such as *Reynolds v. Sims*,[151] to help ensure that We the People have a more effective voice in choosing our elected representatives.

Chapter 4 focuses on the information ecosystem. A healthy democracy requires a healthy information ecosystem. We the People cannot exercise responsible control over our government if we do not have accurate information. Therefore, one of the core purposes of judicial review in the modern digital age should be to nurture the growth of an information ecosystem in which truth prevails over lies in the marketplace of ideas. Instead, the Supreme Court has weaponized the First Amendment[152] to help create an information ecosystem in which lies prevail over truth.[153] From the 1930s until 1987, the Federal Communications Commission (FCC) applied a set of rules known as the fairness doctrine. In 1969, in *Red Lion Broadcasting v. FCC*, the Supreme Court ruled unanimously that the fairness doctrine did not violate the First Amendment.[154] However, less than two decades later, in *Syracuse Peace Council*, the FCC repudiated the fairness doctrine, concluding that the doctrine does violate the First Amendment.[155] Surprisingly, the Supreme Court allowed that FCC decision to stand,[156] despite the obvious conflict between the FCC ruling and the Court's earlier decision in *Red Lion*. The Court's failure to reverse the FCC decision – an example of passive, antidemocratic judicial review – is largely responsible for the current dysfunction in our information ecosystem.[157] The Court exacerbated the problem in *U.S. v. Alvarez*, where it suggested (but did not hold) that the First Amendment protects the right to disseminate lies in roughly the same way that it protects the right to disseminate truthful statements.[158]

The Supreme Court cannot, by itself, create an information ecosystem in which truth prevails over lies. Federal legislation is needed to restrict the ongoing electronic amplification of lies that is undermining American democracy.[159] However, the Court can and should revise its First Amendment doctrine to remove the constitutional handcuffs that currently prevent Congress from enacting effective legislation in this area. In particular, the Court should repudiate the libertarian approach to the First Amendment that has dominated Supreme Court thinking in recent decades, and embrace what scholars have called a "Madisonian approach" to the First Amendment.[160] Chapter 4 develops this argument in more detail.

It bears emphasis that the theory presented in this book calls for a revolutionary change in Supreme Court doctrine. The Court's current approach to popular control over the government vacillates between passive, antidemocratic judicial review (as in *Rucho v. Common Cause* and *Syracuse Peace Council*) and active, antidemocratic judicial review (as in *Buckley v. Valeo* and *Shelby County v. Holder*). For the Supreme Court to make a positive contribution to reversing the process of democratic decay in the United States, it will need to rethink structural constitutional law to emphasize the division of power between the government and We the People. And it will need to rethink its rights jurisprudence to emphasize the affirmative, collective right of We the People to exercise control over our government.

Individual Rights

In the modern era, the Supreme Court routinely applies the Bill of Rights and the Fourteenth Amendment to protect individual rights. The idea that the Court must apply the Constitution aggressively to protect both minority rights and fundamental rights has become deeply rooted in American legal and political culture. Even so, that idea is fundamentally misguided. During the first century of American constitutional history, the Court routinely applied statutes, international law, and common law – but rarely constitutional law – to protect individual rights.[161] (Chapter 2 presents data to support this claim.) The nineteenth-century approach was consistent with the Constitution's commitment to legislative primacy. Under that approach, the people's elected representatives had the last word on most major public policy controversies because Congress retained the power to override judicial decisions based on statutes and international law. In contrast, the modern system of judicial imperialism is at odds with the principle of legislative primacy because it gives unelected judges the last word on major public policy controversies. Moreover, strong judicial review is not necessary to protect individual rights because the Supreme Court in the twenty-first century can provide robust protection for individual rights by applying federal statutes and human rights treaties in accordance with a system of weak judicial review.

Ely's theory drew a sharp distinction between "minority rights" and "fundamental rights" (which he called "fundamental values"). I group those two sets of issues together under the label of "individual rights" and I advocate a system of weak judicial review for both sets of rights.

Ely believed that strong judicial review was necessary to protect minority rights. The basic theory is intuitively appealing: The democratic process does not provide adequate protection for minority rights because minorities are systematically under-represented in the political process. Therefore, strong judicial review is necessary to correct a flaw in the nature of representative government.[162] Although Ely's argument is theoretically plausible, judicial practice for the past few decades runs counter to the theory. Since the 1990s, the Supreme Court has consistently undermined minority rights by invalidating legislation designed to protect minorities. Leading examples include *Shelby County v. Holder*,[163] *Parents Involved in Community Schools v. Seattle School Dist. No. 1*,[164] and *City of Boerne v. Flores*.[165] One lesson from these cases is clear: When legislatures enact laws designed to protect minority rights, courts should defer to our elected representatives. There is no good reason for courts to invalidate laws designed to protect racial or religious minorities.

But what if legislative or executive officials discriminate against racial or religious minorities? Both Congress and state legislatures have enacted numerous statutes prohibiting such discriminatory conduct.[166] Moreover, the United States is now a party to two major international human rights treaties that provide broad protection against government discrimination: the Convention on Elimination of Racial Discrimination (CERD)[167] and the International Covenant on Civil and Political Rights (ICCPR).[168] Like nineteenth-century courts, modern courts should enforce those treaties and statutes aggressively to protect discrete and insular minorities. (Chapter 5 documents the fact that federal courts in the nineteenth century routinely applied treaties to protect both minority rights and fundamental rights from government infringement.) If Congress responds by enacting legislation to override human rights treaties, or to weaken protections under federal civil rights statutes, the primary remedy under our constitutional system is to "vote the rascals out." However, if we can correct the flaws in our electoral system and our information ecosystem discussed in Chapters 3 and 4, I am confident that the American people will not elect legislative majorities at the national level who would pass laws to weaken existing statutory and treaty-based protections for minority rights. Chapter 6 analyzes minority rights in greater detail.

Ely believed that courts should defer to legislatures in cases involving claims of fundamental rights, such as abortion rights and gun rights.[169] Neither women nor gun owners are "discrete and insular minorities."[170] Both women and gun owners have the capacity to mobilize politically to use the democratic process to promote their interests (assuming that we can correct key malfunctions in the political marketplace). Ely was essentially right in this respect. His argument carries even more force after U.S. ratification of the ICCPR in 1992.[171] The ICCPR provides broad protection for universally recognized human rights, including the right to marry and the right of privacy. (Neither the right to marry nor the right of privacy is explicitly mentioned in the U.S. Constitution. Both are explicitly included in the ICCPR.[172])

Under Article VI of the Constitution, the ICCPR is the "supreme law of the land; and the judges in every state shall be bound thereby."[173]

However, when the United States ratified the ICCPR, we added a declaration that the treaty's substantive provisions are "not self-executing."[174] The non-self-executing declaration was intended, among other things, to prevent U.S. courts from applying the ICCPR to override state law. The underlying theory is that it is more "legitimate" for courts to apply the Constitution, and not treaties, to override state law.[175] However, that theory is precisely backward. Courts should apply the ICCPR to protect fundamental rights because Congress can provide a democratic check on judicial power when they do so. Congress can enact laws to override judicial decisions based on the ICCPR.[176] In contrast, Congress cannot enact laws to override judicial decisions based on the Constitution. Therefore, if we want to restore a system of judicial review that is consistent with the Constitution's core commitment to legislative primacy, we need a revolution in American legal culture to reduce judicial reliance on the Constitution, and increase judicial reliance on human rights treaties, as a source of protection for fundamental human rights. Chapter 6 develops this argument in greater detail.

Federalism

Professor Herbert Wechsler published an influential article in 1954 on the "political safeguards of federalism."[177] Wechsler acknowledged that the Constitution divides power between the states and the federal government. However, he argued forcefully that the Supreme Court should not apply strong judicial review (my term) to protect state autonomy from Congress's legislative power because states have ample resources to protect themselves from congressional overreach through their participation in the federal legislative process.[178] Wechsler's political safeguards theory reflected a broad national consensus that prevailed from 1937 until the 1990s. Indeed, between 1937 and 1994, the Supreme Court did not issue a single decision that invalidated federal legislation on the grounds that it exceeded the scope of Congress's power under the Commerce Clause.[179] When Ely published *Democracy and Distrust* in 1980, the idea that courts should defer to Congress and rely on the political process to preserve the Constitution's division of power between the states and the federal government was so well settled that Ely did not feel the need to address the issue in his *magnum opus*. Even so, there is no doubt that Ely would have endorsed Wechsler's theory.[180]

The Supreme Court emphatically rejected Wechsler's theory in *United States v. Lopez*,[181] holding for the first time in almost sixty years that federal legislation exceeded the scope of Congress's power under the Commerce Clause. *Lopez* was one of a series of decisions in the 1990s in which the Court revived strong judicial review of federal legislation for the ostensible purpose of protecting state autonomy from federal overreach and preserving the Constitution's division of power between the states and the federal government. Between 1992 and 2000, the Court established new constitutional limits on Congress's enumerated powers under the Commerce Clause[182] and Section 5 of the Fourteenth Amendment.[183] It also created new constitutional rules based loosely on the Tenth[184] and Eleventh Amendments[185] to strengthen constitutional protection for state autonomy.

The theory underlying the Court's revival of strong, judicially enforced federalism-based limits on Congress is rooted in Federalist 48, where Madison said: "The legislative department is everywhere extending the sphere of its activity, and drawing all power into its impetuous vortex."[186] The problem with this theory today is that Congress is actually much weaker than Madison feared, and the Supreme Court is much stronger than Madison could have envisioned. Today, it is the Court that draws all power into its "impetuous vortex."[187] The federalism jurisprudence that the Court has developed over the past thirty years exacerbates this problem. Although the Court's federalism doctrines are ostensibly designed to protect the states from congressional overreach, in practical effect, those doctrines transfer federal policymaking authority from Congress to the Supreme Court, in violation of separation of powers principles.[188]

Moreover, the Court's modern federalism jurisprudence has had almost no practical effect in protecting state autonomy from overreaching federal power because the main threat to state autonomy comes not from Congress, but from the Court itself. During the Warren Court era, the Court developed a doctrine known as "incorporation doctrine" that radically shifted the balance of power between the states and the federal government by transferring decision-making authority in a wide variety of areas from state governments to federal courts.[189] As a practical matter, incorporation doctrine has done much more to expand federal power and restrict state autonomy than any single piece of legislation enacted by Congress. Incorporation doctrine aggrandizes federal judicial power at the expense of the states; it has no basis in the text or original understanding of the Fourteenth Amendment.[190] If the Court was truly serious about protecting state autonomy from federal overreach, it would endorse the logic of Justice Harlan's dissenting opinions in the incorporation cases and repudiate incorporation doctrine in its entirety.[191] Instead, since 2010, the Court has doubled down on incorporation doctrine, expanding the reach of federal judicial power into additional areas that were previously reserved to the states under the Tenth Amendment.[192]

Chapter 7 presents a critique of the Court's modern federalism jurisprudence. I argue that the Court should adopt a deferential approach to judicial review of federal legislation that allegedly infringes on state autonomy, leaving these matters to be resolved by the political branches in accordance with Wechsler's political safeguards theory. Moreover, if the Court wants to do more than merely pay lip service to the constitutional principle of state autonomy, it should repudiate incorporation doctrine to limit its own power and return power to the states in areas that were previously reserved to the states under the Tenth Amendment.

The rights-protecting function of incorporation doctrine can be served through judicial application of human rights treaties because most rights in the Bill of Rights are also protected under the ICCPR.[193] It is preferable to apply the ICCPR to the states under the Supremacy Clause – rather than applying the Bill of Rights under the Fourteenth Amendment – because the treaty-based approach preserves the option of congressional override, consistent with the principle of legislative primacy. For the small number of incorporated rights that are not covered by the ICCPR,[194] the Court should return power to the states to promote state autonomy. However, I advocate an exception to this approach for property rights. For the reasons explained in Chapters 6 and 7, I argue that the Court should continue applying the Takings Clause to the states under incorporation doctrine.

The proposals summarized over the last several pages – and described in more detail later in this book – if implemented, would entail revolutionary changes in constitutional doctrine, as well as dramatic legislative reforms. Readers may think that the changes I am proposing are unrealistic. Chapter 8 addresses that concern. From a theoretical perspective, the chapter draws on Professor Ackerman's idea of a "triggering election" that sparks a set of constitutional and legislative reforms.[195] Realistically, in the near term, the legislative reforms I propose will not happen unless the Democratic Party secures majorities in both the House and the Senate, along with a Democratic President. An election that yields a Democratic "trifecta" could serve as a triggering election in Professor Ackerman's terms, especially if the Senate is willing to eliminate the filibuster as an obstacle to legislative reform. Even then, some of the legislation I propose might well be ruled unconstitutional, absent changes in Supreme Court personnel. Accordingly, Chapter 8 summarizes a legislative proposal for Supreme Court reform that would allow a two-term Democratic President to appoint four new Justices in eight years.[196] In sum, Chapter 8 charts a path for constitutional revolution that would enable We the People to reclaim our rightful place as sovereigns in a democratic, constitutional order. I believe that path is realistic – if we elect a two-term Democratic President, the Democratic Party maintains a majority in both Houses of Congress during at least half of that eight-year period, and Congress enacts legislation authorizing the President to appoint four new Justices in eight years.

2

Four Revolutions in Constitutional Law

Chapter 1 asserted that there have been four previous revolutions in constitutional law. It would require an entire book to present a detailed defense of that claim. This chapter presents an abbreviated history of constitutional law, and of judicial review, divided into the six time periods that are summarized in Table 1.2. (To reiterate, the division of constitutional history into six discrete time periods is necessarily somewhat arbitrary, but it is useful for the quantitative analysis presented in this chapter.) The book, as a whole, presents a normative argument for a future revolution in constitutional law. This chapter demonstrates that the call for revolution is not unprecedented. Constitutional law is continuously changing and evolving. The history of constitutional law suggests that future revolutions are almost inevitable. What form those revolutions will take remains to be seen, but history can provide some clues.

Before focusing on specific time periods, this chapter highlights two broad trends that are illustrated in Figures 2.1 to 2.3. (These figures are derived from two databases that I created. More detailed data is included in the Appendix, along with information about how I created the databases.[1]) Figure 2.1 shows that the Supreme Court shifted its primary focus from private law to public law between the late nineteenth century and the mid twentieth century. I define the term "public law cases" to include "litigated cases involving a dispute between a private party and a government actor in which the private party alleges that the government actor committed, or threatened to commit, a violation of some established legal norm."[2] From 1801 to 1888, public law cases never comprised more than 40 percent of the Supreme Court's caseload. From 1936 to the present, public law cases have consistently accounted for about 70 percent of the Court's caseload. In the nineteenth century, the Court focused primarily on resolving individual disputes between private parties. Since the New Deal period, the Court has focused primarily on resolving issues that can fairly be described as public policy issues. Clearly, there is no bright line that separates constitutional law from public policy issues, but the shift from private to public law exacerbated the counter-majoritarian difficulty because the Court began to focus more on issues in the grey area that straddles the line between public policy and constitutional law.

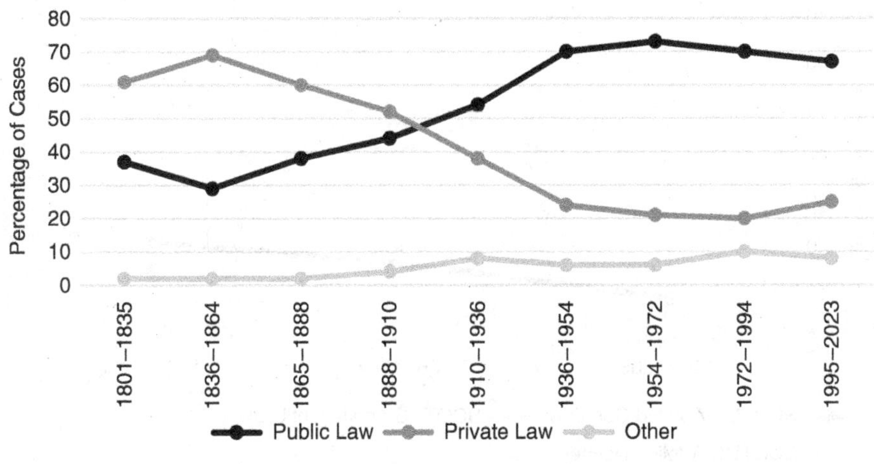

FIGURE 2.1 The Rise of Public Law

Meanwhile, the type of law that the Court applies to decide public law cases has also changed. Figures 2.2 and 2.3 depict the extent to which the Court relied on constitutional law vs. international law vs. other sources of law to decide public law cases in different time periods. The two figures, respectively, address the period before the *Lochner* era and the period after the *Lochner* era. In the nineteenth century, the Court typically applied a mix of international law, statutes, and common law – but rarely constitutional law – to decide public law cases.[3] By applying sources of law other than constitutional law, the Court was engaging in weak judicial review. In Ely's terms, the practice of weak judicial review ensured "that the channels of political participation and communication are kept open" for subsequent action by democratically elected legislators.[4] Since the Warren Court era, the Court has consistently applied constitutional law in more than 50 percent of public law cases. Application of constitutional law typically involves strong judicial review. When the Court applies constitutional law to decide public law cases, Congress cannot override Supreme Court decisions related to major public policy controversies.

The combination of these two trends – the shift from private to public law, and the constitutionalization of public law – has eroded the fundamental constitutional norm of legislative primacy. The Constitution is designed to ensure that We the People have the power to elect new representatives when our government makes decisions we do not like. When Congress retains a power of legislative override, the government is accountable to the people because we retain our power to vote them out of office. The Court's increasing power to decide public policy issues, without the possibility of legislative override, is antithetical to the basic constitutional design because the Court is not accountable to the People. This chapter documents the revolutionary change from a system of weak review in the nineteenth century to a system of strong review that has prevailed since the early twentieth century. Chapter 5 presents a more detailed account of the nineteenth century practice of weak review.

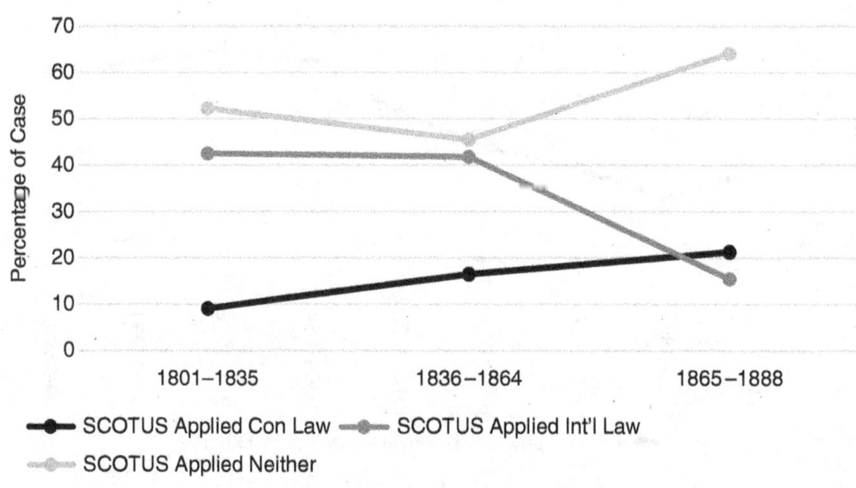

FIGURE 2.2 Before the Lochner Era

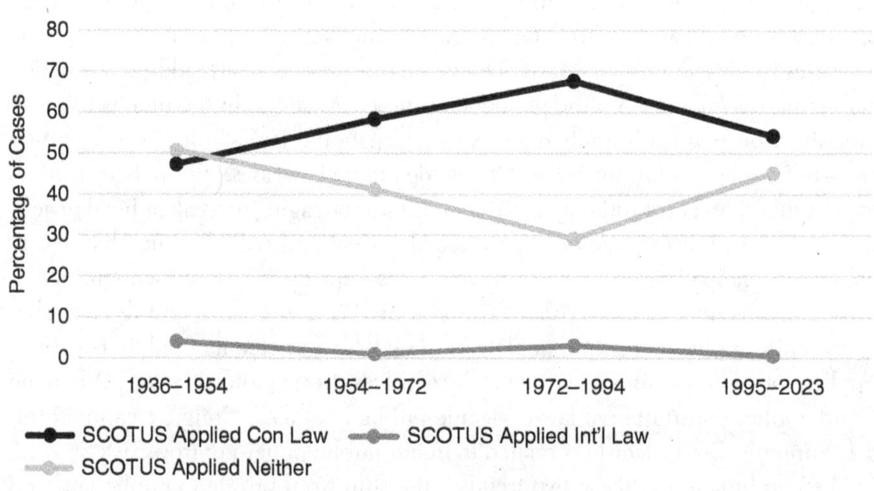

FIGURE 2.3 After the Lochner Era

PENNOYER AND CONSTITUTIONALIZATION

"Constitutionalization" is the process whereby constitutional law displaced international law as the dominant public law discourse in federal courts.[5] The Supreme Court's classic decision in *Pennoyer v. Neff* illustrates the process of constitutionalization.[6] *Pennoyer* involved a default judgment issued by an Oregon state court. Neff, the losing defendant in state court, sued Pennoyer in federal court to challenge the validity of the default judgment, claiming that he "was a non-resident of the State … [who] was not personally served with process, and did not appear therein."[7]

The state court served Neff by publication in a newspaper – a service method apparently authorized by statute in Oregon. Despite statutory authorization for service by publication, the Supreme Court held that the "judgment recovered in the State court of Oregon against the plaintiff herein … was without any validity."[8]

The Court rested its decision on "two well-established principles of public [international] law."[9] First, "that every State possesses exclusive jurisdiction and sovereignty over persons and property within its territory." And second, "that no State can exercise direct jurisdiction and authority over persons or property without its territory."[10] The Court cited two international law treatises as authority – Story's treatise on Conflict of Laws, and Wheaton's treatise on International Law. The Court also stated: "The international law … as it existed among the States in 1790, was that a judgment rendered in one State, assuming to bind the person of a citizen of another, was void within the foreign State, when the defendant had not been served with process or voluntarily made defence."[11] In short, the Court held that the state court judgment was void because it conflicted with principles of international law.

It remains unclear why the Court thought it could apply customary international law to invalidate a state court judgment. One view is that the Court decided *Pennoyer* on state law grounds, using international law to support a narrowing construction of Oregon's personal jurisdiction statute.[12] An alternative view is that the Court applied international law as federal common law to invalidate the Oregon statute that authorized service by publication.[13] Regardless, the Court did not apply federal *constitutional* law to nullify the state court judgment. (The Court's opinion mentioned the Fourteenth Amendment Due Process Clause. However, the Court did not base its holding on the Fourteenth Amendment because the state court judgment was rendered in February 1866 and the Fourteenth Amendment was not ratified until 1868.[14]) If one construes *Pennoyer* as a decision interpreting state law, then the Oregon legislature could have modified the jurisdictional rule. If one construes *Pennoyer* as an application of federal common law, Congress could have modified the *Pennoyer* rule. Either way, *Pennoyer* is a case of weak judicial review, not strong judicial review, because some legislative body retained the power to authorize state courts to exercise jurisdiction in contravention of *Pennoyer*'s territorial rule.

Subsequent Supreme Court decisions transformed the *Pennoyer* rule from a principle of international law to a federal constitutional rule: The Court constitutionalized the *Pennoyer* rule by linking it to the Fourteenth Amendment Due Process Clause.[15] In so doing, the Court replaced weak judicial review with strong judicial review. The transformation of *Pennoyer*'s territoriality principle from an international rule to a constitutional rule illustrates two general points about constitutionalization. First, constitutionalization has produced numerous judge-made constitutional rules that have little or no basis in the actual text of the Constitution. The text of the Due Process Clause says nothing about territorial limits on state court jurisdiction. Similarly, much of modern constitutional doctrine consists of judge-made rules that are at best loosely related to the actual constitutional text.[16]

Second, the process of constitutionalization, and the corresponding shift from weak to strong judicial review, transferred lawmaking power from state and federal legislatures to federal courts. In 1878, when the Court decided *Pennoyer*, either Congress, or state legislatures (or both) retained the power to authorize state courts to exercise jurisdiction over nonresident defendants in contravention of *Pennoyer*'s territoriality rule. By 1900, though, neither Congress nor state legislatures had the power to legislate contrary to the *Pennoyer* rule because the Court had constitutionalized that rule by incorporating it into the Due Process Clause. Thus, there is a significant tension between constitutionalization (strong judicial review) and the Constitution's commitment to the principle of legislative primacy.

THE FIRST HUNDRED YEARS (BEFORE 1890)

Writing in 1885, then-Professor Woodrow Wilson called Congress "unquestionably, the predominant and controlling force, the centre and source of all motive and all regulative power" in the federal government.[17] This statement was clearly true in the 1880s. The division of power among the three branches at that time was consistent with the constitutional norm of legislative primacy. Both the judicial and executive branches were fairly weak; power resided primarily in the legislative branch.

As between the federal government and the states, power resided primarily in state governments. The federal government was much weaker than it is today. On paper, the Civil War Amendments transferred substantial power from the states to the federal government. However, in the *Civil Rights Cases*,[18] the Supreme Court adopted an extremely narrow construction of the scope of congressional power under the Thirteenth and Fourteenth Amendments, thereby depriving those amendments of much of their transformative potential for the next seventy to eighty years.

Throughout this period, the United States maintained a dual-track system for protection of fundamental rights. It was well settled that the Bill of Rights constrained the federal government, but did not constrain the states.[19] Accordingly, federal courts applied the U.S. Constitution as a constraint on the federal government, but individuals who sought judicial protection from infringement of fundamental rights by state governments relied primarily on state courts and state constitutional law to protect their rights.[20] Moreover, cases in which the Supreme Court applied the Bill of Rights as a constraint on the federal government occupied only a fraction of one percent of the Supreme Court's docket.[21]

One reason that the Court rarely applied the Bill of Rights to constrain federal power is that, throughout the nineteenth century, the Supreme Court's docket consisted primarily of private disputes between private parties, rather than public law disputes involving government actors. When John Marshall was Chief Justice (1801–35), about 37 percent of the Court's cases were public law cases. When Roger Taney was Chief Justice (1836–64), that percentage declined to about 29 percent. (See Figure 2.1 and Table A.1 in the Appendix.) In short, before 1890, the Supreme

Court was predominately a private law court, not a public law court. The focus on private law tended to limit the power of the Supreme Court, relative to Congress, because the Court was rarely asked to second-guess Congress's judgment on major public policy issues.

Moreover, within the category of public law cases, the Court frequently relied on international law, rather than constitutional law, as a rule of decision. "Between 1801 and 1864, the Supreme Court applied international law in about 42% of the public law cases decided on the merits. During that period, the Court applied constitutional law in only about 13% of the public law cases decided on the merits."[22] The Court's reliance on international law declined somewhat during the period after the Civil War. However, between 1865 and 1888, the Court still applied constitutional law in only about 21 percent of public law cases. (See Figure 2.2 and Table A.2 in the Appendix.) Judicial application of international law was broadly consistent with the constitutional norm of legislative primacy because Congress retained the power to override judicial decisions based on international law.[23]

One reason that the Supreme Court applied international law more frequently than it applied constitutional law during this period is that – in nineteenth-century public law litigation – private litigants raised international law claims more frequently than they raised constitutional law claims. (See Table A.2 in the Appendix.) Courts typically decide cases by applying the law that litigants use to frame their claims. For most of the nineteenth century, lawyers framed their claims in terms of international law because that was the dominant "public law discourse" in the United States.[24] Until about the 1870s or 1880s, most lawyers did not attend law school; they received their legal training through apprenticeships. Apprentices "read the law." *James Kent's Commentaries on American Law* was one of the most influential treatises for training young lawyers.[25] Kent devoted the first book of his *Commentaries* – roughly 30 percent of the entire treatise – to "The Law of Nations" (the nineteenth-century term for international law).[26] Thus, lawyers framed public law claims in terms of international law, and courts applied international law to decide public law controversies because that reflected their legal training.

The most striking fact about the early history of judicial review in the United States is that the Supreme Court rarely engaged in strong judicial review of federal legislation before 1890. Professor Keith Whittington has done a comprehensive study of Supreme Court decisions in which the Court evaluated the constitutionality of a federal statute.[27] For that project, he created a publicly available database of Supreme Court decisions.[28] Table 2.1 is derived from that database. It shows that the Supreme Court invalidated federal statutes at a rate of less than one case every two years between 1789 and 1889, a much lower rate than any subsequent period in U.S. history.

Moreover, many of the nineteenth-century decisions that Prof. Whittington identifies as cases where the Court invalidated a federal statute involved weak review, not strong review. Consider, for example, *Mossman v. Higginson*,[29] a case that Prof.

TABLE 2.1 *Judicial Review of Congress Over Time*

	# Cases Upholding Validity of Federal Statute	# Cases Invalidating Federal Statute	Ratio (Valid:Invalid)	# Years in Period	# Cases Per Year Invalidating Federal Statutes
1789–1889	126	44	2.86:1	101	.44
1890–1936	302	89	3.39:1	47	1.89
1937–1953	171	20	8.55:1	17	1.18
1954–1971	99	49	2.02:1	18	2.72
1972–1994	199	66	3.02:1	23	2.87
1995–2022	74	84	0.88:1	28	3.00
Total (Average)	971	352	Avg. = 2.76:1 (for all 6 periods)	234	Avg. = 1.50 (for all 6 periods)

Source: Keith E. Whittington, The Judicial Review of Congress Database, 1789–2022 (July 2022).

Whittington identifies as a pre-*Marbury* example of judicial review.[30] Article III of the Constitution grants federal courts jurisdiction to adjudicate claims between a citizen and a foreigner (but not between two foreigners). The Judiciary Act of 1789 authorized federal courts to adjudicate claims in which "an alien is a party to the suit."[31] Higginson, the plaintiff, was a British citizen, but the pleadings did not state explicitly that defendants were U.S. citizens. The Court said that the statute did not authorize federal courts to adjudicate claims between two foreigners, because that construction of the statute would be inconsistent with Article III.[32] The record does not reveal what happened after the Supreme Court dismissed the case, but it seems likely that Mossman was a U.S. citizen.[33] If that is true, Higginson could easily have brought his claim in federal court by amending the pleading to specify that Mossman was a citizen. This is an example of ultra-weak judicial review: The plaintiff retained the power to reverse the outcome of the Supreme Court decision by correcting an error in the pleading.

When litigants tried to persuade the Court to engage in strong judicial review, the Court frequently rebuffed those efforts. For example, in *Hurtado v. California*, petitioner urged the Court to rule that the Fifth Amendment Grand Jury Clause is binding on state governments.[34] The Court refused to do so, in the process providing a ringing endorsement of the principle of legislative primacy. Justice Matthews, writing for a unanimous Court, said that the greatest security for "those fundamental principles of liberty and justice which lie at the base of all our civil and political institutions ... resides in the right of the people to make their own laws [through their elected representatives], and alter them at their pleasure."[35]

Before 1890, the Court was much more active in invalidating state and local laws than it was with respect to federal laws. The Congressional Research Service has published a list of U.S. Supreme Court decisions holding that a state or federal law is unconstitutional.[36] That list identifies 122 cases decided before 1890 where the Court held that a state or local law was unconstitutional. Analysis of those cases reveals a pattern of judicial review that is strikingly different than modern judicial review. Ninety-seven of the 122 cases involved application of either the Contracts Clause or the Dormant Commerce Clause.[37] Judicial application of the Dormant Commerce Clause is a paradigmatic example of weak judicial review because Congress retains the power to authorize state action that would otherwise violate the Clause, as interpreted by the Supreme Court.[38] Moreover, it was well settled by 1827 that the Contracts Clause does not restrict the power of state legislatures to regulate future contracts; the Clause applies only to legislation that interferes with preexisting contracts.[39] Thus, Supreme Court decisions applying the Contracts Clause did not restrict the power of state legislatures to enact legislation governing future behavior.

In sum, the practice of judicial review before 1890 was broadly consistent with the constitutional norm of legislative primacy because the Court rarely engaged in strong judicial review. In Professor Whittington's terms, the Court did not stand "as a significant veto point that was likely to obstruct the legislative efforts of unified political majorities."[40] The practice of strong judicial review – as a routine judicial practice – did not take root until the *Lochner* era.

FIRST REVOLUTION: THE LOCHNER ERA (1890–1936)

Many historical accounts of the *Lochner* era focus on dramatic doctrinal changes during this period – especially the Court's use of economic substantive due process doctrine to restrict state legislative power, and its application of the doctrine of limited, enumerated powers to restrict federal legislative power. Those doctrinal developments were undoubtedly important, but their influence was only temporary because the New Deal Court repudiated key *Lochner* era doctrines. This section focuses on more enduring changes – in particular, the growth of federal judicial power and the erosion of the constitutional norm of legislative primacy. During this period, the Court chipped away at legislative primacy by expanding its own power over domestic affairs and by augmenting the President's power over foreign affairs.[41]

Professor Chemerinsky notes that the *Lochner* era "was the first time that the Supreme Court aggressively used its power of judicial review to invalidate federal and state laws."[42] Quantitative data supports that claim. Table 2.1 shows that, during this period, the Court invalidated federal statutes at a rate of 1.89 cases per year, more than four times the rate of the previous period. Of course, the Court also upheld many state and federal laws during this period.[43] Table 2.1 shows that the Court upheld the validity of federal laws roughly three times as often as it invalidated federal laws. Even so, the *Lochner* era was the first time that the Supreme Court made a sustained effort to replace the traditional system of legislative primacy with a new system of judicial primacy.[44] (See Table 1.2, p. 24.)

Congress supported the rise of judicial power by enacting statutes in 1891 and 1925 that expanded the Supreme Court's authority to control its own docket.[45] Before 1891, the Supreme Court decided the cases it was required to decide under controlling federal legislation that governed the Court's jurisdiction. That system was broadly consistent with the constitutional norm of legislative primacy because Congress controlled the Court's docket. Since Congress enacted the Judges' Bill of 1925,[46] the Supreme Court has had almost complete discretion not only to choose which cases it takes but also to choose which issues it decides.[47] Congress enacted the 1925 statute at the urging of William Howard Taft, who was then serving as Chief Justice. "This legislation codified Taft's vision – then new, now so entrenched that modern lawyers struggle to imagine an alternative – that the Supreme Court should oversee the federal judiciary by focusing on cases that raised *constitutional* questions...."[48] Given control over its docket, the Court started to behave less like a court (in the sense that courts typically decide cases presented by litigants), and more like a legislative body (which sets its own agenda by deciding which policy issues are sufficiently important to merit its attention).[49]

After Congress gave the Supreme Court the power to set its own agenda, the Court chose to focus more on public law controversies, rather than private law claims. Between 1865 and 1888, public law cases accounted for only 38 percent of the Court's docket. In contrast, between 1936 and 1954, public law cases accounted for about 70 percent of the Court's docket. (See Figure 2.1 and Appendix, Table A.1.) Additionally, after gaining control of its docket, the Court increasingly relied on constitutional law, rather than other sources of law, to resolve public law controversies. Between 1865 and 1868, the Court applied constitutional law in only about 21 percent of public law cases. In contrast, between 1936 and 1954, the Court applied constitutional law in about 47 percent of public law cases. (See Figures 2.2 and 2.3 and Appendix, Table A.2.) Both these trends – the shift from private to public law and the constitutionalization of public law – eroded the norm of legislative primacy by transferring power over public policy issues from legislatures to courts. The Court's increasing focus on public law meant that it devoted more of its time to reviewing legislative decisions. The constitutionalization of public law, and the corresponding shift from weak to strong review, meant that the Court decided more cases on grounds that were insulated from legislative override.

As noted previously, the federal government was fairly weak in 1890, relative to state governments. Between the end of the Civil War and 1900, the American economy was transformed from a largely rural, agrarian economy to an urban, industrial economy. Congress began to regulate the growing national economy by enacting the Interstate Commerce Act in 1887 and the Sherman Anti-Trust Act in 1890.[50] Congress enacted many other statutes over the next few decades to assert its control over the national economy. During the *Lochner* era, the Court sometimes supported federal legislative power by upholding the validity of federal statutes.[51] Frequently, though, the Court restricted federal legislative power by engaging in strong judicial review to impose federalism-based limits on Congress's enumerated powers. In particular, the Court enforced a narrow view of the scope of Congress's power under the Commerce Power[52] and the Taxing Power.[53] It also applied the Tenth Amendment as an external constraint on Congress's legislative powers.[54] The Court's aggressive use of strong judicial review slowed, but did not stop, the steady growth of Congress's power to regulate the national economy.

At the same time that the Court was resisting the growth of federal legislative power, it was eagerly accelerating the transfer of power from state legislatures to the Supreme Court. By 1900, most state legislatures had "adopted measures to control elements of the employer-employee relationship, improve the conditions of factory labor, and expand the liability of employers for workplace injuries."[55] The Court developed the doctrine of economic substantive due process in response to these state laws; that doctrine generally protected the rights of employers and businesses to be free from government regulation. With economic substantive due process doctrine, the Court abandoned the traditional dual track system for protection of fundamental rights. Instead of relying on state constitutions and state courts to protect fundamental rights from infringement by state governments, the Court applied the U.S. Constitution – specifically, the Fourteenth Amendment – to protect fundamental rights from infringement by state governments. (Roughly thirty years before its decision in *Lochner*, the Court explicitly rejected this approach in *Slaughter-House Cases* on the grounds that the Fourteenth Amendment should be construed in harmony with the traditional dual-track system.[56])

According to one commentator, the Court decided about 180 cases during this period that applied the Fourteenth Amendment to invalidate state laws.[57] (Prof. Whittington's database covers only cases where the Court invalidated a federal statute.) In addition to *Lochner v. New York*,[58] which invalidated a New York law that set maximum hours for bakers, the Court applied economic substantive due process doctrine to invalidate state minimum wage laws,[59] and to strike down laws protecting the right of workers to unionize.[60] The Court's application of substantive due process doctrine to invalidate state laws effectively transferred final decision-making authority over major public policy issues from state legislatures to the Supreme Court, simultaneously weakening both the constitutional norm of legislative primacy and the norm of state autonomy.

Critics may argue that I am being unfair to the Court because the Fourteenth Amendment itself transferred power from the states to the federal government. That much is true. However, the Framers of the Fourteenth Amendment clearly intended to vest power in Congress, not the Supreme Court.[61] As Professor Mark Graber notes, the Amendment's authors regarded "Congress as the institution primarily responsible for interpreting and implementing the post-Civil War amendments." They rarely "mentioned the federal judiciary when constitutional reform was on the table."[62] Accordingly, Section 5 of the Fourteenth Amendment states: "The Congress shall have power to enforce … the provisions of this article."[63] It does not say that the Supreme Court "shall have power to enforce" the Amendment. Since the Court never overruled the *Civil Rights Cases* – which imposed severe limits on Congress's power under the Fourteenth Amendment – the *Lochner* era gave us a construction of the Fourteenth Amendment that empowered the Supreme Court, while imposing strict limits on Congress. Not only is that construction contrary to the original public meaning of the Fourteenth Amendment, it is also contrary to the constitutional norms of legislative primacy and state autonomy.[64]

In sum, the *Lochner* Court did almost precisely the opposite of what Ely's theory recommends. Whereas Ely advocated strong judicial review to reinforce popular control over the government, the *Lochner* Court was largely indifferent to the goal of enhancing democratic self-government. Whereas Ely supported deference to the legislature with respect to federalism and fundamental rights, the *Lochner* Court practiced strong judicial review in those areas. This should not be surprising. Although commentators have noted that Ely developed his theory in part as a defense of the Warren Court,[65] it is also true that he developed his theory in part as a critique of the *Lochner* era.

SECOND REVOLUTION: THE NEW DEAL COURT (1937–1953)

Scholars agree that the year 1937 marked a revolutionary change in Supreme Court doctrine. In *West Coast Hotel v. Parrish*,[66] the Court upheld a state minimum wage law for women, overruling *Adkins v. Children's Hospital*[67] and repudiating the doctrine of economic substantive due process. In *NLRB v. Jones & Laughlin Steel Corp.*,[68] the Court upheld key provisions of the National Labor Relations Act, signaling a more expansive view of the scope of congressional power under the Commerce Clause. In *Steward Machine Co. v. Davis*[69] and *Helvering v. Davis*,[70] the Court rejected Tenth Amendment challenges to the Social Security Act, adopting an expansive view of Congress's powers under the Spending Clause. Popular mythology explains these doctrinal changes as a response to President Roosevelt's court packing plan. That explanation is at best simplistic and at worst wrong.[71] Regardless, the Court's decisions in 1937 launched the beginning of a new era of constitutional law.

Perhaps the most dramatic change involved a renewed commitment to judicial deference to Congress, rooted in the constitutional principle of legislative primacy.[72] As Justice Stone declared in 1938, federal "legislation affecting ordinary commercial transactions is not to be pronounced unconstitutional unless in the light of facts made known or generally assumed it is of such a character as to preclude the assumption that it rests upon some rational basis within the knowledge and experience of the legislators."[73] Between 1937 and 1953, the Supreme Court did not invalidate any federal legislation on either federalism or separation of powers grounds.[74] The Court upheld the validity of federal statutes more than eight times as often as it invalidated federal statutes. By that metric, the New Deal period was by far the most deferential period in Supreme Court history. (See Table 2.1.) Measured by the number of cases per year invalidating federal statutes, the New Deal Court was also much more deferential than the *Lochner* Court, or any subsequent period in Supreme Court history. (See Table 2.1.)

Despite the Court's sincere commitment to judicial deference and legislative primacy, two trends that began during the *Lochner* era, and that continued during the New Deal era, contributed to the steady growth of judicial power and the eventual demise of legislative primacy. First, the Court's shift from a private law to a public law focus grew even more pronounced during the New Deal era. (See Figure 2.1.) Second, the constitutionalization of public law – that is, the Court's increasing reliance on constitutional law, rather than other sources of law, to decide public law cases – continued unabated during this period. (See Figures 2.2 and 2.3 and Appendix, Table A.2.) As explained previously, the combination of these trends meant that the Supreme Court was increasingly using its judicial power to resolve major public policy controversies and deciding cases in ways that insulated judicial decisions from legislative override.

Although the New Deal Court firmly repudiated economic substantive due process doctrine, it continued to apply the Fourteenth Amendment Due Process Clause to invalidate state legislation. The Court rejected Justice Black's argument that the Fourteenth Amendment "incorporated" the Bill of Rights,[75] and it sometimes rebuffed efforts to make specific provisions in the Bill of Rights binding on state governments.[76] Even so, the New Deal Court (building on *Lochner* era precedents[77]) held that the Due Process Clause made several provisions in the Bill of Rights binding on state governments, including freedom of assembly,[78] the Free Exercise Clause,[79] the Establishment Clause,[80] the Search and Seizure Clause,[81] and the Sixth Amendment right to a public trial.[82] The Court also decided two cases during this period that recognized new unenumerated rights and made those rights binding on the states under the Fourteenth Amendment: *Skinner v. Oklahoma*[83] and *West Va. State Bd. of Educ. v. Barnette*.[84] Thus, although economic substantive due process was dead, substantive due process survived in precursors to modern incorporation doctrine and in unenumerated rights cases that established important precedents for modern substantive due process.[85] In sum, the Court continued to appropriate power from state legislatures, notwithstanding judicial deference to Congress.

Importantly, all of the cases cited in the previous paragraph and accompanying footnotes, except *Everson v. Board of Educ.*, implicate a process that a coauthor and I have called the "federalization of human rights."[86] The federalization of human rights involved the transfer of regulatory authority over internationally recognized human rights from the states to the federal government. The United Nations adopted the Universal Declaration of Human Rights (UDHR) in 1948. My coauthor and I identified sixty-eight discrete rights that qualify as fundamental human rights under the UDHR.[87] As of 1930, fifty-nine of those sixty-eight rights were subject to either exclusive or primary *state* regulatory authority. By 1976, fifty of those sixty-eight rights were subject to either exclusive or primary *federal* regulatory authority.[88]

As explained in the next section (on the Warren Court), the bulk of that federalization process occurred after 1948. Even so, the federalization of human rights gained momentum under the New Deal Court.

Thus far, I have focused on federalization by the judiciary. However, federal legislation enacted by Congress was arguably the most important mechanism for federalization of human rights during the New Deal period.[89] Congress enacted the Social Security Act[90] and the National Labor Relations Act (NLRA)[91] in 1935. Soon thereafter, it enacted the Housing Act of 1937[92] and the Fair Labor Standards Act (FLSA).[93] All four statutes established federal protection for rights later included in the UDHR.[94] Under the constitutional standards that prevailed during the *Lochner* era, all four statutes were vulnerable to constitutional challenges. Shortly after Congress enacted the statutes, petitioners challenged the constitutionality of the NLRA, the Social Security Act, and the FLSA, arguing that Congress exceeded the scope of its enumerated powers and invaded the reserved powers of the states. In a series of decisions between 1937 and 1941, the Supreme Court upheld the validity of all three statutes.[95] Thus, the Court facilitated the statutory federalization of human rights by adopting a more expansive view of the scope of Congress's enumerated powers and a narrower view of Tenth Amendment limits on federal power.

During the New Deal era, the Court arguably missed an important opportunity to correct its prior mistake in the *Civil Rights Cases*.[96] Instead of (or in addition to) relying on the Commerce Clause, the Court could have upheld both the NLRA and the FLSA, among other statutes, as valid exercises of Congress's power under Section 5 of the Fourteenth Amendment. Section 5 grants Congress the power "to enforce," *inter alia*, "the privileges or immunities of citizens of the United States." Congress could reasonably have determined that the rights protected under the NLRA and the FLSA are privileges of U.S. citizenship.[97] Moreover, under the best construction of the Fourteenth Amendment, Congress has broad powers to determine the scope of rights to be protected under Section 1 of the Amendment.[98]

The Court's 1938 decision in *Erie Railroad v. Tompkins*[99] was arguably one of the New Deal Court's most consequential decisions. *Erie* famously terminated the judicial practice – which had prevailed for the previous century – of applying "general common law" to resolve disputes. Justice Brandeis, who authored the *Erie* opinion, clearly hoped that his opinion would limit federal judicial power.[100] Ironically, though, *Erie* may have had precisely the opposite effect. *Erie* helped shift the path of federal judicial decision-making away from general common law and toward what Professor Henry Monaghan called "constitutional common law."[101] (See Figures 2.2 and 2.3, which depict the rise in judicial reliance on constitutional law and the corresponding decline in judicial reliance on other sources of law, including general common law.) The shift from general common law to constitutional common law enhanced judicial power because judicial decisions based on general common law were subject to legislative override, whereas judicial decisions based on constitutional law are not subject to legislative override.

THIRD REVOLUTION: THE WARREN COURT (1954–1971)

President Eisenhower appointed Earl Warren as Chief Justice in October 1953. The Supreme Court issued its decision in *Brown v. Bd. of Education* in May 1954. *Brown* launched the third revolution in constitutional law. Before commenting on the revolutionary features of the Warren Court, two points bear emphasis. First, the Supreme Court's transition from a private law court to a public law court was essentially complete by this time; roughly 70 percent of the Court's cases during this period were public law cases. (See Figure 2.1 and Appendix, Table A.1.) Second, the constitutionalization of public law continued. The percentage of public law cases in which the Court applied constitutional law increased from about 47 percent during the New Deal period to about 58 percent under the Warren Court. (See Figure 2.3 and Appendix, Table A.2.) As discussed previously, judicial application of constitutional law to resolve public law controversies – as opposed to other sources of law – enhances judicial power over public policy because the Court's constitutional decisions are not subject to legislative override.

One of the most revolutionary features of Warren Court jurisprudence was the fact that the Court used its power of judicial review to promote the goal of political equality. In *Reynolds v. Sims*, the Court held that the Constitution requires "that each citizen [must] have an equally effective voice in the election" of our elected legislators.[102] Chapter 3 presents a detailed analysis of *Reynolds* and the principle of political equality. Here, it bears emphasis that *Reynolds* and related Warren Court decisions provided the foundation for Ely's argument that the Court should engage in aggressive judicial review to correct malfunctions in the political marketplace.[103] Unfortunately, this feature of the Warren Court revolution had a short lifespan. In 1976, in *Buckley v. Valeo*,[104] the Court emphatically rejected the idea that courts should utilize their power of judicial review to promote political equality. Chapter 3 develops the argument that *Reynolds* was right and *Buckley* was wrong in this respect.

As noted in Chapter 1, one of the Warren Court's key legacies is that its 1958 decision in *Cooper v. Aaron*[105] established judicial supremacy as an entrenched feature of constitutional practice.[106] The Court had clearly flirted with judicial supremacy in earlier periods but then retreated (at least partially) during the New Deal era. During the decades after Earl Warren retired, a more conservative Court repudiated certain aspects of Warren Court jurisprudence, but it never retreated from its commitment to judicial supremacy. (See Table 1.2, p. 24.)

Chapter 1 referred to Herbert Wechsler's famous article on the political safeguards of federalism.[107] Consistent with Wechsler's article and with the practice of the New Deal Court, the Warren Court relied on political safeguards, rather than judicial safeguards, to govern the division of power between Congress and the states. Between 1954 and 1971, the Supreme Court decided only one case that invalidated federal legislation on federalism grounds.[108]

Although the Court generally deferred to Congress on federalism questions, the Warren Court invalidated federal statutes at a much higher rate than the New Deal Court. The Warren Court invalidated federal statutes at a rate of 2.72 cases per year, more than twice the rate during the New Deal period. Similarly, the ratio of cases upholding federal statutes to cases invalidating federal statutes was about 2.02:1, less than one-fourth the ratio during the New Deal era. (See Table 2.1.) In short, the Warren Court largely abandoned the New Deal Court's principled commitment to judicial deference to Congress.

The story of the Warren Court is often described as a legacy of enhanced protection for individual rights. For example, the Court strengthened protection for African-Americans under the Equal Protection Clause,[109] expanded First Amendment rights,[110] revived substantive due process doctrine,[111] and expanded protections for criminal defendants under the Fourth, Fifth, and Sixth Amendments.[112] In light of these decisions, the Warren Court revolution is often called a "civil rights revolution,"[113] but it could also be described as a "human rights revolution."[114] Arguments based on international human rights law featured prominently in written briefs filed in *Brown v. Board of Education* and its companion case, *Bolling v. Sharpe*.[115] The Court chose not to address those arguments in its opinion, at least partly for political reasons.[116] Even so, during the next two decades after *Brown*, the Court silently incorporated numerous international human rights norms into federal constitutional law without explicitly citing international human rights instruments.[117]

As noted in the previous section, a coauthor and I constructed a list of sixty-eight discrete rights that qualify as fundamental human rights under the UDHR.

> As of 1948, state governments exercised primary or exclusive regulatory authority for 71% of those rights (48 of 68), whereas the federal government exercised primary or exclusive regulatory authority for only 29% (20 of 68). By 1976, the allocation of authority between state and federal governments had flipped. As of 1976, the federal government exercised primary or exclusive regulatory authority for 74% of those rights (50 of 68), and state governments exercised primary or exclusive regulatory authority for only 26% (18 of 68).[118]

The bulk of that federalization process occurred between 1954 and 1971. Federalization of human rights was essentially complete by 1976. Although the scope of protection for human rights has changed substantially since 1976, the division of regulatory authority between the states and the federal government is virtually the same today as it was in 1976.[119] (*Dobbs* returned authority over abortion rights to the states,[120] but the right to have an abortion is not one of the sixty-eight rights included in our list.[121]) Thus, the Warren Court era gave us the federalization of human rights. It sounded the death knell for the traditional dual-track approach to protection of fundamental rights, which had prevailed from the Founding through the New Deal era. (Recall that, under the traditional dual-track approach, litigants relied primarily on state courts and state law to protect fundamental rights from infringement by state governments.)

During the Warren Court era, the Supreme Court and Congress worked together as partners to enhance protection for human rights. Whereas the *Lochner* Court asserted judicial primacy, and the New Deal Court restored legislative primacy, during this period the Court and Congress developed a partnership model for promotion and protection of fundamental human rights. In Mark Tushnet's words, "the Court saw itself as collaborating with Congress to develop a set of fundamental principles that would permanently order U.S. society. Sometimes Congress would push the ball forward, and the Court would approve.... On other occasions, Congress would actively seek out the Court's assistance."[122]

Indeed, many of the landmark statutes that Congress enacted during this period contributed to the federalization of human rights. The most well-known examples are the 1965 Voting Rights Act,[123] the 1964 Civil Rights Act,[124] and the 1968 Fair Housing Act.[125] Perhaps less well known is that, during this period, Congress also enacted statutes providing federal protection for a range of rights that are classified under international human rights law as socioeconomic rights, rather than civil and political rights. Leading examples include the Social Security Amendments Act of 1956,[126] the Social Security Amendments Act of 1965,[127] and the Occupational Safety and Health Act of 1970.[128] These and other federal statutes enacted during this period codified federal statutory protection for universal human rights recognized in the UDHR.[129]

A PERIOD OF TRANSITION (1972 TO 1994)

In 1968, President Johnson nominated Associate Justice Abe Fortas to replace Earl Warren as Chief Justice. Senate deliberations proceeded in the midst of the politically charged 1968 presidential campaign. The Republican nominee, Richard Nixon, worked behind the scenes with Senate Republicans to defeat Fortas' nomination and ultimately force his resignation.[130] Nixon took office in January 1969, determined to alter the ideological composition of the federal judiciary. He promptly appointed Warren Burger as Chief Justice to replace Earl Warren. By January 1972, he had also appointed three new Associate Justices – Harry Blackmun, William Rehnquist, and Lewis Powell – to replace Abe Fortas, Hugo Black, and John Harlan. Those four appointments moved the Court significantly to the right.[131]

Even so, the term "conservative" meant something different for Nixon's Supreme Court nominees than it did for later nominees. Conservative Justices in the 1970s and 1980s, for the most part, pursued incremental change, not revolutionary change. Both the New Deal Court and the Warren Court adopted a deferential approach to judicial enforcement of federalism limits on Congress's enumerated powers, consistent with Herbert Wechsler's article on the political safeguards of federalism.[132] The Burger Court briefly experimented with more aggressive judicial enforcement of the

Tenth Amendment in *National League of Cities*,[133] but overruled that decision nine years later in *Garcia v. San Antonio Metropolitan Transit Authority*,[134] returning to a deferential approach that relied on political safeguards. Thus, when William Rehnquist became Chief Justice in 1986, the law governing federalism-based limits on Congress's enumerated powers was essentially unchanged from the late 1930s.

The Court also left incorporation doctrine unchanged after early Burger Court decisions incorporated the Fifth Amendment Double Jeopardy Clause[135] and the Eighth Amendment Excessive Bail Clause.[136] After the Court decided *Schilb v. Kuebel* in 1971, the Bill of Rights provisions that bound the states under incorporation doctrine remained unchanged for four decades, until the Court's landmark decision in *McDonald v. City of Chicago* in 2010.[137] Congress and the Supreme Court collaborated to complete the federalization of human rights in the early 1970s by strengthening federal constitutional and statutory protection against gender discrimination,[138] and by establishing a federal statutory right for disabled children to obtain free elementary education.[139] As noted in the previous section, the division of authority between the federal government and the states over internationally recognized human rights has remained essentially unchanged since 1976.[140]

During this period, although the Court often praised the virtues of judicial restraint, it continued to invalidate federal statutes at roughly the same rate as the Warren Court. From 1954 to 1971, the Court invalidated federal statutes at a rate of 2.72 cases per year. From 1972 to 1994, that rate increased slightly to 2.87 cases per year. The ratio of cases upholding federal statutes to cases invalidating federal statutes increased from 2.02:1 to 3.02:1, indicating that the Court was somewhat more deferential to Congress than it was in the preceding period. (See Table 2.1, p. 40.) However, in one of those cases, *INS v. Chadha*,[141] Justice White noted in dissent that the Court struck down "in one fell swoop provisions in more laws enacted by Congress than the Court has cumulatively invalidated in its history."[142] Thus, *Chadha* arguably foreshadowed the subsequent rise of judicial imperialism and the ultimate demise of the constitutional norm of legislative primacy.

During this period, the Court continued its march toward the constitutionalization of public law. In the preceding period (1954–71), the Court applied constitutional law to decide about 58 percent of public law cases. In the period from 1972 to 1994, it applied constitutional law to decide about 68 percent of public law cases. (See Figure 2.3 and Appendix, Table A.2.) At the risk of excessive repetition, it bears emphasis that reliance on constitutional law augments judicial power because the Court's constitutional decisions are not subject to legislative override. Thus, the steady rise of judicial power continued unabated.

Petitioners in many of the landmark Warren Court cases relied on two federal statutes to advance their claims: 42 U.S.C. §1983 and the federal habeas statute.[143] Rather than overruling Warren Court precedents that strengthened protection for constitutional rights, the Court achieved a similar result by restricting the availability of remedies under these two statutes.[144] In a series of decisions establishing qualified immunity for government officers, the Court made it increasingly difficult for civil rights plaintiffs to bring successful claims against government officers under section 1983.[145] Similarly, in cases such as *Stone v. Powell*,[146] *Wainwright v. Sykes*,[147] and *Teague v. Lane*,[148] the Court erected hurdles that limited the availability of federal habeas relief for state prisoners.

During this period, the Court also restricted the availability of remedies for criminal defendants. In *Mapp v. Ohio*,[149] the Warren Court held that the Fourth Amendment exclusionary rule binds the states. *Mapp* enabled many defendants in state criminal trials to avoid conviction by filing successful motions to exclude incriminating evidence obtained from unlawful searches. In *United States v. Leon*,[150] the Burger Court created a "good faith exception" to the exclusionary rule. *Leon* did not overrule *Mapp*, but it carved out a giant exception to *Mapp*.[151] Similarly, in *Miranda v. Arizona*,[152] the Warren Court held that evidence obtained from police interrogation is inadmissible at trial unless the police give suspects the required warnings before commencing the interrogation. In *Oregon v. Elstad*,[153] the Burger Court did not overrule *Miranda*, but it weakened the *Miranda* rule by allowing police to skip *Miranda* warnings in the first interview, then conduct a second interview after issuing the required warnings, and then "use the second interview as a vehicle to recapitulate the information that had been gained in the first, putatively illegal interview."[154]

The one aspect of Supreme Court jurisprudence during this period that might be considered revolutionary was the introduction of antidemocratic judicial review.[155] Two cases decided during this period initiated the trend toward antidemocratic judicial review, a trend that accelerated under the Fed Soc Court. First, in *Buckley v. Valeo*,[156] the Court rejected the idea that the Constitution embodies a commitment to political equality,[157] thereby abandoning one of the central elements of Warren Court jurisprudence (without actually overruling any earlier decisions). Chapter 3 analyzes *Buckley* in greater detail. Second, in 1987, the Federal Communications Commission (FCC) repudiated the fairness doctrine[158] – an important regulatory doctrine that helped maintain a healthy information ecosystem from the 1930s until its demise under the Reagan Administration. The FCC concluded that the fairness doctrine violated the First Amendment, even though the Supreme Court had ruled unanimously two decades earlier in *Red Lion* that the fairness doctrine *did not* violate the First Amendment.[159] The Supreme Court allowed that FCC decision to stand,[160] despite the apparent conflict between the FCC ruling and the Court's earlier decision in *Red Lion*. Chapter 4 shows that the demise of the fairness doctrine was a major factor contributing to democratic decay in the United States.

FOURTH REVOLUTION: THE FED SOC COURT (1995 TO PRESENT)

I refer to the current Supreme Court as the "Fed Soc Court" because the Federalist Society has exerted tremendous influence over judicial appointments for at least the past two decades. In his history of the Federalist Society, Professor McGinnis celebrates the Society's influence in securing the appointments of Chief Justice Roberts and Justice Alito.[161] Another source claims that "every single federal judge appointed by the two Presidents Bush was either a member or approved by members of the society, including four Supreme Court Justices: Antonin Scalia, Clarence Thomas, John Roberts and Samuel Alito."[162] All of President Trump's Supreme Court appointees had close ties to the Federalist Society before becoming judges.[163]

The Fed Soc Court launched the so-called federalism revolution with its 1995 decision in *United States v. Lopez*,[164] holding for the first time since 1936 that federal legislation exceeded the scope of Congress's power under the Commerce Clause. Three years earlier, in *New York v. United States*,[165] the Court foreshadowed the federalism revolution by inventing a new "anti-commandeering" principle that is loosely based on the Tenth Amendment. Within five years after *Lopez*, the Court had revolutionized the body of constitutional doctrine governing the relationship between Congress and the states by imposing new limits on Congress's enumerated powers under the Commerce Clause[166] and the Fourteenth Amendment,[167] extending the anti-commandeering principle to encompass state executive action as well as state legislative action,[168] and rewriting Eleventh Amendment sovereign immunity doctrine in a way that is completely divorced from the actual text of the Eleventh Amendment.[169]

The ostensible purpose of these doctrinal changes was to limit federal power in order to strengthen state autonomy. However, as explained in Chapter 7, the federalism revolution has had almost no practical effect in protecting state autonomy from federal interference, in part because the Supreme Court continues to intervene actively in areas that were previously reserved to the States under the Tenth Amendment. For example, the Court has issued constitutional rulings that impose severe restrictions on the power of state and local governments to enact gun control regulations,[170] regulate marriage,[171] and establish their own rules for public elementary and secondary schools.[172] Hence, as explained in Chapter 7, the Fed Soc revolution has strengthened the Supreme Court and weakened Congress without actually enhancing state autonomy. The net effect is profoundly antidemocratic: The Court has transferred federal lawmaking power from elected legislators to unelected judges.

Chapter 1 introduced the concept of antidemocratic judicial review. To reiterate, "a judicial decision is an act of [anti-democratic] judicial review if it has a significant negative impact on the minimum core of electoral democracy."[173] For the first time in this nation's history, the Fed Soc Court institutionalized antidemocratic judicial review as a staple feature of Supreme Court jurisprudence. Chapter 3 presents a detailed analysis of three cases from this period where the Court abused its power of judicial review to undermine core features of electoral democracy: *California Democratic Party v. Jones* (elevating the interests of political parties over the interests of voters),[174] *Shelby County v. Holder* (invalidating a key provision of the Voting Rights Act),[175] and *Rucho v. Common Cause* (holding that partisan gerrymandering claims are nonjusticiable).[176] One could add several other cases to this list, such as *Citizens United v. Fed. Election Comm'n* (invalidating limits on corporate campaign expenditures).[177] Professor Richard Hasen, a leading election law scholar, notes that the Court has weakened campaign finance regulation to the point that "sophisticated, large-scale players can essentially contribute and spend whatever they want to influence campaigns."[178]

Scholars agree that one of the core purposes of the First Amendment is to enhance democratic self-government.[179] However, the Fed Soc Court has embraced a libertarian view of the First Amendment – which critics have dubbed "First Amendment Lochnerism"[180] – that has converted First Amendment doctrine into a weapon for subverting democratic self-government. For example, in *United States v. Alvarez*,[181] the Court suggested that the First Amendment protects the right to disseminate lies in roughly the same way that it protects the right to disseminate truthful statements. Moreover, as explained in Chapter 4, the Court has refused to accord any constitutional significance to the critical distinction between ordinary speech (which, at most, reaches an audience of thousands), and commercial services for electronic amplification of speech, which enable speakers to transmit their messages instantaneously to millions of people. Consequently, we now have an information ecosystem in which lies spread faster than truth.[182] Chapter 4 demonstrates that our information ecosystem, nurtured by the Fed Soc Court's libertarian First Amendment jurisprudence, poses significant risks for the future of democratic self-government in this country.

Chapter 1 drew a distinction between judicial supremacy and judicial imperialism. The rise of judicial imperialism – which can be traced to the Court's decisions in *United States v. Lopez* (1995) and *City of Boerne v. Flores* (1997) – is perhaps the most distinctive feature of the Fed Soc revolution. Under the current system of judicial imperialism, the Court has transformed a broad range of public policy issues into questions of constitutional law. Suppose Congress wants to improve the health care system in the United States. It must obtain the Court's approval.[183] Suppose the Environmental Protection Agency wants to combat climate change. It too must obtain the Court's approval.[184] Under our current system of judicial imperialism, it is difficult to identify any major public policy issue that does not give rise to constitutional litigation. The Supreme Court is "everywhere extending the sphere of its activity, and drawing all power into its impetuous vortex."[185]

Data from Professor Whittington's database supports the claim that the Fed Soc Court is more "imperialist" than any of its predecessors. Measured by the number of decisions per year in which the Court invalidates federal statutes, the Fed Soc Court does not appear to be significantly different from the Warren Court or the transition period from 1972 to 1994. (See Table 2.1, p. 40.) However, if one focuses on the ratio of cases upholding federal statutes to cases invalidating federal statutes, the Fed Soc Court is truly an outlier. The period from 1995 to the present is the only period in Supreme Court history when the Court has invalidated more statutes than it has upheld. (See Table 2.1, p. 40.) The higher rate of invalidation is directly attributable to the fact that the Fed Soc Court applies strong judicial review for individual rights, federalism, and separation of powers claims, whereas the Warren Court adopted a more deferential approach for federalism and separation of powers claims. (See Table 1.2, p. 24.)

Professor Mark Lemley notes that the imperial Supreme Court has enhanced its own power "by simultaneously stripping power from every political entity except the Supreme Court itself."[186] He wrote those words in 2022. A slight amendment is necessary to account for decisions from the Court's October 2023 term: The Court has stripped power from every entity except itself and the President. In *Trump v. United States*,[187] the Court issued a shockingly broad decision along strictly partisan lines that grants the President broad discretion to violate the law with impunity.[188] It bears emphasis that the Court's newly minted immunity doctrine is at odds with both the text and original understanding of the Constitution.[189] Meanwhile, in the other major Trump case from the October 2023 term,[190] the Court refused to decide whether Donald Trump is eligible to be President, even though the text and original understanding support a powerful argument that he is disqualified under Section 3 of the Fourteenth Amendment.[191] In sum, the Fed Soc revolution has given us an imperial Court, an imperial Presidency, and an enfeebled Congress that incurs the risk of judicial invalidation by an unpredictable Court whenever it enacts politically controversial legislation.

The last few pages have been very critical of the Fed Soc Court, but it is important to give the Justices their due. The Fed Soc Court deserves credit for reinvigorating active judicial review to enforce structural features of the Constitution. The central problem is that the Court has focused on the *wrong* structural features. We need strong judicial review to enforce the Constitution's division of power between the government and We the People. Absent such strong review, We the People are powerless when the government deploys "the awesome power of the State"[192] to manipulate election-related rules in a way that impairs our affirmative, collective right to "vote the rascals out" and choose new representatives. With respect to the structural division of power between the government and the People, the Fed Soc Court has given us antidemocratic review instead of strong review. In contrast, the Fed Soc Court has given us strong review to enforce the Constitution's division of power between the federal government and the states. But we do not need strong judicial review to protect state autonomy from unwarranted congressional interference because – as explained in Chapter 7 – the primary federal threat to state autonomy comes not from Congress, but from the Supreme Court itself.

Chapter 3 presents several proposals for the Court to apply strong judicial review to enforce the Constitution's division of power between the government and the People, and to protect our affirmative, collective right to exercise control over our government.

3

Elections

Chapter 3 develops the argument in favor of strong judicial review to correct malfunctions in our electoral system. The first section analyzes flaws in our current electoral system. The next reviews the Warren Court's decisions in key malapportionment cases: *Wesberry v. Sanders* and *Reynold v. Sims*. I then present a critique of four election law decisions since 1976 where the Supreme Court has engaged in antidemocratic judicial review. The final section presents several proposals for new constitutional rules that build on the principles articulated in *Wesberry* and *Reynolds* that are designed to enhance the quality of self-government in the United States today.

THE CENTRAL PATHOLOGY OF OUR CURRENT ELECTORAL SYSTEM

The final section of this chapter proposes new constitutional rules that are designed to correct malfunctions in the political marketplace. This section analyzes the pathology that the rules are designed to correct. The central pathology, in brief, is that the market for elected office is not sufficiently competitive. Only through a "robustly competitive market … can one of the central goals of democratic politics be realized: that the policy outcomes of the political process be responsive to the interests and views of citizens."[1] In a constitutional system that divides power between the government and We the People, a competitive market for elective office is essential to preserve the power of the people to exercise control over the government.

In a well-designed electoral system, candidates compete for the vote of the median voter.[2] To appreciate this point, visualize a group of voters who are spread along a spectrum from left to right. Assume that the distribution of voter preferences resembles a normal bell curve, with many voters near the center of the distribution and small tails on either end. In a two-person contest between a far-left candidate and a center-right candidate, the center-right candidate will win the most votes because she appeals to voters in the center as well as voters on the right. More generally, when elections are truly competitive, incumbents face a threat of removal. "This threat of removal has an important disciplining effect on the incumbent politician – if she wants to stay in office, she needs to be responsive to voters' first order concerns."[3] To win elections, she needs to appeal to the median voter.

Some scholars claim that "a candidate whose policy position is equal to the median voter's also maximizes the satisfaction of a symmetric electorate as a whole."[4] If the distribution of voter preferences resembles a normal bell curve, this claim makes intuitive sense. Suppose, though, that voter preferences are deeply polarized, with a large group on the far left, and a large group on the far right, and very few voters in the middle of the spectrum. In those circumstances, will middle-of-the-road policies still maximize the satisfaction of the electorate as a whole? Or would centrist policies simply leave everyone dissatisfied?

The answer is unclear. However, it bears emphasis that a large body of empirical research shows that "American voters are less ideologically polarized than they think they are."[5] Here, it is important to distinguish between "affective polarization" and "ideological polarization." Affective polarization measures the degree to which Democrats dislike Republicans and Republicans dislike Democrats. Affective polarization has increased dramatically since about the 1980s.[6] "Americans [today] harbor strong dislike for members of the other party."[7]

Ideological polarization has also increased in the sense that the ideological gap between the median Democrat and the median Republican has grown wider, as shown in Figure 3.1. However, roughly 43 percent of voters identify as independents.[8] Figure 3.2 strips away information about party affiliations and depicts ideological polarization in the electorate as a whole. As of 1994, the distribution of voter ideology closely resembled a normal bell curve. In 2017, we no longer had a normal bell curve, but it was still true that a majority of voters were in the center of the ideological spectrum, neither consistently liberal nor consistently conservative. (See Figure 3.2.) In light of that fact, there is no doubt that a competitive electoral system – in which candidates must appeal to the median voter to win elections – would minimize voter dissatisfaction.

To appreciate this point, look again at the picture in Figure 3.2 for 2017. Imagine vertical lines at 25, 50, and 75 percent. A candidate who is positioned either at the 25 percent line (liberal) or the 75 percent line (conservative) will leave more than 50 percent of the voters dissatisfied; they will feel like "my representative does not actually represent me." In contrast, a candidate positioned at the 50 percent line will leave most of the voters at least moderately satisfied. Given high degrees of affective polarization, Democrats will be dissatisfied with a Republican representative, and vice versa. Even so, Democrats will be less dissatisfied with a centrist Republican and Republicans will be less dissatisfied with a centrist Democrat. Thus, competitive elections – in which candidates must compete for the votes of median voters – reduce voter dissatisfaction in the aggregate.[9]

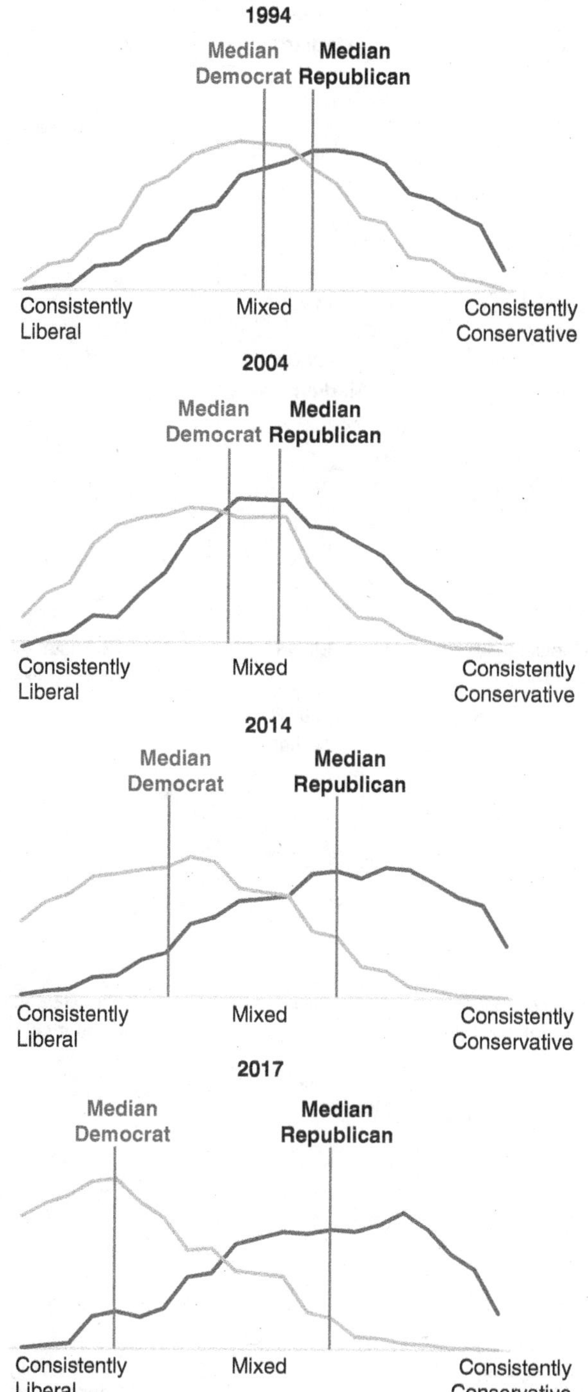

FIGURE 3.1 Political Polarization by Party, 1994–2017
Data source: Pew Research Center surveys conducted in 1994, 2004, 2014, and 2017

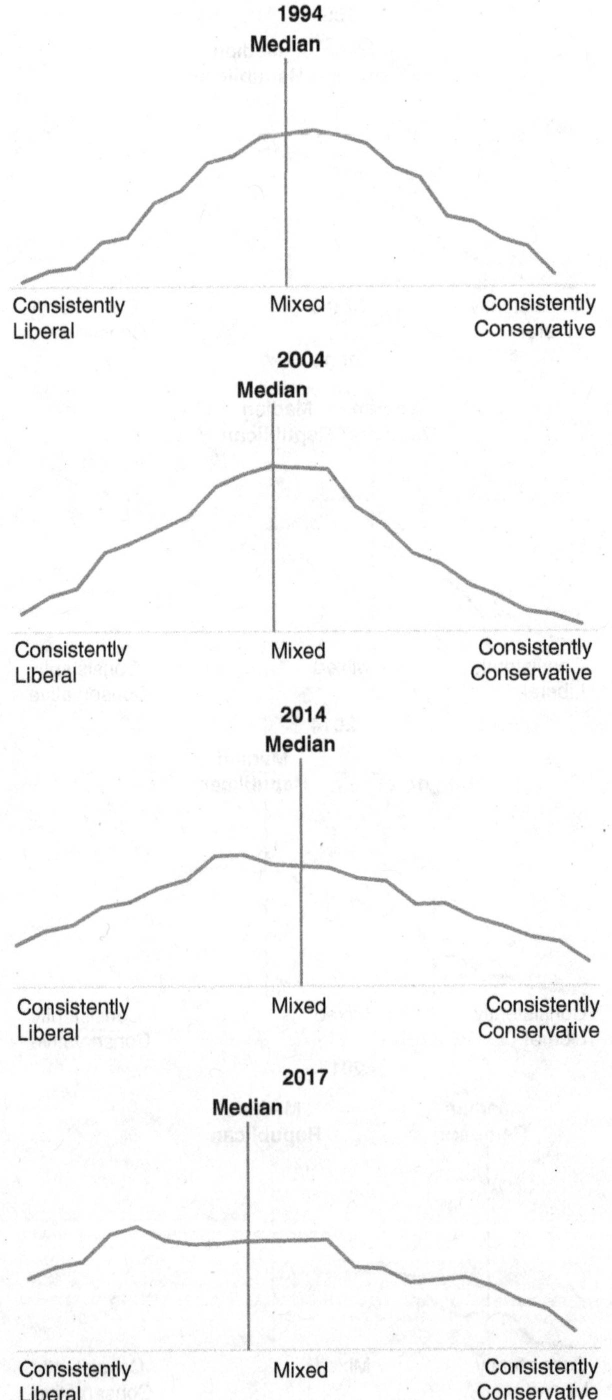

FIGURE 3.2 Political Polarization of Total Population, 1994–2017
Data source: Pew Research Center surveys conducted in 1994, 2004, 2014, and 2017

The central problem with the U.S. electoral system today is that most candidates for national and statewide offices do not have an incentive to compete for the vote of the median voter because most elections are not competitive. Figure 3.3 depicts changes in the ideological composition of the US House of Representatives over a period of about forty years. In 1973–74, many Members of Congress were centrists. They held views that aligned with the views of the median voter because we had a system of fairly robust electoral competition. However, by 2011–12 the center had virtually disappeared. House Members have become much more ideologically polarized. Indeed, our elected representatives are much more ideologically polarized than the citizens whom they are supposed to represent.[10]

Candidates for the House of Representatives no longer compete for the votes of the median voter. For most seats in the House of Representatives, the primary election is the only election that matters because only one party has a realistic chance of winning the general election. "Instead of candidates competing for the median voter of the entire electorate, they compete for the median voter of the primary electorate – either Democratic or Republican."[11] Voters who participate in primary elections are more ideologically polarized than the electorate as a whole. Thus, Republican candidates compete in primary elections for the votes of party activists, who are further to the right than the average Republican, and Democratic candidates compete in primaries for the votes of their party activists, who are further to the left than the average Democrat.[12] That type of electoral competition yields the results depicted in Figure 3.3. Independent voters in the center of the ideological spectrum are not being represented effectively in Congress because candidates are no longer competing for the votes of median voters. Hence, a poll conducted in fall 2023 showed that "57% of independents say that they usually feel that none of the candidates represent my views very well."[13]

John Adams wrote in 1776 that a representative assembly "should be in miniature an exact portrait of the people at large. It should think, feel, reason and act like them."[14] However, if one compares Figures 3.2 and 3.3, it is evident that the pictures are strikingly different. The center of the ideological spectrum remains strong in Figure 3.2, but it has disappeared from Figure 3.3. The House of Representatives does not come anywhere close to being "an exact portrait of the people" because the underlying conditions that give us healthy electoral competition have largely disappeared. "Centrifugal forces pulling candidates toward the extremes are growing stronger relative to the centripetal forces pulling candidates toward the median voter's preferences."[15]

The sharp contrast between high levels of ideological polarization among elected officials (Figure 3.3), compared to much lower levels of ideological polarization among average citizens (Figure 3.2), does not just harm voters in the middle of the ideological spectrum. It hurts all of us because the growing ideological gap between Democrats and Republicans in Congress has made it increasingly difficult to strike

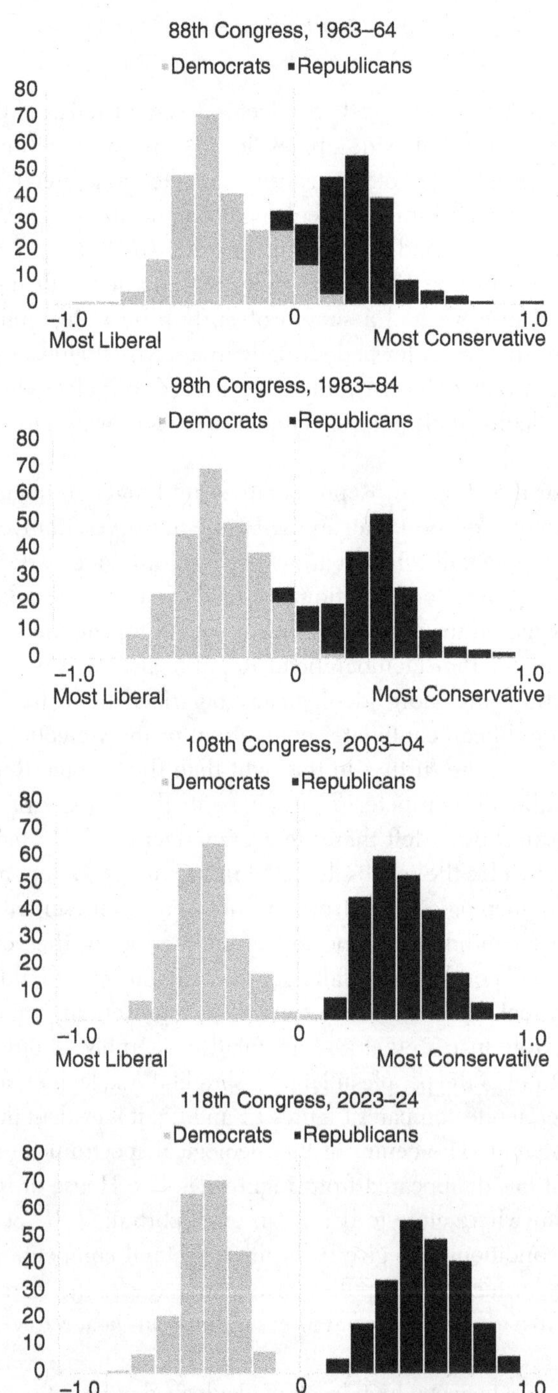

FIGURE 3.3 Ideological Score Distribution, House of Representatives
Data source: Lewis, Jeffrey B., Keith Poole, Howard Rosenthal, Adam Boche, Aaron Rudkin, and Luke Sonnet (2024). Voteview: Congressional Roll-Call Votes Database. https://voteview.com/

the types of bipartisan deals that are necessary for Congress to enact legislation to promote the public interest.[16]

Three features of our current electoral system create the pathology highlighted here. First, the process for drawing the boundaries between electoral districts – which is controlled by partisan actors in most states – creates too many safe seats. Second, most states conduct partisan primary elections as the first stage of a two-stage election process. Third, almost every state uses a first-past-the-post (FPTP) system for the general election, which permits a candidate to win with less than 50 percent of the total votes. The combination of these three factors creates a system in which the two major parties tend to elect more ideologically extreme candidates in their partisan primaries, and the independent voters who would prefer a more centrist candidate are left with no viable choice in the general election. The proposals presented later in this chapter address each of these three features of our electoral system separately. However, it is important to bear in mind that the dynamic interaction among all three factors creates the basic pathology. That pathology is a direct result of the Supreme Court's constitutional rules, which allocate power to political parties at the expense of We the People. The Court can, and should, correct the pathology by adopting different constitutional rules that reduce the power of political parties and increase the power of We the People to choose elected representatives who actually represent us.

MALAPPORTIONMENT CLAIMS IN THE WARREN COURT

In *Colegrove v. Green*, voters challenged the districting scheme in Illinois for elections to the U.S. House of Representatives. The Court said that plaintiffs' claims raised nonjusticiable political questions that federal courts are powerless to adjudicate.[17] However, in *Baker v. Carr*, the Court overruled *Colegrove*.[18] *Baker* involved elections to the state legislature in Tennessee, not the U.S. Congress. The Court held that federal courts have jurisdiction to adjudicate malapportionment claims, but did not identify the proper legal standard for adjudicating such claims.

Within nine months after the Court decided *Baker*, plaintiffs had filed lawsuits in thirty-four states to challenge malapportionment in state legislatures.[19] The underlying problem was similar in many states. States used county lines to create legislative districts. Many states had large numbers of rural counties and smaller numbers of urban counties. In the early twentieth century, there was large-scale migration from rural areas to cities, but state legislatures failed to redraw their maps. Consequently, voters in rural counties had greater representation in state legislatures – and in the U.S. House of Representatives – than their urban and suburban counterparts. The Supreme Court decided two cases in 1964 that established federal constitutional standards for malapportionment claims. *Wesberry v. Sanders* addressed federal congressional districts.[20] *Reynolds v. Sims* addressed state legislatures.[21]

In *Wesberry*, the Court held that voters in Georgia's Fifth congressional district were underrepresented in Congress because the Congressman from that district represented more than 800,000 people, whereas Congressmen from other districts in Georgia, on average, represented fewer than 400,000 people. Justice Hugo Black wrote the opinion. He invoked Article I, Section 2 of the Constitution, which states: "The House of Representatives shall be composed of Members chosen … by the People of the several states."[22] Justice Black analyzed the records of the 1787 Constitutional Convention to show that the Framers believed that the House of Representatives should "represent the people … *on a basis of complete equality for each voter*."[23] Black acknowledged that the Constitution does not require mapmakers "to draw congressional districts with mathematical precision."[24] Even so, *Wesberry* established the "one person, one vote" principle that still governs elections to the House of Representatives.

Reynolds extended the "one person, one vote" principle to state legislatures. Chief Justice Warren wrote the opinion; he described it as the "most important opinion" he ever wrote.[25] That point bears emphasis: Chief Justice Warren, famous for his opinion in *Brown v. Board of Education*, thought that *Reynolds* was even more important than *Brown*. *Reynolds* involved legislative districting for the Alabama Senate and House of Representatives. Plaintiffs alleged that "the Legislature of the State of Alabama has failed and continues to fail to reapportion itself since 1900,"[26] despite substantial demographic changes. As a result, the largest Senate district had about forty times as many people as the smallest district. The largest House district had about sixteen times as many people as the smallest one.[27] Legislators from rural districts resisted any change to the system because malapportionment gave them more power than their urban colleagues.

Article I, sec. 2 of the Constitution did not apply in *Reynolds* because that provision applies only to federal elections. Hence, the Court relied on the Equal Protection Clause. Warren emphasized the fundamental importance of voting rights. He said: "No right is more precious in a free country than that of having a voice in the election of those who make the laws…. Other rights, even the most basic, are illusory if the right to vote is undermined."[28] The Court held that the Equal Protection Clause "requires that the seats in both houses of a bicameral state legislature must be apportioned on a population basis. Simply stated, an individual's right to vote for state legislators is unconstitutionally impaired when its weight is in a substantial fashion diluted when compared with votes of citizens living in other parts of the State."[29] The rule does not require perfect mathematical equality, but states must create districts "as nearly of equal population as is practicable."[30]

The Court's decisions in *Wesberry* and *Reynolds* are models for the type of strong review this book advocates: strong judicial review to correct defects in the electoral process. The primary goal of such judicial review should be to help ensure that our elected representatives in Congress and in state legislatures effectively represent the people they are elected to represent. To implement this approach, it is necessary to articulate a theory of effective representation. The following passage from *Reynolds* provides the kernel of such a theory:

> [R]epresentative government is in essence self-government through the medium of elected representatives of the people, and each and every citizen has an inalienable right to full and effective participation in the political processes of his State's legislative bodies.... Full and effective participation by all citizens ... requires, therefore, that each citizen have an *equally effective voice* in the election of members of his state legislature.[31]

Professor Cass Sunstein refers to the idea that every citizen is entitled to an "equally effective voice" as the ideal of political equality.[32] In *Wesberry*, the Court found a textual basis for political equality in Article I, sec. 2 of the Constitution. In *Reynolds*, the Court found a textual hook for the principle in the Equal Protection Clause.

The juxtaposition of *Wesberry* and *Reynolds* highlights what Professor Guy-Uriel Charles has called the "rights-structure debate" in election law.[33] *Wesberry* relied on Article I, sec. 2, which is a structural provision. *Reynolds* relied on the Equal Protection Clause, which is an individual rights provision. Both cases endorsed the principle of political equality. Professor Charles contends that "political rights are best thought of as dual rights: they are individualist at the core but also structural."[34] He is undoubtedly correct to reject the idea of an "either-or" choice between rights and structure. However, the rights at issue are best conceived as affirmative, collective rights, rather than negative, individual rights.

The best defense of the principle of political equality relates to the Constitution's division of power between The People and the government. As explained in Chapter 1, the Constitution is designed to ensure that We the People, collectively, maintain effective control over our government. This is a core structural feature of the Constitution; it is also an affirmative, collective right. Moreover, as James Madison explained in Federalist No. 10, one of the Framer's key goals was to ensure (as far as possible) that government would serve the common good, rather than serving the interest of a particular "faction."[35] In Madison's words, the term "faction" refers to "a number of citizens ... who are united and actuated by some common impulse of passion, or of interest, adverse to the rights of other citizens, or to the permanent and aggregate interests of the community."[36] If our electoral system grants disproportionate influence to one faction, while simultaneously diminishing the influence of competing factions, then government will serve factional interests instead of promoting the common good. Thus, *Wesberry* and *Reynolds* stand for the proposition that vigorous judicial enforcement of the principle of political equality – the idea that each citizen is entitled to an equally effective voice – is necessary to ensure that our elected representatives represent We the People, rather than representing factional interests based on race, wealth, geography, or partisan affiliations. (As discussed later in this chapter, the best way for the Court to implement this principle is to create constitutional rules that require states to design electoral systems that incentivize candidates to compete for the vote of the median voter.)

Several passages in *Reynolds* support this interpretation. For example, Chief Justice Warren wrote: "The concept of 'we the people' under the Constitution visualizes no preferred class of voters but equality among those who meet the basic qualifications."[37] Similarly, he said: "The theme of the Constitution is equality among citizens in the exercise of their political rights. The notion that one group can be granted greater voting strength than another is hostile to our standards for popular representative government."[38] Warren never said that the Court was enforcing the Constitution's structural division of power between the People and the government. However, he clearly endorsed the ideal of political equality. Moreover, the strongest defense of the claim that the Constitution manifests a principled commitment to political equality relies on the structural division of power between the People and the government.

Critics may argue that the original Constitution rejected the ideal of political equality. Both the Senate and the Electoral College give greater weight to the citizens of small states, compared to larger states. Under the original Constitution, neither Blacks nor women had the right to vote. This is all true. However, We the People have amended the Constitution several times to expand the class of people who are eligible to vote. That group now includes Blacks,[39] women,[40] D.C. citizens,[41] and eighteen year olds.[42] Other constitutional amendments abolished poll taxes[43] and provided for direct election of Senators.[44] This entire series of constitutional amendments shows that the Constitution, as it exists today, is best understood to embody a principled commitment to political equality. Granted, the Senate and the Electoral College operate as limitations on that principle, but those features of our system cannot reasonably be construed to support a claim that constitutional doctrine should repudiate the principle of political equality.

In the past thirty years, the Supreme Court has made dramatic changes in constitutional doctrine to give greater emphasis to structural features of the Constitution – namely, federalism and separation of powers – that are not linked to individual constitutional provisions, but that are woven into the very fabric of the Constitution. Since the Warren Court era, though, the Court has largely ignored the other key structural feature of the Constitution: The division of power between the government and We the People. It is past time to remedy that oversight. The Court should recognize the division of power between citizens and government as a core structural feature of the Constitution. It should also recognize that vigorous judicial enforcement of the principle of political equality is necessary to vindicate our affirmative, collective right to exercise control over our government.

ANTIDEMOCRATIC JUDICIAL REVIEW

As noted in Chapter 1, a judicial decision involves antidemocratic judicial review if it has a significant negative impact on the quality of electoral democracy.

The Court has decided several election law cases over the past few decades that involve antidemocratic judicial review. This section highlights four such cases: *Buckley v. Valeo*,[45] *California Democratic Party v. Jones*,[46] *Shelby County v. Holder*,[47] and *Rucho v. Common Cause*.[48] In all four cases, the Court did the opposite of what Ely's theory (and this book) recommends: instead of correcting malfunctions in the electoral process, the Court used its judicial power to erode the quality of electoral democracy.

Buckley v. Valeo

In 1974, largely in response to the Watergate scandal, Congress enacted amendments to the Federal Election Campaign Act (FECA).[49] The 1974 legislation was the most significant federal campaign finance legislation since the 1907 Tillman Act.[50] In *Buckley v. Valeo*, a group of candidates and political parties raised a broad set of constitutional challenges to FECA, including challenges to statutory restrictions on monetary contributions, expenditures, and various disclosure and reporting requirements.[51] In a *per curiam* opinion, the Court upheld the validity of FECA's disclosure requirements and limits on monetary contributions, but it held that restrictions on campaign expenditures violated the First Amendment.

The Court's opinion in *Buckley* addressed three distinct expenditure provisions: a restriction on expenditures by persons other than candidates,[52] a restriction on expenditures by candidates drawn from personal or family assets,[53] and a limitation "on overall campaign expenditures by candidates seeking" federal office.[54] The Court invalidated all three provisions. The vote was 6–2 for the provision dealing with family assets; it was 7–1 for the other two provisions. (Justice Stevens did not participate.) The Court identified three distinct goals that FECA was intended to promote: to prevent corruption and the appearance of corruption; to "equalize the relative ability of all citizens to affect the outcome of elections"; and to place "a brake on the skyrocketing cost of political campaigns."[55] The Court characterized the anticorruption goal as FECA's "primary interest." It described the other two goals as "ancillary interests."[56] In one passage, the Court even implied that the goal of equalizing the relative influence of citizens was illegitimate. It said: "[T]he concept that government may restrict the speech of some elements of our society in order to enhance the relative voice of others is wholly foreign to the First Amendment."[57]

The contrast between *Buckley* and *Reynolds* is jarring. In *Reynolds*, the Court insisted that the Constitution mandates that "each citizen [must] have an *equally effective voice* in" the electoral process.[58] Just twelve years later, though, in *Buckley*, the Court thought that Congress's attempt to guarantee each citizen an equally effective voice was constitutionally suspect; it was "wholly foreign to the First Amendment."[59] Only three Justices who sat on the Court in 1964, when *Reynolds* was decided, remained on the Court in *Buckley*: Justices William Brennan, Potter Stewart, and Byron White. Both Brennan and Stewart joined the Court's opinion in full. Justice White dissented in part; he voted to uphold all three expenditure provisions that the Court invalidated.[60] However, White's opinion barely mentioned the ideal of political equality.[61] Instead, he emphasized the importance of judicial deference to Congress.

As Professor Pamela Karlan has noted, the Warren Court was very deferential to Congress when the Court thought Congress was acting to promote core constitutional values.[62] For example, in *South Carolina v. Katzenbach*[63] and *Katzenbach v. Morgan*,[64] the Court upheld key provisions of the 1965 Voting Rights Act. In both cases, the Court affirmed the constitutional validity of statutory provisions that were designed, among other things, to promote the goal of political equality. More broadly, the Warren Court often viewed Congress as a partner, not an adversary, in advancing constitutional goals.[65] Justice White's deferential approach in *Buckley* was entirely consistent with Warren Court jurisprudence in this respect. In contrast, the majority's refusal to defer to Congress – its tendency to view Congress as an adversary, not a partner – marked a sharp break with the Warren Court.

The Court's refusal to defer to Congress in *Buckley* relates to one other key issue: the distinction between speech and conduct. The government argued – persuasively, in my view – that "what the Act regulates is conduct, and that its effect on speech and association is incidental."[66] The Court rejected this argument, stating that "the Act's expenditure ceilings impose direct and substantial restraints on … political speech."[67] Justice White, somewhat mockingly, described the majority's position as the view "that money is speech."[68] Of course, the claim that "money is speech" is patently false. Moreover, the majority's assertion that expenditure limits constitute "direct restraints" on speech is equally false, or at best misleading. However, the majority apparently thought it was necessary to describe the expenditure restrictions as "direct restraints" on speech to justify application of "exacting scrutiny," rather than deferential review.[69]

In FECA, Congress sought to promote the goal of political equality. As discussed previously, political equality is a core constitutional value because it is necessary for all citizens to have an equally effective voice, as far as practicable, to help ensure that We the People do not relinquish control over our government to some faction or factions. Unfortunately, rather than recognizing political equality as a core constitutional value, the *Buckley* Court decided that Congress's effort to promote that goal was an unconstitutional infringement of free speech. *Buckley* is a paradigmatic example of antidemocratic judicial review. The Court undermined popular sovereignty by invalidating legislation that was clearly designed to enhance democratic self-governance.

One might legitimately ask whether – if the Court had upheld the expenditure provisions in *Buckley* – those provisions would have had the intended effect of equalizing the relative ability of all citizens to influence electoral outcomes. The honest answer is that we don't know. There are legitimate reasons to fear that statutory limits on campaign expenditures would systematically harm challengers and benefit incumbents. That is a good reason for courts to scrutinize any such statutory limits carefully. However, if we want to enhance the quality of democratic self-government in this country, Congress must be able to experiment with different approaches to campaign finance regulation to determine what succeeds and what fails. In *Buckley* – and in subsequent campaign finance cases – the Court has imposed unwarranted constitutional constraints on Congress's power to regulate campaign expenditures.[70] We do not know what type of legislation might best promote the goal of political equality because the Court has not permitted Congress to experiment. Meanwhile, public trust in Congress has declined dramatically and a large number of U.S. citizens have concluded that the entire system is "rigged."

California Democratic Party v. Jones

State laws regulating the conduct of primary elections vary widely. In a state with closed primaries, one must register as a Republican to vote in the Republican primary. In a state with open primaries, any registered voter is allowed to vote in the Republican primary. There are several variations. According to the National Conference of State Legislatures, "primaries can be categorized as closed, partially closed, partially open, open to unaffiliated voters, open, or multi-party."[71] In 1996, California voters approved Proposition 198, which replaced the state's closed primary system with a "blanket primary."[72] In a blanket primary system, an individual voter could choose, for example, to vote in "the Republican primary for governor, the Democratic primary for attorney general, [and] the Libertarian primary for treasurer."[73] (In contrast, in an open primary system, a person who identifies as a Democrat may register to vote in the Republican primary, but he/she may not vote in the Republican primary for one office and the Democratic primary for a different office.)

In *California Democratic Party v. Jones*,[74] the California Democratic Party, California Republican Party, and two minor parties challenged the constitutionality of Proposition 198. Exit polls indicated that 61% of Democrats, 57% of Republicans, and 69% of independents supported Proposition 198.[75] Thus, in a very real sense, *Jones* pitted the interests of political parties against the interests of voters. The Supreme Court, in a 7–2 decision, ruled in favor of the parties. The Court held that the blanket primary law violated political parties' freedom-of-association rights under the First Amendment, because "the State of California … [was] forcing political parties to associate with those who do not share their beliefs."[76] Justices Stevens and Ginsburg were the only dissenters.

In evaluating the Court's opinion in *Jones*, it is helpful to recall that, in Madison's view, political parties are the paradigmatic example of the "factions" that pose a threat to republican government.[77] Sounding this Madisonian theme, California defended Prop. 198 on the grounds that it would produce "elected officials who better represent the electorate" because "officials elected under blanket primaries stand closer to the median policy positions of their districts than do those selected only by party members."[78] Empirical studies based on actual elections support the claim that blanket primaries "in fact produced more moderate candidates."[79] Even so, Justice Scalia, writing for the Court, rejected the state's argument. In his view, California's asserted interest in electing officials who better represent the voters was "nothing more than a stark repudiation of freedom of political association."[80]

Justice Scalia's contemptuous dismissal of California's interest in ensuring that elected officials actually represent the people constitutes a complete inversion of constitutional values. The Court's analysis gives great weight to the asserted First Amendment rights of political parties, even though the First Amendment does not explicitly mention a right to freedom of association.[81] (It is noteworthy that Justice Scalia – who claimed to be both a textualist and an originalist, and who generally disparaged unenumerated rights – authored an opinion that exalts the importance of an unenumerated right, without so much as a nod to constitutional text or original public meaning.) Conversely, the Court trivializes the peoples' right to effective representation, even though the idea that elected officials are supposed to represent the people is one of the central premises of our entire system of representative democracy.[82]

Professor Pildes argues persuasively that the underlying problem in *Jones* – and in some other cases involving the First Amendment rights of political parties – is that "the Court assesses the rights of parties through individual rights frameworks borrowed from other areas of constitutional law but ill-suited to determining the distinct role of political parties in democratic politics."[83] The better approach is for the Court to "address structural problems and enforce structural values concerning the democratic order as a whole."[84] However, Pildes fails to mention that the Court's current doctrinal framework for structural constitutional law is equally ill-suited to the task because that doctrinal framework focuses exclusively on the division of power among government actors. Since political parties, *qua* parties, are not government actors, the Court's structural constitutional doctrine mostly ignores political parties.

As I argued in the Introduction, the Court's approach to structural constitutional law should be much more attentive to the division of power between the government and the people. Political parties play a vital role in mediating the relationship between the government and citizens, but the structural relationship among citizens, political parties, and the government is complex. On one hand, political parties provide an important mechanism that enables citizens to act collectively to assert popular control over the government.[85] On the other hand, once a political party has obtained governmental power, it often uses that power to advance partisan interests, rather than promoting the common good. "This constantly looming pathology of democratic systems … means that the vitality of democracy depends upon external institutions that can contain this disease."[86] In a well-functioning democracy, We the People would use political parties as an instrument to help us exercise control over the government. In our current system, political parties use the government as an instrument to control voters.

Extreme partisan polarization is one of the main threats to the vitality of American democracy today.[87] In Proposition 198, California voters enacted a law designed to help heal the disease of partisan polarization. The law may or may not have achieved its desired result. We do not know because the Court invalidated the law. Like *Buckley v. Valeo, Jones* is an example of antidemocratic judicial review. There is no legitimate reason for the Court to invalidate a law designed to enhance the quality of democratic self-government, absent compelling evidence that the law will actually yield the opposite result, or that the ostensible pro-democracy objective is actually a smokescreen. When legislators (or voters) enact a law designed to make representative democracy work better, courts should apply a strong presumption of constitutionality.

The Court partially reversed the harmful effects of *Jones* in its later decision in *Washington State Grange v. Washington State Republican Party.*[88] In that case, the state Republican Party challenged the constitutionality of a Washington state law that established a nonpartisan primary system. Under the Washington law, it was at least theoretically possible for the primary election to yield a result in which two Democratic candidates would compete against each other in the general election.[89] The Court upheld the constitutional validity of the state law, saying that it did not "impose a severe burden on political parties' associational rights."[90] *Washington State Grange* was a step in the right direction, insofar as it gave states greater leeway to experiment with alternatives to traditional partisan primaries. Even so, the Court's current doctrine is flawed because it gives greater weight to the associational rights of political parties than it does to the affirmative, collective right of We the People to exercise control over our government.

Shelby County v. Holder

In *Shelby County v. Holder*, the Court invalidated a key provision of the 1965 Voting Rights Act.[91] Section 2 of the Voting Rights Act bans any "standard, practice, or procedure" that "results in a denial or abridgement of the right of any citizen … to vote on account of race or color."[92] Section 5 establishes a "pre-clearance" procedure that applies only to "covered jurisdictions." If a "covered jurisdiction" wants to change its election laws, it may not implement proposed changes without prior authorization from either the U.S. Attorney General or a federal court. Section 4(b) provides a formula for determining which jurisdictions qualify as "covered jurisdictions." Under the original statute, covered jurisdictions included South Carolina, as well as "Alabama, Alaska, Georgia, Louisiana, Mississippi, [and] Virginia," as well as certain counties in other states.[93] With later amendments, Arizona and Texas were added to the list of covered jurisdictions, along with several counties in other states.[94]

In sum, Section 2's prohibition on racial discrimination in voting applies to all fifty states. However, Section 5's pre-clearance procedure – which bars state and local governments from changing their election laws without prior federal authorization – applies only to state and local governments that qualify as "covered jurisdictions" under Section 4(b). In *Shelby County*, the Court left Section 2 of the Voting Rights Act untouched, but held that Section 4(b) is unconstitutional. As a formal matter, Section 5 remains valid, but the pre-clearance procedure in Section 5 does not apply to any state or local governments unless/until Congress enacts a new coverage formula to replace Section 4(b). Today, more than ten years after *Shelby County*, Congress has still not enacted a new coverage formula.[95]

Perhaps more than any other recent Supreme Court decision, *Shelby County* illustrates the radical change from the Warren Court to the Roberts Court in the implicit theories guiding the Court's exercise of its power of judicial review. Ely's theory of judicial review identified two situations where strong judicial review is necessary: to remedy harms to democracy and to protect discrete and insular minorities. An important corollary is that the Court should be especially deferential to Congress when it enacts legislation to remedy harms to democracy or to protect discrete and insular minorities. In the 1965 Voting Rights Act, Congress sought to accomplish both goals simultaneously. Accordingly, when the Warren Court assessed the constitutionality of the Voting Rights Act, it was very deferential to Congress. In contrast, the Roberts Court treated Congress with contempt, rather than deference.

South Carolina challenged the constitutionality of the Voting Rights Act soon after its enactment. In *South Carolina v. Katzenbach*, the Supreme Court upheld the statute.[96] Consistent with Ely's theory, Chief Justice Warren adopted a very deferential approach to judicial review. He quoted Chief Justice Marshall's famous line from *McCulloch v. Maryland*: "Let the end be legitimate, let it be within the scope of the constitution, and all means which are appropriate, which are plainly adapted to that end, which are not prohibited, but consist with the letter and spirit of the constitution, are constitutional."[97] South Carolina objected that the Voting Rights Act infringed state sovereignty. Warren responded: "The language and purpose of the Fifteenth Amendment ... and the general doctrines of constitutional interpretation, all point to one fundamental principle. As against the reserved powers of the States, Congress may use any rational means to effectuate the constitutional prohibition of racial discrimination in voting."[98]

Congress reauthorized the Voting Rights Act in 1970, 1975, and 1982. The Court repeatedly upheld the statute against constitutional challenges.[99] Congress again reauthorized the Voting Rights Act in 2006.[100] *Shelby County* involved a constitutional challenge to the 2006 statute. Chief Justice Roberts wrote the opinion for a 5–4 majority. Like Warren, Roberts quoted the famous language from *McCulloch v. Maryland*.[101] However, unlike Warren, Roberts explicitly rejected *McCulloch*'s deferential approach to judicial review, insisting that more aggressive judicial review was necessary to vindicate "the fundamental principle of equal sovereignty."[102] In *Katzenbach*, the Warren Court held that the coverage formula in Section 4(b) – which made the pre-clearance requirement applicable to some states, but not others – did not violate the doctrine of equal sovereignty because "that doctrine applies only to the terms upon which States are admitted to the Union, and not to the remedies for local evils which have subsequently appeared."[103] *Shelby County* silently overruled that holding in *Katzenbach* by relying on *dicta* from the Court's 2009 decision in *Northwest Austin* – where the Court suggested, for the first time, that the principle of equal sovereignty applies to situations other than admission of new states to the Union.[104]

In *Shelby County*, the Court's nondeferential approach to Congress extended to questions of both law and fact. When Congress enacted the 1965 Voting Rights Act and subsequent amendments, it relied on its power under Section 2 of the Fifteenth Amendment. Section 1 of the Fifteenth Amendment bans racial discrimination in voting. Section 2 states: "The Congress shall have power to enforce this article by appropriate legislation."[105] The text of Section 2 is virtually identical to Section 2 of the Thirteenth Amendment and Section 5 of the Fourteenth Amendment, both of which empower Congress to "enforce" those amendments with "appropriate legislation."

As Professor Michael McConnell has demonstrated, the authors of the Civil War amendments understood that Congress's enforcement power included a power to interpret the substantive provisions of those amendments.[106] However, in 1997, the Supreme Court declared in *City of Boerne v. Flores* that the Constitution grants the Supreme Court the *exclusive* authority to interpret the substantive provisions of the Fourteenth Amendment.[107] It bears emphasis that the Court's claim of exclusive interpretive authority is contrary to both the text and the original understanding of the Civil War amendments.[108] It is also contrary to the overall design of the Constitution, which divides the power to interpret the Constitution among the three branches of the federal government. Nevertheless, the majority opinion in *Shelby County* relied implicitly on *Boerne* to support its unstated assumption that Section 2 of the Fifteenth Amendment does not grant Congress any interpretive authority, and that therefore the 2006 reauthorization of the Voting Rights Act cannot possibly be justified as an exercise of such authority. Chief Justice Roberts made no attempt to defend or explain that unstated assumption, but his entire opinion hinges on that mistaken assumption. Hence, Justice Ginsburg's dissenting opinion in *Shelby County* aptly described the majority opinion as an act of judicial "hubris."[109]

The majority in *Shelby County* was equally dismissive of Congress's factual findings. When Congress reauthorized the Voting Rights Act in 2006, it "compiled thousands of pages of evidence" to support reauthorization.[110] Based on that evidence, the text of the statute includes the following factual findings, among others. "The evidence clearly shows the continued need for Federal oversight in jurisdictions covered by the Voting Rights Act of 1965."[111] Similarly, "[d]espite the progress made by minorities under the Voting Rights Act of 1965, the evidence before Congress reveals that 40 years has not been a sufficient amount of time to eliminate the vestiges of discrimination."[112] Even so, the Court faulted Congress for failing to make factual findings to support its decision to retain the old coverage formula in Section 4(b), rather than replacing it with a new coverage formula.[113]

In essence, the Court ruled that Section 4(b) was unconstitutional because Congress failed to make detailed factual findings that were specifically responsive to the new constitutional standard that the Court first announced in *dicta* in *Northwest Austin* – three years after Congress passed the 2006 reauthorization. As Professor Nathaniel Persily has shown, Congress was on notice when it debated the 2006 statute that the Court's 1997 decision in *Boerne* established a need for factual evidence to support reauthorization.[114] But *Boerne* provided very little useful guidance about what type of factual evidence was necessary. Thus, as of 2006, Congress was forced to make an educated guess about the type of factual information that was needed, but the Court reserved the right to tell Congress after the fact that it had gathered the wrong type of evidence.[115] Given the ambiguity in the law that was a direct result of the Court's decision in *Boerne*, Congress made a reasonable decision "to develop an evidentiary record for the principal purpose of explaining why the covered jurisdictions should remain covered, rather than justifying the coverage of certain jurisdictions but not others."[116] Then, in *Shelby County*, the Court said: "Sorry, you guessed wrong."

Unfortunately, the Court's decision in *Shelby County* yielded utterly predictable results. "Over the past decade, since the Supreme Court suspended preclearance, nearly 30 laws that make voting more difficult have gone into effect in states formerly covered under Section 5."[117] A Brennan Center report presents a detailed empirical analysis of the "racial turnout gap" – that is, the difference between White and Black voter turnout – for "every county in the country for each election between 2008 and 2022."[118] The report concludes that the racial turnout gap is "wider now than at any point in at least the past 16 years" and "the gap is growing most quickly in parts of the country that were previously covered under the preclearance regime … until the disastrous *Shelby County* ruling."[119] If it was possible to sue the Supreme Court for constitutional violations, one could make a compelling argument that the Court itself violated the Fifteenth Amendment in *Shelby County*.

Ultimately, judicial decisions about when to defer to Congress, and when not to defer, involve choices about constitutional values. The Warren Court placed great weight on the constitutional values of democratic self-governance and minority rights. It deferred to Congress in *Katzenbach* because it recognized that the 1965 Voting Rights Act was designed to promote those values. In *Shelby County*, the Roberts Court was not completely indifferent to the values of self-governance and minority rights. However, the Roberts Court refused to defer to Congress because – if you accept the Court's rhetoric at face value – Congress did not give sufficient weight to the value of state sovereignty when it passed the 2006 reauthorization of the Voting Rights Act. It would be a mistake, though, to accept that rhetoric at face value. The Roberts Court applies the rhetoric of state sovereignty aggressively as a constitutional constraint on Congress, but refuses to recognize that state sovereignty imposes any limitation on its own judicial power. Therefore, in practice, the rhetoric of state sovereignty supports judicial imperialism: the privileging of federal judicial power over the legislative power that the Constitution grants expressly to our elected representatives in Congress.

Rucho v. Common Cause

In most states in the United States, state legislators design the maps that divide the state into separate electoral districts; that process is called redistricting. Redistricting determines the boundaries between districts for elections to state legislatures and to the U.S. House of Representatives. Professional mapmakers – aided by huge volumes of data and sophisticated data analysis tools – can draw maps that favor either Republicans or Democrats. If one party controls both houses of the state legislature and the Governor's office, it can draw maps that are deliberately biased in favor of that party. That is partisan gerrymandering. In *Rucho v. Common Cause*,[120] the Supreme Court held that partisan gerrymandering claims are nonjusticiable.

The Court was not writing on a clean slate in *Rucho*. In *Davis v. Bandemer*,[121] Justice O'Connor, writing for herself and two other conservative Justices, argued that "the partisan gerrymandering claims of major political parties raise non-justiciable political questions that the judiciary should leave to the legislative branch."[122] The other six Justices agreed that partisan gerrymandering claims are justiciable, but they could not agree on a legal standard for adjudicating such claims. Twenty years later, *Vieth v. Jubelirer*[123] was in many ways a replay of *Bandemer*. The Court produced five separate opinions in *Vieth* without a majority opinion. Justice Scalia wrote an opinion for himself and three other conservative Justices; they would have overruled *Bandemer* and held that partisan gerrymandering claims are nonjusticiable.[124] However, they could not secure a fifth vote, so partisan gerrymandering claims remained justiciable after *Vieth*. In *Rucho*, the conservatives finally found a fifth vote to support the position that Justice O'Connor initially advocated more than thirty years earlier.

Rucho combined two cases: one challenging a Democratic gerrymander in Maryland and the other challenging a Republican gerrymander in North Carolina. I focus here on North Carolina. In February 2016, a federal court ordered North Carolina to revise its map for elections to the U.S. House of Representatives. At that time, Republicans held majorities in both houses of the state legislature. The legislature created a redistricting committee – chaired by Representative David Lewis and Senator Robert Rucho – whose task was to prepare a revised districting plan. Lewis and Rucho hired Dr. Thomas Hofeller, a professional mapmaker, to assist the committee.[125]

In 2016, North Carolina had thirteen seats in the House of Representatives. Lewis and Rucho instructed Hofeller to prepare maps that would yield votes for ten Republicans and three Democrats in the upcoming election. Lewis said that he proposed maps "to give a partisan advantage to 10 Republicans and 3 Democrats because he did not believe it would be possible to draw a map with 11 Republicans and 2 Democrats."[126] In the 2016 election, Republican candidates won 53 percent of the statewide vote. Even so, Republicans won ten of the thirteen House seats (77 percent), prevailing in precisely those districts that Lewis, Rucho, and Hofeller had designed as safe Republican seats.[127] One expert analyzed 3,000 possible maps, all of which were consistent with North Carolina's redistricting criteria, except for the goal of giving Republicans a partisan advantage. 2,999 of those 3,000 maps would have given Democrats at least one more seat in Congress. Most of those maps would have given Democrats at least six of North Carolina's thirteen House seats, corresponding roughly to the Democrats' 47 percent share of the statewide vote.[128]

The facts in *Rucho* demonstrate clearly that Republican legislators intended to create electoral districts with a strong pro-Republican bias. (In simple terms, "partisan bias" means that the votes of individuals are not equally weighted. If electoral maps are biased in favor of Democrats, the votes of individuals who vote for Democratic candidates are worth more than the votes of individuals who vote for Republican candidates. Scholars have proposed several different techniques for measuring partisan bias.[129] Under any of the proposed measurement techniques, the maps at issue in *Rucho* in both Maryland and North Carolina were extremely biased.) The Republican plan produced the results that the legislators intended. The North Carolina delegation to the U.S. House of Representatives for the 115th Congress included approximately one Republican representative for every 244,000 Republican voters, and one Democratic representative for every 721,000 Democratic voters.[130] These results are impossible to square with the ideals of the Constitution's Framers, who believed that "it would be unfair, unjust, and contrary to common sense to give a small number of people as many … Representatives as were allowed to much larger groups."[131]

Chief Justice Roberts wrote the majority opinion in *Rucho*, holding that partisan gerrymandering claims are nonjusticiable. Justice Kagan wrote a powerful dissent, joined by Justices Ginsburg, Breyer, and Sotomayor. One key passage in Roberts' opinion exposes the central flaw in his argument. He wrote: "But determining that lines were drawn on the basis of partisanship does not indicate that the districting was improper. A permissible intent – securing partisan advantage – does not become constitutionally impermissible … when that permissible intent 'predominates.'"[132] The Chief Justice's key assumption – that the intent to secure partisan advantage is a permissible intent – is profoundly mistaken for three reasons.

First, we elect legislators to serve the common good. James Madison said that one of the chief criticisms of "popular governments" is "that the public good is [often] disregarded in the conflicts of rival parties."[133] The Constitution's Framers knew that they could not completely eliminate that problem, but one of their central goals was to "break and control the violence of faction," which Madison described as a "dangerous vice."[134] When elected representatives intentionally create partisan bias in an electoral map, they are not serving the public good. Instead, they are serving the interests of a particular faction. The intent to create partisan bias is illegitimate because it is contrary to one of the primary goals that the Framers sought to accomplish when they adopted the Constitution: to control the violence of faction. As Professor Michael Kang has argued: "Partisanship simply does not count … as a legitimate government interest."[135]

Second, the Constitution does not merely divide power among government actors. It also divides power between the government and We the People. Indeed, the division of power between the government and the people is a core structural feature of our Constitution. Justice Kagan wrote: "If there is a single idea that made our Nation … it is this one: The people are sovereign. The power … is in the people over the Government and not in the Government over the people."[136] Periodic elections are the primary mechanism for the people to exercise their power over the government. When legislators intentionally create partisan bias in the redistricting plans that govern elections, they violate the Constitution by robbing We the People of our power to exercise control over the government. Granted, virtually any mapmaking exercise will yield maps with some degree of partisan bias. However, the fact that small amounts of partisan bias are the accidental byproduct of almost any mapmaking process does not mean that the deliberate attempt to create partisan bias is a legitimate policy objective.

Third, the Constitution grants We the People a collective right to democratic self-governance. This means that we have the right to choose our legislators; they do not have the right to choose their voters. In Justice Ginsburg's words, "the core principle of republican government" is "that the voters should choose their representatives, not the other way around."[137] When legislators intentionally create maps with partisan bias, they violate our collective right to democratic self-governance by designing an electoral system in which legislators choose their voters. For all these reasons, the deliberate intent to create maps with partisan bias is not a legitimate goal. Chief Justice Roberts' assertion that the intent to create partisan bias is "a permissible intent" manifests an alarming failure to appreciate the core values underlying our constitutional system.

The Chief Justice presented two main arguments to support his view that the goal of creating partisan bias is a legitimate goal. First, he cited Article I, Section 4 of the Constitution, which says: "The Times, Places and Manner of holding Elections for Senators and Representatives, shall be prescribed in each State by the Legislature thereof."[138] Relying on this text, the Chief Justice asserted: "To hold that legislators cannot take partisan interests into account when drawing district lines would essentially countermand the Framers' decision to entrust districting to political entities."[139] His argument conflates two distinct issues: Who has the power to make decisions? And what are the legitimate goals they may pursue? Roberts is correct that the Framers made a deliberate choice to grant power over redistricting to state legislators. However, since Article I, sec. 4 says nothing about the goals to be accomplished by redistricting, we must look to the Constitution as a whole to determine what goals are legitimate. The main goals of redistricting should be to promote the common good, to preserve the power of the people over the government, and to vindicate our collective right to democratic self-governance. The deliberate attempt to create partisan bias is antithetical to all three goals.

Roberts also argued that the intent to secure partisan advantage must be a legitimate goal because legislators have been doing it for more than 200 years.[140] That argument is not persuasive. Throughout its history, the Court has invalidated longstanding practices on the grounds that they conflict with core constitutional values. *Reynolds v. Sims* invalidated the longstanding practice of drawing district lines to privilege rural voters over urban voters. The Court did not say: "Well, this must be okay because we've been doing it for a long time." Instead, the Court condemned the practice because it violated the principle of political equality.[141] The fact that legislators have been doing something for a long time cannot justify the practice if it violates core constitutional norms.

Moreover, to quote Justice Kagan: "[B]ig data and modern technology … make today's gerrymandering altogether different from the crude linedrawing of the past…. These are not your grandfather's – let alone the Framers' – gerrymanders."[142] Before the rise of big data and modern computing technology, partisan legislators sometimes produced so-called dummymanders: "gerrymanders that went spectacularly wrong."[143] Modern partisan gerrymandering is much more damaging to our democratic institutions than older gerrymanders because big data and modern technology enable politicians to wield a scalpel, instead of a cluster bomb.

Chief Justice Roberts argued that the central question in partisan gerrymandering cases is "how much partisan dominance is too much?"[144] By framing the question in that way, he implied that partisan gerrymandering is defined primarily by effects, not intent. That framing of the issue follows naturally from his (mistaken) view that the intent to create partisan bias is legitimate. The Court justified its central holding – that partisan gerrymandering claims are nonjusticiable – by arguing that the "how much is too much" question requires a political answer, rather than a legal answer, because any answer to that question necessarily involves arbitrary line drawing.[145]

If one accepts the premise that partisan gerrymandering should be defined in terms of effects, not intent, Roberts' argument seems plausible. Moreover, most Supreme Court Justices who have argued that partisan gerrymandering claims are justiciable have advocated some version of an effects test, or a test that combines intent plus effects.[146] On this point, I part company with Justice Kagan and the other Justices who have analyzed partisan gerrymandering in terms of its effects. The basic test should be an intent test, not an effects test, because the intent to create partisan bias is an illegitimate goal. If one frames the test in terms of intent, not effects, the answer to the "how much is too much" question is simple. Any deliberate attempt to create partisan bias in the context of redistricting is illegitimate and therefore unconstitutional. (In contrast, a deliberate attempt to undo the partisan bias of a previous mapmaking exercise is entirely legitimate.[147])

Admittedly, my proposed constitutional rule creates one problem. In *Rucho* and other recent cases, legislators and mapmakers did not try to conceal their partisan goals because they believed that their intent to create partisan bias was legitimate. In such cases, it is easy for plaintiffs to prove partisan intent; they can simply use the legislators' own words against them. However, if the Court rules that the intent to create partisan bias is unconstitutional, legislators and mapmakers may continue to pursue partisan goals, but they will probably attempt to conceal their true objectives.

In those circumstances, it will be more difficult for plaintiffs to prove that legislators and mapmakers acted with the intent to create partisan bias. Therefore, courts will need to consider partisan effects as indirect evidence of partisan intent. This type of approach is common. For example, in a murder case, the prosecution must prove that the defendant acted with intent to kill. Typically, the prosecution lacks direct evidence of intent, such as a tape recording of the killer's statements. Thus, the prosecution uses evidence of the killer's actions and the effect of those actions (a dead body) to prove intent. Similarly, to prove intent in partisan gerrymandering cases, plaintiffs will need evidence of the legislators' actions and the effects of those actions – in this case, maps that manifest extreme partisan bias. In such cases, the "how much is too much" question returns, but in a different form. If the judge or jury concludes that the degree of partisan bias is so great that it is implausible to believe that mapmakers created that bias accidentally, then the judge or jury may infer that the mapmakers acted with deliberate intent. In sum, the constitutional test for partisan gerrymandering should be an intent test, not an effects test, because any deliberate attempt to create partisan bias is illegitimate. However, in cases where direct evidence of intent is lacking, evidence of extreme partisan effects could be used to support an inference that the legislators and mapmakers acted with wrongful intent.

* * * * *

The preceding analysis supports three specific proposals for constitutional reform. First, the Court should overrule *Buckley v. Valeo* and give Congress greater leeway to experiment with restrictions on campaign expenditures. Second, the Court should overrule *Shelby County* and direct the Attorney General to reinstate the pre-clearance regime. Third, the Court should overrule *Rucho* and declare unequivocally that partisan gerrymandering is unconstitutional. The Court is unlikely to adopt any of these proposals until a future President appoints new Supreme Court Justices who are committed to using their judicial power to enhance the power of We the People to exercise control over our government. Chapter 8 explores a potential pathway for constitutional change in which Congress and the Supreme Court could collaborate as partners to enhance popular control over the government. *California Democratic*

Party v. Jones raises complex issues about the role of political parties in our electoral system. Much of the remainder of this chapter explores those issues in greater detail.

ONE SIMPLE PROPOSAL

Before delving into issues related to political parties, I want to suggest one fairly simple constitutional rule that would help restore confidence in election procedures. The Court should declare that the Constitution requires states to appoint nonpartisan officials to oversee election administration, including the counting and certification of ballots.[148] The United States is one of the few countries in the world that entrusts election administration to partisan officials.[149] As of this writing, there is no evidence from recent elections that any of those officials have deliberately manipulated vote counts to favor their own parties. However, a significant minority of U.S. citizens believe that elections are not being administered fairly. A poll conducted in June 2023 found that "30% of respondents believe Biden's victory came thanks to voter fraud, while 59% say he won the election fair and square."[150] Moreover, the perception of fairness is almost as important as actual fairness. Vesting authority in nonpartisan officials to oversee the mechanics of election administration "should help bolster the perception that elections are administered neutrally."[151]

In *Democracy and Distrust*, John Hart Ely reminded us that "constitutional law appropriately exists for those situations where representative government cannot be trusted, not those where we know it can."[152] The elected representatives who control state governments have no apparent incentive to initiate a shift from partisan to nonpartisan election administration. Congress could use its power under Article I, sec. 4 to mandate nonpartisan election administration for federal elections. However, based on current constitutional understandings, Congress lacks the power to mandate nonpartisan election administration for state and local elections. (If the Court overrules *City of Boerne v. Flores*, Congress could use its power under Section 5 of the Fourteenth Amendment to regulate state and local elections.) Hence, judicial intervention is needed to correct a malfunction in the political marketplace. The strongest rationale for a constitutional prohibition on partisan election administration relies on the Constitution's structural division of power between the government and the people, and the need to reinforce popular control over the government. To restore confidence in fair elections, citizens who fear voter fraud must be persuaded that officials responsible for election administration serve We the People, not partisan interests.

THREE PROPOSED RULES

I propose three new constitutional rules that, taken together, are designed to enhance the power of We the People to exercise control over our government through the electoral process. More specifically, the rules are designed to correct the central pathology in our current electoral system (described at the beginning of this chapter), nurture robust competition in the political marketplace, and incentivize candidates to compete for the votes of median voters. In formulating these rules, I assume that it is not realistically feasible to amend the Constitution. Therefore, I rely on constitutional construction, rather than constitutional amendment, to achieve constitutional reform. Given the existence of the Electoral College and the Twelfth Amendment, this chapter does not address rules for Presidential elections.[153]

The three proposed rules are as follows. First, the Court should declare that the Constitution requires officials responsible for redistricting to maximize the number of competitive seats. Second, the Court should ban partisan primaries and require primaries to be conducted so that at least three candidates proceed to the general election. Third, the Court should hold that the Constitution requires ranked choice voting (RCV) in the general election, and that states must use a ballot tabulation method in which the "Condorcet winner" wins the election, unless there is no Condorcet winner. (As explained in more detail later, the "Condorcet winner" is the candidate whom the most voters dislike the least.) The first rule should apply to all seats for state legislatures and for the U.S. House of Representatives. The second and third rules operate together: They should apply to all elections for Governors and U.S. Senators, as well as elections for state legislatures and the House of Representatives. In elaborating these rules, I rely heavily on the work of two leading election law scholars: Professors Edward Foley and Richard Pildes.[154]

Insofar as the proposed rules address federal elections, Article I, Section 4 grants Congress the power to enact legislation to codify the rules. Insofar as the rules address elections for Governors and state legislatures, Congress arguably lacks any such power, unless the Supreme Court overrules *City of Boerne Flores* and adopts a broader construction of Congress's power under Section 5 of the Fourteenth Amendment. From the standpoint of democratic theory, it would be preferable for Congress to enact the proposed rules through legislation. However, as a practical matter, strong judicial review may be necessary because the incentives that drive elected politicians to seek reelection raise doubts about whether those same politicians would support legislation designed to increase competition in the political marketplace. In states that permit citizens to enact new statutes or constitutional amendments by voter referenda or initiatives, change may be possible without judicial intervention. However, only about half the states allow these types of citizen-led statutory and/or constitutional reforms.[155] Therefore, new federal constitutional rules provide the most promising pathway to nurture robust electoral competition on a national basis.

In *Wesberry v. Sanders* and *Reynolds v. Sims*, strong judicial review was necessary to fix a broken electoral system that our elected representatives wanted to preserve for purely self-interested reasons. Similarly, active judicial intervention may be necessary today to fix a broken electoral system that the two dominant political parties are incentivized to preserve for mostly partisan reasons. Even so, in addressing these issues, the Court should formulate rules designed to ensure "that the channels of political participation and communication are kept open" for subsequent action by democratically elected legislators.[156] Specifically, rules for federal elections should be grounded in what Professor Foley has called the "Dormant Elections Clause."[157] That approach would enable Congress to act under Article I, Section 4, to flesh out the details of principles articulated by the Court.[158] In formulating constitutional rules for elections to state offices, the Court could maintain open channels for political participation by basing its decisions on the Equal Protection Clause (as in *Reynolds v. Sims*) and inviting Congress to use its Section 5 power to flesh out the details for implementing judicially formulated constitutional principles.

Maximize Competitive Seats

The first proposed rule is a constitutional mandate for officials in charge of redistricting to maximize the number of competitive seats for both state legislatures and the House of Representatives, subject to constraints imposed by traditional districting criteria, such as compactness, contiguity, and county lines. State legislatures would still be free to enact laws establishing redistricting criteria, but those criteria could not include any that are explicitly or implicitly intended to protect safe seats. The constitutional mandate would require mapmakers to draw maps to maximize the number of competitive seats within the constraints imposed by state statutory criteria. Those statutory criteria, themselves, would be subject to constitutional challenge if they violated constitutional rules on racial gerrymandering or partisan gerrymandering, or if they were secretly intended to maximize the number of safe seats.

Professor Pildes says: "From the early 1970s to the early 1990s, around 35 percent of congressional districts were extremely competitive. But by 2022, 84 percent of candidates to the U.S. House were elected from safe seats."[159] The proposed rule, by itself, could potentially restore the level of competition that existed in the 1970s to 1990s. When combined with the other proposed rules discussed later in this chapter, even greater gains in electoral competitiveness should be possible.

Note that a ban on partisan gerrymandering, by itself, would not maximize electoral competition. Consider the case of North Carolina, which currently has fourteen seats in the House of Representatives. According to Cook Political Report, that figure includes ten seats that are solid Republican, three seats that are solid Democrat, and one tossup.[160] A ban on partisan gerrymandering would shift the balance between solid Republican seats and solid Democratic seats, but it might not yield any more competitive seats. In contrast, a constitutional mandate to maximize the number of competitive seats would likely yield a map with at least three or four competitive seats.[161]

One potential problem with a constitutional mandate to maximize the number of competitive districts is that the Court would need to establish a standard or rule for competitiveness. "Competitive districts have generally been defined as those in which the winning candidate receives 55 percent of the vote or less."[162] Professor Pildes notes: "Given increasing partisan loyalty among voters ... swing districts today might have to include no more than 53 percent of likely voters for one party to be competitive."[163] To help avoid protracted litigation, the Court should set a bright-line rule for competitiveness in the range of 53 to 55 percent, but the Court should make clear that its rule is subject to congressional modification.

Clearly, the rule would need to be framed in terms of projected electoral outcomes, not past electoral outcomes. In other words, the rule would require mapmakers to draw electoral districts to maximize the number of seats, subject to statutory districting criteria, where the winning party is expected to secure no more than [53][55] percent of the vote. With big data and sophisticated data analysis tools, mapmakers today have the capacity to project electoral outcomes on a district-by-district basis with a high degree of precision. If plaintiffs who challenge a redistricting plan prove by a preponderance of the evidence that mapmakers could have created more competitive seats, courts could order states to redraw their maps, or simply issue court-ordered maps.

An alternative constitutional rule would require states to use independent redistricting commissions to draw boundaries between electoral districts. The data in Table 3.1 suggests that this approach would increase the number of competitive seats. Table 3.1 combines information from two sources. The Brennan Center for Justice provides information about who controls the redistricting process in every state.[164] The Cook Political Report provides detailed information about which seats in the House of Representatives were competitive in the 2024 elections.[165] In the most recent redistricting cycle, partisan legislators controlled the redistricting process for 226 seats. Only 12 of those 226 seats (about 5 percent) are competitive. (See Table 3.1.) In contrast, independent courts or commissions controlled the redistricting process for 173 seats. Twenty-eight of those 173 seats (about 16 percent) are competitive. (See Table 3.1.) Thus, a constitutional rule requiring independent redistricting commissions would almost certainly increase the number of competitive seats.

However, a rule requiring independent commissions would likely be more difficult to implement than a rule requiring states to maximize competitive seats, because it is hard to determine whether a commission is truly independent. The Brennan Center says that four states use "independent commissions," whereas five other states use "political commissions."[166] The line separating independent commissions from political commissions is hard to define. Moreover, not all "independent" commissions are created equal. The Brennan Center classifies Arizona, California, Colorado, and Michigan as states with independent commissions. Common Cause – a leading group that advocates for fair redistricting – publishes a "report card" on state redistricting plans.[167] California earned an A minus; Colorado and Michigan earned Bs; and Arizona scored a B minus. Asking judges

TABLE 3.1 *Independent Redistricting Commissions and Competitive Seats*

	Number of States	Number of House Seats	Number of Competitive Seats	Percentage of Seats that are Competitive
Republican Legislature Controlled Redistricting	19	177	7	4.0%
Democratic Legislature Controlled Redistricting	7	49	5	10.2%
Court-Ordered Redistricting	8	91	15	16.5%
Independent Commission	4	82	13	15.9%
One At-large Seat[168]	6	6	1	16.7%
Other	6	30	4	13.3%
Total	50	435	45	10.3%

to establish criteria for evaluating "independence" and then apply those criteria would probably lead to protracted litigation. In contrast, if the Court establishes a bright-line rule for competitiveness in the range of 53 to 55 percent, it would be fairly simple for lower courts to administer that rule. Moreover, the proposed rule would address the central issue – increasing electoral competitiveness – directly, rather than indirectly.

All-Candidate Primaries and Ranked Choice Voting

At this point in the argument, it is worth recapping a few key principles before analyzing election procedures. First, the Constitution divides power between the government and We the People. It is designed to empower We the People to control our government. It is also designed to minimize the risk that a particular faction will exercise power in a manner that deprives the people of control over the government. One central purpose of judicial review is to preserve popular control of the government. The Court affirmed these principles in *Reynolds v. Sims* when it declared that the Constitution requires "that each citizen have an equally effective voice in the election of members of his state legislature."[169] Political scientists have shown that the best way to minimize the harmful influence of factions and to guarantee every citizen an equally effective voice is to design election procedures that incentivize candidates to compete for the votes of median voters.

Based on these principles, the Court should hold that the Constitution requires states to: (a) conduct all-candidate primaries in which at least three candidates move on to the general election; and (b) conduct general elections that use ranked choice voting (RCV) procedures, along with a ballot tabulation method ensuring that the "Condorcet winner" will win the election, unless there is no Condorcet winner.[170] These rules would require states to use RCV, but states would retain discretion to choose among several possible variants of RCV, unless Congress enacts legislation requiring states to adopt a specific variant. The Court should mandate this type of two-stage election process for Senate seats, House seats, gubernatorial elections, and state legislative elections.

The Marquis de Condorcet was an eighteenth-century French philosopher and mathematician who developed important insights about democratic election procedures. In an election with three or more candidates, the Condorcet winner is the candidate whom a majority of voters prefer over each of the other candidates in a pairwise comparison.[171] In less technical terms, the Condorcet winner is the least polarizing candidate – the candidate whom the most voters dislike the least. An electoral system that is designed to produce a Condorcet winner provides the strongest possible incentive for candidates to compete for the vote of the median voter.[172]

No state currently uses election procedures that are fully consistent with the proposed rules, but Alaska's system is close. Alaska adopted a top-four system in 2020, which took effect in 2022. Under that system, candidates first compete in a nonpartisan primary. The top four vote-getters then move on to the general election.[173] Alaska uses instant runoff voting (IRV) for the general election. IRV is a specific type of RCV procedure. Under IRV, voters rank their preferences on the ballot, designating each of the candidates as 1, 2, 3, or 4. The candidate with the lowest number of first-choice votes is eliminated in round one. The votes of the people who chose that candidate as their first choice are then transferred to each voter's second preference and the votes are tabulated again. If all candidates are still below 50 percent, a second candidate is eliminated in round two and votes are again transferred to each voter's second choice.[174]

In Alaska, the nonpartisan primary in 2022 yielded four candidates for a U.S. Senate seat: Lisa Murkowski, the incumbent Republican (a moderate); Kelly Tshibaka, a Trump-endorsed Republican; Buzz Kelley, also a Republican; and Patricia Chesbro, the Democratic candidate. Despite strong opposition from Donald Trump, Murkowski won the election after Buzz Kelley was eliminated in round one and Patricia Chesbro was eliminated in round two. Chesbro, the Democrat, received about 28,000 votes in the first round. When she was eliminated, more than 20,000 votes were transferred to Murkowski, but only 2,200 were transferred to Tshibaka.[175] In the final round, Murkowski won with 54 percent of the vote, compared to 46 percent for Tshibaka. The Democrats who picked Chesbro as their first choice overwhelmingly preferred Murkowski (a moderate Republican) compared to Tshibaka (a MAGA Republican). In the end, under its top-four system, Alaska's voters elected the candidate whose views were closest to the preferences of the median voter. Senator Murkowski would have been the Condorcet winner if Alaska adopted a Condorcet system.[176]

Compare Alaska to Wyoming, which uses a closed partisan primary election, followed by first past the post (FPTP) in the general election.[177] In 2022, Harriet Hageman challenged Liz Cheney for Wyoming's seat in the House of Representatives. Donald Trump strenuously opposed Cheney's reelection; he supported Hageman in the Republican primary. Hageman won the Republican primary with 66 percent of the votes; she then won the general election with 68 percent of the votes. If Wyoming adopted Alaska's electoral system, Cheney might possibly have won reelection.[178] Conversely, if Alaska conducted partisan primaries followed by FPTP, Ms. Tshibaka almost certainly would have won the Republican primary and the general election.[179] The contrast between Alaska and Wyoming illustrates a broader point. Election procedures matter. Partisan primaries and FPTP favor more ideologically extreme candidates. All-candidate primaries and RCV favor candidates whose views are closer to the median voter in most cases.[180]

Mandate All-Candidate Primaries

In the vast majority of states, the state employs its government apparatus to support separate primary elections for the Democratic Party and the Republican Party. At present, Alaska, California, and Washington are the only states that conduct nonpartisan primary elections for federal offices.[181] (Louisiana and Nebraska conduct nonpartisan primaries for some state offices.[182]) Both California and Washington use a top-two system; the two candidates with the most votes in the primary compete head-to-head in the general election. As discussed previously, Alaska uses a top-four system that sends four candidates to the general election.

Professor Pildes says: "The traditional party primary has become a significant force fueling the rise and success of more ideologically extreme candidates."[183] To counter the rise of ideologically extreme candidates and help foster the growth of a more competitive electoral system that favors candidates who appeal to the median voter, the Supreme Court should hold that the Constitution requires states to conduct all-candidate primaries for both state and federal offices.[184] The Constitution's structural division of power between the government and We the People provides the foundation for the proposed rule. The Constitution is designed to ensure that We the People, acting collectively, maintain control over our government. State-run partisan primaries enable partisan factions to exercise control over the government for the benefit of their factions, to the detriment of the common good. By allowing political parties to utilize the instruments of state power to conduct partisan elections as the first stage of a two-stage election process, states are effectively robbing We the People of a power that the Constitution vests in us and transferring that power to factional political parties.

A constitutional rule mandating all-candidate primaries would still allow political parties to conduct their own primary elections if they chose to do so. The rule would simply prohibit state governments from using the instruments of state power to support partisan primaries. Therefore, the rule does not interfere with the freedom-of-association rights of political parties.

There are two important corollaries to the rule requiring all-candidate primaries. First, the Court should hold that states must conduct primaries in a manner that yields at least three candidates to compete in the general election. A top-two system (like the systems currently in place in California and Washington) replicates the problems associated with partisan primaries because it tends to eliminate the likely Condorcet winner in the first round of voting. A rule requiring at least three candidates in the general election – when combined with a rule requiring RCV in the general election – would provide a powerful incentive for candidates to compete for the vote of the median voter.

The second corollary is for the Court to hold that so-called sore-loser laws are unconstitutional. "Sore-loser laws prohibit a candidate who loses a party primary from running in the general election; currently, forty-seven states have such laws."[185] Sore-loser laws restrict the power of voters to choose their preferred candidates; such laws effectively transfer power over the electoral process from voters to political parties. Assuming that the Constitution requires all-candidate primaries, states will need rules to determine who is eligible to appear on the primary ballot. States might opt for the California approach, which allows multiple Democrats and multiple Republicans to compete in the primary election. Alternatively, states would have the discretion to adopt rules that allow only one Democratic candidate and one Republican candidate to appear on the ballot for the primary election. And states would be free to designate those candidates with the labels D and R. However, a constitutional ban on sore-loser laws would ensure that a candidate who lost in the (privately operated) Democratic or Republican primary could still appear on the ballot in the state-run primary as an independent candidate, provided that she qualifies under general ballot eligibility rules. Preserving spots on the ballot for such candidates would incentivize Democratic and Republican candidates to compete for the votes of median voters.

General Elections and Ranked Choice Voting

The *Washington Post* reported in October 2024 that "referendums in the District [of Columbia], Colorado, Idaho, Nevada and Oregon will ask voters in November whether they want to institute ranked choice [voting]."[186] I have suggested that the Court should hold that the Constitution requires states to conduct general elections that use RCV, along with a ballot tabulation method that guarantees that the Condorcet winner will win the election, unless there is no Condorcet winner. The proposed rule would promote competitive elections by providing a powerful incentive for candidates to compete for the vote of the median voter. As noted previously, if and when the Court adopts a rule along these lines, it should make clear that the rule is subject to congressional modification – under a "Dormant Elections Clause" theory for federal elections, and under a theory rooted in Section 5 of the Fourteenth Amendment for state elections.

One obvious objection is that the rule, as stated, is confusing. A much simpler version of the rule would merely require states to conduct general elections that use RCV. However, this simple rule would not actually achieve the goal of promoting competitive elections. Under the simple rule, many states would probably opt for IRV. Indeed, in the places where state and local governments are experimenting with RCV, IRV appears to be the most common ballot tabulation method. Unfortunately, "IRV will tend to produce outcomes that deviate from the preferences of states' median voters.... [This problem] is greatly exacerbated as the electorate's polarization increases."[187]

A simple example illustrates the point. Consider an election with three candidates: L, R, and C (left, right, and center). Citizens are given a ranked choice ballot and told to rank the candidates. Forty percent of voters choose L as their first choice; they all choose C as their second choice. Forty percent choose R as their first choice; they all choose C as their second choice. The other 20 percent choose C as their first choice. Within that group, 12 percent choose L as their second choice and 8 percent choose R. C is clearly the Condorcet winner because 60 percent of voters prefer C to L, and 60 percent of voters prefer C to R. However, in an IRV election, C will be eliminated in the first round because C received the fewest first-round votes. (This phenomenon is known as the "center squeeze.") In this example, L will win by a 52–48 margin in round two, despite the fact that 60 percent of voters prefer C to L. Thus, IRV does a poor job of incentivizing candidates to compete for the vote of the median voter. Moreover, "the effect is most pronounced in the most polarized states."[188]

Consider a different possible formulation of the proposed rule: States must conduct general elections that use RCV and that yield a Condorcet winner. This rule is simpler to state than my proposed rule, but it is impossible to implement. Without doing a deep dive into electoral math, suffice it to say that under any RCV system with three or more candidates, there is a risk that no candidate will be the Condorcet winner. If "there is no Condorcet Winner and instead each candidate prevails in only one pairwise comparison ... there needs to be a method to break this ... tie among the candidates."[189] My proposed rule would give states flexibility to experiment with different approaches to breaking a tie if there is no Condorcet winner. Even so, it would provide a powerful incentive for candidates to compete for the vote of the median voter by insisting that states must adopt rules that guarantee victory for the Condorcet winner if there is one.

In theory, the Court could announce a new constitutional rule that requires states to use a very specific type of election procedure in all general elections for Senators, Congressmen, Governors, and state legislatures. For example, the Court could mandate use of the top-three system that Professor Foley has proposed.[190] That rule would require states to conduct primary elections that yield precisely three candidates to compete in the general election. It would also require states to adopt a tie-breaker rule in which the candidate who comes closest to being a Condorcet winner is declared the victor if there is no Condorcet winner.[191]

This type of constitutional rule could be described as the election law equivalent of the *Miranda* rule. *In Miranda v. Arizona*,[192] the Court held that police officers must use a specific verbal formulation to advise criminal defendants of their constitutional rights. *Miranda* is generally understood as a prophylactic rule: Although the Constitution itself does not mandate a precise verbal formulation, there were compelling practical reasons for the Court to mandate a precise verbal formulation to avoid endless disputes about whether a particular warning issued by police is "good enough" to satisfy the Constitution. Similarly, if the Court mandated the use of a very specific type of election procedure, it could potentially avoid lengthy disputes about whether a particular state election law is "Condorcet compliant."

Even so, a new federal constitutional rule that mandated the use of a very specific type of electoral process would rightly be criticized as heavy-handed judicial lawmaking. For more than two centuries, the Constitution has been construed to grant states a large degree of flexibility to design their own election procedures.[193] The problem today is that the two dominant political parties have captured the machinery of state government and used their power over state governments to design electoral rules that promote partisan interests at the expense of the common good. Strong judicial review is necessary to wrest power away from the political parties and return power over the electoral process to We the People. My proposed rule strikes a balance. It gives states some freedom to experiment, while also requiring states to design their election laws in a way that incentivizes candidates to compete for the vote of the median voter.

Granted, the phrase "Condorcet winner" does not easily roll off the tongue of the average American voter. Ideally, if the Court is going to announce a new constitutional rule, that rule should be easy for the general public to understand. Professor Foley has suggested the phrase "maximum convergence voting" to describe an electoral process that favors the Condorcet winner.[194] Regardless of what terminology is used, the critical point is that the Supreme Court must explain the rule in a way that is comprehensible to state election officials so that they know which types of election procedures do, and do not, comply with the rule. My proposed rule satisfies that test because the concept of a Condorcet winner can be easily explained to state election officials. Thus, the proposed rule would avoid protracted litigation because state election officials would know what types of procedures are, or are not, permissible.

4

Election-Related Misinformation

The Introduction to this book noted that the United States is currently undergoing a process of democratic decay. Leading scholars who have studied democratic decay in other countries warn that "the guardrails of American democracy are weakening."[1] The parallels between sociopolitical conditions in the United States today and conditions in other countries that have descended from democracy to dictatorship are alarming.[2]

On January 6, 2021, a violent mob stormed the Capitol. For the first time since the Civil War, a group of citizens resorted to violence in an attempt to prevent the peaceful transfer of power from an outgoing President to his duly elected successor. Moreover, the January 6 attack was merely one element of a broader scheme by President Trump to prevent President Biden from taking office.[3]

Citizens attacked the Capitol because they believed the "Big Lie": the claim that Joe Biden stole the election from Donald Trump, who (in their view) was the rightful winner.[4] There was essentially no evidence to support Trump's claim. In fact, "Trump and his allies lost sixty-one of sixty-two cases [raising challenges to the results in the 2020 election], and Trump's sole win was a minor one."[5] Nevertheless, millions of Americans still believe the Big Lie. A CNN poll conducted in August 2023 found that 38 percent of Americans, and 69 percent of "Republicans and Republican-leaners," believed that President Biden's victory in the 2020 election was "not legitimate."[6] They believed the Big Lie in January 2021, and they continue to believe it today, because several large media and information technology companies amplified and repeated Donald Trump's false claims over and over again. Empirical research demonstrates that "the more [a claim] is repeated, the more viewers will believe it (even if the claim that is being repeated is not true)."[7]

It bears emphasis that – but for the electronic amplification of misinformation – the January 6 attack on the Capitol would not have happened. Donald Trump could not have rallied the troops to assault the Capitol without help from companies that provide "electronic amplification services," enabling speakers to deliver content to millions of people almost instantaneously. (I have drafted a proposed statute that defines "electronic amplification services" to mean "content distribution and content aggregation services that enable speakers to deliver their messages to large audiences almost instantaneously."[8]) Therefore, this chapter begins with the premise that the electronic amplification of false and misleading election-related claims poses a significant threat to American democracy. We urgently need government regulation of companies that provide electronic amplification services to address that threat. However, the Supreme Court has created a body of First Amendment doctrine that places Congress in a constitutional straightjacket, making it almost impossible for Congress to enact the legislation that is necessary to prevent the United States from following Weimar Germany down the path from democracy to dictatorship.

Standard accounts of the First Amendment emphasize two core goals that the Amendment is designed to accomplish: enhancing the quality of democratic self-government and helping ensure that truth prevails over lies in the marketplace of ideas.[9] If our information ecosystem functioned properly, then American citizens would receive truthful, accurate, election-related information, advancing both of these goals simultaneously. Unfortunately, though, the United States currently has an information ecosystem in which lies often prevail over truth – including, but not limited to, election-related lies.[10]

Several factors have contributed to the growth of our dysfunctional information environment. Many people blame the advent of new communications technologies, such as social media, and Congress's utter failure to regulate those technologies.[11] I agree that Congress and social media companies are partly to blame. However, that explanation is incomplete. Empirical research demonstrates that a narrow focus on social media is misplaced because cable TV and talk radio are key channels for the dissemination of election-related disinformation.[12] Moreover, this chapter contends that the Supreme Court – in particular, the Court's misguided First Amendment doctrine – deserves a large share of the blame. Specifically, First Amendment doctrine fails to appreciate the constitutional significance of the distinction between ordinary speech and the electronic amplification of speech.[13] Moreover, First Amendment doctrine fails to recognize that government regulation of speech is sometimes necessary to prevent what Professor Deborah Pearlstein calls "democracy harms."[14]

Modern First Amendment doctrine emphasizes the negative function of the First Amendment: The Amendment imposes restrictions on government based on a general distrust of government regulation of speech.[15] In prior work, I have highlighted the distinction between "Madisonian" and "libertarian" views of the First Amendment.[16] Madisonians emphasize the affirmative goals of the First Amendment; they believe that some government regulation of the information ecosystem is necessary to accomplish the twin goals of truth seeking and democracy promotion. Libertarians emphasize the negative First Amendment. They tend to be skeptical of any government effort to regulate the information marketplace.[17] Most libertarians would presumably support the goal of creating an information ecosystem that provides citizens accurate, truthful, election-related information. However, libertarians tend to think that the best way to accomplish that goal is to rely on the private sector because we cannot trust government to regulate speech. Although Congress and the Supreme Court generally shared a Madisonian perspective from the 1930s to the 1970s, libertarian thinking has dominated the Court's First Amendment doctrine since the 1980s.

Karl Loewenstein developed the theory of militant democracy in Germany in the 1930s.[18] According to Professor Neil Netanel, "Loewenstein placed primary emphasis on preventing fascists and other totalitarian forces from exploiting liberal democratic rights of speech, association, and political participation to subvert democracy."[19] A key insight underlying Loewenstein's theory is that democracy is an indispensable prerequisite for the effective exercise of free speech rights. If the United States – or any other country – allows authoritarian forces to exploit free speech to subvert democracy, it will lose both democracy and free speech. Moreover, if the Supreme Court continues to apply its current libertarian approach to the First Amendment, the Court will prevent Congress from enacting the type of legislation that is urgently needed to protect our democracy, and therefore to protect free speech. In the words of Hannah Arendt: "Freedom of opinion is a farce unless factual information is guaranteed and the facts themselves are not in dispute."[20]

This chapter proceeds as follows. The first section describes the media ecosystem in the United States from the 1930s to the 1980s. I then discuss the demise of the fairness doctrine in the 1980s. Next, I address the rise of the "right-wing media ecosystem"[21] and the resultant harm to democratic self-government. The following section sketches the outlines of a proposed federal statute that would restrict the electronic amplification of election-related misinformation. Finally, I explain why any statute along those lines – indeed, any statute that might be moderately effective in protecting American democracy from the threat posed by the electronic amplification of misinformation – would almost certainly be deemed unconstitutional under the Court's current First Amendment doctrine. Therefore, the Court must revise its First Amendment doctrine to save American democracy.

Before proceeding further, one preliminary point is in order. Article 19 of the International Covenant on Civil and Political Rights (ICCPR) states: "Everyone shall have the right to freedom of expression; this right shall include freedom to seek, receive and impart information of all kinds, … through any other media of his choice." Article 19 also specifies that the exercise of these rights "carries with it special duties and responsibilities."[22] Accordingly, Article 19 authorizes governments to enact some legal restrictions on freedom of expression to promote the common good. Chapter 6 develops the argument that U.S. courts should rely more on the ICCPR and less on the Bill of Rights, to protect individual rights. In this chapter, though, I analyze the electronic amplification of misinformation through a First Amendment lens, setting aside international law arguments for later chapters.

FROM THE 1930S TO THE REAGAN ADMINISTRATION

Congress created the Federal Communications Commission (FCC) in the Communications Act of 1934.[23] Leading public intellectuals at the time recognized that government regulation of electronic amplification services was necessary to promote First Amendment values because they knew from experience that "information was supremely susceptible to manipulation and control" by large media companies.[24] Walter Lippman, perhaps the leading journalist of his day, argued that "the most important questions about communication in the public sphere were about the institutional structure of political communication, not about individuals' free speech rights," because "inhabitants of a mass society were exceedingly vulnerable to quacks, charlatans, and worse."[25] Consistent with Lippman's views, the 1934 Act granted the FCC broad powers to regulate radio (and later television) stations to promote "the public interest."[26]

The Golden Age of Broadcast News

The FCC first authorized commercial television broadcasts in 1941. "By 1955, half of American households owned television sets."[27] NBC launched the first television news broadcast in 1956, the *Huntley-Brinkley Report*. For the next three or four decades, most Americans received most of their news from network television. There were only three networks: NBC, ABC, and CBS. They all reported roughly the same news in roughly the same way. A 1972 poll identified Walter Cronkite, the anchor for *CBS Evening News*, as "the most trusted man in America."[28] In contrast to the modern era of media fragmentation, the fact that most Americans received their news from a small set of trusted gatekeepers meant that American voters generally operated on the basis of a set of shared facts (or shared assumptions) that provided a basis for reasoned discussion about public policy issues. On the other hand, those shared assumptions tended to reflect the perspectives of the White, male, middle-class journalists who dominated the three major networks.

Several factors contributed to the homogeneity of the news reported by the three networks. First, the FCC codified the Fairness Doctrine in a 1949 report, *In re Editorializing by Broadcast Licensees*.[29] The doctrine imposed two main obligations on radio and televisions stations. First, licensees were required to "devote a reasonable portion of broadcast time to the discussion and consideration of controversial issues of public importance." Second, they must "affirmatively endeavor to make … facilities available for the expression of contrasting viewpoints."[30] The Fairness Doctrine, and the accompanying threat of enforcement by the FCC, provided a strong incentive for television news networks to report the news in a way that was broadly accepted as objective and impartial.

Second, the Society of Professional Journalists adopted a Code of Ethics in 1926 that called for "journalistic impartiality, meaning that news reports should be free from opinion or bias of any kind."[31] Newspaper journalists, who dominated news reporting in the 1920s, soon embraced the new code of journalistic ethics. As radio and television became important sources of news over the next few decades, radio and TV journalists followed suit. The combination of a professional sense of journalistic ethics, combined with the Fairness Doctrine and FCC oversight, exerted a centripetal force that pulled network news toward the political center.

The scarcity of news sources also contributed to homogeneity.[32] Cable television began in the late 1940s. However, anticompetitive behavior by the three major networks stymied the growth of cable TV until the Carter Administration began to deregulate cable in the late 1970s.[33] Even after deregulation, it took time for cable news to emerge as a competitor to the network news broadcasts. Ted Turner launched CNN, the first cable news channel, in 1980. As of 1980, though, cable "reached just over nineteen million households. By contrast, 79.9 million households received broadcast signals."[34] Four years later, in 1984, "31.4 million out of 85.5 million households [nationwide] were signed up for cable television."[35] Fox Broadcasting Company did not launch the Fox News Channel until 1996.[36]

The Evolution of Supreme Court Doctrine

In 1969, in *Red Lion Broadcasting v. FCC*, the Supreme Court ruled unanimously that the fairness doctrine did not violate the First Amendment.[37] Red Lion Broadcasting Company operated WGCB radio station in Pennsylvania. In November 1964, WGCB aired a fifteen-minute broadcast in which Reverend Billy James Hargis made a series of derogatory statements about Fred Cook, the author of a recent book about Barry Goldwater. (Goldwater was the Republican nominee for President in 1964.) Hargis claimed that Cook had written his book "to smear and destroy Barry Goldwater."[38]

At that time, the fairness doctrine included a rule known as the "personal attack rule." The rule required broadcasters in some circumstances to offer individuals an opportunity to respond when "an attack is made upon the honesty, character, [or] integrity ... of an identified person or group."[39] Cook asked WGCB to let him respond to Hargis, but the station refused to set aside air time for his response. The FCC subsequently ruled that Red Lion violated the fairness doctrine by denying Cook his right to respond to Hargis' personal attack. Red Lion appealed the FCC ruling and the case went to the Supreme Court. Although the case before the FCC focused primarily on the personal attack rule, the Supreme Court combined it with a separate case that raised a broader challenge to the fairness doctrine. Thus, the Court had to decide whether "the fairness doctrine and its specific manifestations in the personal attack and political editorial rules" violate First Amendment protections for freedom of speech and of the press.[40]

Red Lion argued that the fairness doctrine violated the constitutional rights of broadcasters because "the First Amendment protects their desire to use their allotted frequencies … to broadcast whatever they choose, and to exclude whomever they choose from ever using that frequency."[41] The Court acknowledged that the First Amendment protects radio and television companies. However, the Court said, "[i]t is the right of the viewers and listeners, not the right of the broadcasters, which is paramount." Moreover, "the people as a whole retain … their collective right to have the medium [i.e., radio] function consistently with the ends and purposes of the First Amendment."[42] (The Court's emphasis on the collective right of the people parallels the Warren Court's jurisprudence on malapportionment, discussed in Chapter 3.)

The Court emphasized two distinct First Amendment goals that the fairness doctrine was designed to promote. First, "It is the purpose of the First Amendment to preserve an uninhibited marketplace of ideas in which truth will ultimately prevail." Second, "the right of the public to receive suitable access to social, political … and other ideas … is crucial" because "speech concerning public affairs … is the essence of self-government."[43] In sum, the Court rejected the libertarian argument that government regulation of broadcasting companies was a threat to their First Amendment rights. Instead, the Court embraced the Madisonian view that government regulation of radio and television was necessary to protect the First Amendment rights of viewers and listeners – in particular, their right to participate in democratic self-government and in a "marketplace of ideas in which truth will ultimately prevail." In the Court's words, the fairness doctrine "enhance[s] rather than abridge[s] the freedoms of speech and press protected by the First Amendment."[44]

Five years later, in *Miami Herald Publishing Co. v. Tornillo*, the Court addressed a constitutional challenge to a Florida statute that granted political candidates a right to reply to personal attacks printed in a newspaper.[45] The Court held unanimously that the Florida statute violated the First Amendment. The Court quoted Zechariah Chafee for the proposition that the "liberty of the press is in peril as soon as the government tries to compel what is to go into a newspaper."[46] Justice White, who wrote the unanimous opinion in *Red Lion*, penned a separate concurring opinion in *Miami Herald*. He said that, under the First Amendment, "the government may not force a newspaper to print copy which, in its journalistic discretion, it chooses to leave on the newsroom floor."[47]

Viewed together, *Red Lion* and *Miami Herald* teach that the government may compel a radio station to broadcast a reply to a personal attack, but the government may not compel a newspaper to print a reply to a personal attack. Curiously, although the Justices published three separate opinions in *Miami Herald*, none of those opinions mentioned *Red Lion*. The Court simply assumed that there is a constitutionally significant difference between print media and broadcast media, without explaining why the First Amendment applies differently to newspapers and broadcasters. Moreover, the Court left unresolved the tension between its libertarian approach in *Miami Herald* and its Madisonian approach in *Red Lion*.

Conventional wisdom today holds that broadcast media differ from print media because broadcast frequencies are a scarce resource. Indeed, the Court stated in *Red Lion* that "broadcast frequencies constituted a scarce resource whose use could be regulated and rationalized only by the Government."[48] Today, though, newspapers are also a scarce resource. The "lack of reporting about towns, suburbs, and rural areas is now creating 'news deserts' across the country." "Newspaper newsrooms lost 45 percent of their employees between 2008 and 2017."[49] The scarcity of broadcast frequencies is a function of the electromagnetic spectrum and its interaction with broadcast technology. In contrast, the scarcity of newspapers is primarily a function of economic factors and the rise of the internet. Although the underlying causes of scarcity differ, both newspapers and broadcast stations are scarce resources. Therefore, in the current media environment, the scarcity rationale does not provide a convincing justification for differential treatment between print and broadcast media under the First Amendment.

Four years after *Miami Herald*, the Court decided *FCC v. Pacifica Foundation*.[50] In *Pacifica*, Justice Stevens presented the Court's most detailed defense of the view that the First Amendment applies differently to broadcasters and newspapers. In that case, a New York radio station owned by Pacifica Foundation broadcast a monologue by the comedian, George Carlin, entitled "Filthy Words." In his monologue, Carlin explicitly identified several words that one should never say on radio or television. "He proceeded to list those words and repeat them over and over again in a variety of colloquialisms." The monologue was humorous. Indeed, the Court noted that the recording "indicates frequent laughter from the audience."[51] The radio station aired the program at 2:00 PM on a weekday. A man who was driving his car with his young son heard the broadcast and complained to the FCC. The FCC noted "that certain words depicted sexual and excretory activities in a patently offensive manner," and that the program was "broadcast at a time when children were undoubtedly in the audience."[52] The FCC chose not to impose sanctions on Pacifica Foundation, but warned that it might impose sanctions in the future if the station continued to broadcast indecent material.

In *Red Lion*, the Court said that "differences in the characteristics of new media justify differences in the First Amendment standards applied to them."[53] A decade later, in *Pacifica*, the Court explained why the intrusiveness of broadcast media justifies differential treatment. Justice Stevens said that "broadcast media have established a uniquely pervasive presence in the lives of all Americans." He then compared offensive speech on the radio to an assault. "To say that one may avoid further offense by turning off the radio when he hears indecent language is like saying that the remedy for an assault is to run away after the first blow."[54] In sum, the potential harm caused by exposure to "bad" speech on electronic media is greater than the potential harm caused by exposure to "bad" speech in print media because electronic media assaults our senses in a way that print media does not. I will refer to this argument as the intrusiveness rationale.

Notably, the intrusiveness rationale applies with even greater force to subsequent technological developments, such as cable television and social media. However, the intrusiveness rationale has effectively disappeared from the Court's First Amendment jurisprudence. Consequently, the Court tends to treat both cable TV and social media more like newspapers in *Miami Herald* than like broadcasters in *Red Lion*.

SYRACUSE PEACE COUNCIL AND THE DEMISE OF THE FAIRNESS DOCTRINE

In March 1979, Columbia Pictures released a hit movie called *The China Syndrome*, starring Jane Fonda and Michael Douglas. The movie depicted a fictional nuclear accident at a nuclear power plant. Less than two weeks later, there was a partial nuclear meltdown at the Three Mile Island (TMI) nuclear power plant in Pennsylvania. The TMI accident was then – and is still today – the worst accident in the history of civilian nuclear power in the United States. The accident sparked the growth of a powerful protest movement that attempted to halt further development of nuclear power in the United States.

Three years after the TMI accident, WTVH radio in Syracuse, New York, ran a series of advertisements "arguing that the Nine Mile II nuclear power plant was a sound investment for New York."[55] Syracuse Peace Council was an antinuclear group. It complained to the FCC that Meredith Corporation – the company that operated WTVH radio – violated the fairness doctrine by failing to provide listeners a balanced perspective on the policy debates related to the construction of the Nine Mile II facility.[56]

In its initial ruling, the FCC agreed with the Peace Council, holding that WTVH violated the fairness doctrine.[57] Meredith Corp. argued that the fairness doctrine violated the First Amendment. However, the FCC declined to rule on Meredith's constitutional argument, reasoning that "Congress and the courts are more appropriate venues for reacting to the constitutional questions."[58] Meredith appealed the Commission's decision. On appeal, the D.C. Circuit remanded the case to the FCC for reconsideration because the FCC had "failed to give adequate consideration to Meredith's constitutional argument."[59]

President Reagan appointed six new FCC commissioners between 1981 and 1986.[60] While *Syracuse Peace Council* was being litigated, the FCC conducted a comprehensive review of the fairness doctrine under the leadership of Chairman Mark Fowler (a Reagan appointee), leading to publication of the 1985 Fairness Report.[61] When the Commission reconsidered the Syracuse Peace Council complaint in 1987, it relied heavily on the 1985 Fairness Report to support its conclusion that the fairness doctrine violates the First Amendment rights of broadcasters.[62]

In its 1987 decision, the FCC said that "the policy and constitutional considerations in this matter are inextricably intertwined," so that "it would be difficult, if not impossible, to isolate the policy considerations from the constitutional aspects underlying the doctrine."[63] In one portion of its opinion, the FCC purported to "evaluate the constitutionality of the fairness doctrine under the standard enunciated in *Red Lion*."[64] The FCC noted that the Supreme Court in *Red Lion* had expressed a willingness to "reconsider its holding if experience with the administration of the fairness doctrine indicates that it has the net effect of reducing rather than enhancing the volume and quality of coverage of controversial issues of public importance."[65] Relying on the 1985 Fairness Report, the FCC concluded that "the fairness doctrine, in operation, thwarts the purpose that it is designed to promote. Instead of enhancing the discussion of controversial issues of public importance ... the fairness doctrine ... provides broadcasters with a powerful incentive not to air" programs addressing controversial issues.[66]

The FCC said that the Supreme Court in *Red Lion* had relied expressly on "the scarcity of broadcast frequencies" to justify its holding that television and radio broadcasters deserve weaker First Amendment protection than newspapers.[67] However, the FCC said, there had been "an explosive growth in both the number and types of [information] outlets in every market since the 1969 *Red Lion* decision." The Commission added: "Not only has the number of television and radio stations increased ... but the advent and increased availability of such other technologies as cable and satellite television services have dramatically enhanced that access."[68] Accordingly, the FCC concluded that the scarcity rationale – which, in its view, was central to the Court's holding in *Red Lion* – could no longer justify the fairness doctrine's restrictions on the editorial discretion of broadcasters.

The FCC stated explicitly that the constitutional "standard applied in *Red Lion* should be reconsidered and that the constitutional principles applicable to the printed press should be equally applicable to the electronic press."[69] In contrast to the Court's Madisonian analysis in *Red Lion*, the Commission's approach was entirely libertarian. "[A] cardinal tenet of the First Amendment is that governmental intervention in the marketplace of ideas of the sort involved in the enforcement of the fairness doctrine is not acceptable and should not be tolerated."[70] Whereas the Court in *Red Lion* emphasized the affirmative right of listeners and viewers to receive truthful information and to participate in self-government, the FCC emphasized "the rights of the public to receive information unencumbered by government intrusion."[71] The FCC did not mention *Pacifica*'s intrusiveness rationale. Instead of worrying about the intrusiveness of electronic communications technology, it focused on the intrusiveness of government regulation.

In sum, the Commission in *Syracuse Peace Council* claimed that its analysis was entirely consistent with *Red Lion*, but the Commission inverted First Amendment values by substituting its own libertarian approach for the Court's Madisonian approach in *Red Lion*. When Syracuse Peace Council appealed, the D.C. Circuit declined to reach the merits of the constitutional issue, holding instead that "the Commission's public interest determination was an independent basis for its decision and was supported by the record."[72] That claim was somewhat disingenuous. After all, the FCC said that "the policy and constitutional considerations in this matter are inextricably intertwined," so that "it would be difficult, if not impossible, to isolate the policy considerations from the constitutional aspects underlying the doctrine."[73]

After the Supreme Court denied cert., the fairness doctrine was officially dead.[74] (Congress enacted legislation designed to revive the fairness doctrine, but President Reagan vetoed that legislation.[75]) Three Justices who were on the Court when it decided *Red Lion* in 1969 remained on the Court when it denied cert. in *Syracuse Peace Council*: Justice White (the author of *Red Lion*), Justice Brennan, and Justice Marshall. No Justice dissented from the denial of cert. No Justice defended the Madisonian vision that animated the Court's *Red Lion* decision. In their silence, the Justices relegated the pursuit of truth and self-government to a (mostly) unregulated marketplace of media and communications technology companies.

FRAGMENTATION AND POLARIZATION

In 2018, three Harvard scholars published a sophisticated, data-driven analysis of how propaganda and misinformation spread in our current information ecosystem.[76] It is worth quoting their key findings at length.

> There is no left-right division, but rather a division between the right and the rest of the media ecosystem. The right wing of the media ecosystem behaves precisely as the echo-chamber models predict – exhibiting high insularity, susceptibility to information cascades, rumor and conspiracy theory, and drift toward more extreme versions of itself. The rest of the media ecosystem, however, operates as an interconnected network anchored by organizations … that adhere to professional journalistic norms.[77]

As of 2018, Breitbart and Fox News were the two most influential players in the right-wing media ecosystem. The *New York Times*, *Washington Post*, and CNN were among the most influential players in the mainstream media ecosystem.[78] However, the mainstream media also includes "traditionally conservative publications like the *Wall Street Journal* or *Forbes*."[79]

Information consumers "seek out [identity] confirming information [and] reject or discount disconfirming evidence."[80] In both the right-wing and mainstream media, there is a tension between a truth-seeking norm and an identity confirmation norm. However, the right-wing media ecosystem is "oriented more toward offering identity-confirming information to partisan audiences," whereas the mainstream media "strive for accuracy and aspire to neutrality."[81] Thus, the mainstream media ecosystem imposes "reputational costs on sites and authors who propagate rumor and provides avenues for relatively rapid fact checking, criticism of false claims, and rapid dissemination of … corrected narratives."[82] In contrast, the right-wing media ecosystem "creates positive feedbacks for bias-confirming statements as a central feature of its normal operation."[83]

Thus, when election-related misinformation appears in the mainstream media, it does not spread very far or very fast because it is subject to fact-checking and correction. In contrast, the right-wing media ecosystem amplifies election-related misinformation that confirms the preexisting biases of the people who inhabit that media environment. For example, in summer 2024, Elon Musk reportedly spread misleading election-related claims on X that were viewed 1.2 billion times.[84] Sources associated with the mainstream media engage in fact-checking in an effort to debunk lies and half-truths circulating in the right-wing media ecosystem, but their fact-checking efforts have little impact because denizens of the two different media ecosystems occupy different factual universes.

The end of the fairness doctrine sparked a chain of causation that gave rise to the right-wing media ecosystem. After the demise of the fairness doctrine, "the media landscape was transformed. The driving force was talk radio. In 1960, there were only two all-talk radio stations in America; by 1995, there were 1130."[85] Rush Limbaugh was the dominant force in right-wing talk radio in the 1990s. "By 1994, he had an audience of 20 million Americans tuning in on some 650 stations."[86] Rush Limbaugh provided the model on talk radio that Fox News would later adapt to cable TV. Professor Brian Leiter says: "Beginning in the early 1990s, hyper-partisan media, devoted to an alternative (and often false) view of reality and the debunking of epistemic authority, became widespread in America: Rush Limbaugh on radio, then Fox News on television."[87] Leiter notes that "Rush Limbaugh would not have survived" under the fairness doctrine. "Much of Fox News would not have survived either."[88] Neither Limbaugh nor certain Fox News hosts met a key requirement of the fairness doctrine: the obligation "to provide reasonable opportunities for the presentation of contrasting views on controversial issues of public importance."[89] (Technically, the fairness doctrine never applied to cable channels, such as Fox News. However, with the requisite political will, the doctrine could easily have been adapted to apply to cable TV.)

The rise of the right-wing media ecosystem, and the bifurcation between mainstream media and the right-wing ecosystem, has led to "the collapse of epistemic authority."[90] An epistemic authority "is someone who tells people what they ought to believe, and in so doing, makes it much more likely that those people will believe what is true … than if they were left to their own devices."[91] During the "golden age" of broadcast television, Walter Cronkite and other news anchors served as important epistemic authorities. Today, there is no comparable source of news and information who is trusted across the political spectrum.

A YouGov poll conducted in May 2024 reveals a sharp divide between Democrats and Republicans concerning the news sources that they deem trustworthy.[92] Table 4.1 presents selected information from that poll. Positive scores indicate that respondents trust a particular source; negative scores indicate that they distrust that source.

TABLE 4.1 *Trusted Information Sources*

	Overall	Democrats	Republicans
The Weather Channel	+43	+58	+36
BBC	+25	+57	+3
Wall Street Journal	+22	+43	+11
CBS	+15	+58	−20
New York Times	+13	+53	−22
CNN	+2	+54	−41
Fox News	−10	−34	+28

For four of the listed sources – CBS, the *New York Times*, CNN, and *Fox News* – there is a large gulf between Democratic and Republican scores. *The Weather Channel* is the only listed source that is widely trusted across the political spectrum, but it does not cover political news. The fact that the BBC earns positive scores from both Democrats and Republicans is noteworthy: The BBC is subject to regulation in the UK similar in certain respects to the fairness doctrine.[93] It is unclear why *The Wall Street Journal* earns positive scores from both Democrats and Republicans. Perhaps that is because readers consult WSJ primarily for business and economic news, rather than political news. Or perhaps it is because WSJ's news department, which aspires to journalistic objectivity, is independent from its conservative editorial department. Most likely, a combination of both factors is at play.

Regardless, it is questionable whether American democracy can survive the collapse of epistemic authority. To be clear, the problem is NOT that Americans are able to choose among a broad range of news and information sources with diverse perspectives. That feature of our current information ecosystem is an improvement over the "golden age," when the three major networks presented the same bland diet of commentary that was neither too far left nor too far right. The problem today is that democracy cannot function effectively without agreement on shared facts. The rise of the right-wing media ecosystem has undermined agreement on shared facts because denizens of the right-wing media ecosystem occupy a different factual universe than citizens who rely primarily on the mainstream media as a source of news and information. The polling data cited at the beginning of this chapter – showing that 69 percent of Republicans and Republican-leaners believe that President Biden's victory in the 2020 election was "not legitimate"[94] – reinforces this point.

Authoritarian governments provide their citizens perceived epistemic authority by suppressing all voices that challenge the government's narrative. That approach is clearly incompatible with democratic self-government. Libertarians place their faith in Justice Holmes' theory "that the best test of truth is the power of the thought to get itself accepted in the competition of the market."[95] Although that theory may have been plausible when Holmes was alive, it is no longer defensible in the modern age of electronic amplification technology. Social psychology research demonstrates that consumers trust news and information sources that confirm their preexisting biases, regardless of whether the information they receive is truthful or accurate.[96] Large media and information technology companies earn billions of dollars in profits every year by giving consumers the content they want – again, regardless of whether that content is truthful or accurate.[97]

To restore epistemic authority in the United States and to reestablish the agreement on shared facts that is an essential foundation for democratic self-governance, we need a system for regulating electronic amplification services that is neither libertarian nor authoritarian. The next section sketches the contours of such a regulatory system. Granted, there is no realistic chance that Congress will enact legislation along these lines while Republicans control even one House of Congress. But suppose that Democrats gain control of both Houses and try to enact meaningful legislation to regulate electronic amplification services. The final portion of this chapter explains why the Supreme Court's First Amendment doctrine – its stubborn adherence to a libertarian, rather than a Madisonian approach – presents an almost insuperable hurdle to enacting the type of legislation that is urgently needed to reverse our ongoing descent from democracy to dictatorship.

A PROPOSED REGULATORY SYSTEM

Let me begin by introducing some terminology, all of which is adapted from a statute I drafted.[98] The term "electronic amplification services" refers to content distribution and content aggregation services that enable speakers to deliver their messages almost instantaneously to large audiences. The term "electronic megaphone companies" (EMCs) refers to companies that provide electronic amplification services for individuals (and other companies), including by means of radio, television, social media, blogs, and podcasts. The term "persons with large electronic megaphones" (PLEMs) refers to individuals whose messages reach very large audiences through the medium of radio, television, social media, blogs, and/or podcasts. (An actual statute would need to establish specific numerical thresholds for each type of media.) The term "PLEM" also includes specific shows or programs, such as ABC World News Tonight. (*The New York Times* would likely qualify as a PLEM because it operates a social media account that reaches a very large audience.)

Millions of Americans believe the Big Lie because there are a fairly small number of PLEMs who disseminated the Big Lie to large audiences and repeated that lie over and over again until their audiences accepted it as true.[99] Accordingly, a statutory scheme designed to restrict the electronic amplification of election-related misinformation should: (1) empower the government to (2) coerce EMCs to (3) deny or restrict the availability of electronic amplification services for PLEMs who continue to disseminate false or misleading election-related claims after receiving multiple warnings to cease and desist. (My proposed statute provides a detailed definition of the term "election-related communication" that builds on the current statutory definition of "electioneering communication."[100]) I have presented three different variants of this proposal over the past few years.[101] Prior versions did not include the element of government coercion because I was trying to work within the framework of existing First Amendment doctrine.[102] However, a statute lacking any provision for government coercion would likely be ineffectual. Given the magnitude of the current threat to democracy, we need to reconceptualize the First Amendment and permit some degree of government coercion to enable Congress to address that threat.

As will become clear shortly, I am not proposing a "Ministry of Truth." However, I am suggesting that the First Amendment, properly construed, protects freedom of speech, not "freedom of reach."[103] If I repeat an election-related lie in a face-to-face conversation with a friend or neighbor, the harm to democracy is negligible. However, when Donald Trump repeats an election-related lie on social media – and that lie is disseminated instantaneously to tens of millions of people – the harm to democracy is potentially enormous. Accordingly, Professor Pearlstein has argued that First Amendment doctrine should recognize a categorical exception for "democracy harms," analogous to the exceptions for incitement, true threats, and so on that are recognized under current doctrine.[104] My proposal is similar, but somewhat narrower, in that I would recognize an exception for electronic amplification services to enable Congress to regulate EMCs in order to prevent or mitigate democracy harms. There are sound policy reasons for nurturing the growth of an information environment that enables individuals to utilize electronic amplification services to maximize their freedom of reach. However, Congress has a constitutional responsibility to protect the integrity of American democracy. To fulfill that responsibility, Congress must regulate – and must have the constitutional authority to regulate – EMCs to restrict the provision of electronic amplification services to PLEMs who repeatedly use their electronic megaphones to spread false/misleading election-related claims to large audiences.

There is an important distinction between substantive and procedural election-related claims. Suppose my neighbor tells me that I am not allowed to vote by mail in California. That is a (false) claim about election procedures. We can, and should, rely on government officials to tell us whether a claim about election procedures is true or false. Substantive election-related claims are different. J.D. Vance recently claimed that Kamala Harris is "calling for an end to the child tax credit." According to FactCheck.Org, that claim is incorrect.[105] Most Americans would presumably agree that we do not want to rely on government officials to tell us whether such claims are true or false. For these types of claims, it makes sense to rely on independent, nongovernmental fact-checkers. In sum, we can rely on government officials as epistemic authorities for at least some procedural, election-related claims, but we need independent, nonpartisan, nongovernmental organizations to serve as epistemic authorities for substantive, election-related claims. Without such epistemic authorities, it is very difficult, if not impossible, for the average American citizen to distinguish between true and false claims.

The proposed statute would create a National Endowment for Fact-Checking (NEFC), modeled on the National Endowment for Democracy (NED). The NED is an independent, nongovernmental foundation established in 1983 to strengthen democratic institutions around the world.[106] Similarly, NEFC's mission would be to strengthen democracy at home. Like the NED, the NEFC would distribute federal funds to grantees – in this case, independent, nonpartisan organizations that monitor public communications and perform key fact-checking functions. The proposed statute includes several provisions designed to ensure that both NEFC and its grantees are truly nonpartisan.[107] For example, the statute provides that the NEFC Board of Directors must have an equal number of Democratic and Republican Directors; it prohibits Directors from interfering with operational decisions by NEFC staff or NEFC grantees. The statute also requires NEFC to ensure that all grantees operate in accordance with the code of principles adopted by the International Fact-Checking Network.[108] No statutory scheme is perfect. Even if NEFC operates in a nonpartisan fashion, it will inevitably be accused of partisan leanings. However, if the professional staff do their jobs well, the institution will (hopefully) gain the public's trust over time.

Under the proposed statute, independent fact-checking organizations would issue warnings to PLEMs who disseminate false or misleading election-related claims. If a PLEM heeds the warning and stops disseminating such claims, that is the end of the matter. No government coercion is involved. If a particular PLEM refuses to heed warnings, the statute lays out a series of escalating measures to apply increasing pressure. The first step would be for NEFC itself to encourage (but not require) relevant EMCs to restrict the availability of electronic amplification services for PLEMs who continue to disseminate false or misleading claims after receiving repeated warnings. Companies could comply with such a request by denying electronic amplification services altogether, or by implementing technical measures that would restrict freedom of reach without blocking freedom of speech. As above, no government coercion is involved at this stage because NEFC is not a government agency and it has no power to impose fines or penalties on private companies.[109]

Suppose, however, that a particular EMC refuses to comply with an NEFC request to limit electronic amplification services for a particular PLEM who has repeatedly disseminated false/misleading election-related claims. For example, Fox News is an EMC; it provides electronic amplification services for "Jesse Watters Primetime," which would presumably be deemed a PLEM, depending on the precise numerical threshold established by statute for determining who qualifies as a PLEM. ("Jesse Watters Primetime was Fox's top show in July [2024], reeling in 4.4 million total viewers."[110]). In May 2024, PolitiFact reported that Jesse Watters Primetime made false claims about the judge overseeing Donald Trump's New York state criminal trial.[111]

Assume, hypothetically, that Kamala Harris wins the Presidential election in 2028, but her Republican opponent claims that she stole the election and that the Democrats committed widespread fraud. Jesse Watters uses his Primetime slot to disseminate claims of election fraud to millions of viewers. Independent fact-checking organizations determine that such claims are false or misleading. Based on the enactment of the new statute, they issue warnings to Jesse Watters, but he ignores those warnings. Fox News refuses to take action against Watters, despite strong encouragement from NEFC. The next logical step in the chain of escalation is for some government agency to intervene by imposing, or threatening to impose, a fine or penalty on Fox News, unless it takes concrete steps to restrict the electronic amplification of Jesse Watters Primetime. (If Fox News is technologically dependent upon some other EMC – and that EMC has the technical capacity to limit the dissemination of Fox News content to a mass audience – the government could potentially achieve the same objective without imposing any fine or penalty by encouraging that EMC to restrict electronic amplification services for Jesse Watters Primetime.)

As explained in the next section, a statute granting a government agency the power to impose a penalty on Fox News in such circumstances would almost certainly violate the First Amendment, as currently interpreted by the Supreme Court. Yet, in my view, some government agency must have that power. Absent such power, the government would be incapable of protecting our democracy from the threat posed by electronic amplification of election-related misinformation. In short, we should view the First Amendment through the lens of a theory of militant democracy.[112] Militant democracy recognizes the need for limits on freedom of expression when such limitations are necessary to protect democracy. If we allow individuals to abuse free speech rights to destroy democracy, we will lose both democracy and freedom of speech.

THE LIBERTARIAN FIRST AMENDMENT

In an article published in 1992, then-Professor Kathleen Sullivan argued that the Court was divided between Justices of rules and standards.[113] In constitutional doctrine, this division manifests as a tension between categorization and balancing.[114] Balancing involves a standard-like approach; courts decide cases by weighing competing factors. Categorization involves a rule-like approach; courts decide cases by assigning them to preexisting categories and applying the rule associated with the relevant category. In the past thirty years, in the area of First Amendment doctrine, categorization has won. Balancing is dead. Leading scholars have advocated a revival of balancing (also called proportionality) in First Amendment doctrine,[115] and in constitutional law more broadly,[116] but to no avail. Justice Breyer consistently advocated a balancing approach in First Amendment cases,[117] but he was a minority voice and he retired in 2022.

Professor Sullivan argued that neither a rule-like approach nor a standard-like approach necessarily produces either liberal or conservative outcomes. The relationship between the categorization versus balancing dichotomy and the political valence of decisions is context dependent and historically contingent.[118] That claim is undoubtedly true as a general matter. However, in the three decades since she wrote that article, the Court has employed a categorical approach in First Amendment cases to promote a libertarian agenda.

The most important categorical First Amendment rule is that content-based speech regulations trigger application of strict scrutiny. For example, in *Reed v. Town of Gilbert*, the Court evaluated a local ordinance enacted by the town of Gilbert, Arizona that regulated "the manner in which people may display outdoor signs."[119] The local ordinance prohibited "the display of outdoor signs anywhere within the Town without a permit, but it then exempt[ed] 23 categories of signs from that requirement."[120] A town official cited Clyde Reed, the pastor of a small church, for violating the ordinance by posting signs advertising Sunday church services. All nine Justices agreed that the town violated the church's First Amendment rights, but they did not agree on a rationale.

Justice Thomas, writing for the majority, held "that these provisions are content-based regulations of speech that cannot survive strict scrutiny."[121] Justices Ginsburg, Breyer, and Kagan concurred in the result. Justice Kagan said: "We apply strict scrutiny to facially content-based regulations of speech … when there is any realistic possibility that official suppression of ideas is afoot."[122] However, "when that is not realistically possible, we may do well to relax our guard so that entirely reasonable laws imperiled by strict scrutiny can survive."[123] She noted that "thousands of towns have" ordinances similar to the one at issue here, "many of them entirely reasonable."[124] Under the majority's rationale, "courts will have to invalidate one after the other…. And courts will strike down those democratically enacted local laws even though no one – certainly not the majority – has ever explained why the vindication of First Amendment values requires that result."[125]

Justice Kagan's critique is entirely justified. The majority rationale is wooden and formalistic. The majority categorized the town ordinance as a content-based speech restriction. Laws in that category require application of strict scrutiny. Strict scrutiny is "strict in theory but fatal in fact."[126] From the majority's perspective, case-by-case analysis of First Amendment values is not necessary, because the Court can dispose of First Amendment claims by assigning cases to categories and applying the relevant rule associated with that category. Under that approach, though, one First Amendment value – namely, distrust of government regulation – consistently trumps all other First Amendment values.[127] Under the majority approach in *Reed*, the negative value of distrusting government prevailed over the affirmative value of promoting democratic self-government, even though thousands of democratically elected local governments have enacted sign ordinances, and despite the fact that there is no reason to believe, as a general matter, that local governments are abusing their power over signs to suppress disfavored ideas. In sum, the rigid categorical rule that content-based speech regulations trigger strict scrutiny represents the triumph of the libertarian First Amendment. It demonstrates the Court's willingness to sacrifice the affirmative goal of promoting democratic self-government on the altar of libertarians' instinctive distrust of government regulation.

Current First Amendment doctrine permits governments to enact content-based regulations for certain categories of low-value speech where strict scrutiny does not apply. These include incitement to violence,[128] fighting words,[129] consumer fraud,[130] defamation,[131] obscenity,[132] and child pornography.[133] Content-based speech restrictions within these categories are presumptively constitutional because speech in these categories is not protected by the First Amendment.[134] The Court developed First Amendment doctrine in these areas through a series of incremental, common-law-like decisions from the early 1940s to the early 1980s. However, despite transformative changes in information and communications technology, and despite emergent threats to democratic self-government, the evolution of constitutional common law in this area has been frozen for the past forty years. The Court has not recognized a new category of unprotected speech since its 1982 decision in *New York v. Ferber*, which declared that child pornography does not merit First Amendment protection. (In particular, the Court has not recognized a distinct category for harms to democracy,[135] or for electronic amplification.[136])

Consider, for example, *United States v. Stevens*.[137] The defendant in *Stevens* was convicted for violating a federal criminal statute that imposes a penalty on "anyone who knowingly creates, sells, or possesses a depiction of animal cruelty if done for commercial gain in interstate or foreign commerce."[138] When Congress enacted the statute, it was primarily concerned with "crush videos": videos that "feature the intentional torture and killing of helpless animals."[139] In contrast, *Stevens* involved videos that depicted "pit bulls engaging in dogfights and attacking other animals."[140] It bears emphasis that the underlying conduct depicted in both crush videos and dogfighting videos is unlawful in all fifty states. Moreover, the expressive content of crush videos and dogfighting videos has no positive social value. The videos exist solely to enable people who engage in criminal conduct to make money from that criminal conduct. Nevertheless, the Court held in *Stevens* that the statutory ban on the depiction of animal cruelty violated the First Amendment.

The government argued that "the banned depictions of animal cruelty, as a class, are categorically unprotected by the First Amendment."[141] Chief Justice Roberts, writing for an 8–1 majority, emphatically rejected that argument. Justice Alito was the sole dissenter. He argued – persuasively, in my view – that the Court's rationale in *New York v. Ferber* supported a conclusion that crush videos and dogfighting videos are not protected by the First Amendment.[142] In contrast, the Chief Justice argued that the Court's prior decisions recognizing discrete categories of unprotected speech "cannot be taken as establishing a freewheeling authority to declare new categories of speech outside the scope of the First Amendment."[143] He acknowledged that there may be "some categories of [unprotected] speech that … have not yet been specifically identified or discussed as such in our case law. But if so, … 'depictions of animal cruelty' is [not] among them."[144]

Under the majority's analysis in *Stevens*, the Court will not recognize any new category of unprotected speech unless the government can demonstrate that a particular law fits within a category of speech restrictions that have historically been recognized as valid restrictions on freedom of expression "from 1791 to the present."[145] Almost by definition, any law targeting a novel problem that did not exist in 1791 will fail this test. In particular, a law targeting the electronic amplification of misinformation will fail this test because the problem did not exist in 1791. (The printing press could be described as eighteenth-century "amplification technology," but it did not enable speakers to deliver their messages to millions of people instantaneously. Technologies enabling instantaneous transmission to mass audiences call for a novel type of government regulation to mitigate harms to democracy – a fact that Congress recognized when it enacted the Communications Act of 1934.[146])

Here, let us compare child pornography to electronic amplification of misinformation. As explained previously, the electronic amplification of election-related misinformation undermines the two most important affirmative First Amendment goals: promoting truth and enhancing democracy. All agree that child pornography is low-value speech, but child pornography does not subvert the First Amendment's affirmative goals. Even so, under the Court's rigid, categorical approach to doctrinal analysis, the fact that electronic amplification of misinformation undermines affirmative First Amendment values is wholly irrelevant. Those values do not factor into the Court's analysis because First Amendment analysis relies entirely on categorization. Electronic amplification of misinformation does not qualify as a category of unprotected speech because it did not exist in 1791. A restriction that focuses on *election-related* misinformation is necessarily content based. All content-based restrictions automatically trigger strict scrutiny. Therefore, any content-based restriction on electronic amplification of misinformation will be subject to strict scrutiny. Truth-seeking and democracy promotion have disappeared from doctrinal analysis because there is no place for those First Amendment values within the Court's rigid, categorical framework.

In *Stevens*, Chief Justice Roberts expressed concern about the Court's "freewheeling authority to declare new categories of speech outside the scope of the First Amendment."[147] From a Madisonian perspective, the Justices should be much more concerned about the Court's freewheeling authority to declare that new categories of laws are prohibited by the First Amendment. The term "freewheeling authority" is appropriate here because, under the Court's categorical approach, it has the authority to declare any restriction on free expression unconstitutional – without even considering the law's impact on First Amendment values – if the law is content based and it does not fit within one of the previously recognized categories of unprotected speech. This approach promotes libertarian values by imposing constitutional handcuffs on legislators that make it exceedingly difficult for them to enact novel laws to deal with novel problems.

Alvarez, Lies, and the First Amendment

The Stolen Valor Act is a federal statute that imposes criminal penalties on individuals who falsely claim to have received a Congressional Medal of Honor. Xavier Alvarez was convicted for violating the statute. On appeal, he argued that the statute violated the First Amendment.[148] The Supreme Court noted that Alvarez's "claim to hold the Congressional Medal of Honor was false. There is no room to argue about interpretation or shades of meaning."[149] In short, he clearly violated the Act. Nevertheless, the Court reversed his conviction on the grounds that the Act violated the First Amendment.

The Court did not produce a majority opinion in *Alvarez*. Justice Kennedy wrote a plurality opinion, joined by Chief Justice Roberts and Justices Ginsburg and Sotomayor. Justice Kennedy's analysis was based on rigid categorization. He explicitly rejected balancing, saying that "this Court has rejected as startling and dangerous a free-floating test for First Amendment coverage based on an ad hoc balancing of relative social costs and benefits."[150] He classified the Stolen Valor Act as a content-based speech restriction. In his view, "the Constitution demands that content-based restrictions on speech be presumed invalid and that the Government bear the burden of showing their constitutionality."[151] Content-based restrictions may avoid strict scrutiny "only when confined to the few historic and traditional categories of expression long familiar to the bar."[152] Those categories do not include a "general exception to the First Amendment for false statements."[153] The plurality acknowledged that "there are instances in which the falsity of speech bears upon whether it is protected," citing perjury as an example.[154] However, in Justice Kennedy's view, the Stolen Valor Act was subject to strict scrutiny because it is a content-based speech restriction that does not fit within any of the traditional categories of unprotected speech. Moreover, the law did not survive strict scrutiny because, in his view, "the Act is not actually necessary to achieve the Government's stated interest."[155]

Justice Breyer, writing for himself and Justice Kagan, agreed with the result, but not with the plurality's rationale. Justice Breyer, before his retirement, was the only Justice in this century who consistently advocated a balancing approach to First Amendment analysis. Accordingly, he said, "I do not rest my conclusion upon a strict categorical analysis."[156] The key question, in his view, was "whether the statute works speech-related harm that is out of proportion to its justifications."[157] He concluded that the Stolen Valor Act violates the First Amendment because "the statute as written risks significant First Amendment harm" and it would be possible "to achieve the Government's objectives in less burdensome ways."[158] However, in contrast to the plurality, Justice Breyer rejected the idea that content-based speech restrictions should always trigger strict scrutiny. As he wrote in *Reed v. Town of Gilbert*, "the category 'content discrimination' is better considered in many contexts … as a rule of thumb, rather than as an automatic strict scrutiny trigger, leading to almost certain legal condemnation."[159]

Justice Alito wrote a dissenting opinion, joined by Justices Scalia and Thomas. Like the plurality, Justice Alito applied a categorical approach to analyze the Stolen Valor Act. However, in his view, the First Amendment "does not protect false factual statements that inflict real harm and serve no legitimate interest."[160] He noted that "many kinds of false factual statements have long been proscribed without raising any constitutional problem."[161] He listed several examples, including fraud, perjury, defamation, and more.[162] In his view, "false statements of fact merit no First Amendment protection in their own right," unless they serve some valid purpose.[163] Thus, in his view, the Stolen Valor Act, as applied to Alvarez, did not violate the First Amendment because his false statements served no valid purpose and inflicted real harm on individuals who actually did receive a Congressional Medal of Honor.

What does *Alvarez* teach about the constitutionality of a possible statute targeting the electronic amplification of election-related misinformation? Under Justice Kennedy's plurality analysis, the proposed statute would clearly trigger strict scrutiny because it is a content-based speech restriction that is not "confined to the few historic and traditional categories of expression long familiar to the bar."[164] Strict scrutiny is likely to be "strict in theory but fatal in fact."[165] The proposed statute might well survive a constitutional challenge under Justice Breyer's proposed proportionality analysis, but Justice Breyer has retired, and it is unclear whether Justice Kagan – who joined his opinion in *Alvarez* – would apply a balancing approach to a statute targeting electronic amplification of misinformation.[166]

At first blush, Justice Alito's analysis in *Alvarez* appears to offer a promising path for defending the validity of a new federal statute targeting election-related misinformation because, in Alito's view, "false statements of fact merit no First Amendment protection in their own right," unless they serve some valid purpose.[167] However, I suspect that Justice Alito would distinguish between the Stolen Valor Act and my proposed statute on electoral misinformation. For example, he might argue that the claim that Democrats "stole" the 2020 Presidential election, and similar claims, are not "false statements of fact," but merely statements about matters of opinion. Moreover, he might argue, any effort to suppress such opinions would constitute impermissible viewpoint discrimination.

Clearly, any legislation targeting election-related misinformation must distinguish between false statements of fact and disagreements about matters of opinion. The International Fact-Checking Network has published a Code of Principles that addresses this point.[168] Under my proposed statute, all NEFC grantees would be required to operate in accordance with those principles, which are specifically designed to minimize the risk of viewpoint discrimination. Even so, based on Justice Alito's opinion in *Alvarez*, it is unclear whether he or other members of the Court's conservative wing could be persuaded that the safeguards built into the NEFC statute are sufficient to address valid concerns about the risk of viewpoint discrimination.

Moody v. NetChoice *and Social Media*

In *Moody v. NetChoice*,[169] the Court considered First Amendment challenges to Texas and Florida laws that regulated the content-moderation functions of social media platforms. Texas attempted to justify its law by arguing that the content-moderation practices of social media companies "skewed against politically conservative voices." Texas argued that government regulation was needed "to balance the [ideological] mix of speech on Facebook's News Feed and similar platforms."[170]

NetChoice is a trade association whose members include Facebook and YouTube, among others. NetChoice brought facial challenges to both the Texas and Florida laws. The Court explained that the decision "to litigate these cases as facial challenges … comes at a cost." In a facial challenge, the plaintiff must prove that "the law's unconstitutional applications substantially outweigh its constitutional ones."[171] Justice Barrett, in a concurring opinion, noted that this is "a daunting, if not impossible task."[172] The Court remanded both cases to lower courts, without reaching a final decision on the merits, because both lower courts failed to perform the appropriate analysis for a facial challenge. All nine Justices agreed with the decision to remand the cases for further analysis.

Justice Kagan's majority opinion sought to provide guidance for the lower courts. In a portion of her opinion joined only by four other Justices, she was especially critical of the lower court decision in the Texas case, where the Fifth Circuit reversed a preliminary injunction that would have temporarily barred application of the Texas law. She said: "The Fifth Circuit got its likelihood-of-success finding wrong. Texas is not likely to succeed in enforcing its law against the platforms' application of their content-moderation policies to the feeds that were the focus of the proceedings below."[173] Texas was unlikely to succeed because the goal of its legislation was "not valid, let alone substantial."[174] Justice Kagan said: "The government may not, in supposed pursuit of better expressive balance, alter a private speaker's own editorial choices about the mix of speech it wants to convey."[175]

Although I agree with much of what Justice Kagan wrote, certain aspects of her opinion raise doubts about the constitutionality of any potential federal law to regulate the electronic amplification of election-related misinformation. Justice Kagan's opinion relies heavily on *Miami Herald*;[176] it does not even mention *Red Lion*. (Recall that *Miami Herald* involved newspapers, whereas *Red Lion* involved radio.) In a separate concurring opinion, Justice Jackson cited *Red Lion* for the proposition that "differences in the characteristics of new media justify differences in the First Amendment standards applied to them."[177] The Court produced five separate opinions in *Moody*. None of them cited *Pacifica*, or made any reference to *Pacifica*'s "intrusiveness" rationale as a possible justification for applying different First Amendment standards to electronic media versus print media. To the contrary, Justice Kagan said: "Whatever the challenges of applying the Constitution to ever-advancing technology, the basic principles of the First

Amendment do not vary."[178] That statement is difficult to square with either *Red Lion* or *Pacifica*. Justice Kagan's majority opinion in *Moody* makes it difficult, but not impossible, for the Court to hold in a future case that the First Amendment applies differently to electronic media than it does to print media. (I use the term "print media," rather than "newspapers," because publications such as the *New York Times* likely fit within the definition of an "electronic megaphone company" under the proposed NEFC statute.)

Second, Justice Kagan's analysis focuses almost exclusively on the First Amendment rights of private companies to exercise editorial discretion. Her opinion barely mentions the First Amendment rights of social media users. The Court in *Red Lion* said that "the people as a whole retain their … collective right to have the medium function consistently with the ends and purposes of the First Amendment. It is the right of the viewers and listeners, not the right of the broadcasters, which is paramount."[179] Texas advanced a similar argument in *Moody*, claiming that its law was designed to create "an expressive realm in which the public has access to a wide range of views."[180] Justice Kagan agreed that the asserted goal is consistent with the goals of the First Amendment. However, she said, the government may not pursue that goal by "stop[ping] private actors from speaking as they wish … [or] prohibit[ing] speech to improve or better balance the speech market."[181]

These statements, on their face, seem to suggest that the government may not order social media companies to restrict the electronic amplification of election-related lies to help ensure that citizens receive truthful, accurate information about electoral procedures and candidates for elective offices. Of course, Justice Kagan might reasonably distinguish between: (a) government efforts to achieve ideological balance on social media platforms (which was the main point at issue in *Moody*); and (b) government efforts to restrict the electronic amplification of election-related lies. That distinction makes sense because any government effort to achieve ideological balance is fraught with difficulties, whereas government regulation to curb the electronic amplification of election-related lies is essential to protect democracy. However, Justice Kagan would probably have to disavow some of the dicta in *Moody* to defend that distinction.

SUMMARY

The electronic amplification of election-related misinformation poses a significant threat to American democracy. The Supreme Court's current First Amendment doctrine makes it virtually impossible for Congress to enact the type of legislation that is necessary to address that threat. Therefore, the Court should rethink its doctrine to give Congress greater leeway to enact legislation in this area. Three distinct options merit consideration.

First, the Court should relax the rule that content-based speech regulations automatically trigger strict scrutiny. Strict scrutiny is appropriate where "content discrimination [is] an unconstitutional method for suppressing a viewpoint," and where "rules governing a traditional public forum are, in fact, not a neutral way of fairly managing the forum."[182] However, when Congress or a state legislature enacts a law designed to promote the First Amendment's affirmative goals – in particular, truth seeking and/or democracy promotion – intermediate scrutiny is more appropriate. Applying intermediate scrutiny in these circumstances would enable courts to engage in balancing, weighing the extent to which the legislation actually helps advance affirmative First Amendment goals against any factors indicating that government cannot or should not be trusted in particular circumstances.[183] If the Court pursues this pathway, it should signal lower courts, and potential litigants, that facial challenges to such laws will be viewed with great skepticism. Courts have the capacity to engage in the type of balancing I am suggesting when they are presented with as-applied challenges. It is much more difficult for courts to undertake this type of balancing in cases presenting facial challenges.[184]

A second possible option would be for the Court to carve out a narrow exception for laws targeting election-related misinformation. The Court would not have to go so far as to say that election-related misinformation is unprotected speech. It could simply acknowledge that laws targeting election-related misinformation, at least presumptively, advance two important First Amendment goals: truth seeking and democracy promotion. The Court could craft a special-purpose balancing test that applies exclusively to laws targeting election-related misinformation. To avoid the difficulties associated with facial challenges, it could specify that the special-purpose test would apply only to as-applied challenges, not to facial challenges. Of the three options under consideration here, this one involves the least drastic change to current First Amendment doctrine.

Third, the Court could acknowledge that companies that provide electronic amplification services are engaged in commercial activity that has an expressive element. Insofar as electronic amplification services are commercial activities, regulation of those services warrants rational basis review. Insofar as electronic amplification services have an expressive element, some form of heightened scrutiny under the First Amendment is appropriate. However, the First Amendment guarantees freedom of speech; it does not guarantee an individual right to exploit commercial technologies to deliver a message instantaneously to millions of people. Content-based laws that restrict electronic amplification, without abridging freedom of speech, do not warrant strict scrutiny unless there is a "realistic possibility that official suppression of ideas is afoot."[185] Therefore, some type of intermediate scrutiny standard makes sense for laws that regulate electronic amplification services.

The third option is consistent with the Court's general approach in both *Red Lion* and *Pacifica*. To paraphrase Justice Stevens in *Pacifica*, we have a right not to be "assaulted" with a steady stream of election-related lies and misinformation.[186] Per *Red Lion*, We the People retain a "collective right to have [electronic media] function consistently with the ends and purposes of the First Amendment."[187] We have a right to receive truthful, accurate information about electoral procedures and about candidates for elective offices. Protection of this collective right is essential to preserve the Constitution's structural division of power between the government and the people. In a bygone era, the Supreme Court actually cared about these rights. It is long past time for the Court to rediscover the wisdom in some of its older First Amendment cases.

5

Individual Rights under International Law

There is a widespread misconception that "traditional" international law did not protect individual rights. That claim is false. As noted in Chapter 1, *Ware v. Hylton* was one of the first cases in which the Supreme Court exercised its power of judicial review to invalidate a state law. In *Ware*, the Court applied a treaty with Britain (the peace treaty that ended the Revolutionary War) to protect the rights of British creditors by invalidating a Virginia law that discriminated against those creditors in favor of American debtors.[1]

Chapter 6 presents a normative argument in favor of a system of weak judicial review to protect individual rights that relies heavily on international human rights treaties as a source of judicially enforceable rules. This chapter presents historical analysis to support two key points that lay a foundation for that argument. First, throughout the nineteenth century, courts applied a system of weak judicial review in which they enforced treaty-based rules to protect individual rights from government infringement. Therefore, the type of system I am proposing has deep historical roots in American public law. Second, due to a largely invisible constitutional transformation that occurred between 1945 and 1965, international human rights treaties are not currently available to U.S. courts as a source of judicially enforceable rights. However, under current constitutional understandings, Congress has the power to make those treaties judicially enforceable by enacting an appropriate statute to that effect.

The remainder of this chapter is divided into four sections. The first section presents a case study of pre-Civil War litigation involving real property claims in territories that the U.S. acquired by means of treaties with Spain and France. The next section analyzes a set of habeas corpus cases filed on behalf of Chinese immigrants in the late nineteenth and early twentieth centuries. The two case studies illustrate the use of weak judicial review to constrain government power and to protect both minority rights (Chinese immigrants) and fundamental rights (ownership of real property).

The third section analyzes the "de facto Bricker Amendment":[2] a de facto constitutional amendment that occurred between 1945 and 1965 that produced a new constitutional understanding concerning the domestic effect of treaties under the Supremacy Clause. The final section addresses U.S. ratification of international human rights treaties in the 1990s. The last two sections document U.S. resistance to judicial application of international human rights law in domestic courts. The resistance to judicial enforcement of human rights treaties (which would entail weak judicial review) channeled human rights advocacy onto a path of strong judicial review, based on enforcement of constitutional rights. That resistance has typically been justified by pro-democracy rhetoric. Ironically, though, the resultant system of strong judicial review is more antidemocratic than the alternative of weak judicial review because judicial enforcement of constitutional rights is not subject to legislative override.

REAL PROPERTY CLAIMS IN LOUISIANA AND FLORIDA: 1830 TO 1860

The United States acquired Louisiana from France under an 1803 treaty;[3] it acquired Florida from Spain under an 1819 treaty. Both treaties protected the property rights of individuals who owned land under the prior sovereign.[4] The treaties restated principles of customary international law, which held that transfer of territory between sovereign states does not affect individual property rights. Chief Justice Marshall summarized the law as follows:

> The people change their allegiance; their relation to their ancient sovereign is dissolved; but their … rights of property, remain undisturbed…. Had Florida changed its sovereign by an act containing no stipulation respecting the property of individuals, the right of property in all those who became subjects or citizens of the new government would have been unaffected by the change; it would have remained the same as under the ancient sovereign…. The king cedes that only which belonged to him; lands he had previously granted, were not his to cede.[5]

From Marshall's standpoint, this was not merely a principle of international law; it was also a matter of fundamental rights. He said: "That sense of justice and of right which is acknowledged and felt by the whole civilized world would be outraged, if private property should be generally confiscated, and private rights annulled."[6]

The principle was easier to state than to apply. Two factors presented difficulties. First, many claimants produced ostensible titles tainted by fraud.[7] Given widespread allegations of fraud, Congress established administrative tribunals, known as land commissions, to distinguish between valid and fraudulent claims, and provided for judicial review of administrative decisions.[8] The laws governing land commissions varied by region, but the commissions typically reported to Congress, whereupon Congress enacted statutes confirming individual titles as recommended by the commissioners.[9]

Second, the varied practices of French and Spanish officials who issued land grants before the U.S. acquisitions of Louisiana and Florida gave rise to a bewildering array of imperfect, or inchoate, titles.[10] Supreme Court doctrine that developed between 1830 and 1850 established that individuals who held complete, or perfect, titles before the relevant treaty of cession did not have to present their claims to land commissions; the treaties confirmed the validity of perfect titles.[11] However, individuals who held inchoate titles had to apply to land commissions, pursuant to procedures established by Congress, before the government would confirm their titles.[12]

Between 1830 and 1860, the Supreme Court decided approximately 100 cases involving land disputes arising from the Louisiana and Florida treaties.[13] Some were private disputes between private parties, but most were public law disputes between the federal government and individuals who asserted titles based on French or Spanish grants. "In the whole of the Louisiana Purchase, there were between 13,000 and 14,000 such claims."[14] Claims arising from the Louisiana Purchase covered about seven million acres.[15] Supreme Court decisions in the Florida cases affected title to "fifteen million acres … covering about one-third of the state."[16] The stakes were high because, during this period, "for all the growth of industry and steady accumulation of capital in other forms, land was the principal form and source of wealth in the country."[17]

The Role of International Law

Litigants in the Louisiana-Florida land cases routinely invoked rights protected by international law. Federal statutes governed the procedural rules, but claimants' substantive rights depended on foreign and international law. In most cases, French or Spanish law determined the validity of the initial land grant.[18] However, neither French nor Spanish law protected individuals from adverse claims by the federal government. In every case, the individual's substantive rights vis-à-vis the United States depended on treaties, customary international law, or both. Under international law, any individual who had a valid claim against the French or Spanish government before the treaty of cession had an equally valid claim against the United States after the change of sovereignty.[19] Conventional wisdom holds that nineteenth-century international law did not protect U.S. citizens from their own government, but that view is mistaken. The Louisiana-Florida cases rarely specified the citizenship of claimants, but many of them were undoubtedly U.S. citizens. Moreover, citizenship was irrelevant. Both citizens and noncitizens were protected by relevant rules of international law.

The Supreme Court decision in *United States v. Arredondo* is illustrative.[20] The grant at issue in *Arredondo* "covered an area of 289,645 acres.… It embraced nearly the entire northeastern coast of Florida, including Jacksonville and other cities."[21] Former Attorney General William Wirt and Attorney General Roger Taney argued the case for the government. Daniel Webster and former Attorney General John

Berrien represented the private claimants.[22] "The government attacked the claim as fraudulent, denied the legal power of the Cuban army intendant to make the grant, [and] argued that the lands were within the Indian boundary and not subject to grant."[23] The Supreme Court rejected all these arguments, ruling decisively for the private claimants. The Court emphasized that "[t]he treaty and the acts of Congress were to be liberally construed, [and] the acts of foreign public officers were presumed to be lawful."[24]

Later commentators noted that *Arredondo* "served as the most important legal precedent for the entire body of Louisiana, Florida, and later California land cases."[25] *Arredondo* established a key legal precedent for protecting property rights from government infringement. However, the Court did not apply constitutional law to protect individuals from government overreaching. Instead, the Court applied international and foreign law to constrain federal executive power and protect individual property rights. Summarizing the body of precedent derived from *Arredondo*, the Supreme Court later said: "the claims shall be adjudged, and the equities of claimants determined and settled according to the law of nations, the stipulations of the treaty, and … the laws and ordinances of the government from which the claims are alleged to have been derived."[26] In short, the Court engaged in weak judicial review to resolve individual claims against the government. The system involved weak judicial review because Congress retained the authority to change the governing law and to exercise its power of eminent domain to seize private property, subject only to the Takings Clause requirement to pay just compensation.

Private litigants had great success litigating property claims against the federal government. Between 1832 and 1836, Joseph Mills White, the foremost U.S. expert on Spanish land law, represented private claimants before the Supreme Court in twenty-four cases involving the Louisiana and Florida treaties.[27] He won a partial or total victory in twenty-three of twenty-four cases,[28] relying on international and foreign law to protect individual rights from government infringement. Few, if any, modern Supreme Court litigators can claim a comparable success rate. In sum, the history of Louisiana/Florida property disputes demonstrates that a system of weak review can provide strong protection for fundamental rights.

Comparison to Modern Public Law Cases

The Louisiana-Florida land cases are similar in several respects to modern public law litigation. The land cases involved judicial review of administrative decisions made pursuant to federal statutes creating specialized tribunals (the land commissions). The cases raised generic conflicts between private parties and federal officials whose mission was to safeguard public goods without adversely affecting private rights. Consider an analogy to modern disability cases. In those cases, private claimants assert an entitlement to public goods (federal dollars).[29] Federal officers have a statutory duty to protect public goods from unworthy claimants and to distribute those goods to worthy claimants. Similarly, in the nineteenth-century land cases, private claimants asserted an entitlement to public goods (federal lands). Federal officers had a statutory duty to protect those public goods from unworthy claimants,[30] but they also had a duty (under treaties and customary international law) to confirm the titles of worthy claimants. Thus, the nineteenth-century land cases are structurally similar to certain modern administrative law cases.

One surprisingly modern feature of the nineteenth-century land cases was the prevalence of "cause lawyering." In the mid nineteenth century, the Court was ideologically divided between Justices sympathetic to individuals who asserted property rights based on French or Spanish grants, and Justices who favored the federal government's power to distribute land to its chosen grantees.[31] Joseph Mills White represented individual claimants before the Supreme Court in at least twenty-four land cases.[32] Daniel Webster argued several cases on behalf of private claimants,[33] joining White as co-counsel in two very significant cases.[34] White represented individual claimants because he was committed to the "Jeffersonian belief … in small landholding as the secret to the creation and maintenance of a viable democracy."[35] Similarly, Webster represented individual claimants because he believed, based on "[f]irst principles of justice drawn from natural law," that "government must recognize claims of title to ownership … and must assure a large measure of freedom in the uses of property."[36]

Modern lawyers might frame property rights claims against the government as Fifth Amendment Takings claims. However, the lawyers who litigated the Louisiana-Florida property cases rarely invoked constitutional law to advance their arguments, and the Court rarely applied constitutional law to decide the cases. In the pre-Civil War era, a constitutional claim challenging a governmental taking of private property might well have failed because key legal precedents supported the government's power to seize private property without paying compensation.[37] Regardless, claimants did not need constitutional law to protect their rights from government infringement because the courts protected their rights through vigorous enforcement of international law.

CHINESE HABEAS LITIGATION[38]

Between 1882 and 1905, Chinese petitioners seeking admission into the United States filed thousands of habeas corpus petitions in federal courts.[39] Despite restrictive immigration laws designed to exclude Chinese immigrants, petitioners won a very high proportion of those cases.[40] Judicial decisions relied primarily on international law, not constitutional law, to support the entry rights of Chinese petitioners. The Supreme Court did not invalidate any federal laws restricting Chinese immigration during this period.[41] Thus, the analysis shows that courts can provide robust protection for minority rights in a manner consistent with the principle of legislative primacy by applying international law to constrain executive power and protect individual rights. The following narrative is divided into three time periods.

Period One: 1868–1888

China and the United States concluded the Burlingame Treaty in 1868.[42] Evoking natural law, the treaty affirmed the "inherent and inalienable right of man to change his home." Both countries promised to allow "free migration and emigration of their citizens and subjects, respectively, from the one country to the other, for purposes of curiosity, of trade, or as permanent residents."[43] By 1880, more than 100,000 Chinese nationals were living in the United States.[44] The influx of immigrants produced a political backlash, resulting in a wave of anti-Chinese legislation. Responding to political pressure to restrict Chinese immigration, President Hayes appointed a commission to renegotiate the treaty with China.[45]

The new treaty, concluded in 1880, allowed the United States to restrict, but not prohibit, immigration of Chinese laborers "[w]henever in the opinion of the Government of the United States, the coming of Chinese laborers to the United States, or their residence therein, affects or threatens to affect the interests of that country, or to endanger the good order of the said country."[46] Although the treaty permitted restrictions on immigration of Chinese laborers, "[t]he limitation … shall apply only to Chinese who may go to the United States as laborers, other classes not being included in the limitations."[47] The treaty provided that "teachers, students, [and] merchants," as well as laborers who resided in the United States before entry into force of the treaty, "shall be allowed to go and come of their own free will and accord."[48] Thus, the new treaty attempted to balance the populist desire to exclude Chinese immigrants with the natural law commitment to the "inherent and inalienable right of man to change his home."[49]

After conclusion of the 1880 treaty, Congress enacted the Chinese Exclusion Act of 1882, suspending immigration of Chinese laborers for ten years, as permitted by the treaty.[50] The Act gave primary enforcement responsibility to customs collectors at ports of entry.[51] The collector in San Francisco "adopted a very strict reading of the act" and denied entry to numerous prospective immigrants.[52] The Chinese responded by filing habeas petitions in the Northern District of California. The federal court adopted a more expansive view of Chinese entry rights than the customs collector. Consequently, "[w]ithin fourteen months of the act's passage … the federal courts were directly or indirectly responsible for the entry of one-third of all Chinese landed during that period."[53] Judicial decisions granting habeas petitions invoked treaties with China as the primary source of rights for Chinese immigrants.[54]

In 1884, Congress amended the Chinese Exclusion Act to create additional hurdles for prospective immigrants.[55] Under the 1880 treaty and the 1882 statute, Chinese laborers who lived in the United States before passage of the 1882 Act retained the right to exit and return. Not surprisingly, customs collectors had difficulty distinguishing between Chinese who actually resided in the United States before 1882, and those who falsely claimed prior residence to gain entry.[56] The 1882 Act addressed this problem by allowing Chinese laborers to obtain a certificate before leaving the country. The certificate entitled Chinese laborers to "re-enter the United States upon producing and delivering the same to the collector of customs."[57] The 1884 amendment tightened the rules by providing that "said certificate shall be *the only evidence permissible* to establish this right of re-entry."[58]

Despite the clear statutory mandate, the Supreme Court soon decided two cases holding that "said certificate" was not the only evidence permissible to establish a right of entry. In *Chew Heong v. United States*, the Court held that a Chinese laborer who resided in the United States before passage of the 1882 Act, left the country without a certificate before enactment of the 1884 amendment, and then sought reentry after passage of the 1884 amendment, was entitled to enter the country without a certificate.[59] The Court stated: "[Because] the purpose avowed in the act was to faithfully execute the treaty, any interpretation of its provisions would be rejected which imputes to congress an intention to disregard the plighted faith of the government, and, consequently, the court ought, if possible, to adopt that construction which recognized and saved rights secured by the treaty."[60] Similarly, in *United States v. Jung Ah Lung*, the Court held that a Chinese laborer who claimed that his certificate was stolen was entitled to reenter if he could prove prior residence by other means.[61]

Between passage of the Chinese Exclusion Act in 1882 and passage of the Scott Act in 1888, federal courts consistently adopted a more generous view of Chinese entry rights than the customs collector in San Francisco.[62] By 1888, "4091 Chinese had petitioned the federal courts for a hearing." The courts granted petitioners entry rights in 85 percent of Chinese habeas cases.[63] Although the Chinese Exclusion Act was clearly intended to restrict immigration, the courts construed the Act broadly to protect the treaty-based entry rights of Chinese immigrants. Courts justified their decisions by invoking the principle that statutes should be construed in conformity with U.S. treaty obligations. In sum, the courts provided robust protection for Chinese entry rights without applying constitutional law and without invalidating any federal legislation governing Chinese immigration.

Period Two: 1888–1894

Congress enacted the Scott Act in 1888.[64] The 1882 and 1884 Acts could plausibly be construed consistently with the 1880 treaty. In the Scott Act, though, Congress made unmistakably clear that it did not intend to comply with the treaty. Although the 1880 treaty guaranteed Chinese laborers who resided in the United States before 1880 the right to "go and come of their own free will," the Scott Act provided that "it shall be unlawful for any Chinese laborer who shall at any time heretofore have been … a resident within the United States, and who shall have departed, or shall depart, therefrom, and shall not have returned before the passage of this act, to return to … the United States."[65] To avert any possible misinterpretation, Congress added that "every certificate heretofore issued … is hereby declared void … and the Chinese laborer claiming admission by virtue thereof shall not be permitted to enter the United States."[66]

In *Chae Chan Ping v. United States*, a Chinese laborer who held a certificate under the 1884 Act tried to reenter the United States.[67] The customs collector denied him entry in reliance on the Scott Act because the Act declared the certificate void. Chae Chan Ping challenged the constitutionality of the Act, arguing that it constituted an illegal "expulsion from the country of Chinese laborers, in violation of existing treaties between the United States and the government of China, and of rights vested in them under the laws of Congress."[68] The Supreme Court upheld the Act. The Court acknowledged that the Act contravened "express stipulations of the treaty of 1868, and of the supplemental treaty of 1880." Nevertheless, the Court ruled that "the last expression of the sovereign will must control."[69] The Court's opinion is replete with language affirming the principle that courts must give judicial effect to statutes enacted by democratic legislatures.

After *Chae Chan Ping*, Chinese nationals could no longer enter the country as laborers. Nevertheless, Chinese immigrants continued to litigate habeas petitions with great success by claiming a right to enter the country as merchants,[70] U.S. citizens,[71] or the wives or children of merchants or citizens.[72] In December 1890, a customs inspector testified that, between passage of the Scott Act and November 30, 1890, the federal court in San Francisco granted almost 2,000 habeas petitions filed by Chinese immigrants, but denied only 157 petitions.[73] Thus, Chinese petitioners won almost 93 percent of the habeas petitions filed within the first twenty-six months after passage of the Scott Act. Overall, between 1882 and 1891, "the Chinese filed more than seven thousand petitions for habeas corpus, and the court attracted the wrath of the public and administrative officials by allowing the vast majority of these Chinese to enter freely."[74]

Congress enacted a new immigration law in 1891.[75] The 1891 Act barred judicial review of administrative decisions denying entry to noncitizens.[76] However, the prohibition of judicial review did not apply to Chinese immigrants.[77] Consequently, federal courts continued to grant Chinese habeas petitions. Professor Salyer determined that the federal district court in San Francisco granted Chinese habeas petitions at an annual rate of 73 percent in 1891, 88 percent in 1892, 66 percent in 1893, and 80 percent in 1894.[78]

Lau Ow Bew v. United States illustrates the types of cases litigated in the early 1890s.[79] Petitioner had lived in the United States for seventeen years. During that time, he was "engaged in the wholesale and importing mercantile business in the city of Portland," Oregon.[80] He departed the country in September 1890 to visit relatives in China, returning in August 1891. When he returned, he produced documents to show that he was a merchant. As a merchant, the treaties protected his right to enter the country. The customs collector denied reentry, invoking a statute requiring Chinese merchants to "obtain the permission of ... the Chinese Government ... in each case to be evidenced by a certificate issued by such Government."[81]

Chief Justice Fuller asked: "Does the section apply to Chinese merchants, already domiciled in the United States, who, having left the country for temporary purposes ... seek to re-enter it on their return to their business and their homes?"[82] The Court concluded that it was absurd to require a merchant who had lived in the United States for seventeen years to obtain a certificate from the Chinese government granting him permission to return to the country. Chief Justice Fuller applied standard principles of statutory interpretation to support this conclusion. He also invoked petitioner's rights under "general international law" and the United States' treaties with China.[83] Finally, he quoted the Court's prior decision in *Chew Heong*: "[S]ince the purpose avowed in the [Chinese Exclusion] act was to faithfully execute the treaty, any interpretation of its provisions would be rejected which imputed to congress an intention to disregard the plighted faith of the government; and, consequently, the court ought, if possible, to adopt that construction which recognized and saved rights secured by the treaty."[84]

In sum, federal courts applied a combination of statutes and treaties to provide judicial protection for the treaty-based rights of Chinese immigrants.[85] By applying statutes and treaties, rather than constitutional law, the courts preserved Congress's prerogative to modify the governing legal rules. Thus, Chinese habeas litigation provides an example of weak judicial review that combines robust protection for individual rights with genuine judicial respect for legislative primacy.

Period Three: 1894–1905

In 1894, the United States and China concluded a new treaty prohibiting entry of Chinese laborers into the United States "for a period of ten years."[86] The treaty reaffirmed that "[t]he provisions of this Convention shall not affect the right ... of Chinese subjects, being officials, teachers, students, merchants or travelers for curiosity or pleasure, but not laborers, of coming to the United States and residing therein."[87] Thus, as before, the 1894 treaty balanced the populist desire to exclude Chinese laborers with the natural law commitment to international freedom of movement.

Meanwhile, the public was concerned that Chinese petitioners were repeatedly using habeas corpus to overturn administrative decisions denying them admission.[88] Accordingly, in August 1894 Congress enacted an amendment barring judicial review of exclusion decisions. The statute provided: "In every case where an alien is excluded from admission into the United States ... the decision of the appropriate immigration or customs officers, if adverse to the admission of such alien, shall be final, unless reversed on appeal to the Secretary of the Treasury."[89] Thus, the statute extended to Chinese immigrants the bar on judicial review that previously applied to other noncitizens under the 1891 Act.

In *Lem Moon Sing v. United States*,[90] a Chinese merchant with a "permanent domicile" in the United States filed a petition challenging a customs officer's decision denying him admission when he returned home after a temporary business trip to China. The Supreme Court affirmed the lower court's decision denying habeas relief, concluding that the 1894 Act precluded judicial review of the customs officer's decision.[91] The Court relied on its prior decision in *Nishimura Ekiu*, which upheld the validity of the 1891 statute barring judicial review of administrative decisions in non-Chinese cases.[92] Justice Harlan, writing for the majority in *Lem Moon Sing*, said there was no principled basis for distinguishing between the 1891 statute at issue in *Nishimura Ekiu* and the 1894 statute at issue in *Lem Moon Sing*.[93]

Respectfully, the Court's decision in *Lem Moon Sing* was mistaken. *Lem Moon Sing* and *Nishimura Ekiu* are readily distinguishable. In *Nishimura Ekiu*, the petitioner was "a person without means of support, without relatives or friends in the United States … unable to care for herself, and liable to become a public charge."[94] She was therefore ineligible to enter under the 1891 statute. In contrast, Lem Moon Sing was a Chinese merchant with a permanent domicile in the United States who – based on the facts in the Supreme Court opinion – had a clear right to enter under the 1894 treaty. The Court's opinion in *Lem Moon Sing* provides no indication of any statutory basis for the customs officer's decision to deny entry; his decision may have been entirely arbitrary and capricious. Even so, said Justice Harlan, the 1894 statute barred judicial review by way of habeas corpus.[95] That conclusion is troubling. The Court could easily have held that Congress did not intend to bar judicial review in cases where the immigration inspector's decision was arbitrary, capricious, or contrary to clearly established law.[96]

Lem Moon Sing appeared finally to bar judicial review of habeas petitions in Chinese exclusion cases. However, the courts continued to entertain habeas petitions from people of Chinese descent who claimed to be U.S. citizens. In *United States v. Wong Kim Ark*, the Court held that "a child born in the United States, of parents of Chinese descent, who at the time of his birth … have a permanent domicile and residence in the United States … becomes at the time of his birth a citizen of the United States, by virtue of" the Fourteenth Amendment.[97] Because the 1894 statute merely barred judicial review in cases "where an alien is excluded from admission,"[98] persons of Chinese descent who claimed birthright citizenship under the Fourteenth Amendment could still obtain judicial review.

Surprisingly, federal courts continued to grant habeas relief in most cases. Between 1895 (when *Lem Moon Sing* was decided) and 1904, the Northern District of California entertained 1,559 habeas petitions filed by persons of Chinese descent who sought admission to the country. The court granted relief in about 55 percent of those cases.[99] Chinese habeas litigation finally ended in 1905 when the Supreme

Court ruled in *United States v. Ju Toy* that federal courts lacked jurisdiction to entertain habeas petitions filed by persons of Chinese descent who claimed birthright citizenship under the Fourteenth Amendment.[100]

One can legitimately criticize the decisions in *Lem Moon Sing* and *Ju Toy* on the grounds that the Court caved too quickly to legislative efforts to bar judicial review of administrative decisions. The Court could potentially have done more to preserve limited judicial review without invalidating statutes approved by Congress. Still, the overall record of weak judicial review between 1882 and 1905 reveals a federal judiciary that was committed to both minority rights and legislative primacy, and that did a creditable job mitigating the tension between those competing values.

THE FUJII CASE AND THE BRICKER AMENDMENT

Both state and federal courts continued to adjudicate treaty-based individual rights claims between 1900 and 1945.[101] However, claims based on customary international law largely disappeared from federal courts during this period. In 1900, in *The Paquete Habana*, the Court famously declared: "International law is part of our law, and must be ascertained and administered by the courts of justice of appropriate jurisdiction as often as questions of right depending upon it are duly presented for their determination."[102] Even so, much of the nineteenth-century litigation involving direct application of customary international law by federal courts involved "pirates, prizes, and privateers."[103] Those cases "largely disappeared as professional navies took over the conduct of high-seas warfare." Additionally, several other factors contributed to the waning of customary international law in U.S. federal courts between 1900 and 1945.[104]

The United States ratified the UN Charter in 1945. In the Charter, the United States undertook a binding treaty obligation to promote "universal respect for, and observance of, human rights and fundamental freedoms for all *without distinction as to race*, sex, language, or religion."[105] Three years later, the United Nations adopted the Universal Declaration of Human Rights (UDHR). The UDHR, which was a nonbinding declaration, proclaimed "the equal and inalienable rights of all members of the human family."[106] Together, the Charter and the UDHR gave birth to modern international human rights law.

The advent of international human rights law had a profound effect on the development of constitutional law in the United States in two distinct ways. First, as discussed in Chapter 2, the Charter and the UDHR triggered the federalization of human rights in the United States – the transfer of authority over human rights issues from the states to the federal government.[107] Second, the Charter and the UDHR sparked a process of constitutional change that I call the "de facto Bricker Amendment."[108] This section first addresses the *Fujii* case and then the de facto Bricker Amendment.

The Fujii Case[109]

In *Fujii v. California*, Mr. Sei Fujii, a Japanese national, challenged the validity of California's Alien Land Law.[110] The California statute did not explicitly target Japanese for discriminatory treatment. Instead, the statute barred all noncitizens from owning land in California unless they were eligible to become naturalized citizens.[111] Federal law, not California law, determined who was eligible for naturalization. Under then-existing federal law, Japanese were one of the few groups ineligible for citizenship because of their nationality. Moreover, of those national groups who were ineligible for citizenship, Japanese were the only group with a sizeable population in California. Therefore, the main practical effect of the Alien Land Law was to preclude Japanese from owning land in California. Fujii was well aware of these facts; he was determined to end California's longstanding practice of discriminating against Japanese people.

The trial court upheld the validity of the Alien Land Law and Fujii appealed. His appellate brief contended that the Alien Land Law violated the Fourteenth Amendment Equal Protection Clause. From a modern perspective, it seems obvious that a state law barring Japanese nationals from owning property violates the Equal Protection Clause. However, it was not obvious in 1949. To the contrary, the California Attorney General cited a long string of decisions by the U.S. Supreme Court and the California Supreme Court upholding the validity of the Alien Land Law.[112] Thus, in terms of legal precedent, Fujii faced an uphill battle.

Perhaps recognizing the weakness of his Equal Protection claim, Fujii also argued that the Alien Land Law conflicted with "the exalted principles and high resolutions of our nation as expressed in the United Nations Charter."[113] Two Charter provisions are especially relevant for *Fujii*. Article 55 states: "the United Nations shall promote … universal respect for, and observance of, human rights and fundamental freedoms for all without distinction as to race, sex, language, or religion." Under Article 56, Member States "pledge themselves to take joint and separate action … for the achievement of the purposes set forth in Article 55."[114] Thus, Articles 55 and 56 obligate the United States to take "separate action" to promote "human rights … for all without distinction as to race." But this statement raises several questions. Is the right to own property a "human right"? If so, what type of "separate action" must the United States take to promote that right? Is a statutory distinction between citizens and noncitizens a "distinction as to race" within the meaning of Article 55 if, in practice, the statute has a disparate impact on Japanese nationals?

Finally, assuming there is an actual conflict between the Alien Land Law and the UN Charter, should a California court apply the statute to decide the case, or should it apply the Charter? The Constitution's Supremacy Clause addresses that question. The Clause specifies that treaties ratified by the United States are "the supreme Law of the Land; and the Judges in every State shall be bound thereby, any Thing in the Constitution or Laws of any State to the Contrary notwithstanding."[115]

Thus, if there is a conflict between a ratified treaty and state law, the Supremacy Clause directs "Judges in every State" to apply the treaty. Therefore, if Fujii's equal protection argument failed, the combination of the UN Charter and the Supremacy Clause provided an alternative legal rationale for invalidating the Alien Land Law.

The California Court of Appeal issued its decision in April 1950.[116] The court easily dismissed Fujii's equal protection argument, citing a string of decisions by the U.S. Supreme Court and the California Supreme Court upholding the validity of the Alien Land Law. The court concluded that portion of its opinion as follows: "This opinion might well be terminated under the doctrine of *stare decisis* with a reaffirmation of the former decisions, since upon constitutional questions we deem ourselves obliged to follow the decisions of the Supreme Courts of the United States and of this State until one of those courts should announce the overruling of its own decisions."[117]

The court then addressed Fujii's human rights argument. It held that California's Alien Land Law was invalid because California law conflicted with the Charter's human rights provisions, and the Supremacy Clause required state courts to apply the treaty.[118] The court's decision sent a shock wave through the U.S. political system whose effects are still felt today.

The Court of Appeal issued its decision on April 24, 1950. An article the next day in the *Los Angeles Times* described *Fujii* as a "precedent-setting decision."[119] The *Los Angeles Daily Journal*, a newspaper written primarily for the legal profession, correctly described *Fujii* as "the first decision in which the Charter of the United Nations has been invoked to invalidate a law of a State."[120] The *San Francisco Chronicle* and *New York Times* also published short stories about the case.

On April 28, 1950, four days after the court's decision, Senator Forrest Donnell, a Republican from Missouri, warned his Senate colleagues about the dangers of *Fujii*. The fact that the Senate devoted floor time to a discussion of the *Fujii* case is extremely unusual. U.S. Supreme Court decisions routinely attract the Senate's attention. The Senate sometimes heeds decisions by state supreme courts or lower federal courts. However, *Fujii* was a decision by an intermediate appellate court in California – a state court, not a federal court. Intermediate appellate courts throughout the United States issue hundreds or thousands of decisions every day. The Senate rarely notices any of them. Even so, the Senate spent approximately one hour of its valuable time on April 28, 1950, discussing the implications of *Fujii*.[121]

Senator Donnell read a statement quoting several paragraphs from the Court of Appeal's decision. He summarized the case as follows: "Mr. President, the opinion from which I have just read holds … that a valid treaty, which is, by the Constitution of the United States, the supreme law of the land, invalidates the law of a state which is in conflict with said treaty."[122] Senator Homer Ferguson (R-MI) was not prepared to concede that the court's decision was correct. However, if the decision was correct, he noted, the effect of the Charter "may be to nullify or make void all statutes in any State in relation to distinctions made between the sexes; and, in addition, we may find that by that means equal rights have already been established in the United

States."[123] He did not need to state explicitly – because it was obvious to everyone present – that the Charter would also invalidate Jim Crow laws. If *Fujii* was right, the United States had effectively abrogated Jim Crow laws throughout the South by ratifying the UN Charter.

Senator Donnell recalled the 1920 Supreme Court decision in *Missouri v. Holland*.[124] He explained that *Holland* held that "the adoption of a treaty on a given subject matter which is within the treaty power and as to which subject matter there had been no previous grant to Congress of legislative power causes Congress … to be possessed of power to legislate to carry into effect such treaty."[125] Senator George Malone (R-NV) responded: "If I correctly understand the Senator's interpretation … it does open the door to Congress to legislate on subjects which were never given by the States through the Constitution of the United States to the Congress in the first place."[126] Donnell said, "That is precisely correct." Malone replied, "To that extent, it is dangerous." Donnell agreed: "To my mind, it is highly dangerous" because "the effect of a treaty may possibly be to vest in the Congress of the United States a vast reservoir of power to legislate on matters which perhaps previously had been confined to the States."[127]

The perceived danger did not stem from the *Fujii* decision itself. From Donnell's perspective, the real danger lay in the Constitution's Supremacy Clause, which meant that treaties ratified by the United States automatically invalidated conflicting state laws. Additionally, the Supreme Court's prior decision in *Missouri v. Holland* was dangerous because it meant that the federal government could utilize the Treaty Power to extend Congress' legislative powers into areas previously reserved to the States. Still, *Fujii* was a dramatic reminder that ratification of the Charter opened the door to legal arguments by aggrieved groups who sought to invalidate state laws that discriminated on the basis of "race, sex, language, or religion."[128]

While Senators discussed *Fujii*'s implications, the State was preparing its next move in the litigation. Two weeks after the Court of Appeal's decision, the California Attorney General filed a petition for rehearing.[129] Three days later, the American Civil Liberties Union (ACLU) and the American Jewish Congress (AJC) filed a joint *amicus curiae* brief opposing the petition for rehearing.[130] They contended that the Court of Appeal's decision was correct: The Alien Land Law was invalid because it conflicted with the Charter's human rights provisions. A few days later, the Japanese American Citizens' League and the NAACP filed an application to join the ACLU/AJC brief, stating that the brief "is in accordance with the views of these petitioning amici curiae and petitioning amici curiae join therein."[131] *Fujii* was one of many cases during this period where groups that we now identify as "domestic civil rights" organizations invoked the Charter's human rights provisions to support their preferred outcomes in domestic civil rights cases.[132]

The Court of Appeal denied the petition for rehearing on May 22, 1950.[133] That decision effectively closed the first chapter of the *Fujii* litigation. By that time the battle lines were drawn. The ACLU, the NAACP, and other civil rights organizations supported judicial application of the UN Charter to invalidate discriminatory state laws. Senate Republicans, state governments, and others feared that judicial application of the Charter would disrupt the racial status quo in the Jim Crow South and upset the constitutional balance between the federal and state governments.

The De Facto Bricker Amendment[134]

When the Constitution's Framers met in Philadelphia in 1787, one of their primary objectives was to persuade European powers that the United States could be trusted to fulfill its international obligations.[135] In the decade since adoption of the Declaration of Independence, the United States had repeatedly violated treaty obligations owed to European states.[136] The failure to fulfill its international obligations created serious problems for the young nation. The Framers included the Supremacy Clause in the Constitution to help rectify those problems.

The Clause specifies that treaties are "the supreme Law of the Land" and that "the Judges in every State shall be bound thereby."[137] From the Founding until World War II, the treaty supremacy rule was uniformly understood to be a mandatory rule consisting of two elements. First, all valid, ratified treaties supersede conflicting state laws. Second, courts have a constitutional duty to apply treaties when they have jurisdiction over a justiciable claim involving a conflict between a treaty and state law.[138] Thus, the court's application of the Supremacy Clause in *Fujii* was entirely consistent with the traditional understanding of the treaty supremacy rule.

Congress and the courts began developing a doctrine of "non-self-executing" (NSE) treaties as early as the 1790s. However, NSE doctrine did not affect the operation of the treaty supremacy rule because NSE doctrine and treaty supremacy doctrine addressed two discrete sets of nonoverlapping issues. NSE doctrine was primarily concerned with the division of power over treaty implementation between Congress and the President.[139] Treaty supremacy doctrine addressed conflicts between treaties and state law. Before World War II, there was no exception to the treaty supremacy rule for NSE treaties because self-execution doctrine was simply not relevant to treaty supremacy cases.[140]

The American Law Institute (ALI) published its Restatement (Second) of Foreign Relations Law in 1965.[141] The Restatement asserted that NSE treaties do not supersede conflicting state laws.[142] Whereas the traditional treaty supremacy rule was a mandatory rule, the Restatement treated it as an optional rule: The treaty makers (i.e., the President and Senate, acting together under Article II) could opt out of the treaty supremacy rule by declaring that a particular treaty is not self-executing. Thus, the ALI recognized an NSE exception to the treaty supremacy rule.[143] That exception was potentially problematic because it allowed state and local governments to violate U.S. treaty obligations. Thus, the optional supremacy rule was in tension with the Framers' goal of designing a constitution that precluded state governments from breaching national treaty obligations, absent congressional authorization.

What changed between 1945 and 1965? Why did the ALI endorse a doctrine that was at odds with the original understanding of the treaty supremacy rule and with the vast weight of legislative, executive, and judicial authority from the Founding until World War II? The central story line can be summarized as follows. With adoption of the UN Charter in 1945 and the UDHR in 1948, the norms of universality and nondiscrimination were incorporated into modern international law. Universality means that all human beings have certain fundamental rights. Nondiscrimination means that governments may not discriminate on the basis of race, gender, or other prohibited factors in making decisions about the scope of protection to be accorded for human rights. The new international norms exerted a powerful magnetic pull, sparking an explosion of human rights activism in the United States. Between 1945 and 1954, human rights activists litigated dozens of cases, like the *Fujii* case, in which claimants asked U.S. courts to apply the UN Charter's human rights provisions in conjunction with the treaty supremacy rule to invalidate discriminatory state laws.[144]

The explosion of human rights activism produced a conservative reaction. Activists gathered support within the American Bar Association (ABA) for a proposed constitutional amendment to abolish the treaty supremacy rule.[145] Senator John Bricker, working closely with the ABA, rallied support within the U.S. Senate for a similar amendment, known as the Bricker Amendment.[146] Conservatives in the ABA and the Senate cited *Fujii* repeatedly as "exhibit number one" in support of the proposed Bricker Amendment. Bricker's supporters feared that application of human rights norms in conjunction with the treaty supremacy rule would abrogate Jim Crow laws throughout the South and produce a fundamental change in the balance of power between state governments and the federal government. They argued that a constitutional amendment to abolish the treaty supremacy rule was necessary to avert that danger.[147]

The Eisenhower Administration opposed the Bricker Amendment on the grounds that it would erode the federal government's control over the conduct of foreign policy.[148] Internationalists within the ABA shared that concern. Opponents of the Bricker Amendment argued that a constitutional amendment was unnecessary because Bricker's fears could be addressed by including language in human rights treaties, or in unilateral declarations attached to those treaties, stipulating that the treaties would not supersede state laws unless Congress enacted implementing legislation.[149] Implicit in this argument was an unstated assumption that the treaty supremacy rule is optional – that is, that Article II grants the treaty makers an affirmative power to opt out of the treaty supremacy rule by declaring that the treaty is not self-executing. In the early 1950s, when Bricker's opponents first introduced this argument, the proposition that the treaty supremacy rule is optional was a novel idea. Even so, the optional supremacy rule rapidly gained acceptance as settled law.

The California Supreme Court endorsed the optional treaty supremacy rule in its 1952 decision in *Fujii v. State*,[150] the appeal from the lower court decision in *Fujii*. The California Supreme Court decision in *Fujii* was the first published judicial decision in U.S. history to hold that NSE treaties do not supersede conflicting state laws.[151] Senior members of the Eisenhower Administration issued a series of statements in 1953 – in Senate testimony during the Bricker Amendment hearings – in which they also endorsed the NSE exception to the treaty supremacy rule.[152] However, statements by senior executive officials were not readily accessible to courts, so most courts continued to apply the traditional treaty supremacy rule until the ALI published its Restatement of Foreign Relations Law in 1965.[153] As a practical matter, the ALI codified the new constitutional understanding that developed within the Eisenhower Administration during the Bricker Amendment debates.[154] Once that new understanding was codified in the Restatement, state courts and lower federal courts began to apply the optional supremacy rule.

I refer to the transformative process that gave rise to a new constitutional understanding as the "de facto Bricker Amendment." Other scholars have written about the "de facto ERA."[155] In the ERA example, advocates of women's equality pursued their goals by means of a constitutional amendment (the ERA). The amendment was not approved, but ERA supporters achieved some of their goals by triggering a transformative process that yielded a new constitutional understanding. In the Bricker example, human rights advocates pursued their goals by litigating claims based on the UN Charter and the treaty supremacy rule. Their political adversaries mobilized support for the proposed Bricker Amendment in an attempt to abolish the treaty supremacy rule. As in the case of the de facto ERA, the proposed amendment was never approved, but Bricker's supporters achieved some of their goals by triggering a transformative process that effectively converted the treaty supremacy rule from a mandatory rule to an optional rule.

Several factors help explain why the optional treaty supremacy rule gained acceptance between 1950 and 1965. One such factor was the widespread belief in "American exceptionalism" – a view that the United States has the best constitutional system in the world. In cases where human rights claimants raised treaty supremacy arguments based on the UN Charter, they also raised Fourteenth Amendment equal protection claims. The lower court in *Fujii* held that a discriminatory California law violated the UN Charter, but did not violate the Equal Protection Clause.[156] That decision was impossible to reconcile with the public faith in American exceptionalism. As one prominent commentator stated in response to *Fujii*: "It would seem, indeed, a reproach to our constitutional system to confess that the values it establishes fall below any requirement of the Charter. One should think very seriously before admitting such a deficiency."[157] The NSE exception to the treaty supremacy rule provided courts a convenient rationale for dodging the treaty supremacy argument altogether. By dodging that argument, courts helped preserve the faith in American exceptionalism by avoiding any ruling that implied that international human rights standards provided more robust protection against racial discrimination than did the Equal Protection Clause.

Two key events in 1954 helped solidify the new constitutional understanding that there is an exception to the treaty supremacy rule for NSE treaties. On February 26, the Senate voted 60–31 in favor of one version of the Bricker Amendment.[158] The tally was one vote short of the requisite two-thirds majority, but it was sufficiently close to convince any remaining doubters that Bricker's supporters constituted a potent political force. Then, on May 17, the Supreme Court issued its landmark decision in *Brown v. Board of Education*,[159] which revolutionized constitutional equal protection doctrine. In *Bolling v. Sharpe*,[160] a companion case to *Brown*, petitioners argued forcefully that racial segregation in the District of Columbia public schools violated U.S. treaty obligations under the UN Charter, and that the Charter superseded local law under the Supremacy Clause.[161] The Supreme Court ducked the treaty supremacy argument in *Bolling*, relying instead on equal protection doctrine to support its holding that racial segregation was unconstitutional.

By applying equal protection doctrine to invalidate discriminatory state laws, instead of applying the UN Charter and the treaty supremacy rule, the Supreme Court helped preserve the public faith in American exceptionalism. U.S. diplomats supported domestic civil rights reform because racial discrimination at home was undermining the nation's Cold War foreign policy by providing ammunition for foreign critics who condemned the United States' racist policies and practices.[162] The executive branch supported application of equal protection doctrine, rather than the treaty supremacy rule, because expanded human rights protection under the Equal Protection Clause promoted the goals of Cold War foreign policy by helping U.S. diplomats sell the virtues of our constitutional system to a skeptical global audience.[163]

In light of the Senate vote on the Bricker Amendment and the Supreme Court decisions in *Brown* and *Bolling*, human rights activists who had previously invoked the UN Charter and the treaty supremacy rule in domestic civil rights litigation changed their strategy. They abandoned international human rights claims and focused, instead, on constitutional equal protection claims. *Brown* and *Bolling* meant that their constitutional claims were more likely to succeed. And the Senate vote on the Bricker Amendment persuaded them that judicial decisions applying the UN Charter and the treaty supremacy rule would have the unwanted effect of mobilizing support for their political adversaries. Consequently, international human rights litigation in U.S. courts largely disappeared after 1954. Even so, the human rights litigation of the late 1940s and early 1950s had a powerful impact on constitutional history. The UN Charter's antidiscrimination norm had been a part of the "paper Constitution" in the United States since adoption of the Fourteenth Amendment. That norm did not become a part of the "living Constitution" until after the Fourteenth Amendment was subjected to the magnetic pull of international human rights law. As explained in Chapter 2, the United States federalized international human rights norms between 1948 and 1976 by silently incorporating those norms into federal law.[164]

NON-SELF-EXECUTING DECLARATIONS AND HUMAN RIGHTS TREATIES

The United Nations adopted the UDHR in 1948. Over the next two decades, the UN Commission on Human Rights completed work on two major international human rights treaties that codified the rights included in the UDHR into legally binding treaty obligations: the International Covenant on Civil and Political Rights (ICCPR),[165] and the International Covenant on Economic, Social, and Cultural Rights (ICESCR).[166] During that same period, the Commission also drafted the Convention on Elimination of Racial Discrimination (CERD).[167] After concluding work on those treaties, the Commission drafted the Convention on Discrimination against Women (CEDAW),[168] the Convention against Torture (CAT),[169] and the Convention on the Rights of the Child (CRC).[170] Meanwhile, the Organization of American States adopted the American Convention on Human Rights (ACHR) in 1969.[171] Table 5.1 presents key information about the six UN treaties. (The "date of adoption" is the date when the text was finalized. Entry into force occurs after a minimum number of states have ratified the treaty. The minimum number varies by treaty; it is specified in the text of the treaty.)

TABLE 5.1 *Major Global Human Rights Treaties*

Name of Treaty	Date of Adoption	Date of Entry into Force	Number of Parties*	U.S. Status
Convention on Racial Discrimination (CERD)	1965	1969	182	Party since 1994
Covenant on Civil and Political Rights (ICCPR)	1966	1976	173	Party since 1992
Covenant on Economic, Social, and Cultural Rights (ICESCR)	1966	1976	171	Not a party
Convention on Discrimination against Women (CEDAW)	1979	1981	189	Not a party
Convention against Torture (CAT)	1984	1987	173	Party since 1994
Convention on the Rights of the Child (CRC)	1989	1990	196	Not a party

* Data on the number of parties is taken from Office of the High Commissioner of Human Rights, Status of Ratification: Interactive Dashboard, available at https://indicators.ohchr.org/ (last visited August 13, 2024).

During Senate debates over the Bricker Amendment, then-Secretary of State John Foster Dulles made a political commitment that the United States would not become a party to any human rights treaty.[172] His statement helped opponents of the Bricker Amendment defeat the proposed amendment.[173] The statement manifested an "allergy" to human rights treaties that carried sufficient political force that the United States did not ratify a major international human rights treaty for almost forty years.

President Carter submitted four human rights treaties to the Senate in 1978: the ICCPR, the ICESCR, the American Convention, and the Race Convention.[174] However, the Senate did not vote on the treaties during the Carter Administration, due to "domestic and international events at the end of 1979, including the Soviet invasion of Afghanistan and the hostage crisis in Iran."[175] The Senate took no significant action on human rights treaties for the next decade. The United States signed the Torture Convention in 1988; President Reagan promptly submitted it to the Senate.[176] The United States ultimately ratified the ICCPR in 1992. We ratified the Race Convention and the Torture Convention in 1994.[177] We have not ratified the ICESCR, the ACHR, CEDAW, or CRC.

For all three treaties that the United States ratified in the early 1990s, the President and Senate adopted a set of "reservations, understandings, and declarations," commonly referred to as RUDs. For all three treaties, the Department of Justice (DOJ) analyzed treaty obligations to determine the extent to which we could achieve treaty compliance by relying on preexisting constitutional and statutory provisions, and to identify specific treaty obligations for which we would need to change U.S. law to comply with the treaty. The President and Senate adopted either reservations or understandings – which have the effect of limiting the scope of our treaty obligations under international law – for all treaty provisions where the DOJ determined that we would need to change U.S. law to achieve compliance. Thus, the RUDs were designed to allow the United States to comply with its treaty obligations, as limited by the RUDs, without having to make any changes in domestic law.[178]

For all three treaties (the ICCPR, CAT, and CERD), the United States also adopted declarations specifying that the substantive provisions of the treaties are "not self-executing." Implicit in the adoption of these "NSE declarations" is the assumption that the Constitution's treaty supremacy rule is optional, not mandatory. By adopting the NSE declarations, the President and Senate expressed their intention to opt out of the treaty supremacy rule. Thanks to the de facto Bricker Amendment, which had crystallized a new constitutional understanding by the time that the ALI published its Restatement in 1965, there was broad consensus in the early 1990s that the treaty makers had the power, under Article II of the Constitution, to opt out of the treaty supremacy rule.[179]

However, even today, it remains unclear what exactly it means to opt out of the treaty supremacy rule. Recall that the treaty supremacy rule has two elements: treaties are supreme federal law ("Law of the Land"); and judges have a constitutional duty to enforce treaties in appropriate circumstances (judges are "bound thereby").[180] Some scholars argue that the NSE declarations are best construed to mean that human rights treaties ratified by the United States are the "supreme Law of the Land," but that judges are not "bound thereby" because that portion of the treaty supremacy rule is optional, and the treaty makers opted out by adopting NSE declarations.[181] However, as I have shown in detail elsewhere, current law manifests no less than eight different variants of NSE doctrine.[182] Detailed analysis of Senate materials associated with treaty ratification demonstrates that the Senate has manifested different understandings of NSE declarations at different times, such that those declarations might reasonably be construed in accordance with one of three different variants of NSE doctrine.[183] Regardless, two points are clear. First, the NSE declarations were intended to restrict, if not completely prohibit, direct judicial application of human rights treaties by U.S. courts. Second, the declarations have had the intended effect: Over the past thirty years, U.S. courts have not applied human rights treaties directly as a rule of decision to resolve contested issues in litigation. (Courts apply treaties "directly" when they apply a treaty as a rule of decision. Courts apply treaties "indirectly" when they apply a treaty as an aid to statutory interpretation.)

President Carter first proposed a package of RUDs for human rights treaties when he transmitted four human rights treaties to the Senate in 1978.[184] From that time onward, until the Senate consented to ratification of the Race Convention in June 1994, both the Senate and the Executive Branch invoked pro-democracy rhetoric to justify adoption of the RUDs. For example, a senior State Department official told the Senate in 1992: "If the Congress desires to change existing domestic laws, it will undoubtedly want to do so by statute, in the customary, legislative process."[185] Similarly, in its report on the ICCPR, the Senate Foreign Relations Committee said:

> The Committee recognizes the importance of adhering to internationally recognized standards of human rights. Although the U.S. record of adherence has been good, there are some areas in which the U.S. law differs from the international standard.... In areas such as these, it may be appropriate and necessary to question whether changes in U.S. law should be made to bring the United States into full compliance at the international level. However, the Committee anticipates that changes in U.S. law in these areas will occur *through the normal legislative process.*[186]

The reference to the "normal" legislative process implies that there is something "abnormal," perhaps even "undemocratic," about using self-executing treaties to make changes in domestic law. However, the President and Senate have been using the Article II treaty power to make changes in domestic law since the eighteenth century. Indeed, the Framers included treaties in the Supremacy Clause precisely because they wanted (and expected) courts to apply treaties directly to override conflicting state laws.[187]

Regardless, if the goal was to ensure that Congress would take the lead in making changes to U.S. law to achieve compliance with international human rights standards, the actual result has been almost precisely the opposite. The Supreme Court, not Congress, has taken the lead in making changes to U.S. law – not through democratic, legislative processes, but through undemocratic constitutional lawmaking. Consider, for example, the juvenile death penalty. Article 6(5) of the ICCPR states: "Sentence of death shall not be imposed for crimes committed by persons below eighteen years of age."[188] When the United States ratified the ICCPR, we adopted a reservation that exempted us from the obligation to comply with this provision, ostensibly because we wanted to ensure that changes to U.S. law would occur only through "the normal legislative process." At the time of treaty ratification, the governing constitutional rule barred application of the death penalty to children below sixteen years old.[189] However, a decade after we ratified the ICCPR, the Court overruled *Stanford v. Kentucky* and brought U.S. law into alignment with the international standard by holding, in *Roper v. Simmons*, that the Eighth Amendment bars application of capital punishment to anyone who was under eighteen at the time he or she committed the crime.[190]

If the United States had ratified the ICCPR without the juvenile death penalty reservation, and without the NSE declaration, it would have had essentially the same effect as the Court's decision in *Roper v. Simmons*: It would have changed the governing rule under federal law from a sixteen-year-old floor to an eighteen-year-old floor. However, if the United States changed the governing rule by treaty ratification, instead of doing it by constitutional decree, Congress would have retained the power to alter the rule "through the normal legislative process."[191] Thus, the package of RUDs – which was ostensibly intended to preserve a role for Congress in making changes to federal law – ultimately excluded Congress from the federal lawmaking process. The RUDs themselves are a legacy of the Bricker Amendment debates and the U.S. allergy to international human rights law that is a byproduct of those debates. Senator Bricker failed in his effort to preserve Jim Crow and protect state autonomy from the federalization of human rights. Nevertheless, the "ghost of Senator Bricker" survives in a federal system of human rights protection that privileges judicial lawmaking over democratic lawmaking.[192]

Chapter 6 contends that Congress could strengthen democratic control over federal lawmaking, without weakening protection for human rights, by removing the NSE declarations from human rights treaties and encouraging courts to apply those treaties, instead of applying the Constitution, to protect fundamental human rights.

6

Weak Review, Strong Rights[1]

Ely's theory distinguished sharply between minority rights and fundamental rights. In his view, courts should apply strong judicial review to protect minority rights, at least insofar as particular minority groups are systematically underrepresented in the political process.[2] Judicial protection of discrete and insular minorities rights is a paradigmatic example of judicial review designed to correct a malfunction in the political process. In contrast, Ely argued that courts should generally defer to legislatures on questions of fundamental rights because we can trust the democratic process to protect fundamental rights.[3] After all, if a right is truly "fundamental" – in the sense that all human beings have a moral entitlement to that right – strong democratic majorities can be expected to support that right.

In contrast to Ely, this chapter contends that courts should apply a system of weak review for both minority rights and fundamental rights. Most of the rights included in the Bill of Rights and the Fourteenth Amendment – and most of the unenumerated rights that are protected under the Court's current constitutional doctrine – are listed explicitly in the International Covenant on Civil and Political Rights (ICCPR).[4] (See Tables 6.1–6.3, comparing constitutional rights to treaty rights). The United States has been a party to the ICCPR since 1992. Under established doctrine, Congress has the power to enact legislation to authorize judicial enforcement of the rights included in the ICCPR.[5] If Congress enacts such legislation, and the courts practice constitutional avoidance, the net result would be a system of weak judicial review that is functionally similar to what Professor Stephen Gardbaum calls "the new Commonwealth model of constitutionalism" – a model that applies with some variations in Australia, Canada, New Zealand, and the United Kingdom.[6]

Under the proposed system of weak review, federal courts would rely heavily on international human rights treaties to protect both minority rights and fundamental rights. They would practice constitutional avoidance in all cases where judicial enforcement of treaties provides a viable substitute for judicial enforcement of the Constitution. The proposed system of weak review would provide judicial protection for rights that is substantially equivalent to – and in some cases better than – the current system of strong review. Moreover, the proposed system of weak review offers several advantages over the current system. First with weak review, Congress could override judicial decisions it disapproves. The option for legislative override is consistent with the constitutional norm of legislative primacy; in contrast, the current system of strong review is fundamentally at odds with that norm. Legislative primacy is necessary to preserve the power of We the People to exercise control over our government, a core structural feature of the Constitution that is largely ignored in the current system. As shown in Chapter 5, a treaty-based approach has strong historical antecedents in the nineteenth century. Indeed, weak review was the dominant approach to judicial protection of individual rights before the *Lochner* revolution, which gave rise to the constitutionalization of American public law.[7]

Additionally, reliance on international human rights treaties as a substitute for judicial enforcement of constitutional rights provides a much stronger textual foundation for judicial enforcement of individual rights. With respect to minority rights, the treaty texts provide much more detailed guidance for courts than the vaguely worded Equal Protection Clause, which simply invites judicial lawmaking. With respect to fundamental rights, it is important to distinguish between enumerated and unenumerated rights. Many of the fundamental rights that U.S. courts enforce today are not specifically enumerated in the text of the Constitution. In contrast, almost all of the key unenumerated rights are specifically enumerated in the text of the ICCPR.[8] Moreover, even with respect to enumerated rights, the judicial decision to make those rights binding on state governments via incorporation doctrine lacks textual support in the text of the Fourteenth Amendment (as explained in Chapter 7). In contrast, the Supremacy Clause provides explicit textual support for making international human rights treaties binding on state governments. Granted, human rights litigation will invariably raise issues where the text of human rights treaties is open to conflicting interpretations, and judicial construction is therefore necessary. However, the option for Congress to override treaty-based judicial decisions preserves a vital check on unrestrained judicial lawmaking – a check that is missing from the current system of strong review.

I said previously that "most" constitutional rights are listed explicitly in the ICCPR. Table 6.1 identifies the primary exceptions. The most important exception is the Fifth Amendment Takings Clause. As I have argued elsewhere, the property rights protected by the Takings Clause qualify as "fundamental rights" under the traditional natural law test,[9] which specifies that a right is fundamental if it implicates "immutable principles of justice which inhere in the very idea of free government."[10] Protection for property rights is included in the Universal Declaration of Human Rights (UDHR).[11] However, when the United Nations translated the broad principles of the UDHR into legally binding treaties, those rights were codified in two separate treaties: the ICCPR and the International Covenant on Economic, Social, and Cultural Rights (ICESCR).[12] Property rights ended up in the ICESCR, a treaty that the United States has not ratified. Hence, unlike most other fundamental human rights, there is no treaty-based substitute for judicial enforcement of the Takings Clause. Absent a treaty-based substitute, and given that property rights are properly classified as "fundamental rights," courts should continue to apply the Takings Clause to protect property rights. Here, it bears emphasis that judicial application of the Takings Clause differs markedly from most other examples of strong judicial review in that the Takings Clause does not actually prevent governments from taking private property[13]: It merely requires governments to incur a cost for doing so.

The remainder of this chapter is divided into three sections. The first section addresses minority rights. The next section presents a proposal for federal legislation to make human rights treaties judicially enforceable. The final section addresses two objections to my proposal for legislating human rights. First, sovereigntists argue that U.S. courts should apply the Constitution to protect individual rights, rather than applying international law, precisely because it is "our Constitution." Second, civil libertarians worry that a system of weak review, which allows legislatures to override courts, will not provide adequate protection for individual rights. The final section of this chapter presents detailed responses to both objections.

MINORITY RIGHTS

Ely's argument for strong judicial review for minority rights is intuitively appealing: We need courts to protect discrete and insular minorities because they consistently lose in legislative processes dominated by democratic majorities. However, Ely's theory has not proved to be true in practice. During the Warren Court era, the Supreme Court consistently applied its power of judicial review to benefit discrete and insular minorities.[14] Since the 1970s, though, legislatures have generally provided more protection for minority rights than have courts.

In fact, since the 1970s, the Court has frequently used its power to invalidate or weaken laws and policies designed to benefit disadvantaged minority groups.[15] Consider, briefly, two examples that are analyzed in greater detail in Chapters 1 and 3. First, in *City of Boerne v. Flores*,[16] the Court invoked a federalism rationale to invalidate a federal statute, the Religious Freedom Restoration Act, that was specifically intended to benefit minority religious groups.[17] Similarly, in *Shelby County v. Holder*,[18] the Court invented a novel doctrine of "equal sovereignty" that significantly weakened enforcement of the 1965 Voting Rights Act, the landmark federal statute designed to enhance protection for minority voting rights.[19]

These are not isolated examples. Beginning with its 1978 decision in *Regents of Univ. of California v. Bakke*,[20] the Court has construed the Equal Protection Clause to create judge-made obstacles for legislators and policymakers who seek to enact or implement race-conscious programs to benefit discrete and insular minorities. The fact that the Equal Protection Clause has become, in the hands of a conservative Court, an obstacle to such programs is deeply ironic, because those programs are generally designed to promote one of the core goals of the post-Civil War Amendments: namely, benefiting historically disadvantaged racial minorities.[21]

This section analyzes the Supreme Court's race-based Equal Protection jurisprudence since *Bakke*, with a special focus on programs designed to promote racial integration in public schools. The key takeaway is clear. Professor Ely – and Justice Stone before him in *Carolene Products* – was wrong to assume that aggressive judicial review is necessary to protect discrete and insular minorities from legislative majorities. To the contrary, the record for the past several decades shows that legislatures and other policymakers have frequently tried to protect discrete and insular minorities,[22] but the Supreme Court has created judge-made obstacles that impede their efforts to do so. If courts would simply get out of the way and let other government actors do their jobs, the concrete benefits for historically disadvantaged minorities would likely be very substantial.

Affirmative Action: Theory and Doctrine

For the past several decades, Equal Protection doctrine and scholarship have been pulled in opposite directions by the tension between the "anticlassification" principle and the "antisubordination" principle. Proponents of the anticlassification principle (also called the "color-blind" principle) argue that the Equal Protection Clause forbids racial classifications, period. Proponents of the antisubordination principle (also called the "anti-caste" principle) counter that the Clause merely forbids racial classifications that have the purpose or effect of harming historically disadvantaged minority groups.[23] "The anticlassification school – associated overwhelmingly with constitutional conservatives – holds that affirmative action violates the Constitution because the programs treat students differently based on race."[24] In contrast, "the antisubordination school – identified predominantly with legal liberals – contends that affirmative action passes constitutional muster because the programs treat no one as racially inferior."[25]

The text of the Fourteenth Amendment is indeterminate; it can reasonably be construed in accordance with either the anticlassification view or the antisubordination view. Conservative scholars and judges who favor anticlassification make a superficially plausible argument that historical sources support their view.[26] However, that argument relies on a strategy of selective quotation, while ignoring key sources that point the other direction. Historians have shown that Congress adopted Section 1 of the Fourteenth Amendment in response to widespread racialized violence in the South after the Civil War,[27] and the emergence of so-called black codes, some of which were drafted in racially neutral terms, but which were clearly intended to discriminate against blacks.[28] The anticlassification construction of the Equal Protection Clause is difficult to square with that history, because neither racialized violence nor facially neutral laws violate the anticlassification principle. My point, here, is not that the antisubordination view is necessarily correct.

Rather, I contend that the Constitution's division of power between the legislative and judicial branches – and the associated constitutional norm of legislative primacy – requires courts to defer to legislatures, absent evidence of a clear constitutional violation. Given the indeterminacy of the Equal Protection Clause, racial discrimination claims that rely solely on the anticlassification principle do not satisfy that "clear violation" standard, absent evidence that the conduct at issue also violates the antisubordination principle (as in *Brown v. Board of Education*).

In *Regents of Univ. of California v. Bakke*,[29] the Supreme Court held in a 5–4 vote that the U.C. Davis Medical School acted unlawfully by adopting an admissions program that reserved 16 out of 100 places in its entering class for members of minority groups. Justice Stevens, writing for himself, Chief Justice Burger, and Justices Stewart and Rehnquist, rested that conclusion on Title VI of the Civil Rights Act, without reaching the Equal Protection claim.[30] Justices Brennan, White, Marshall, and Blackmun argued that "racial classifications designed to further remedial purposes" should be subject to intermediate scrutiny, not strict scrutiny,[31] and that the U.C. Davis program violated neither Title VI nor the Equal Protection Clause.[32] Justice Powell was the key swing vote. He argued (only for himself) that affirmative action programs, like the one adopted by U.C. Davis Medical School, should be subject to strict scrutiny under the Equal Protection Clause.[33] Moreover, he concluded that the U.C. Davis program violated the Fourteenth Amendment.[34] However, in a portion of his opinion joined by Justices Brennan, White, Marshall, and Blackmun, he wrote that "the State has a substantial interest [in creating a diverse student body] that legitimately may be served by a properly devised admissions program involving the competitive consideration of race and ethnic origin."[35] In short, racial quotas are unlawful, but institutions of higher education may lawfully consider race as a factor in their efforts to create a diverse student body.

Although Justice Powell wrote only for himself in *Bakke*, his opinion was very influential, setting the Court on a path toward its decision in *Adarand Constructors, Inc. v. Pena*,[36] where the Court held unequivocally that "all racial classifications, imposed by whatever federal, state, or local governmental actor, must be analyzed by a reviewing court under strict scrutiny."[37] *Adarand* arguably represented the triumph of anticlassification over antisubordination, insofar as it held that racial classifications designed to benefit historically disadvantaged minority groups are subject to the same "strict scrutiny" standard applied to classifications intended to harm those minority groups. However, Justice O'Connor, the author of the main opinion in *Adarand*, left a slight opening. She said: "Finally, we wish to dispel the notion that strict scrutiny is strict in theory, but fatal in fact. The unhappy persistence of both the practice and the lingering effects of racial discrimination against minority groups in this country is an unfortunate reality, and government is not disqualified from acting in response to it."[38]

During the next three decades after *Adarand*, the Supreme Court applied strict scrutiny in a series of cases involving affirmative action in higher education. In

Gratz v. Bollinger,[39] the Court invalidated the University of Michigan's undergraduate admissions program. However, in both *Grutter v. Bollinger*[40] and *Fisher v. University of Texas*,[41] the Court upheld the constitutionality of affirmative action programs in state universities. Finally, in 2023, the Court sounded the death knell of affirmative action in higher education in *Students for Fair Admissions v. Harvard*,[42] strongly suggesting that strict scrutiny is indeed "fatal in fact," at least in the context of higher education.

The remainder of this section addresses efforts by local public schools to promote racial integration. Before turning to that topic, though, it is worth citing relevant international human rights law. Article I, paragraph 1 of the Convention on Elimination of Racial Discrimination (CERD) – an international human rights treaty that the United States ratified in 1994 – defines the term "racial discrimination" to mean "any distinction, exclusion, restriction or preference based on race ... or national or ethnic origin *which has the purpose or effect* of nullifying or impairing the recognition, enjoyment or exercise, on an equal footing, of human rights and fundamental freedoms...."[43] Although the text does not explicitly endorse the antisubordination principle, the "purpose or effect" clause makes clear that the treaty rejects the anticlassification principle.

The treaty also includes a specific provision to address affirmative action. "Special measures taken for the sole purpose of securing adequate advancement of certain racial or ethnic groups or individuals requiring such protection as may be necessary to ensure such groups or individuals equal enjoyment or exercise of human rights and fundamental freedoms shall not be deemed racial discrimination."[44] In other words, affirmative action programs designed to benefit historically disadvantaged groups do not constitute "racial discrimination." However, the language quoted above is followed by a proviso: "provided, however, that such measures ... shall not be continued after the objectives for which they were taken have been achieved."[45] That proviso is similar to Justice O'Connor's admonition in *Grutter v. Bollinger*: "[R]ace-conscious admissions policies must be limited in time.... We see no reason to exempt race-conscious admissions programs from the requirement that all governmental use of race must have a logical endpoint."[46]

Thus, in affirmative action cases, if U.S. courts applied the CERD as a substitute for the Equal Protection Clause (weak review), the resulting jurisprudence would strengthen judicial protection for racial minorities, because affirmative action programs would be presumptively valid, assuming the government could demonstrate that "the objectives for which [the program was adopted] have [not yet] been achieved."[47] In other words, the switch from strong review to weak review would actually benefit historically disadvantaged minorities. Critics of affirmative action programs contend that such programs harm racial minorities. I concede that such programs may harm minorities in particular cases. However, under the Court's current doctrine, courts adopt an almost-irrebuttable presumption that affirmative action harms minorities in all cases. That presumption is not supported by evidence and is fundamentally at odds with the proper division of power between courts and legislatures. Under the standards articulated in the Race Convention, courts would need to consider fact-based arguments on a case-by-case basis, rather than adopting a conclusive presumption that race-based affirmative action is universally harmful.

It bears emphasis that the CERD is the "Supreme Law of Land" under the Supremacy Clause. The treaty does not take precedence over the Equal Protection Clause. However, the Supreme Court certainly can (and should) take account of the Convention in its construction of the Equal Protection Clause. The Court's failure to consider the relevance of the treaty impoverishes its Equal Protection jurisprudence.

Parents Involved v. Seattle School District

Parents Involved combined two cases in a single opinion: one from Seattle, Washington, and the other from Louisville, Kentucky.[48] In the Seattle case, a non-profit group challenged a plan adopted by the local school district that was designed to reduce racial segregation in public high schools. In the Louisville case, the parent of a school-age child challenged a school district plan designed to reduce racial segregation in elementary schools.[49]

As a policy matter, I am agnostic as to whether the benefits of plans like the Seattle and Louisville plans outweigh the costs. Efforts by local school boards to promote greater racial integration, raise a complex set of empirical, moral, and practical issues that vary substantially by locality. That is one reason why the Constitution, properly construed, vests substantial discretion in local governments to resolve these issues on a local level, free from unwarranted interference by the federal judiciary. The Court has warned, in a very different context, that the federal government must not "obliterate the distinction between what is national and what is local."[50] The Court would do well to heed that warning itself.

In *Parents Involved*, the Court divided sharply along ideological lines. Chief Justice Roberts, joined by Justices Scalia, Thomas, and Alito, applied strict scrutiny and concluded that both the Seattle and Louisville plans violated the Equal Protection Clause.[51] Justice Kennedy agreed that strict scrutiny was the proper standard, and he agreed with the result, but he declined to join large portions of the Chief's opinion that relied on a strict anticlassification rationale. He objected to the Chief's opinion insofar as it implied "an all-too-unyielding insistence that race cannot be a factor in instances when, in my view, it may be taken into account."[52] Justice Breyer wrote the principal dissent, joined by Justices Stevens, Souter, and Ginsburg. He argued that "the Constitution *permits* local communities to adopt desegregation plans even where it does not *require* them to do so."[53] He also argued that "the law requires application here of a standard of review that is not 'strict' in the traditional sense of that word."[54] Finally, he argued that both the Seattle and Louisville plans were constitutional under the version of strict scrutiny that the Court applied in both *Gratz* and *Grutter*.[55]

The plurality and the dissent disagreed about which prior Supreme Court decisions established the key precedents for evaluating the school district plans. The plurality thought that the Court's affirmative action cases – including *Adarand, Gratz v. Bollinger*, and *Grutter v. Bollinger* – were the most important precedents.[56] In contrast, the dissent argued that the Court's older school desegregation cases were the most relevant precedents. For example, Justice Breyer quoted the Court's 1971 decision in *Swann v. Charlotte-Mecklenburg Bd. of Ed.*[57] as follows:

> School authorities are traditionally charged with broad power to formulate and implement educational policy and might well conclude, for example, that in order to prepare students to live in a pluralistic society each school should have a prescribed ratio of Negro to white students reflecting the proportion for the district as a whole. To do this as an educational policy is within the broad discretionary powers of school authorities.[58]

Chief Justice Roberts dismissed this language as mere "dicta."[59] However, Justice Breyer argued persuasively that the quoted language was a core principle that guided the lower federal courts in dozens, if not hundreds, of school desegregation decisions for several decades after the Court's landmark decision in *Brown*.[60] The plurality attempted to distinguish the older school desegregation cases by claiming that "the distinction between segregation by state action and racial imbalance caused by other factors has been central to our jurisprudence in this area for generations."[61] Thus, according to the plurality, local governments may employ race-conscious measures to remedy *de jure* segregation, but they may not use racial classifications as part of a plan for remedying *de facto* segregation.

One problem with this argument is that the purported distinction between *de jure* and *de facto* segregation is largely illusory. In most metropolitan areas in the United States today, racial segregation in public schools is the direct result of racial segregation in housing. Moreover, "racial segregation in housing ... was a nationwide project of the federal government in the twentieth century."[62] Indeed, the research "demonstrates that racially explicit government policies to segregate our metropolitan areas are not vestiges, were neither subtle nor intangible, and were sufficiently controlling to construct the ... segregation that is now with us in neighborhoods and hence in schools."[63]

In sum, Chief Justice Roberts argued that race-conscious policies to desegregate public schools are permissible only as a remedy for purposeful government discrimination; such policies are not permissible to counteract the effects of voluntary, private choices that (accidentally) produced racially segregated housing patterns. However, the best available research demonstrates that racially segregated housing patterns – and the consequent racial segregation of public schools – are not simply the product of voluntary, private choice. They are the direct consequence of deliberate government policies that persisted for decades and that were intended to produce, and did produce, the racially segregated housing that we see in much of the United States today. Therefore, under the logic of the plurality opinion in *Parents Involved*, the Court should have held that the racial desegregation plans in Seattle and Louisville were constitutional because they were designed to remedy the ongoing effects of government policies that were purposefully designed to create racially segregated housing in the United States.

In the final analysis, Chief Justice Roberts' color-blind construction of the Equal Protection Clause led him to engage in fact-blind analysis. Rather than confronting the ugly history of racial discrimination in the United States, he pretended that he could make it disappear by waving the magic wand of a Supreme Court opinion. The Court is powerful, but it is not that powerful. The Court can shield its eyes from the facts, but it cannot make those facts disappear. Racial segregation in public schools today is the direct result of deliberate government policies designed to promote racial segregation in residential housing. If the Court wants to realize the promise of *Brown v. Board of Education*, it must begin by acknowledging the relevant facts.

Finally, it is important to note a critical distinction between cases involving affirmative action in higher education and cases, like *Parents Involved*, involving racial segregation in public schools. As I have emphasized throughout this book, the Constitution embodies a norm of legislative primacy. Judicial respect for that norm – manifested in judicial deference to legislative judgments – is essential to preserve the power of We the People to exercise control over our government. Cases involving affirmative action in higher education do not implicate the norm of legislative primacy because the key government decision-makers are university administrators, not legislators. In contrast, in the public-school desegregation cases, the key government decision-makers are democratically elected legislators – namely, the elected members of local school boards. Therefore, even if one assumes that strict scrutiny is the proper standard of review for higher education, there are compelling reasons for courts to adopt a more deferential approach in the public-school desegregation cases. In *Parents Involved*, the plurality violated separation-of-powers restrictions on its own judicial power by substituting its own, subjective policy judgment for the better-informed policy judgments of local, democratically elected school boards.

LEGISLATING HUMAN RIGHTS

The United States ratified the ICCPR in 1992. We ratified the CERD in 1994. As explained in Chapter 5, the United States adopted "NSE declarations" for both treaties; those declarations limit judicial enforcement of the treaties.[64] Under the Necessary and Proper Clause, as construed by the Supreme Court in *Missouri v. Holland*,[65] Congress has the power to make the treaties judicially enforceable, in whole or in part, by enacting a federal statute through the ordinary, bicameral legislative process.[66]

This chapter contends that Congress should make specific provisions of both treaties judicially enforceable. With such legislation in place, the vast majority of individual rights claims that are currently litigated as constitutional claims could be brought as human rights claims under one or both treaties. Courts would continue to apply constitutional law (strong review) in those few areas where there is no treaty-based substitute for a constitutional right. However, in areas where there is a treaty-based substitute, the federal courts should adopt a consistent practice of constitutional avoidance – applying treaty-based rights (weak review) whenever possible as a substitute for judicial enforcement of constitutional rights. The combination of human rights legislation and constitutional avoidance would establish a system of weak judicial review that would provide substantive protection for individual rights broadly similar to our current system. However, from the perspective of democratic theory, the new system of weak review would be far superior to our current system of strong review for the reasons explained at the beginning of this chapter.

This section first compares enumerated rights under the Constitution to analogous provisions in the ICCPR and CERD. It then compares unenumerated rights that are firmly established in US constitutional jurisprudence to explicit, textual provisions in the ICCPR. The analysis shows that the vast majority of both enumerated and unenumerated rights have explicit, textual support in human rights treaties. The final subsection analyzes some of the issues Congress would need to consider in drafting legislation to make human rights treaties judicially enforceable.

Enumerated Rights

The original Constitution – before adoption of the Bill of Rights – included a small number of individual rights provisions in Sections 9 and 10 of Article I. Section 9 bars the federal government from enacting a "Bill of Attainder or ex post facto law."[67] Section 10 imposes identical restrictions on state governments.[68] Article 15(1) of the ICCPR prohibits ex post facto laws.[69] Article 14(1) is similar to the Bill of Attainder clauses, which bar criminal punishment without a trial. Article 14(1) says: "In the determination of any criminal charge against him … everyone shall be entitled to a fair and public hearing by a competent, independent and impartial tribunal established by law."[70]

Section 9 of Article I bars suspension of "the privilege of the Writ of Habeas Corpus."[71] The writ of habeas corpus enables an individual deprived of his liberty to challenge the lawfulness of his detention. Article 9(4) of the ICCPR provides similar protection. It states: "Anyone who is deprived of his liberty … shall be entitled to take proceedings before a court, in order that that court may decide without delay on the lawfulness of his detention."[72] The Suspension Clause is rarely invoked.[73] However, when it applies, it provides stronger protection than the ICCPR because the Suspension Clause precludes Congress from "suspending" the writ.

Article I, Section 10 precludes state governments from enacting any "law impairing the obligation of contracts."[74] The Article IV Privileges and Immunities Clause generally limits "the ability of a state to discriminate against out-of-staters with regard to fundamental rights or important economic activities."[75] The ICCPR does not include analogues for those provisions. In sum, the ICCPR provides a complete, treaty-based substitute for the Bill of Attainder and Ex Post Facto clauses, but it does not provide a treaty-based substitute for the Suspension Clause, the Contracts Clause, or the Article IV Privileges and Immunities Clause. It bears emphasis that the Suspension and Contracts Clauses are rarely invoked in modern constitutional litigation.[76]

The Bill of Rights contains extensive protections for individual rights. Table 6.1 lists all of the Bill of Rights provisions that are binding on the states under current incorporation doctrine. It also lists the comparable provisions in the ICCPR, where applicable. Note that the ICCPR provides a treaty-based substitute for eighteen of the twenty-four discrete rights listed in Table 6.1.[77] For most of those eighteen rights, the treaty language is very similar to the language used in the Constitution.[78] Here, I want to highlight two specific provisions where the texts differ significantly, but the substantive protections are quite similar. First, the Eighth Amendment prohibits "excessive bail." Art. 9(3) of the ICCPR states: "It shall not be the general rule that persons awaiting trial shall be detained in custody, but release may be subject to guarantees to appear for trial."[79] Both provisions discourage, but do not prohibit, pretrial detention.

Second, the First Amendment guarantees a right "to petition the Government for a redress of grievances." There is no directly comparable provision in the ICCPR. However, the ICCPR protects "freedom of expression" (art. 19), the "right of peaceful assembly" (art. 21), "the right to freedom of association" (art. 22), and the right "to take part in the conduct of public affairs" (art. 25). Collectively, these treaty provisions offer substantive protection similar to the First Amendment right to petition the government. Therefore, I conclude that the ICCPR does provide a treaty-based substitute for the right to petition the government.

Table 6.1 identifies six specific rights for which there is no comparable provision in the ICCPR: the Establishment Clause, the right to bear arms, the exclusionary rule, the Takings Clause, the Sixth Amendment right to a jury trial,[80] and the Excessive Fines Clause. As noted earlier in this chapter, the Court's Takings doctrine should be preserved because there is no treaty-based substitute and the property right protected under the Takings Clause qualifies as a "fundamental right." Chapter 7 contends that the other five rights listed above do not qualify as "fundamental rights" under any reasonable definition of that term. Therefore, to restore the proper constitutional division of power between the states and the federal government, the Court should reverse its prior incorporation decisions for those rights and return power to the states.[81] Under this approach, federal courts would continue to enforce the Establishment Clause, the Second Amendment, the exclusionary

TABLE 6.1 *Incorporated Rights*

Amendment	Right	ICCPR Provision
First	Establishment Clause	n.a.
First	Free Exercise Clause	Art. 18, para. 1
First	Freedom of Speech	Art. 19, para. 2
First	Freedom of the Press	Art. 19, para. 2
First	Freedom of Assembly	Art. 21
First	Right to Petition Government	Arts. 19, 21, 22, 25
Second	Right to Bear Arms	n.a.
Fourth	Search and Seizure	Art. 17
Fourth	Warrant Requirement	Art. 9, para. 1
Fourth	Exclusionary Rule	n.a.
Fifth	Double Jeopardy	Art. 14, para. 7
Fifth	Self-Incrimination	Art. 14, para. 3(g)
Fifth	Takings Clause	n.a.
Sixth	Speedy Trial	Art. 14, para. 3(c)
Sixth	Public Trial	Art. 14, para. 1
Sixth	Impartial Tribunal	Art. 14, para. 1
Sixth	Jury Trial	n.a.
Sixth	Informed of Charges	Art. 14, para. 3(a)
Sixth	Confront Witnesses	Art. 14, para. 3(e)
Sixth	Compulsory Process	Art. 14, para. 3(e)
Sixth	Assistance of Counsel	Art. 14, para. 3(d)
Eighth	Excessive Bail	Art. 9, para. 3
Eighth	Excessive Fines	n.a.
Eighth	Cruel and Unusual Punishment	Art. 7

rule, the Sixth Amendment jury trial right, and the Excessive Fines Clause against the federal government, but those provisions would not bind state governments.

Three specific provisions in the Bill of Rights have not been incorporated: the Third Amendment rule on quartering soldiers, the Fifth Amendment Grand Jury Clause, and the Seventh Amendment right to a jury trial in civil cases. The Third Amendment is effectively a dead letter. The Grand Jury Clause is part of the standard operating procedure for federal courts in criminal cases.[82] Seventh Amendment doctrine is an incoherent mess.[83] The ICCPR does not provide a treaty-based substitute for any of those provisions. The proposed legislation would preserve the status quo for all three.

Finally, the Civil War Amendments added five more enumerated rights to the list of individual rights that are explicitly protected under the Constitution. Table 6.2 lists those rights and identifies analogous provisions in the treaties. The Thirteenth Amendment prohibits both slavery and involuntary servitude. Similarly, Article 8 of the ICCPR prohibits slavery, the slave trade, and servitude, as well as "forced or compulsory labour."[84] The Supreme Court has construed the Fourteenth Amendment Privileges or Immunities Clause to protect the right to interstate travel.[85] Similarly,

TABLE 6.2 *Rights Arising from Civil War Amendments*

Amendment	Right	Treaty Provisions
Thirteenth	Freedom from slavery	ICCPR, art. 8
Fourteenth	Privileges/immunities	ICCPR, art. 12
Fourteenth	Due process	Various
Fourteenth	Equal protection	ICCPR, art. 2, 26 CERD, art. 1–6
Fifteenth	Ban racial discrimination in voting	ICCPR, art. 2, 25 CERD, art. 5

Article 12 of the ICCPR states: "Everyone lawfully within the territory of a State shall, within that territory, have the right to liberty of movement and freedom to choose his residence."[86] The Fifteenth Amendment bars racial discrimination in voting. Similarly, Article 5 of CERD prohibits racial discrimination "in the enjoyment of … the right to participate in elections – to vote and to stand for election – on the basis of universal and equal suffrage."[87] Articles 2 and 25 of the ICCPR, read together, also prohibit racial discrimination in voting. (Article 2 prohibits discrimination with respect to "the rights recognized in the present Covenant." Article 25 protects the right "to vote and to be elected at genuine periodic elections which shall be by universal and equal suffrage.")

Under current Supreme Court doctrine, the Due Process Clause has both a substantive and a procedural component. Substantive due process is addressed in the next section on unenumerated rights. Insofar as procedural due process addresses criminal trials, most of the key treaty provisions are cited in Table 6.1; three specific procedural rights that relate to criminal defendants are included in Table 6.3.[88] For civil cases, the core components of due process are notice,[89] the opportunity to be heard,[90] and an impartial decision-maker.[91] The ICCPR includes similar, substantive protections. It says: "All persons shall be equal before the courts and tribunals. In the determination of … his rights and obligations in a suit at law, everyone shall be entitled to a fair and public hearing by a competent, independent and impartial tribunal established by law."[92] Under a system of weak judicial review, courts could provide essentially the same procedural due process protections by applying the ICCPR as they currently provide under the Due Process Clause.[93]

The Supreme Court has construed the Equal Protection Clause to restrict discrimination on the basis of race, national origin, gender, alienage (in some cases), and sexual orientation.[94] (I address sexual orientation in the section on unenumerated rights.) Similarly, Article 26 of the ICCPR prohibits discrimination "on any ground such as race, colour, sex, language, religion, political or other opinion, national or social origin, property, birth or other status."[95] Article 2 of the ICCPR makes clear that discrimination on any of these grounds is prohibited with respect to all of "the rights recognized in the present Covenant."[96] Under Article 5 of CERD, states are obligated "to guarantee the right of everyone, without distinction as to race, colour, or national or ethnic origin, to … the enjoyment of the following rights."[97] The treaty then enumerates a long list of civil, political, economic, and social rights as to which discrimination is prohibited. In sum, the ICCPR and CERD, taken together, provide substantially stronger protection against discrimination than is available under the Equal Protection Clause.[98] Some (but not all) of those treaty-based protections duplicate statutory protections available under federal civil rights statutes.

Assuming that Congress decides to enact legislation to make portions of the ICCPR and CERD judicially enforceable, it may choose to limit judicial enforcement of treaty-based antidiscrimination norms so that judicial protection does not extend beyond the protections currently available under federal statutory and constitutional law. In other words, Congress might wish to act on a retail basis, not a wholesale basis, to make specific antidiscrimination provisions judicially enforceable. Regardless, under a treaty-based approach, there is no doubt that judicial enforcement of human rights treaties could provide a complete substitute for all of the rights identified in Table 6.2.

Unenumerated Rights

Current Supreme Court doctrine protects a wide range of rights that are not specifically enumerated in the text of the Constitution. As I have argued elsewhere,[99] the distinction between enumerated and unenumerated rights is somewhat fuzzy at the margins because it depends partly on how broadly or narrowly one construes a particular textual right. Regardless, the distinction is widely recognized and is analytically useful. Table 6.3 lists the most important unenumerated rights that are firmly established in Supreme Court jurisprudence. For each entry, the table includes the name of the case where the right was first recognized, a label for the right at issue, and the treaty provision corresponding to that right. It bears emphasis that the ICCPR provides clear textual support for all of the rights listed in Table 6.3. Accordingly, one crucial benefit associated with switching from the current system of strong review to a treaty-based system of weak review is that the treaty-based system provides a stronger textual foundation for key rights that are currently enforced as unenumerated rights.

Article 17 of the ICCPR states: "No one shall be subjected to arbitrary or unlawful interference with his privacy, family, home or correspondence." Insofar as Article 17 addresses "home or correspondence," it overlaps to some extent with the Fourth Amendment. Insofar as it addresses privacy and family, it provides a textual foundation for many of the rights that are currently enforced under substantive due process doctrine. Article 23, which protects marriage and family, also provides a textual basis for many of the unenumerated rights listed in Table 6.3.

In light of the Supreme Court decision in *Dobbs v. Jackson Women's Health Organization*,[100] Table 6.3 does not list abortion as an unenumerated right. Whether the ICCPR protects a woman's right to choose is debatable. As I have argued in detail

TABLE 6.3 *Unenumerated Rights*

Case (Year)	Right	ICCPR
Meyer v. Nebraska (1923) Pierce v. Society (1925)	Parents' right to direct child's education	Article 18(4)
Skinner v. Oklahoma (1942)	Right to procreate	Article 23(2)
West Virginia State Bd. v. Barnette (1943)	Freedom of opinion	Article 19(1)
Griffin v. Illinois (1956)	Right to appeal a criminal conviction	Article 14(5)
NAACP v. Alabama (1958)	Freedom of association	Article 22(1)
Gideon v. Wainwright (1963)	Right to state-appointed counsel	Article 14(3)(d)
Griswold v. Connecticut (1965)	Right to use contraception	Article 17, 23(2)
Loving v. Virginia (1967)	Interracial marriage	Articles 2(1), 23(2)
In re Winship (1970)	Right to be presumed innocent	Article 14(2)
Moore v. East Cleveland (1977)	Right to protection for family	Article 23(1)
Lawrence v. Texas (2003)	Right to private, consensual sexual activity	Articles 17, 26
Obergefell v. Hodges (2015)	Same-sex marriage	Articles 2(1), 23(2)

elsewhere, there are plausible arguments on both sides.[101] For present purposes, suffice to say that the Constitution's commitment to democratic self-government and legislative primacy means that these issues are best decided by popular referenda or elected legislators, not by unelected judges.[102]

Article 14(2) of the ICCPR states: "Everyone charged with a criminal offence shall have the right to be presumed innocent until proved guilty according to law." The Supreme Court first recognized this right under the Due Process Clause in *In re Winship*.[103] Article 14(3(d) protects the right to counsel, including the right "to have legal assistance assigned to him … without payment by him in any such case if he does not have sufficient means to pay for it." The Supreme Court first recognized this right in *Gideon v. Wainwright*.[104] Article 14(5) says: "Everyone convicted of a crime shall have the right to his conviction and sentence being reviewed by a higher tribunal according to law." The Constitution does not explicitly guarantee criminal defendants a right of appeal, but *Griffin v. Illinois* established federal constitutional protection for the right to appeal state criminal convictions.[105]

Article 19(1) states: "Everyone shall have the right to hold opinions without interference." Although the Constitution does not include a comparable provision, the Court first recognized this right in *West Virginia State Bd. of Educ. v. Barnette*.[106] Article 22(1) states: "Everyone shall have the right to freedom of association with others." The Constitution does not explicitly protect freedom of association. Even so, the Court first recognized this right in *National Ass'n for Advancement of Colored People v. Alabama*.[107] Article 18(4) explicitly protects "the liberty of parents and, when applicable, legal guardians to ensure the religious and moral education of their children in conformity with their own convictions." Although the Constitution does not include any such provision, the Court first established this right in *Meyer v. Nebraska*[108] and *Pierce v. Society of Sisters.*[109]

Article 23(1) of the ICCPR states: "The family is the natural and fundamental group unit of society and is entitled to protection by society and the State." It provides a clear textual basis for the holding in *Moore v. City of East Cleveland,*[110] where the Court held that a local government could not prohibit a grandmother from living with her two grandsons. Article 23(2) protects the right "to found a family." It provides a textual foundation for *Skinner v. Oklahoma,*[111] where the Court invalidated a state law that authorized forced sterilization as a form of criminal punishment. Article 23(2), read in conjunction with Article 17 (which prohibits arbitrary interference with privacy and family), also supports the Supreme Court decision in *Griswold v. Connecticut.*[112] *Griswold* launched the modern substantive due process revolution by recognizing a constitutional right to privacy and invalidating a state law that prohibited married couples from using contraceptives. Articles 17 and 23(2) support the *Griswold* decision because a state law that prevents married couples from using contraceptives constitutes arbitrary interference with privacy and infringes the right of a married couple to postpone having children until they are ready.

Article 23(2) also states: "The right of men and women of marriageable age to marry … shall be recognized." Article 2(1) states: "Each State Party … undertakes to respect and to ensure to all individuals within its territory … the rights recognized in the present Covenant, without distinction of any kind, such as race, colour, sex … or other status." Read together, these two articles clearly protect the right of interracial marriage, which the Court first recognized in *Loving v. Virginia.*[113] The phrase "other status" in Article 2(1) is open to conflicting interpretations, but it has been construed to bar discrimination on the basis of sexual orientation.[114] Read in that way, the combination of Articles 2(1) and 23(2) also protect the right to gay marriage, which the Court first recognized in *Obergefell v. Hodges.*[115] Finally, the combination of the Article 17 right to privacy and the Article 2(1) antidiscrimination norm provides a firm textual basis for *Lawrence v. Texas,*[116] where the Court held that the state could not interfere with the right of two adult, gay men to engage in private, consensual sexual activity.

In sum, the Court's legitimacy is most vulnerable when it applies the Constitution to protect rights that are not specifically enumerated in the Constitution's text. The ICCPR provides clear textual support for all of the key unenumerated rights that are currently recognized under Supreme Court doctrine. Under the proposed system of weak review, courts would continue to protect all of those rights, but they could do so in a way that is less vulnerable to charges of illegitimate judicial lawmaking.

A Few Thoughts on Legislative Drafting

Federal legislation – enacted through the ordinary, bicameral legislative process – should reverse the effects of the NSE declarations by making a broad range of remedies available for violations of a specific list of treaty-based rights. With respect to the ICCPR, the legislation should specifically identify all of the treaty rights listed in Tables 6.1–6.3, as well as the treaty provisions that correspond to the Ex Post Facto and Bill of Attainder Clauses. Judicial remedies should be available for violations of all of those rights.

Available remedies should include: suits against state and local government officers under 42 U.S.C. § 1983, suits against federal officers under the Administrative Procedures Act (APA),[117] habeas corpus relief under federal habeas corpus statutes,[118] and declaratory relief under the Declaratory Judgment Act.[119] Additionally, the legislation should specify that defendants in civil and/or criminal actions initiated by federal, state, or local governments are entitled to raise treaty-based defenses. These remedies should be available in both state and federal courts, as applicable. Congress should consider whether to create a private cause of action for money damages for suits against federal officers alleging violations of treaty-based rights.[120] Finally, to avoid potential conflicts with civil rights statutes, the legislation should specify that it does not authorize any remedies in suits against private parties.[121]

Congress could also consider adding protections for treaty-based rights that are not covered under current Supreme Court doctrine. For example, in criminal cases, the ICCPR guarantees defendants "the free assistance of an interpreter if he cannot understand or speak the language used in court."[122] Several lower federal courts have recognized a constitutional right to an interpreter under the Due Process Clause,[123] but the Supreme Court has not explicitly decided this issue. This is just one example where the ICCPR provides more robust (or more explicit) rights protection than current Supreme Court doctrine. Congress may wish to proceed incrementally in providing judicial remedies for violations of such treaty-based rights.

Judicial enforcement of the Race Convention raises more complex questions. The treaty defines racial discrimination to include "any distinction, exclusion, restriction or preference based on race, colour … which has the *purpose or effect* of nullifying or impairing the recognition, enjoyment or exercise, on an equal footing, of human rights and fundamental freedoms."[124] Some civil rights statutes provide remedies for government actions that produce discriminatory effects, but the Equal Protection Clause, as interpreted by the Supreme Court, does not bar government action that causes discriminatory effects unless the law is facially discriminatory or the plaintiff can prove discriminatory purpose.[125] Congress should consider whether to endorse the international definition of race discrimination, thereby giving rise to judicial remedies for government conduct that produces discriminatory effects.

Article 5 of the Race Convention "guarantee[s] the right of everyone, without distinction as to race, colour, or national or ethnic origin, to equality before the law, notably in the enjoyment of the following rights." It then provides a long list of rights, including: "the right to equal treatment before the tribunals and all other organs administering justice"[126]; "the right to security of person"[127]; a set of political rights that goes beyond the simple right to vote[128]; a long list of "other civil rights"[129];

and a list of specific "economic, social and cultural rights."[130] If Congress adopted the treaty's definition of discrimination (including discriminatory effects) – and provided judicial remedies for violations of all of the specific rights covered in Article 5 – the statute would significantly enhance protection against racial discrimination. If Congress defined racial discrimination narrowly to cover only government actions that are facially discriminatory and/or motivated by a discriminatory purpose – and it selectively included some, but not all, of the rights specified in Article 5 – it could provide a treaty-based substitute for current Equal Protection doctrine related to race discrimination (outside the affirmative action context), without enhancing protection against racial discrimination.

The proposed statute should include language that encourages, but does not require, federal and state courts to practice constitutional avoidance in all cases where a litigant's constitutional claim or defense could be resolved by applying a treaty provision that is judicially enforceable under the statute. The classic statement of the canon of constitutional avoidance says: "The Court will not pass upon a constitutional question although properly presented by the record, if there is also present some other ground upon which the case may be disposed of."[131] The proposed statute would provide a treaty-based substitute for the vast majority of individual rights claims under the Constitution, thus facilitating the practice of constitutional avoidance. I have argued elsewhere that Congress has the power to mandate constitutional avoidance in such cases[132] but that argument is controversial. In this context, it makes sense for Congress to begin with a recommendation, rather than a statutory mandate. If the courts persistently ignore Congress's suggestion to practice constitutional avoidance, then Congress could consider more forceful measures in a subsequent amendment.

Implementation of this proposal will invariably raise cases where courts are required to address conflicts, or perceived conflicts, between treaty rules and constitutional rules. Both the ICCPR and CERD contain one, but only one, rule that obligates the United States to take action that is constitutionally prohibited under current doctrine: Both treaties require states to ban hate speech.[133] Hate speech is constitutionally protected under the First Amendment.[134] Accordingly, the United States adopted reservations for both treaties that exempt us from the treaty obligation to ban hate speech.[135] The legislation should make clear that U.S. courts must apply the treaties as modified by the reservations, understandings, and declarations (RUDs) that the United States adopted when it ratified the treaties, unless or until Congress acts to remove any RUDs. That approach will avoid any direct conflict between the treaties and the Constitution.

Other cases might arise where treaty-based rules differ from constitutional rules, but there is no direct conflict, in the sense that the treaty requires what the Constitution prohibits. Realistically, Congress cannot anticipate all such cases, so courts will need to address these types of conflicts on a case-by-case basis. Even so, the legislation should articulate four general principles for addressing such cases. First, courts should construe treaty provisions liberally (in favor of broad rights protection), absent contrary guidance from Congress. Second, courts should defer to Congress's legislative judgment when Congress has enacted legislation that explicitly addresses the issue presented. Third, courts are permitted to consult foreign and international sources for guidance in interpreting specific treaty provisions, but U.S. courts are not bound by foreign or international sources. Fourth, courts may construe treaty provisions in harmony with established constructions of similar constitutional provisions, unless there is explicit treaty language to the contrary (as there is, for example, in the case of affirmative action).

TWO PRINCIPAL OBJECTIONS

I have argued that Congress should establish a system of weak review for judicial enforcement of both minority rights and fundamental rights by enacting legislation that would make human rights treaties judicially enforceable and encourage courts to practice constitutional avoidance. If courts actually do practice constitutional avoidance, the legislation would help revitalize the constitutional norm of legislative primacy – and strengthen the power of We the People to exercise control over our government – by creating a system of judicial review for individual rights that would enable Congress to override judicial decisions. Moreover, the proposed statute would provide a more secure textual foundation for a range of rights that are not specifically enumerated in the Constitution's text.

This proposal is likely to provoke opposition from both liberals and conservatives. Conservatives may object that judicial application of international treaties as a substitute for constitutional rights is "un-American," and that it would infringe our national sovereignty by "offshoring" rights protection to international bodies. Liberals may object that the proposed system of weak judicial review will not provide sufficient protection for individual rights. The remainder of this chapter addresses these objections.

The Sovereigntist Objection

In his dissenting opinion in *Atkins v. Virginia*, Justice Scalia said: "We must never forget that it is a Constitution for the United States of America that we are expounding.... [W]here there is not first a settled consensus among our own people, the views of other nations, however enlightened the Justices of this Court may think them to be, cannot be imposed upon Americans through the Constitution."[136] Justice Scalia has a fair point. Imposing foreign values on Americans through constitutional construction is antidemocratic. However, that objection is not applicable to the proposal presented here. The United States has ratified both the ICCPR and the CERD. Both treaties are the supreme Law of the Land under the Supremacy Clause. If Congress enacts legislation to make the treaties judicially enforceable, the democratic pedigree of such legislation is unassailable. (Professor John Yoo has challenged the democratic pedigree of self-executing treaties on the grounds that self-executing treaties exclude the House of Representatives from federal lawmaking,[137] but his critique does not apply to bicameral legislation that provides for judicial enforcement of treaties.)

Professor John McGinnis has raised concerns about treaty-based delegations of authority to international institutions.[138] Again, those concerns are valid, but they do not apply to the legislative proposal presented in this chapter. The ICCPR does not delegate binding decision-making authority to any international institution.[139] Article 22 of the Race Convention does enable states to raise treaty-related disputes before the International Court of Justice. However, the United States adopted a reservation to Article 22, specifying that "the specific consent of the United States is required in each case" before a dispute may be submitted to the ICJ.[140] Nothing in the proposed legislation requires the United States to accept international dispute resolution procedures, nor would it require U.S. courts to defer to the views of international or foreign tribunals on treaty interpretation questions. The legislation simply authorizes state and federal courts to enforce specific provisions in treaties that the United States has ratified. U.S. courts would be free to consider the views of international and foreign tribunals on treaty interpretation questions,[141] but they would not be required to do so.

Others may object that judicial reliance on human rights treaties as a substitute for constitutional litigation is at odds with U.S. constitutional traditions. However, as Chapter 5 demonstrated, U.S. courts relied heavily on international treaties as a source of protection for both minority rights and fundamental rights throughout the nineteenth century.[142] Indeed, before the Civil War – and to a lesser extent in the late nineteenth century – the Supreme Court applied international law much more frequently than it applied constitutional law to resolve public law controversies.[143]

Granted, increased judicial reliance on human rights treaties as a substitute for constitutional litigation would be a sharp departure from more recent constitutional traditions. However, as explained in Chapter 5, the modern "allergy" to domestic judicial enforcement of human rights treaties is largely a legacy of the Bricker Amendment controversy in the early 1950s.[144] Supporters of the Bricker Amendment were motivated to a large extent by their desire to ensure that domestic courts would not apply international human rights treaties to invalidate Jim Crow laws in the South.[145] That is hardly a convincing rationale for opposition to judicial enforcement of human rights treaties today. Senator Bricker's antipathy to human rights treaties was also rooted in federalism concerns. However, as explained in Chapter 2, those concerns are baseless today because the United States federalized protection for human rights in the period between 1948 and 1976.[146] In fact, if Congress and the Supreme Court implemented the proposals set forth in this chapter and in Chapter 7,[147] they would partially reverse the process of federalization and return power to the states.

As explained in Chapter 5, the United States ratified three major human rights treaties in the 1990s. We adopted a set of RUDs for all three treaties.[148] The Senate Foreign Relations Committee justified the RUDs, in part, by saying that any changes in domestic law should "occur through the normal legislative process."[149] However, instead of changing U.S. law through a democratic, legislative process, the Supreme Court has changed U.S. law by engaging in judicial lawmaking – in particular, by recognizing a broad range of unenumerated rights,[150] and by establishing a system of judicial imperialism that is antithetical to core constitutional principles.[151] The proposed legislation would implement the stated expectations of the Foreign Relations Committee, and strengthen democratic control over the process of incorporating international human rights norms into domestic law, by empowering courts to apply human rights treaties in a manner that is consistent with the constitutional principle of legislative primacy.

Does Weak Review Mean Weak Rights?

One other objection to a system of weak review is that we need strong review to ensure strong protection for individual rights. The concern here is that, given the option of legislative override, Congress will act aggressively to weaken protection for individual rights. With Congress as presently constituted, that fear is exaggerated because congressional gridlock makes it difficult for Congress to enact any legislation. The proposals discussed in Chapters 3 and 4, if implemented, should help reduce gridlock by reducing polarization. If Congress evolves to become closer to John Adams' ideal – a representative assembly that is "in miniature an exact portrait of the people at large"[152] – the risk that Congress will abuse its power to undermine protection for individual rights is fairly small. However, if changes in the political system reduce gridlock without enhancing the quality of representation, there is a risk that a shift from strong review to weak review could weaken protection for individual rights.

Some comparative data may help reassure skeptics. As noted previously, Australia, Canada, New Zealand, and the United Kingdom all apply variants of weak review to protect individual rights.[153] Table 6.4 presents scores from the V-Dem liberal democracy index for those four countries and the United States, along with the change in scores between 2000 and 2021.[154] The liberal democracy index is arguably the single best quantitative measure of the degree to which a country provides strong legal protection for individual rights. (Higher scores indicate better rights protection.) As shown in Table 6.4, the United States – with its system of strong judicial review – experienced a sharper decline in protection for individual rights than any of the other listed countries. As of 2021, the United States scored lower than any of the other four countries, even though the U.S. is the only country with strong judicial review.[155] Based on this very limited data set, there seems to be an inverse correlation between strong judicial review and strong rights protection. Data from

TABLE 6.4 *Changes in Liberal Democracy Scores over Two Decades*

	Year = 2000	Year = 2021	Change
Australia	.854	.808	−.46
Canada	.758	.755	−.03
New Zealand	.841	.837	−.04
United Kingdom	.795	.782	−.13
United States	.808	.735	−.73

Freedom House presents a similar picture. As of 2022, the United States scored 83 out of 100 on the Freedom House "Freedom in the World" score.[156] The other four countries scored between 93 (the United Kingdom) and 99 (New Zealand). If one measures the decline from 2013 to 2022, the United States experienced the worst decline, dropping ten points, from 93 to 83. The United Kingdom had the second worst decline during that period, dropping from 97 to 93.

One distinctive feature of what Professor Gardbaum calls "the new Commonwealth model of constitutionalism" – which applies with some variations in Australia, Canada, New Zealand, and the United Kingdom – is "mandatory pre-enactment political rights review."[157] In plain language, this means that "both of the elective branches of government … engage in rights review of a proposed statute" before it becomes law to help ensure that the statute does not violate human rights.[158] Critics of weak judicial review may argue that weak review actually undermines protection for individual rights, but the data in Table 6.4 masks that problem because the comparatively higher scores in non-U.S. countries are attributable to the practice of pre-enactment political rights review, which strengthens protection for individual rights. There may be some truth to that argument, but there is no empirical evidence to support the claim that weak judicial review undermines protection for individual rights. Regardless, a federal statute requiring some form of pre-enactment political rights review in the United States could potentially help strengthen protection for individual rights. It seems unlikely that such a statute would make things worse.

In the final analysis, proponents of strong judicial review tend to assume that courts are better than legislatures at protecting individual rights. That may be true in specific cases, but it is difficult to defend that assumption as a general matter. This book has presented detailed analyses of Supreme Court decisions in *City of Boerne v. Flores*,[159] *Shelby County v. Holder*,[160] and *Parents Involved v. Seattle School District*.[161] In all three cases – and one could cite many others – legislatures tried to protect individual rights, and Supreme Court decisions weakened rights protection by invalidating laws enacted by democratically elected legislatures.

Given that both courts and legislatures sometimes act to weaken protection for individual rights, the relative costs and benefits of weak and strong review can be fairly summarized as follows. In a system of weak review, if Congress undermines rights protection by exercising its power of legislative override, We the People can vote the rascals out and replace them with legislators who respect our rights. In a system of strong review, if the Supreme Court weakens rights by invalidating rights-protective legislation, We the People have no remedy in the near term because the Justices have life tenure. Therefore, weak review is better than strong review because it preserves the power of We the People to act collectively through the democratic process to protect our rights.

7

Federalism

The Constitution divides power between the federal government and the states. That much is not controversial. As discussed in Chapter 2, and as illustrated in Table 1.2, for most of U.S. history the Supreme Court deferred to the political branches on federalism questions, letting them decide the proper division of power between Congress and the states. However, in the 1990s, the Fed Soc Court began applying strong judicial review to federalism questions, claiming for itself a central role in policing the Constitution's division of authority between Congress and the states.

This chapter contends that the Court's so-called federalism doctrines are misguided for several reasons. First, those doctrines have had very little practical effect in achieving their stated goal: to protect state autonomy from unwarranted federal interference. Second, under the banner of federalism, the Fed Soc Court has engaged in illegitimate judicial lawmaking by creating a set of judge-made rules that have no basis in the Constitution's text. Third, when the Court speaks of federalism, it conveniently ignores the fact that the Supreme Court, itself, is part of the federal government. If the Court truly wants to protect state autonomy from unwarranted federal interference – which is clearly a legitimate goal – the best way to do so is to exercise self-restraint by limiting the reach of judge-made law that interferes with state autonomy. In particular, the Court should repudiate incorporation doctrine – a judge-made doctrine that was largely invented by the Warren Court that has no basis in the text of the Fourteenth Amendment. As a practical matter, incorporation doctrine imposes much more severe restrictions on state autonomy than all of the federal statutes (viewed in the aggregate) that the Court has invalidated under various federalism doctrines.

This chapter is divided into two parts. The first part analyzes the relationship between Congress and the states. It presents a critique of the Court's federalism jurisprudence and makes the case for deferential judicial review of questions involving asserted violations of federalism limits on Congress's legislative powers. The second part analyzes the relationship between the Supreme Court and the states. It presents a critique of incorporation doctrine. As shown in Table 6.1, the

Court has decreed that twenty-four specific rights included in the Bill of Rights bind the states under incorporation doctrine. Eighteen of those twenty-four rights have analogues in the ICCPR. As explained in Chapter 6, the Court can achieve the critical rights-protecting function of incorporation doctrine by applying those treaty-based rights to the states under the Supremacy Clause, using a system of weak judicial review.

However, for most incorporated rights that do not have analogues in the ICCPR, the Court should return power to the states because those rights do not qualify as "fundamental" rights under any reasonable definition of that term.[1] The only exception involves property rights claims under the Takings Clause. Since the property rights protected by the Takings Clause do qualify as "fundamental" rights under the standard that the Court applied for several decades before the Warren Court era, the Takings Clause does bind the states under the Fourteenth Amendment.

FEDERALISM DOCTRINES

Beginning with its 1992 decision in *New York v. United States*,[2] the Fed Soc Court developed a set of doctrines that are ostensibly designed to protect state governments from congressional overreach, but that, in practice, have distorted the Constitution's division of power between Congress and the Supreme Court. The four most important federalism doctrines involve: (1) limits on Congress's power under the Commerce Clause; (2) limits on Congress's powers under the Civil War Amendments; (3) the state sovereign immunity doctrine, which is loosely based on the Eleventh Amendment; and (4) the anti-commandeering doctrine, which is loosely based on the Tenth Amendment.[3]

This part addresses each of those doctrines separately. Before doing so, three general points merit comment. First, these doctrines have had very little practical impact in advancing the ostensible goal of protecting state autonomy from congressional overreach. Second, in elaborating these doctrines, the Court has violated separation-of-powers limits on its own judicial power by creating a set of arbitrary, judge-made rules that inhibit Congress's ability to exercise the legislative powers that the Constitution explicitly grants to Congress. Third, scholars who defend the Court's federalism doctrines claim that – without these doctrines – there would be no meaningful limit on Congress's legislative powers.[4] That argument ignores the Constitution's division of power between the government and We the People. If Congress oversteps its authority, We the People can vote them out of office. The requirement that elected legislators must compete in periodic elections is the Constitution's primary structural safeguard against congressional overreach. In contrast, the Constitution does not include any similar safeguard against judicial overreach; when the Supreme Court oversteps its authority, we cannot vote them out of office. The Court's federalism doctrines deprive We the People of our constitutional right to exercise control over our government by transferring decision-making authority from elected legislators, who are accountable to the people, to unelected judges, who are not accountable to anyone.

The Commerce Power

Article I grants Congress the power "to regulate commerce with foreign nations, and among the several states."[5] The Commerce Clause is arguably the most consequential congressional power (with the possible exception of the Spending Clause). It provides the constitutional source of authority for a wide variety of federal legislation and regulations. When Congress enacted landmark civil rights legislation in the 1960s, the Supreme Court relied on the Commerce Clause to uphold the validity of that legislation.[6]

In *United States v. Lopez*,[7] the Supreme Court held for the first time in almost sixty years that Congress had exceeded its powers under the Commerce Clause. *Lopez* involved a constitutional challenge to the Gun-Free School Zones Act of 1990. In that statute, Congress made it a federal crime "for any individual knowingly to possess a firearm at a place that the individual knows, or has reasonable cause to believe, is a school zone."[8] The Court noted that its precedents "identified three broad categories of activity that Congress may regulate under its commerce power." The first category involves "the channels of interstate commerce." The second involves "the instrumentalities of interstate commerce, or persons or things in interstate commerce."[9] The Court quickly dismissed both categories as inapplicable to the Gun-Free School Zones Act.

Under the third category, Congress may use its Commerce Power to regulate *intrastate* activity that "substantially affects interstate commerce." The government argued that "possession of a firearm in a local school zone does indeed substantially affect interstate commerce."[10] The Court rejected that argument. It said: "Under the theories that the Government presents … it is difficult to perceive any limitation on federal power, even in areas such as criminal law enforcement or education where States historically have been sovereign."[11] The Court insisted that the Constitution requires "a distinction between what is truly national and what is truly local."[12] If the Court affirmed the validity of the Gun-Free School Zones Act, according to the majority, it would obliterate that distinction.

The majority opinion in *Lopez* emphasized the importance of the Constitution's vertical division of power between the states and the federal government. In fact, the decision had virtually no practical effect on that vertical division of power, but it had a huge impact on the horizontal division of power between the Supreme Court and Congress. Congress responded to *Lopez* by amending 18 U.S.C. § 922(q). The statute now says: "It shall be unlawful for any individual knowingly to possess a firearm *that has moved in … interstate or foreign commerce* at a place that the individual knows, or has reasonable cause to believe, is a school zone."[13] The addition of the italicized language shifts the constitutional analysis from *Lopez*'s third category to its second category: Congress is now regulating "things in interstate commerce."[14] Under that category, it is immaterial whether the regulated activity "substantially affects interstate commerce," provided that a prosecutor can prove that the particular gun that the defendant possessed "moved" in interstate commerce.[15] That fact should be trivially easy to prove in almost every case.

Thus, the Court's decision in *Lopez* did not actually protect state autonomy because it did not prevent Congress from regulating guns in school zones. As Justice O'Connor observed in her dissenting opinion in *Gonzalez v. Raich*, "*Lopez* stands for nothing more than a drafting guide."[16] Justice O'Connor believed that *Lopez* had real teeth. In her view, it was the Court's subsequent decision in *Gonzalez* that reduced *Lopez* to a mere "drafting guide." However, the congressional amendment to 18 U.S.C. § 922(q), passed one year after *Lopez*,[17] demonstrates that *Lopez* itself was a mere drafting guide. The amended statute was substantially equivalent to the original statute in terms of its impact on areas "where States historically have been sovereign."[18] Even so, the amended statute is constitutional because Congress added the phrase "that has moved in … interstate or foreign commerce."[19]

Although *Lopez* did not materially change the division of power between the states and the federal government, it did materially alter the horizontal division of power between Congress and the Supreme Court. A series of cases decided by the New Deal Court in the 1930s and 1940s established that claims challenging legislation under the Commerce Power are subject to deferential judicial review.[20] For example, the Court stated in *Wickard v. Filburn* that "effective restraints" on the Commerce Power "must proceed from political rather than from judicial processes."[21] Under that approach – which prevailed from 1937 until 1995 – Congress had the primary responsibility for determining the appropriate division of legislative authority between the federal government and the states. The Court could not second-guess Congress's judgment unless there was no rational basis for Congress to conclude that a particular intrastate activity – viewed in the aggregate on a national basis – might have a significant impact on interstate commerce.[22] The *Lopez* Court rejected that deferential standard of review and replaced it with a form of heightened scrutiny (strong judicial review). After *Lopez*, it is the Supreme Court, not Congress, who decides "what is truly national and what is truly local."[23]

The *Lopez* Court justified the transfer of authority from Congress to the judiciary by insisting that the constitutional norm of state autonomy requires some "limitation on federal power."[24] (Note that the reference to "federal power" actually means "federal legislative power." *Lopez* implicitly rejected any meaningful limit on federal judicial power.) However, the Court's analysis ignores the actual limitations on federal legislative power that are included in the Constitution's text. For a bill to become law, the bill's proponents must secure a majority vote in both the House of Representatives and the Senate, and the President must sign the law.[25] The *Lopez* majority tacitly assumed – contrary to empirical evidence[26] – that these are easy hurdles to overcome. The *Lopez* majority also ignored the fact that legislators must stand for reelection – every two years in the House[27] and every six years in the Senate.[28] The requirement to secure a majority vote in both Houses, and the requirement for legislators to secure support from voters, are significant constraints on federal legislative power, which are rooted in clear, unambiguous constitutional text.[29] The *Lopez* majority – not satisfied with textual limits on federal legislative power – chose to create its own limits by engaging in illegitimate judicial lawmaking, giving us a new constitutional standard that lacks textual support in the Constitution, is deeply ambiguous, and is easily manipulable by judges in subsequent cases. In sum, although Chapter 1 argued that the Court's 1997 decision in *City of Boerne v. Flores* laid the foundation for modern judicial imperialism, one could argue that *Lopez* (decided two years before *Boerne*) was actually the first case in which the Court embraced judicial imperialism.

The previous paragraph noted that the *Lopez* standard is easily manipulable. The Court's subsequent decisions in *Gonzalez v. Raich*[30] and *Sebelius*[31] illustrate this point. The Court's decisions in *Lopez* and *United States v. Morrison*[32] established an analytic framework that relies heavily on distinguishing between "economic activity" and "noneconomic activity." Accordingly, in *Morrison*, the Court held that a provision of the Violence Against Women Act (VAWA) that enabled rape victims to sue their rapists in federal court exceeded Congress's power under the Commerce Clause because "gender-motivated crimes of violence are not, in any sense of the phrase, economic activity."[33] However, *Lopez* and *Morrison* left a key issue unresolved: In evaluating whether the regulated activity is "economic" or "noneconomic," should the Court adopt the perspective of the regulated party or should it adopt the perspective of the legislators who enacted the law?

Raich and *Sebelius* adopted diametrically opposite approaches to that question. In *Raich*, the question was whether Congress may, under the Commerce Clause, "prohibit the local cultivation and use of marijuana" for medicinal purposes.[34] Diane Monson argued that her activity was "noneconomic" because she "cultivate[d] her own marijuana"[35] for personal consumption, as permitted by California law. However, the Court concluded that the federal law was valid because the Controlled Substances Act "was a lengthy and detailed statute creating a comprehensive framework for regulating the production, distribution, and possession of … controlled substances."[36] In short, the Court adopted the perspective of the legislators – who were clearly regulating economic activity – rather than the perspective of Diane Monson, who was not personally buying or selling marijuana.

In *Sebelius*, petitioners challenged the validity of the "individual mandate" provision in the Affordable Care Act (ACA), which required "most Americans to maintain 'minimum essential' health insurance coverage."[37] Viewed from the perspective of the legislators who enacted the ACA, the statute regulated the national market for buying and selling health insurance, which is clearly economic activity. However, in contrast to *Raich*, the majority in *Sebelius* adopted the perspective of an individual who, absent government regulation, would choose not to buy health insurance. The Court concluded that the individual mandate provision exceeded the scope of Congress's Commerce Power because Congress had attempted "to rely on that power to compel individuals not engaged in commerce to purchase an unwanted product."[38] In sum, under the line of cases from *Lopez* to *Sebelius*, Congress has broad power to regulate economic activity. It has very limited power to regulate noneconomic activity. However, the classification of regulated activity as "economic" or "noneconomic" is almost entirely arbitrary, because it depends primarily upon how the Supreme Court majority chooses to describe the relevant facts.[39]

In the final analysis, the Court's Commerce Clause doctrine is antithetical to the Constitution's division of power between the government and We the People. Under the prior doctrine (pre-*Lopez*), the Court recognized that constitutional limits on the Commerce Power "must proceed from political rather than from judicial processes."[40] That approach left decision-making authority in elected legislators, who are accountable to the People. The *Lopez* doctrine concentrates decision-making authority in unelected judges, who are not accountable to anyone. Under the doctrine that prevailed from the 1930s to the 1990s, We the People could exercise meaningful control over Congress through the electoral process. Modern doctrine deprives citizens of any practical mechanism to exercise control over Supreme Court Justices, who are now the ultimate decision-makers. The Court rules by engaging in arbitrary line-drawing ("economic" vs. "noneconomic"), depriving We the People of our constitutional right to exercise control over our government.

The Civil War Amendments

Section 5 of the Fourteenth Amendment grants Congress the "power to enforce, by appropriate legislation, the provisions of this article."[41] Section 2 of the Thirteenth Amendment and Section 2 of the Fifteenth Amendment include almost identical language.[42] By granting Congress the "power to enforce," the text of all three amendments makes clear that the Amendments' authors regarded "Congress as the institution primarily responsible for interpreting and implementing the post-Civil War amendments."[43] As one Republican Senator explained shortly after adoption of the Fifteenth Amendment: "[T]he remedy for the violation of the fourteenth and fifteenth amendments was expressly not left to the courts. The remedy was legislative."[44] Even so, as described in Chapters 1 and 3, the Supreme Court elevated judicial power over congressional power by adopting a narrow view of congressional power under the Fourteenth Amendment in *City of Boerne v. Flores*[45] and by adopting a narrow view of congressional power under the Fifteenth Amendment in *Shelby County v. Holder*.[46] The Court justified both decisions by invoking federalism principles, claiming that it was protecting state autonomy from unwarranted federal interference.

Both *Boerne* and *Shelby County* share two features in common with *Lopez*. First, in all three cases, the Court violated separation-of-powers limits on its own judicial power by claiming power for itself that – under a correct construction of the Constitution – is properly allocated to Congress. In all three cases, Congress was exercising an enumerated power that the Constitution explicitly grants to Congress: the Commerce Power in *Lopez*, Section 5 of the Fourteenth Amendment in *Boerne*, and Section 2 of the Fifteenth Amendment in *Shelby County*. In all three cases, leading Supreme Court precedents supported a deferential approach to judicial review.[47] In all three cases, the Court rejected deferential judicial review and chose, instead, to apply heightened scrutiny. In sum, the Court engaged in judicial lawmaking in all three cases by creating new limits on Congress's enumerated powers that are not explicitly mentioned anywhere in the Constitution's text.[48]

Second, in both *Boerne* and *Shelby County*, as in *Lopez*, the Court ignored the Constitution's division of power between the government and We the People. In all three cases, the congressional legislation at issue – the Voting Rights Act in *Shelby County*,[49] the Gun-Free School Zones Act in *Lopez*,[50] and the Religious Freedom Restoration Act (RFRA) in *Boerne*[51] – enjoyed strong, bipartisan support in both Houses of Congress. In all three cases, litigants who could not mobilize political majorities to amend or repeal the relevant laws initiated constitutional litigation in an attempt to overcome the will of the majority. Of course, if any of the statutes violated clear, unambiguous constitutional rules that were explicitly stated in the Constitution's text, the Court would have a constitutional duty to invalidate those statutes.[52] However, none of the three statutes violated any explicit constitutional rules. In all three cases, the Court invoked vague principles that lacked textual support in the Constitution to invalidate laws enacted pursuant to specifically enumerated congressional powers. The Constitution empowers We the People, acting through our elected representatives, to amend or repeal federal laws that we dislike. In *Boerne*, *Shelby County*, and *Lopez*, the Court circumvented that process and robbed We the People of our power to exercise control over the government by invalidating laws that enjoyed broad, popular support.[53]

There is one important respect in which *Shelby County* differs from both *Boerne* and *Lopez*. Recall that Congress effectively reversed the specific outcome in *Lopez* by amending 18 U.S.C. § 922(q) to produce a statute that achieved essentially the same substantive result as the prior version of the Gun-Free School Zones Act, but that withstood constitutional challenges. Similarly, Congress partially reversed the specific outcome in *Boerne* by enacting the Religious Land Use and Institutionalized Persons Act of 2000 (RLUIPA).[54] RLUIPA authorized a set of religious freedom claims against state and local officers that was substantially similar to the set of claims authorized by RFRA.[55] Moreover, the Supreme Court upheld the constitutional validity of one portion of RLUIPA,[56] and federal appellate courts have upheld the constitutional validity of RLUIPA against other constitutional challenges.[57] Thus, as with *Lopez*, the Court's decision in *Boerne* failed to accomplish the ostensible goal of protecting state autonomy from congressional interference because Congress responded to *Boerne* by replacing RFRA with RLUIPA.

In contrast to both *Boerne* and *Lopez, Shelby County* has had a significant practical effect in protecting state autonomy from federal "interference." However, that fact is hardly cause for celebration. As noted in Chapter 3, the Court's decision in *Shelby County* increased the racial turnout gap "in parts of the country that were previously covered under the preclearance regime."[58] Moreover, *Shelby County* empowered numerous state governments to enact laws that make it more difficult for eligible voters to vote.[59] Thus, although *Shelby County* might fairly be described as a "win" for state autonomy, it was clearly a loss for the power of We the People to exercise control over our (state) governments.

Representative Terri Sewell (D-AL) introduced the John R. Lewis Voting Rights Advancement Act in August 2021. Among other things, the Act would have reversed the result in *Shelby County* by establishing "new criteria for determining which states and political subdivisions must obtain preclearance" under the Voting Rights Act.[60] The bill passed the House in August 2021, but the Senate failed to muster the three-fifths majority needed to overcome a filibuster.[61] Public opinion polling data from 2015, two years after the Court's decision in *Shelby County*, showed that most Americans believed that the Voting Rights Act was "necessary today to make sure that blacks and other racial minorities were allowed to vote."[62] Thus, even though the Court's decision in *Shelby County* could plausibly be described as an example of weak judicial review – inasmuch as it left the door open for Congress to enact legislation to restore the preclearance regime – filibuster rules enabled Senate Republicans to kill voting rights legislation that probably enjoyed majority support among U.S. citizens.

The Eleventh Amendment and State Sovereign Immunity

The Eleventh Amendment states: "The judicial power of the United States shall not be construed to extend to any suit in law or equity, commenced or prosecuted against one of the United States by Citizens of another State, or by Citizens or Subjects of any Foreign State."[63] By its terms, the Eleventh Amendment limits the power (jurisdiction) of federal courts, but it does not limit the power of Congress. However, the Court held explicitly in *Seminole Tribe of Florida v. Florida*, that the Eleventh Amendment – or, more precisely, the principle of state sovereign immunity – does limit Congress's power.[64] In *Alden v. Maine*, decided three years after *Seminole Tribe*, Justice Kennedy explained that "the sovereign immunity of the States neither derives from, nor is limited by, the terms of the Eleventh Amendment."[65] He continued: "[T]he States' immunity from suit is a fundamental aspect of the sovereignty which the States enjoyed before the ratification of the Constitution, and which they retain today."[66] Notably, the Court decided *Seminole Tribe* in 1996, one year after

Lopez and one year before *Boerne*. That trio of cases – *Lopez, Seminole Tribe*, and *Boerne* – launched the Fed Soc revolution.[67]

The preceding quotation from Justice Kennedy creates the impression that the doctrine of state sovereign immunity provides robust protection for state autonomy. However, that appearance is deceptive. In the words of Professor John Jeffries, "the Eleventh Amendment almost never matters,"[68] because existing doctrine offers numerous work-arounds that allow plaintiffs to sue both states and state officers. First, although the doctrine of sovereign immunity restricts suits by private plaintiffs, it does not bar suits by the federal government to enforce federal law against the states.[69] Second, although sovereign immunity protects state governments, it does not protect local governments from unwanted lawsuits.[70]

Third, under the doctrine of *Ex parte Young*,[71] private plaintiffs may sue state officers for prospective relief to enjoin an officer's threatened or ongoing violation of federal law. Justice Souter has explained that the *Young* doctrine is "indispensable to the establishment of constitutional government and the rule of law."[72] Although the *Young* doctrine is often described as a "legal fiction," given the crucial importance of *Ex parte Young* as a mechanism to help ensure state compliance with federal law, and given the limited practical effect of the Eleventh Amendment, it might be more accurate to say that the Eleventh Amendment is a fiction, but *Ex parte Young* is not. Regardless, the *Young* doctrine does not authorize suits for money damages. The critical question in such cases is whether the plaintiff seeks prospective (forward-looking) relief, which is allowed, or retrospective (backward-looking) relief, which is not allowed.[73]

Although *Ex parte Young* does not authorize suits for money damages, private plaintiffs may sue state officers for money damages under 42 U.S.C. § 1983. As a formal matter, a "suit against a state officer in his or her official capacity ... is barred by the Eleventh Amendment," whereas a "suit against a state officer in his or her personal capacity may go forward under Section 1983."[74] The Court insisted in *Hafer v. Melo* that "the distinction between official capacity suits and personal-capacity suits is more than a mere pleading device."[75] In practice, though, it is a mere pleading device. An empirical survey of Section 1983 suits against state officers showed that courts almost never dismiss a complaint that is properly framed as a "personal capacity suit" on the grounds that it is actually a suit against the officer in his/her official capacity.[76]

In theory, sovereign immunity doctrine is designed to protect state treasuries. "[A] suit by private parties seeking to impose a liability which must be paid from public funds in the state treasury is barred by the Eleventh Amendment."[77] However, the idea that the Eleventh Amendment protects state treasuries from suits by private parties is mostly a fiction. In the vast majority of suits for money damages against state officers in their individual capacities, the state "will bear the cost of defending the action and satisfying any adverse judgment" because the state has indemnification agreements with its employees.[78] Therefore, although the Eleventh Amendment, in theory, protects states from "liability which must be paid from public funds in the state treasury,"[79] state and local governments often dispense public funds pursuant to indemnification agreements with government employees. (As a practical matter, the doctrine of official immunity, which is a common law doctrine, has a very significant effect in protecting state treasuries because it limits the liability of state and local government officers who are sued in their individual capacities under Section 1983. If the individual officers are not liable, then there is no judgment to be paid under an indemnification agreement.)

"If a State waives its immunity and consents to suit in federal court, the Eleventh Amendment does not bar the action."[80] Moreover, even though Congress may not use its Commerce Power to abrogate state sovereign immunity,[81] Congress does have the power to abrogate state sovereign immunity when it legislates under Section 5 of the Fourteenth Amendment.[82] Since its decisions in *Seminole Tribe* and *Alden v. Maine*, the Court has decided several cases upholding the validity of federal statutes that abrogated state sovereign immunity on the grounds that those provisions constituted valid exercises of Congress's Section 5 power.[83]

In the aggregate, the varied options for circumventing state sovereign immunity – suits by the federal government, suits against local governments, suits under *Ex parte Young* and Section 1983, and rules involving abrogation and waiver – mean that the doctrine of state sovereign immunity has more bark than bite. Like the limits on Congress's Commerce Power (*Lopez*), and the limits on Congress's power under Section 5 of the Fourteenth Amendment (*Boerne*), the doctrine of state sovereign immunity has very little practical impact in terms of protecting state autonomy from unwanted federal interference.

However – like the doctrines associated with *Lopez* and *Boerne* – the doctrine of state sovereign immunity distorts the Constitution's horizontal division of power between the Supreme Court and Congress. The Court's decisions regarding Congress's power to abrogate state sovereign immunity illustrate this point. The basic pattern, as explained in the following paragraphs, is that Congress may abrogate state immunity when it seeks to enforce rights created by judicial lawmaking, but not when it seeks to enforce rights created by federal statutes. In short, the Court's decisions on abrogation of sovereign immunity privilege lawmaking by unelected judges over democratic lawmaking by the people's elected representatives.

In *Florida Prepaid*,[84] *Kimel*,[85] and *Garrett*,[86] the Supreme Court held that federal statutes that purported to abrogate state sovereign immunity violated the Eleventh Amendment. In all three cases, Congress had created remedial schemes to enforce rights created by federal statutes. Those federal statutes reflected a congressional judgment that the rights at issue – patent rights (*Florida Prepaid*), protection against age discrimination (*Kimel*), and protection for people with disabilities (*Garrett*) – were sufficiently important that they merited federal protection, even though the rights at issue do not receive heightened protection under the Court's constitutional jurisprudence. In contrast, in both *Hibbs*[87] and *Tennessee v. Lane*,[88] the Court held that federal statutes abrogating state sovereign immunity were constitutionally valid and did not violate the Eleventh Amendment. In both cases, Congress had enacted statutes to enforce rights that receive heightened protection under the Court's constitutional jurisprudence. *Hibbs* involved gender discrimination, which is subject to heightened scrutiny under the Equal Protection Clause. *Lane* involved the right of access to courts, which receives heightened protection under the Due Process Clause.

The Court's decisions manifest an implicit judgment that constitutional rights are more important than statutory rights. Congress may abrogate state immunity to enforce constitutional rights (as in *Hibbs* and *Lane*), but it may not abrogate state immunity to enforce statutory rights (as in *Florida Prepaid*, *Kimel*, and *Garrett*). The idea that constitutional rights are more important than statutory rights is intuitively appealing, but it is deeply misleading.

To appreciate this point, compare the three cases that involve discrimination. *Hibbs* involved gender discrimination; *Kimel* involved age discrimination; and *Garrett* involved disability discrimination. The Equal Protection Clause says that no state may "deny to any person within its jurisdiction the equal protection of the laws." On its face, the text bars all types of discrimination. Nothing in the ratification materials suggests that gender discrimination warrants special treatment under the Equal Protection Clause, compared to discrimination based on age or disability. Current Equal Protection doctrine – which holds that gender discrimination triggers heightened scrutiny, but discrimination based on age and disability receive only rational basis review – is entirely the product of judicial lawmaking. In other words, current Equal Protection doctrine manifests a substantive policy judgment that victims of gender discrimination are more deserving of judicial protection than victims of discrimination based on age or disability.

One may or may not agree with that judgment, but the Constitution clearly empowers Congress, not the Supreme Court, to make that substantive policy judgment. The legislative power vested in Congress under Section 5 of the Fourteenth Amendment necessarily includes the power to make substantive policy judgments about the relative importance of gender versus age versus disability discrimination. The judicial power vested in the Supreme Court under Article III includes the power to enforce the rules codified in federal statutes, not to second-guess congressional judgments about the relative importance of different types of discrimination. The text of the Fourteenth Amendment reinforces the Constitution's basic division of power between the legislative and judicial branches. Section 5 says: "The Congress shall have power to enforce … the provisions of this article." Ten years after adoption of the Fourteenth Amendment, the Supreme Court said: "It is the power of Congress which has been enlarged" by the Civil War Amendments, not the power of the judiciary.[89]

Assuming that the Fourteenth Amendment empowers Congress to abrogate state sovereign immunity, it is preposterous to claim that Congress may do so only when it seeks to enforce rights that the Court thinks are important, but not when it seeks to enforce rights that Congress has decided are important. Since the Equal Protection Clause does not distinguish between gender discrimination, age discrimination, and disability discrimination, and since Section 5 empowers Congress, not the courts, to enforce that Clause, it necessarily follows that Congress has the power to decide whether to provide similar remedies for all three types of discrimination. The Court's decisions regarding Congress's power to abrogate sovereign immunity invert the proper constitutional relationship between Congress and the Supreme Court by privileging lawmaking by unelected judges over democratic lawmaking by the people's elected representatives.

The Anti-commandeering Doctrine and the Tenth Amendment

The Tenth Amendment states: "The powers not delegated to the United States by the Constitution, nor prohibited by it to the States, are reserved to the States respectively, or to the people." The Supreme Court has said that the Tenth Amendment is "essentially a tautology."[90] Even so, in *New York v. United States* – decided three years before *Lopez* – the Court established the principle, based loosely on the Tenth Amendment, that "Congress may not simply commandeer the legislative processes of the States by directly compelling them to enact and enforce a federal regulatory program."[91] In *Printz v. United States*,[92] the Court extended the anti-commandeering principle to state and local executive officials, holding that Congress may not "command the States' officers, or those of their political subdivisions, to administer or enforce a federal regulatory program."[93] Later, in *Sebelius*, the Court applied a variant of the anti-commandeering principle to Spending Clause legislation, invalidating a portion of the Affordable Care Act (ACA) that expanded the federal Medicaid program because Congress had "crossed the line distinguishing encouragement from coercion."[94]

Like the other federalism doctrines discussed earlier in this chapter, the anti-commandeering doctrine offers limited practical protection for state autonomy, because Congress has several other options it can utilize to impose its will on state governments. For example, Congress may use its Spending Power to induce states to enact laws or regulations that conform to federal requirements, provided that inducement does not cross the (rather fuzzy) line that separates encouragement from coercion.[95] Congress may displace state regulatory authority completely in a particular area by enacting a federal law that "occupies the field," and that therefore preempts all state laws within that field.[96] Congress may also adopt a strategy of "conditional preemption" by threatening to preempt state law if a state refuses to enact legislation conforming to federal recommendations. For example, in the Electronic Signatures in Global and National Commerce Act,[97] Congress threatened to preempt state laws governing the use of electronic signatures in contracts but allowed states to avoid preemption by enacting laws consistent with the Uniform Electronic Transactions Act

(UETA), a model law promulgated by the National Conference of Commissioners on Uniform State Laws.[98] In sum, just as sovereign immunity doctrine preserves several options for plaintiffs to sue states and state officers without running afoul of the Eleventh Amendment, anti-commandeering doctrine preserves several options for Congress to regulate states without running afoul of the Tenth Amendment.

Despite the varied legislative options available to Congress, the anti-commandeering doctrine does afford meaningful protection for state autonomy in some cases. For example, the Court's decision in *Sebelius* addressed the "Medicaid expansion" provisions in the ACA[99] (not to be confused with the "individual mandate" provision, which the Court analyzed under the Commerce Clause). The majority distinguished between the "old" Medicaid program and the "new" Medicaid expansion.[100] In the ACA, Congress presented the states with a stark choice: If you refuse to accept the conditions associated with the new Medicaid expansion program, you will no longer be eligible to receive the funding you previously received under the old Medicaid program.[101] The Court concluded that this choice was like "a gun to the head."[102] It was no choice at all because no state could afford to lose the funding associated with the old Medicaid program. The Medicaid expansion provisions in the ACA were unconstitutional because Congress "crossed the line distinguishing encouragement from coercion"[103] by making continued receipt of the old Medicaid funds contingent on acceptance of the new conditions. The Court protected state autonomy by invalidating that linkage, giving states a genuine choice about participating in the Medicaid expansion program.[104]

This chapter has shown that judge-made constitutional doctrines associated with *Lopez*, *Boerne*, and *Seminole Tribe* violate separation-of-powers principles by transferring decision-making authority from elected legislators to unelected judges (and therefore, indirectly, violate the constitutional right of We the People to exercise control over our government). A similar argument applies to the anti-commandeering doctrine, but the anti-commandeering doctrine is more defensible in this respect. Anti-commandeering doctrine, like the other federalism doctrines discussed previously, can be criticized on the ground that it involves an exercise in judicial lawmaking that has little or no basis in the Constitution's text. However, this book contends that such judicial lawmaking can be justified if it is necessary to correct a malfunction in the political process.

That type of political process rationale provides a plausible justification for the anti-commandeering doctrine. In Justice O'Connor's words, "where the Federal Government compels States to regulate, the accountability of both state and federal officials is diminished."[105] If state legislators, acting without federal compulsion, enact a law that reflects certain policy choices, the citizens of that state know who is responsible. "But where the Federal Government directs the States to regulate, it may be state officials who will bear the brunt of public disapproval, while the federal officials who devised the regulatory program may remain insulated from the electoral ramifications of their decision. Accountability is thus diminished when, due to federal coercion, elected state officials cannot regulate in accordance with the views of the local electorate…."[106] Notably, the dissenters in *New York v. U.S.* did not challenge the principle that Congress may not compel state legislators to enact laws conforming to a federal mandate. However, Justice White's dissenting opinion maintained that no such coercion had occurred in that case.[107] In his words: "Unlike legislation that directs action from the Federal Government to the states, the 1980 and 1985 Acts reflected hard-fought agreements among States as refereed by Congress."[108]

Although the political process rationale provides a plausible justification for the rule that Congress may not commandeer state *legislatures*, the extension of that rule to state executive officers in *Printz v. United States* is more problematic.[109] *Printz* involved a provision in the Brady Handgun Violence Prevention Act that required state and local law enforcement officers to conduct background checks on prospective handgun purchasers. The background-check requirement imposed at most a modest burden on state and local law enforcement officers,[110] but the Court concluded that it was unconstitutional because "the Federal Government may not compel the States to implement … federal regulatory programs."[111]

Here, it is instructive to compare the Brady Act with judge-made rules that compel state and local law enforcement officers to implement federal mandates. For example, in *Miranda v. Arizona*, the Court created a new, judge-made rule that requires arresting officers to issue so-called *Miranda* warnings to detainees.[112] Similarly, in *Aguilar v. Texas*, the Court created a new, judge-made rule that imposed the Fourth Amendment warrant requirement on state and local law enforcement officers.[113] (For roughly 175 years, from the Founding until 1964, it was settled law that the Fourth Amendment warrant requirement did not bind state officers. The decision in *Aguilar* to make that requirement binding on state officers was pure judicial fiat.[114]) The Court has never explained why it is permissible for the Supreme Court to "commandeer" state and local law enforcement officers by engaging in undemocratic judicial lawmaking, but it is not permissible for Congress to do essentially the same thing by engaging in legitimate, democratic lawmaking. The previous section noted that the Court's doctrine on abrogation of state sovereign immunity inverts the proper relationship between Congress and the Supreme Court by privileging judicial lawmaking over democratic lawmaking. A similar argument applies here. There is no plausible justification for the Court's unstated assumption that judicial commandeering of state executive officers is permissible, but congressional commandeering of state executive officers is not. The Court's decision in *Printz* – viewed in light of *Miranda* and *Aguilar* – demonstrates the extent to which the implicit framework of judicial imperialism has pervaded the Court's thinking.

INCORPORATION DOCTRINE

Incorporation doctrine holds that the Fourteenth Amendment made most, but not all, of the individual rights provisions in the Bill of Rights binding on the states.

(Under current doctrine, three specific rights in the Bill of Rights do not bind the states: the Third Amendment, the Fifth Amendment Grand Jury Clause, and the Seventh Amendment.) Viewed in terms of its practical impact, incorporation doctrine is arguably the most significant constitutional doctrine that the Court applies today. "During the two Supreme Court terms that ended in June 2021 and June 2022, the Court decided 26 cases applying the Bill of Rights to the states" under incorporation doctrine.[115] Those twenty-six cases comprised "roughly twenty percent of the Court's entire caseload during those two terms, and an even larger percentage of the Court's constitutional cases."[116] The Court's incorporation cases, viewed in the aggregate, impose far more severe restrictions on state autonomy than all of the federal statutes invalidated under all of the federalism doctrines discussed previously in this chapter.

In *McDonald v. City of Chicago*,[117] the Supreme Court held that the Second Amendment binds the states under the Fourteenth Amendment. Under established doctrine, a right included in the Bill of Rights binds the states under the Fourteenth Amendment only if it qualifies as "fundamental." In *McDonald*, the Court said that a right qualifies as "fundamental" for purposes of incorporation doctrine if it is "deeply rooted in this Nation's history and tradition."[118] An ideologically divided Court held, by a 5–4 majority, that the Second Amendment right to bear arms qualifies as "fundamental" under that historical test.

The historical test that the Court applied in *McDonald* is theoretically incoherent. The central question in every case where the Court is asked to impose a new federal constitutional limitation on the states via incorporation doctrine is whether the Court should jettison a consistent historical tradition of state autonomy and replace it with a new federal constitutional rule of "compelled uniformity."[119] For example, in *McDonald*, the Court rejected a consistent historical tradition – which had prevailed for more than 200 years – that granted states virtually unlimited discretion to enact whatever gun control regulations they chose, free from federal interference. The Court replaced the traditional rule of state autonomy with a newly minted constitutional rule that mandated federal uniformity.

It defies logic to argue, as the majority did in *McDonald*, that a deeply rooted historical tradition of state law protection for a particular right justifies judicial creation of a new constitutional rule that mandates federal uniformity. If the historical record demonstrates that there was a consistent, uniform tradition protecting the right at the state level, then a uniform federal constitutional rule serves no purpose, except to deprive states of powers reserved to them under the Tenth Amendment by transferring decision-making authority from elected state legislatures to unelected federal judges. If, on the other hand, the historical record manifests a diversity of state laws on the subject, then that history – combined with our tradition of constitutional federalism – provides a powerful argument *against* replacing the historical tradition of state autonomy with a new rule of compelled federal uniformity. Either way, history cannot provide a theoretically coherent rationale for judicial creation of a new federal constitutional rule in an area that – for 170 or 200 years – was governed exclusively, or almost exclusively, by state law. (I refer to "170 years" because most of the key incorporation cases that made specific provisions in the Bill of Rights binding on the states for the first time were decided in the 1960s, roughly 170 years after ratification of the Bill of Rights.)

In *Adamson v. California* (1947), the Supreme Court held that the Fifth Amendment prohibition on self-incrimination does not bind the states under the Fourteenth Amendment.[120] In his dissenting opinion, Justice Black argued forcefully that "one purpose of those who framed, advocated, and adopted the [Fourteenth] Amendment had been to make the [entire] Bill of Rights applicable to the States."[121] Black's position came to be known as "total incorporation theory" because he argued that the entire Bill of Rights binds the states under the Fourteenth Amendment. That theory finds no support in the text of the Fourteenth Amendment; the text does not say that "all rights in the Bill of Rights shall henceforth be binding on state governments." Justice Black defended his position on originalist grounds.[122] However, in an important law review article published in 1949,[123] Professor Charles Fairman argued persuasively that Black's originalist argument supporting total incorporation was mostly incorrect, or at best unsubstantiated. Due partly to Fairman's influence, the Supreme Court never accepted Black's theory.

Some scholars contend that the Fourteenth Amendment Privileges and Immunities Clause should be construed to support total incorporation – meaning that Section 1 of the Fourteenth Amendment made the entire Bill of Rights automatically binding on the states.[124] As a textual matter, that argument is unpersuasive. Granted, Section 5 of the Fourteenth Amendment, read in conjunction with the Privileges and Immunities Clause, can reasonably be construed to empower Congress to enact legislation to make the Bill of Rights binding on the states. However, for reasons explained previously,[125] the relevant historical materials show – and the text of Section 5 makes clear – that the key architects of the Fourteenth Amendment intended to empower Congress, not the courts. Insofar as modern incorporation doctrine is a judge-empowering doctrine, it is difficult to square with the original public meaning of the Fourteenth Amendment.

Although the Court never endorsed Justice Black's total incorporation theory, his dissenting opinion in *Adamson* marked an important inflection point in the development of incorporation doctrine.[126] Before 1947, the Court rejected arguments for incorporating specific provisions in the Bill of Rights more frequently than it accepted those arguments. After *Adamson*, it almost always ruled in favor of incorporation.[127] Before 1947, the Supreme Court often applied a natural law test to determine which rights qualify as "fundamental" and therefore bind the states under the Fourteenth Amendment. Under the natural law test, rights included in the Bill of Rights bind the states under the Fourteenth Amendment if "neither liberty nor justice would exist if they were sacrificed,"[128] or if they implicate "immutable principles of liberty and justice which inhere in the very idea of free government."[129]

The traditional natural law test was much more protective of state autonomy than modern incorporation doctrine. Table 7.1 illustrates this point. It divides incorporation cases between cases applying a historical test[130] and those applying a natural law test.[131] It also divides cases between cases where the Court held that a specific Bill of Rights provision binds the states and those where the Court rejected incorporation arguments. It bears emphasis that the Court has never applied the historical test to reject application of a Bill of Rights provision to the states. In contrast, when applying the natural law test, the Court was more likely to reject incorporation than it was to support incorporation.

TABLE 7.1 *Comparing Tests for Incorporation*

	Binding on States	Not Binding on States
Natural law test	Chicago, B & Q R. Co. (1897) • Takings Clause De Jonge v. Oregon (1937) • Freedom of assembly	Twining v. New Jersey (1908) • Self-incrimination Palko v. Connecticut (1937) • Double jeopardy Adamson v. California (1947) • Self-incrimination
Historical test	Klopfer v. North Carolina (1967) • Speedy trial Duncan v. Louisiana (1968) • Right to jury trial Benton v. Maryland (1969) • Double jeopardy McDonald v. City of Chicago (2010) • Second Amendment Timbs v. Indiana (2019) • Excessive fines	The Court has *never* applied the historical test to reject incorporation.

Table 7.1 excludes numerous incorporation cases where the Court did not apply either a natural law or a historical test. Those include seven cases where the Court applied a procedural fairness test[132] and four cases where it applied a test that combined history with natural law.[133] Perhaps most surprisingly, the Court decided a total of nine cases between 1925 and 1971 where it simply decreed by judicial fiat – without articulating any rule or standard for distinguishing between "fundamental" and "non-fundamental" rights – that a particular Bill of Rights provision shall henceforth be binding on state governments.[134] In Justice Harlan's words, the Court "merely declares that the clause in question is 'in' rather than 'out'.… The Court has justified neither its starting place nor its conclusion."[135] In sum, the Supreme Court has exploited incorporation doctrine to transfer a huge amount of lawmaking authority from state legislatures to federal courts, but it has not provided a consistent, theoretically coherent justification for that judicial power grab.[136]

Incorporation Doctrine and State Autonomy

This chapter stated previously that the Court's incorporation cases, viewed in the aggregate, impose far more severe restrictions on state autonomy than all of the federal statutes invalidated under all of the federalism doctrines discussed in the first half of the chapter. Admittedly, that claim is impossible to prove in a rigorous, systematic way. Even so, a comparison of the Court's decisions in *United States v. Lopez* and *McDonald v. City of Chicago* shows why the claim is broadly accurate as a general matter.

In *Lopez*,[137] the Court invalidated the Gun Free School Zones Act. Although the Court claimed that the federal statute interfered with state autonomy, it bears emphasis that the statute did not impose any limitation whatsoever on state legislative authority. Instead, the Gun Free School Zones Act imposed federal criminal penalties for conduct that was already prohibited by criminal laws in most states.[138] Nothing in the federal statute barred states from prosecuting criminals under their own criminal statutes.[139] One could argue that the federal criminal prohibition undermined the authority of state legislatures in states that adopted more permissive rules regarding possession of guns near schools, compared to federal law. However, the fact that the federal government sometimes prohibits conduct that is lawful under state law is a defining characteristic of our federal system. It is a feature, not a bug. In sum, the statute at issue in *Lopez* did not impose any significant, practical restriction on state legislative authority.

Compare *Lopez* to *McDonald v. City of Chicago*.[140] Whereas the Gun Free School Zones Act did not impose any material restriction on state legislative authority, the Court's decision in *McDonald* imposed very substantial restrictions on state legislative authority. For more than two centuries before *McDonald*, state and local legislative bodies had virtually unlimited discretion to enact whatever gun control legislation they chose, free from any Second Amendment constraints.[141] By decreeing that the Second Amendment shall henceforth bind the states, the Court's decision in *McDonald* subjected state and local legislatures to a new set of constitutional constraints in an area where, per *Lopez*, "states have historically been sovereign."[142] The Court's subsequent decision in *New York State Rifle and Pistol Ass'n v. Bruen*,[143] which built on the foundation established in *McDonald*, demonstrated that incorporation of the Second Amendment has real bite: *Bruen* invalidated state gun control laws in seven states.[144]

The comparison between *Lopez* and *McDonald* illustrates a more general point. Most laws enacted by Congress do not impose prospective, forward-looking restrictions on state legislative authority. When Congress does impose such restrictions, federal law preempts state law. The Court's key federalism cases relating to the Commerce Clause, the Civil War Amendments, sovereign immunity, and anti-commandeering have not significantly restricted Congress's power to preempt state law. In contrast, many of the Court's incorporation decisions – especially those relating to the First Amendment,[145] the Second Amendment,[146] and the Eighth Amendment[147] – burden states with prospective, forward-looking restrictions on state legislative authority. The most important incident of state sovereignty is the power of state legislatures to make laws governing future behavior. Incorporation doctrine imposes very significant, judicially created restrictions on that power. The federal statutes that the Court has invalidated under its federalism doctrines generally do not. (For the reasons explained earlier in this chapter, the Medicaid expansion provision that the Court invalidated in *Sebelius* is the most important exception to this general claim.)

Incorporation Doctrine, Natural Law, and Fundamental Rights

In prior work, I have defended a modern version of the natural law test for determining which rights qualify as fundamental rights. Recall that, under the traditional test, rights qualify as fundamental if "neither liberty nor justice would exist if they were sacrificed,"[148] or if they implicate "immutable principles of liberty and justice which inhere in the very idea of free government."[149] The justification for federal courts to intervene to protect *those* rights – notwithstanding constitutional protections for state autonomy – is obvious. If federal courts refuse to intervene when state governments violate rights that "inhere in the very idea of free government," then they are failing to fulfill a core mission of courts in a constitutional democracy.

Critics contend that the natural law test is flawed because it encourages judges to decide cases based on subjective values. My proposed test relies on international and comparative law to provide an objective, natural law test for determining which rights are fundamental. Specifically: "A particular right qualifies as "fundamental" under the Due Process Clause if: (a) it is included in the [Universal Declaration of Human Rights[150]], or (b) it is included in the ICCPR, or (c) it is included in the national constitutions of more than 60 percent of the world's nations."[151]

There are several reasons why it makes sense to apply the UDHR as a benchmark for determining which rights are fundamental. First, the UDHR codifies shared moral intuitions about the scope and content of natural rights that transcend geographical, cultural, and religious divides. When the United Nations created a committee to draft the UDHR, it purposely selected committee members from all geographic regions to represent different cultural, religious, and nonreligious perspectives.[152] In Professor Michael Perry's apt phrase, the UDHR laid the foundation for the development of a "global political morality."[153] The UDHR is accepted throughout the world as an authoritative expression of fundamental human rights. Indeed, most states that have either amended their Constitutions or adopted new Constitutions in the past fifty years have used the UDHR as a template for determining which rights to codify in their national Constitutions.[154]

Look again at Table 6.1, which shows that eighteen of the twenty-four rights that bind states under current incorporation doctrine are included in the ICCPR. Those eighteen rights qualify as fundamental rights under the proposed test because they are included in the ICCPR. (All eighteen rights are also included in the UDHR. Ten of the eighteen rights also qualify under the comparative prong of the test because they are included in the national constitutions of more than 60 percent of the world's nations.[155]) However, if Congress enacts the legislation proposed in Chapter 6, all eighteen rights would be judicially enforceable against state governments under the Supremacy Clause. In that case, there would be no need for incorporation doctrine to make those rights binding on states. Moreover, as this book has emphasized, judicial application of treaty-based rights under the Supremacy Clause is preferable to judicial application of the Bill of Rights under incorporation doctrine because the treaty-based approach preserves a democratic check on judicial power. (It bears emphasis that there was no available treaty alternative to incorporation doctrine in the 1960s, when most provisions of the Bill of Rights were incorporated, because the United States did not ratify the relevant treaties until the 1990s.)

What about the six incorporated rights listed in Table 6.1 that are not included in the ICCPR? Table 7.2 shows how the modern, natural law test applies to those rights. Data on national constitutions is derived from the Comparative Constitutions Project (CCP) database.[156] (The term "n.a." in Table 7.2 indicates that the CCP database does not contain information about which national constitutions include either the exclusionary rule or a restriction on excessive fines.) Table 7.2 shows that the property right protected under the Takings Clause qualifies as a fundamental right because it is included in the UDHR, and it is included in about 66 percent of national constitutions. However, none of the other rights listed in Table 7.2 qualifies as a fundamental right under the modern, natural law test. None of those rights are included in the UDHR. None of them come close to the 60 percent threshold under the comparative prong of the test.

TABLE 7.2 *Incorporated Rights Not Included in the ICCPR*

Right (Year Incorporated)	U.S. Const.	UDHR	National Constitutions
Takings Clause (1897)	Fifth Am.	Art. 17	66%
Establishment Clause (1947)	First Am.	No	27%
Exclusionary rule (1961)	Fourth Am. (implied)	No	n.a.
Jury trial (1968)	Sixth Am.	No	18%
Right to bear arms (2010)	Second Am.	No	2%
Excessive fines (2019)	Eighth Am.	No	n.a.

In light of the preceding analysis, U.S. courts should continue to enforce the Takings Clause against the states under incorporation doctrine because that Clause protects a fundamental right and there is no available treaty-based substitute. In contrast, the Court should overrule its prior decisions in *Timbs* (excessive fines),[157] *McDonald* (right to bear arms),[158] *Duncan* (jury trial),[159] *Mapp* (exclusionary rule),[160] and *Everson* (Establishment Clause).[161] All five cases constitute unwarranted federal interference in areas that are properly reserved to the states under the Tenth Amendment. Application of an objective, natural law test demonstrates that the rights at issue in those cases do not qualify as fundamental rights. Insofar as the Court relied on an historical test to support incorporation in those cases,[162] the Court's rationale fails to justify federal intrusion into areas reserved to the states because the historical test is theoretically incoherent. Overruling those five cases, and returning power to the states in those areas, would have a much greater practical effect in promoting state autonomy than any of the Court's decisions in any of the so-called federalism cases analyzed in the first half of this chapter (with the possible exception of the anti-coercion decision in *Sebelius*).[163]

8

A Roadmap for Revolutionary Change

The preceding chapters presented a set of bold, revolutionary proposals for both legislative reforms and changes in Supreme Court doctrine. Readers who have followed the argument to this point might well ask: "Aren't these proposals wildly unrealistic?" Chapter 8 responds to that question. The first section addresses theories of constitutional change, focusing primarily on Professor Ackerman's "movement, party, Presidency" model of constitutional transformation.[1] Following Ackerman's model, this chapter emphasizes the importance of landmark statutes and judicial super-precedents as engines of constitutional revolution.

The remainder of the chapter lays out a program for revolutionary change, based on the assumption that the Democratic Party will gain simultaneous control of the Presidency, the Senate, and the House of Representatives in 2028, or shortly thereafter. (I initially wrote this chapter before the November 2024 elections, then revised it after learning the election results.) Given that assumption, the next section addresses proposals for Supreme Court reform. If the Democratic Party wants to launch a constitutional revolution to place We the People at the center of our constitutional universe, the starting point must entail changes to the composition of the Supreme Court. After discussing proposals for Supreme Court reform, the final two sections, respectively, consider constitutional transformation related to the electoral process and other constitutional changes.

The chapter assumes that the Democratic Party will take the lead in promoting a constitutional revolution. That assumption relates to the claim in the Introduction that we should think about these issues in the context of the ongoing, global struggle between democracy and autocracy. Unfortunately, as of this writing, the Republican Party is generally aligned with the forces of autocracy. Until that changes, the Democratic Party is the only political party in the United States that is capable of leading a pro-democracy constitutional revolution.

THEORIES OF CONSTITUTIONAL CHANGE

Article V of the Constitution establishes procedures for a formal constitutional amendment. Under Article V, a constitutional amendment must be "ratified by the Legislatures of three fourths of the several States, or by Conventions in three fourths thereof, as the one or the other Mode of Ratification may be proposed by the Congress."[2] Apart from the Twenty-Seventh Amendment[3] – which was initially proposed in 1789 but not ratified until 1992 – the states have not approved a constitutional amendment since 1971. Most observers agree that an array of political obstacles have made amendment through the Article V process virtually impossible.[4] Hence, this chapter focuses on informal constitutional change, outside the Article V process.

Professor Bruce Ackerman has elaborated the most comprehensive theory for explaining the mechanics of informal constitutional change. In his most recent work on the subject, he elaborated a six-stage model of constitutional transformation that highlights the role of political parties, elections, and Presidents in driving constitutional transformation.[5] That model provides an elegant explanation of the New Deal revolution. Ackerman's account highlights the election of Franklin Roosevelt in 1936 as a "triggering election" and his reelection in 1940 as a "consolidating election."[6] (His later work refers to the second election as a "ratifying election."[7]) Although the New Deal revolution did not produce any Article V constitutional amendments, it did produce several "landmark statutes" and "judicial super-precedents." In Ackerman's theory, those landmark statutes and super-precedents are the key elements of constitutional transformation.[8]

Professor Ackerman's "movement, party, Presidency" model does not provide a persuasive explanation for every case of informal constitutional change. For example, other scholars have written about the "de facto ERA," a set of changes in the 1970s that provided women stronger protection against gender-based discrimination.[9] The de facto ERA certainly produced judicial super-precedents[10] and arguably also produced at least one landmark statute.[11] However, the de facto ERA was not the product of a triggering election and Presidential leadership played very little role in the process of constitutional change. Instead, according to Professor Reva Siegel's leading account, the de facto ERA resulted primarily from a clash between competing social forces and changes in political culture.[12]

Beginning in the early 2000s, leading scholars began to focus on the role of social movements in sparking informal constitutional transformation.[13] In prior work, I have made a modest contribution to that literature.[14] In the future, social movements will undoubtedly continue to play an important role in informal constitutional change. However, at this particular moment in American history, Professor Ackerman's "movement, party, Presidency" model provides the most realistic pathway for the type of constitutional revolution envisioned in this book.

The current Supreme Court presents a major obstacle to pro-democratic constitutional change. In the 1970s, one factor that contributed to the success of the women's movement was the fact that the Supreme Court was receptive to their constitutional arguments. In contrast, the current Supreme Court is not receptive to the argument that the Constitution is designed to ensure that We the People maintain effective control over our government. Therefore, like the New Deal revolution in the 1930s, a constitutional revolution designed to place We the People at the center of our constitutional universe must begin by changing the composition of the Supreme Court. Moreover, legislation to alter the Court's composition will not be possible without the type of triggering election that is central to Professor Ackerman's theory of constitutional transformation.

Before considering proposals for Supreme Court reform, it is useful to highlight two other features of Ackerman's theory. First, Professor Ackerman says that the revolutionaries who carried out previous, successful constitutional revolutions "failed to follow well-established rules and principles."[15] Both the Reconstruction Republicans in the 1860s and the New Deal Democrats in the 1930s changed "established modes of constitutional revision … in the very process of changing the substance of fundamental values."[16] In contemporary jargon, we might say that they played "constitutional hardball."[17] The Republican Party, led by Senator Mitch McConnell, played constitutional hardball to prevent President Obama from appointing Merrick Garland to the Supreme Court in 2016 and to enable President Trump to appoint Justice Amy Coney Barrett in 2020. If the Democratic Party is going to lead the next constitutional revolution, it must play constitutional hardball to reform the Supreme Court so that the Court does not stand as an insurmountable obstacle to other legislative reforms.[18] Moreover, a Democratic Party that controls the Presidency and that has majorities in both Houses of Congress will need to eliminate the filibuster in the Senate – or significantly restrict its use – so that Republicans cannot use the filibuster to block pro-democratic reforms.

Second, Professor Ackerman argues that a political party interested in revolutionary constitutional change must win at least two successive Presidential elections to implement and consolidate those changes: a triggering election and a ratifying election.[19] That point is undoubtedly correct. Radical constitutional change does not happen overnight. If the Democratic Party is going to play a central role in initiating and carrying out a major constitutional transformation, it must have sufficient popular support to win at least two successive Presidential elections and retain a majority in both Houses of Congress for much of that eight-year period. In contemporary political circumstances, that means the Democratic Party must focus on two key issues that are tangential to the main concerns of this book, but that are critical for sustaining popular support. First, it must develop policies that reduce economic inequality and increase economic opportunity for working class Americans, who have formed a core element of Donald Trump's base since 2016. (Economic inequality has grown steadily in the United States since the 1980s.[20]) Second, it must enact a landmark statute to protect a woman's right to choose; such legislation should be crafted to garner sufficient popular support to survive the next several electoral cycles.[21] The Democratic Party should not try to reinstate *Roe v. Wade* as a constitutional rule; it cannot credibly claim to be the party that supports a democratic check on judicial power if it purposefully selects Supreme Court Justices who are committed to reinstating *Roe v. Wade* by judicial fiat.

SUPREME COURT REFORM

In April 2021, President Biden signed an executive order to create the Presidential Commission on the Supreme Court of the United States [the "Biden Commission"].[22] The Commission issued its Final Report in December 2021.[23] The Final Report presents a detailed analysis of several different proposals for Supreme Court reform. Although the Commission did not recommend any particular reforms, the Final Report presents a very helpful analysis of the pros and cons – and potential constitutional vulnerabilities – of numerous proposals.

In the 118th Congress, two Democratic Senators introduced significant court reform bills. In 2023, Senator Whitehouse introduced S.3096, the "Supreme Court Biennial Appointments and Term Limits Act."[24] The following year, Senator Wyden introduced S.5229, the "Judicial Modernization and Transparency Act."[25] Senator Wyden's bill is more comprehensive in that his bill mandates detailed financial disclosures for all Supreme Court Justices and nominees. It would also increase the number of judges on the lower federal courts and add two new federal circuit courts.[26]

Both bills would expand the size of the Supreme Court and routinize Supreme Court appointments by authorizing Presidents to appoint new Justices in the first and third years of a four-year Presidential term.[27] These provisions are clearly within the scope of congressional authority to regulate the Supreme Court.[28] However, if a Democratic President takes office in January 2029 and is reelected for a second term, and if no current Justice dies or retires, the new appointments (without more) would not establish a liberal majority on the Court until 2035. Neither Senator Whitehouse nor Senator Wyden wants to wait that long. Hence, both bills play constitutional hardball to accelerate the timeline for regaining an effective liberal majority on the Supreme Court, but they use different tactics to accomplish that goal.

The Wyden bill would require a two-thirds majority of "voting justices" to invalidate an Act of Congress.[29] Assume that a Democratic President is elected in November 2028, no current Justices die or retire, and Congress enacts a statute based on Wyden's proposal in early 2029. Then the President appoints one new Justice in 2029. At that point, the Court would have four Justices appointed by Democratic Presidents (call them liberals) and six Justices appointed by Republican Presidents (call them conservatives). The conservatives would need to secure at least one liberal vote to get the two-thirds majority necessary to invalidate an Act of Congress. Progressive legislation passed by a Democratic majority in Congress in 2029 would likely withstand a constitutional challenge, unless at least one liberal Justice voted to invalidate that legislation.

However, the Court might well invalidate the provision in the Wyden bill requiring a two-thirds majority to hold an Act of Congress unconstitutional. Article III of the Constitution provides that the Supreme Court exercises appellate jurisdiction "with such Exceptions, and under such Regulations as the Congress shall make."[30] The Necessary and Proper Clause grants Congress power to enact legislation "for carrying into execution … all other Powers vested by this Constitution in the Government of the United States."[31] One could argue that the combination of the Article III Exceptions Clause and the Necessary and Proper Clause empowers Congress to prescribe decision-making rules for the Supreme Court. However, one could also argue that the proposed two-thirds rule violates separation of powers principles because it constitutes improper legislative interference with the judicial branch. After presenting a detailed analysis of the issue,[32] the Biden Commission concluded: "[I]t seems quite plausible that the Court would find a congressional attempt to impose a supermajority rule on the Court's decisionmaking … to be beyond Congress's power."[33]

The Whitehouse Bill adopts a different approach. In accordance with Article III, Section 2, the bill divides the Supreme Court's docket into original jurisdiction cases and appellate jurisdiction cases. The entire Supreme Court – as many as eighteen Justices – would sit "en banc" for original jurisdiction cases. However, "only the nine most recently appointed Justices of the Supreme Court … shall preside over appellate jurisdiction cases."[34] Again, assume that a Democratic President is elected in November 2028, no current Justices die or retire, and Congress enacts a statute based on the Whitehouse bill in early 2029. Then the President appoints two new Justices in 2029 and 2031. At that point, liberals would have an effective majority because the new Justices would replace Justice Thomas (in 2029) and Chief Justice Roberts (in 2031) for all appellate jurisdiction cases. Beginning in 2031, progressive legislation passed by a Democratic majority in Congress would likely withstand a constitutional challenge, unless at least one liberal Justice voted to invalidate such legislation.

The Whitehouse proposal to exclude the most senior Justices from appellate jurisdiction cases is also subject to constitutional challenge on the grounds that it constitutes improper legislative interference with the judicial branch. However, compared to Senator Wyden's proposal for super-majority voting, the Whitehouse bill is more easily defensible on the grounds that it is an exercise of Congress's express power, under Article III, Section 2, to make "regulations" for the exercise of the Court's "appellate jurisdiction."[35] The Biden Commission described a proposal similar to the Whitehouse bill as a "way of creating the effective equivalent of term limits that might avoid some of the constitutional problems" associated with actual term limits.[36] The Final Report evaluated constitutional arguments for and against the proposal without reaching a definitive judgment regarding its constitutionality.[37]

Although I believe that the Whitehouse proposal is constitutionally valid, I would add one more "hardball" provision to the statute to help insulate it from constitutional challenge. Specifically, the statute should provide that no federal court may decide the merits of any claim challenging the constitutionality of "this statute" until after two new Supreme Court Justices have been appointed under the statute.

This type of provision is often called a "jurisdiction-stripping" provision because it bars federal courts from exercising jurisdiction in a narrow class of cases. As applied to lower federal courts, the proposed jurisdiction-stripping provision is not constitutionally problematic. Indeed, the Biden Commission noted that the Constitution "contemplates broad congressional power to determine and adjust the jurisdiction of the lower federal courts."[38] It is debatable whether the provision is constitutional as applied to the Supreme Court.[39] However, the restriction on lower federal courts would likely preclude any appeal from reaching the Supreme Court until after two new Justices had been appointed (unless plaintiffs litigated a constitutional challenge in state court and the state court moved quickly to expedite an appeal to the U.S. Supreme Court). If a constitutional challenge reached the Supreme Court in the third or fourth year of a Democratic President's first term, after two new Justices had been appointed, the statute would probably survive a constitutional challenge, but the outcome is uncertain.[40]

Two additional points merit comment before concluding this analysis of Supreme Court reform. First, in March 2016, almost eight months before Election Day, President Obama nominated Merrick Garland to fill a vacant seat on the Supreme Court.[41] Senator Mitch McConnell, the Senate majority leader, refused to allow the Senate to vote on Judge Garland's nomination, arguing that the next appointment should be postponed until after the Presidential election. This type of delay tactic presents an obvious problem for a statute that authorizes each President to appoint two new Justices in a four-year term. To prevent abuse of such tactics, the Wyden bill includes a provision to force a Senate vote on all Supreme Court nominees within 180 days.[42] A similar rule would be a useful addition to the Whitehouse bill.

Second, a Democratic President committed to a pro-democracy constitutional revolution will need to consider whether to apply some type of "litmus test" for judicial nominations, and if so, what that test should be. This book has argued that the Constitution divides power between the government and We the People, and that it grants We the People an affirmative, collective right to exercise control over our government. If White House officials are considering a litmus test for judicial appointments, a demonstrated commitment to that principle would be a good test.

CONSTITUTIONAL TRANSFORMATION AND THE ELECTORAL PROCESS

Chapter 3 presented several proposals for improving the electoral process, all of which are designed to make the market for elective office more competitive. For any particular rule, or proposed rule, the nation confronts a systemic choice about whether the rule should be created through legislation or through judicial lawmaking. From the standpoint of democratic theory, it is better for legislatures to make laws, rather than relying on courts to formulate new electoral rules. However, from the perspective of political science, legislators are self-interested, partisan politicians who lack the correct incentives to create electoral rules that maximize competition in the political marketplace. This chapter envisions a constitutional revolution led by the Democratic Party. The primary goal of that revolution is to restore the proper constitutional division of authority between the government and We the People so that citizens exercise greater control over the government. Assuming that the Democratic Party is committed to that goal, in principle, can we trust partisan legislators to promote that goal through legislation? Or do we need strong judicial review to make the market for elective office more competitive, precisely because we cannot trust partisan legislators to do so?

During the Warren Court era, "the Court saw itself as collaborating with Congress to develop a set of fundamental principles that would permanently order U.S. society. Sometimes Congress would push the ball forward, and the Court would approve.... On other occasions, Congress would actively seek out the Court's assistance."[43] A future, pro-democracy constitutional revolution will require a similar partnership model in which Congress and the Supreme Court collaborate to create a more competitive electoral marketplace so that We the People can exercise more effective control over our government. Here, I consider how such a partnership model might operate in three areas: preclearance under the Voting Rights Act; campaign finance reform; and gerrymandering.

Preclearance

Recall that Section 5 of the Voting Rights Act establishes a "pre-clearance" procedure that applies only to "covered jurisdictions." If a covered jurisdiction wants to change its election laws, it may not implement proposed changes without prior authorization from either the U.S. Attorney General or a federal court. Section 4(b) provides a formula for determining which jurisdictions qualify as "covered jurisdictions." In *Shelby County v. Holder*,[44] the Supreme Court invalidated the coverage formula in Section 4(b), but left untouched the pre-clearance procedure in Section 5. Section 5 is still good law, but it will remain inoperative until Congress creates a new coverage formula. Thus, in *Shelby County*, the Court handed the ball to Congress and challenged Congress to devise a coverage formula consistent with the "equal sovereignty" principle that the Court established in *Shelby County*.[45]

The John R. Lewis Voting Rights Advancement Act of 2023 (H.R. 14) responds to that challenge.[46] The bill establishes a detailed coverage formula to determine which states and political subdivisions are subject to pre-clearance.[47] However, the bill has not made it out of the House Judiciary Committee. That Committee is unlikely to vote in favor of the bill as long as the Republican Party controls the House of Representatives.

What if we elect a Democratic President and the Democratic Party secures a majority in both the House and the Senate? In that case, and if the Senate eliminates the filibuster, Congress would very likely enact legislation similar to H.R. 14.

The political incentives for Democratic Party politicians generally align with the primary goal of the legislation: to restore the pre-clearance procedure under the Voting Rights Act. However, absent changes in Supreme Court personnel, the Court might well invalidate the new legislation. The authors of H.R. 14 appear to have made a sincere effort to craft legislation to conform to the equal sovereignty principle that the Court adopted in *Shelby County*. That principle is extremely malleable, though, and the current Court may be even more hostile to the Voting Rights Act than the Court was in 2013 when it decided *Shelby County*.

Two conclusions follow from the preceding analysis. First, the preclearance example reinforces the point that Supreme Court reform is an essential prerequisite for a successful constitutional revolution. Second, legislation like H.R. 14 provides an excellent opportunity for a Democratic majority in Congress to play constitutional hardball. Specifically, to minimize the risk that the Supreme Court would invalidate the legislation, Congress should add a jurisdiction-stripping provision to delay judicial review until after two new Justices have been appointed to the Supreme Court. Assuming that Congress enacts something like the Whitehouse bill for Supreme Court reform, and assuming that such legislation is constitutional, a reconstituted Supreme Court with a liberal majority would almost certainly hold that legislation substantially similar to H.R. 14 is constitutionally valid.

Campaign Finance Reform

Over the past several decades, Congress has enacted important campaign finance legislation, but the Supreme Court has often invalidated that legislation. For example, in *Buckley v. Valeo*,[48] the Court held that provisions in the Federal Election Campaign Act (FECA) that restricted campaign expenditures violated the First Amendment. It bears emphasis that the Court did not divide along ideological lines in *Buckley*. The Court's liberal and conservative Justices joined forces to vote 7–1, and 6–2, in support of the key First Amendment holdings on campaign expenditures.[49] In *Citizens United v. Federal Election Comm'n*,[50] the Court held that provisions in the Bipartisan Campaign Reform Act (BCRA) that restricted corporate campaign expenditures violated the First Amendment. In contrast to *Buckley*, the Court did divide along ideological lines in *Citizens United*. The Court's five most conservative Justices agreed that BCRA's restrictions on corporate campaign expenditures were unconstitutional. The Court's four liberals dissented on that point.[51]

Congressman Sarbanes (D-MD) introduced the Freedom to Vote Act (H.R. 11) in the House in July 2023.[52] H.R. 11 is a mammoth bill that runs to more than 600 printed pages. Titles VI and VII, which comprise about 100 pages, address "campaign finance transparency" and "campaign finance oversight." Although the Freedom to Vote Act is a very ambitious bill, it does not attempt to regulate campaign expenditures in any way that challenges the Court's key holdings in either *Buckley* or *Citizens United*.[53] Chapter 3 argued that the Court should overrule *Buckley* to give

Congress greater flexibility to regulate campaign expenditures. However, campaign finance regulation presents a "first mover" problem. The Freedom to Vote Act suggests that Congress is reluctant to enact legislation inconsistent with the Court's First Amendment rulings in *Buckley* and *Citizens United*, but the Court will not have an opportunity to reconsider those holdings unless Congress enacts legislation to challenge, or test the limits, of those decisions.

Given the first mover problem, a realistic pathway for Congress and the Supreme Court to engage in a collaborative effort to strengthen campaign finance regulation might proceed in three phases. In phase one, Congress could enact something like the campaign finance rules in the Freedom to Vote Act. Those rules would make incremental improvements to current law by enhancing transparency and enhancing government oversight of campaign expenditures. Legislation along these lines would likely be challenged on First Amendment grounds, but it would probably survive a First Amendment challenge, even without any changes to the composition of the Supreme Court.[54]

In phase two, Congress could try to reenact limits on corporate campaign expenditures similar to the BCRA limits that the Court invalidated in *Citizens United*. As the name suggests, Congress enacted the "Bipartisan Campaign Reform Act of 2002" with bipartisan support.[55] It is questionable whether similar legislation would garner bipartisan support today. Regardless, with a majority in both Houses, the Democratic Party would likely unite to support limits on corporate campaign expenditures. After appointment of two new Justices to replace Justice Thomas and Chief Justice Roberts in appellate jurisdiction cases (per the Whitehouse bill), a liberal majority on the Supreme Court would likely overrule *Citizens United* and uphold statutory restrictions on corporate campaign expenditures. If a Democratic Congress wanted to move quickly to enact such legislation – before securing a liberal majority on the Supreme Court – it could include a hardball provision, as discussed previously, that would postpone adjudication of any constitutional challenge to the legislation until after two new Justices have been appointed.

In phase three, Congress could try to reenact limits on campaign expenditures similar to the limits that the Court invalidated in *Buckley v. Valeo*. Legislation along those lines would be a stretch. Even the current liberal Supreme Court Justices might hold that such legislation violates the First Amendment. Thus, in contrast to the corporate expenditure issue, it is questionable whether appointment of two new Justices would be sufficient to secure a Supreme Court majority in favor of upholding such legislation. Moreover, statutory limits on campaign expenditures like those invalidated in *Buckley* might well fracture the Democratic Party coalition in Congress. On one hand, many former Members of Congress say that the need to spend large amounts of time on the unpleasant task of fundraising was a key factor supporting their decision to retire. Indeed, one former Congressman was quoted as follows: "I don't know of a single member that is leaving that does not include the pressures of raising money … as one of the contributing factors."[56] Limits on campaign expenditures would presumably appeal to Members of Congress who would prefer to spend more time legislating and less time fundraising. However, congressional leadership in both parties consists primarily of individuals who are good at fundraising; that is (partly) why they were promoted to leadership positions.[57] Since the most powerful Members of Congress have benefited from a system that places a premium on fundraising, it is questionable whether they have an incentive to change the system.

Gerrymandering

Chapter 3 defended two distinct proposals related to gerrymandering: a ban on partisan gerrymandering and a mandate to maximize the number of competitive seats.[58] For present purposes, it is helpful to divide these two proposals into four: (a) ban partisan gerrymandering in congressional redistricting; (b) ban it in redistricting for state legislatures; (c) maximize competitive seats in congressional redistricting; and (d) maximize competitive seats in redistricting for state legislatures.

Congress clearly has authority under Article I, Sec. 4 of the Constitution to prescribe rules for redistricting for the U.S. House of Representatives. However, Article I does not grant Congress the power to prescribe rules for redistricting in state legislatures. One could argue that Congress does have such a power, either under the Republican Guarantee Clause,[59] or under Section 5 of the Fourteenth Amendment. However, the Supreme Court is unlikely to agree that Congress has the power to regulate redistricting for state legislatures until a new President appoints a sufficient number of new Justices to create a liberal majority on the Court.

Title V of the Freedom to Vote Act (H.R. 11) includes detailed rules designed to eliminate (or sharply curtail) partisan gerrymandering in congressional redistricting.[60] The bill states explicitly: "Nothing in this title … may be construed to affect the manner in which a State carries out elections for State or local office."[61] The quoted language presumably reflects Congress's understanding that it lacks authority under current Supreme Court doctrine to regulate redistricting for state legislatures. The Freedom to Vote Act does not include any provisions designed to maximize the number of competitive seats in Congress. The absence of any such provision is not rooted in a lack of congressional power; it is based primarily (if not exclusively) on political self-interest. Both Democratic and Republican politicians favor "incumbent-protection" gerrymanders, which maximize the number of safe seats and minimize the number of competitive seats.[62] In contrast, Democratic Representatives favor limits on partisan gerrymandering because partisan gerrymandering has benefited Republicans more than Democrats, at least for the past few redistricting cycles.[63] Thus, the Freedom to Vote Act – a bill introduced by Democratic Representatives without any Republican cosponsors – is consistent with the political incentives of Democratic politicians.

This chapter envisions a partnership model in which Congress and the Supreme Court collaborate to enhance democracy. The preceding analysis suggests that it makes sense for Congress to take the lead in banning partisan gerrymandering for congressional elections because Congress has both the constitutional authority and the right political incentives – assuming a Democratic President and a Democratic majority in both Houses. Moreover, unlike the Supreme Court, Congress has the institutional competence to prescribe detailed rules that specify how a ban on partisan gerrymandering should be implemented,[64] and how that ban interacts with other rules, such as provisions in the Voting Rights Act that protect minority groups.[65] In contrast to other proposals discussed previously in this chapter, it is not necessary to include a jurisdiction-stripping provision to postpone judicial review of the ban on partisan gerrymandering, because the proposed legislation falls squarely within the scope of Congress's authority under current Supreme Court doctrine.[66]

Given the misalignment of political incentives for current legislators, the Supreme Court will need to take the lead in crafting a rule requiring officials in charge of congressional redistricting to maximize the number of competitive seats. Here, I assume that a Democratic President has appointed a sufficient number of new Justices to establish a liberal majority. In that case, the Court might consider two alternative rationales for a mandate to maximize competitive seats. First, such a mandate could be grounded in the Constitution's structural division of power between the government and We the People. Second, it could be grounded in what Professor Edward Foley has called the "Dormant Elections Clause."[67] The idea of the Dormant Elections Clause is modeled on the Court's Dormant Commerce Clause doctrine. Although the Commerce Clause is framed as an affirmative grant of power to Congress, the Court has construed that clause to create limits on state power. Dormant Commerce Clause doctrine is a form of weak judicial review; if the Court holds that a state government has violated the Dormant Commerce Clause, Congress retains the power to override that judicial decision.[68]

Article I, Section 4 of the Constitution (the "Elections Clause") specifies that state legislatures shall prescribe the "Times, Places and Manner of holding Elections for Senators and Representatives," but it also grants Congress an affirmative power to "make or alter such Regulations."[69] By analogy to the Dormant Commerce Clause, the Court could reasonably construe the Elections Clause to impose limits on state power – including a requirement to maximize competitive seats in congressional elections – while also preserving congressional power to override a Supreme Court decision based on the Dormant Elections Clause.[70] Given this book's preference for weak judicial review (consistent with the constitutional norm of legislative primacy), the idea that a mandate to maximize competitive seats could be grounded in the Dormant Elections Clause is appealing.

However, bearing in mind John Hart Ely's admonition that judicial review "exists for those situations where representative government cannot be trusted,"[71] and given the political incentive of legislators to maximize the number of safe seats, I think that the proposed mandate to maximize competitive seats is an issue where strong judicial review is necessary. Therefore, the Court should hold that the Constitution's structural division of power between the government and We the People requires officials responsible for redistricting to exercise that responsibility in a manner that maximizes the number of competitive seats, subject to requirements imposed by the Voting Rights Act.[72] A decision along these lines could still signal Congress that the Court would welcome federal legislation under the Elections Clause to work out the details, without granting Congress a power of legislative override (as would be the case under the Dormant Elections Clause).

What about redistricting for state legislatures? In *Reynolds v. Sims*, the Court created a new constitutional rule to govern redistricting for state legislatures. It grounded that rule in the Equal Protection Clause, stating that the Constitution requires "that each citizen have an *equally effective voice* in the election of members of his state legislature."[73] As I argued in Chapter 3, both partisan gerrymandering and incumbent-protection gerrymandering – as applied to state legislatures – violate the "equally effective voice" principle that the Court endorsed in *Reynolds*.[74] Therefore, the Court should hold both that partisan gerrymandering violates the Equal Protection Clause (EPC) and that the EPC requires state governments to implement the redistricting process in a manner that maximizes the number of competitive seats in state legislatures.

Supreme Court rulings based on the Equal Protection Clause typically involve strong judicial review, but the Court can and should frame its decisions in a way that invites Congress to enact implementing legislation. For the reasons articulated in Chapter 1, I believe that the Court should overrule *City of Boerne v. Flores*. However, a Supreme Court decision on partisan gerrymandering in state legislatures – or a mandate to maximize competitive seats – would not need to overrule *Boerne* to preserve a role for Congress. *Boerne*'s "congruent and proportional" test enables Congress to use its power under Section 5 of the Fourteenth Amendment to "enforce" Supreme Court decisions based on the Equal Protection Clause. Thus, in its rulings based on the EPC, the Court could invite Congress to use its Section 5 power to prescribe rules for redistricting in state legislatures to help enforce the Court's decisions on partisan gerrymandering and on maximizing competitive seats. As noted previously, the detailed provisions on partisan gerrymandering for congressional redistricting in the Freedom to Vote Act demonstrate that Congress has greater institutional competence, compared to the Supreme Court, to flesh out detailed rules regarding redistricting.

CONSTITUTIONAL CHANGE UNRELATED TO THE ELECTORAL PROCESS

Earlier chapters proposed several doctrinal changes unrelated to the electoral process that, if adopted by the Supreme Court, would create new super-precedents. In brief, the proposed doctrinal changes are as follows:

- Repudiate incorporation doctrine and replace it with a system that relies on human rights treaties, federal statutes, and the Supremacy Clause to protect individual rights from infringement by state and local governments.[75] (For the reasons explained in Chapter 7, the Court should continue to apply the Takings Clause to the states via incorporation doctrine.)
- Apply deferential, rational basis review for all claims in which litigants raise federalism-based constitutional challenges to congressional legislation, except that federal courts should continue to apply the rule from *New York v. United States*, which prohibits commandeering of state legislatures.[76]
- Practice constitutional avoidance in all cases where it is possible for courts to protect individual rights by applying a treaty-based substitute for the Bill of Rights or the Fourteenth Amendment.[77]
- Repudiate the rule that all content-based speech restrictions trigger application of strict scrutiny. Apply intermediate scrutiny to all state and federal legislation that is designed to promote the affirmative goals of democracy promotion and/or truth seeking.[78]
- Recognize that there is a constitutionally significant difference between ordinary speech and the electronic amplification of speech. Reaffirm the principle that We the People retain a "collective right to have [electronic media] function consistently with the ends and purposes of the First Amendment."[79] Apply a balancing test to state and federal laws that regulate the electronic amplification of misinformation.[80]

In his revolutionary decision in *Erie Railroad Co. v. Tompkins*,[81] Justice Louis Brandeis discarded a century's worth of judicial precedents, replacing the "old way" of thinking about law with a "new way" of thinking about law. One of *Erie*'s key goals was to limit the scope of judicial power by replacing judicial lawmaking with democratic lawmaking. Today, almost ninety years after *Erie*, the Court has developed a system of judicial imperialism that, once again, privileges lawmaking by unelected judges over democratic lawmaking by the peoples' elected representatives. The doctrinal changes summarized in the previous bullet points, taken together, would constitute a revolution in constitutional law comparable in scope to the *Erie* revolution. They would replace the current system of judicial imperialism with a body of constitutional law that places We the People at the center of our constitutional universe. Like the *Erie* revolution, they would restore the constitutional norm of legislative primacy by privileging democratic lawmaking over judicial lawmaking.

In addition to doctrinal changes, Chapters 4 and 6 proposed two statutes not directly related to the electoral process that are properly characterized as "landmark statutes." Chapter 4 proposed a statute to regulate the electronic amplification of misinformation. Hannah Arendt once said: "Freedom of opinion is a farce unless factual information is guaranteed and the facts themselves are not in dispute."[82] For several decades – from the 1930s to the 1980s – the United States had an information ecosystem in which "the facts themselves were not in dispute." Given subsequent developments in information and communications technology, it is not feasible to restore the media ecosystem of the 1960s, nor would it be desirable to do so. Nevertheless, a realistic plan to revitalize American democracy *must include* federal legislation to curb the electronic amplification of election-related misinformation along the lines discussed in Chapter 4. Absent such legislation, lies will continue to prevail over truth in the marketplace of ideas and the epistemic foundations of our democracy will continue to erode.

Since the current Supreme Court would almost certainly hold that the proposed legislation on misinformation violates the First Amendment, Congress should include a constitutional hardball provision specifying that no federal court may exercise jurisdiction over a claim challenging the statute's constitutional validity until after two new Justices have been appointed pursuant to the court reform legislation discussed earlier in this chapter. Alternatively, to minimize the risk of judicial invalidation of the statute, Congress could start with a softer version of the legislation that does not include any government penalties, to be followed later, if necessary, by an amendment that does include such penalties.[83]

Chapter 6 proposed legislation to make human rights treaties judicially enforceable and to encourage courts to practice constitutional avoidance in cases where there is a treaty-based substitute for judicial enforcement of the Bill of Rights or the Fourteenth Amendment. If such legislation is enacted and successfully implemented, it would have a transformative effect on the way that we think about protection for individual rights in the United States. Instead of looking to the Bill of Rights and the Fourteenth Amendment as the primary sources of protection for individual rights, lawyers and judges (and even nonlawyers) would look to international human rights treaties and federal statutes as the primary sources of protection for individual rights – in roughly the same way that nineteenth-century American lawyers relied on international law to protect individual rights from government infringement.[84] Since Congress has the power to override judicial decisions based on treaties and statutes, the legislation would enhance popular control over the government by transferring final decision-making authority for major public policy issues from unelected judges to elected legislators. It would also constrain judicial discretion because – for a range of fundamental rights – human rights treaties provide more explicit and detailed textual provisions than does the U.S. Constitution.[85] Finally, the shift from the Bill of Rights and the Fourteenth Amendment to an international human rights approach would likely strengthen judicial protection for minority rights.[86]

The Biden Commission on Supreme Court reform considered options for a legislative override of the Supreme Court's constitutional decisions.[87] The Commission highlighted the potential pro-democracy benefits of some type of legislative override system. The Final Report noted that "the most straightforward way to adopt a system of legislative overrides would be through constitutional amendment, as was urged during the Progressive and New Deal eras."[88] However, there is no realistic chance of enacting such a constitutional amendment in the foreseeable future. The Final Report added: "Absent constitutional amendment, it is highly likely that the Supreme Court would strike down a statute … setting forth a system for legislative overrides."[89] The legislation outlined in Chapter 6 would create a legislative override system that avoids the constitutional difficulties discussed in the Biden Commission report and that is broadly consistent with the dominant approach to public law litigation that prevailed in federal courts for most of the nineteenth century.

Appendix

Figures 2.1 to 2.3, which are included in Chapter 2, present in graphic form data that is summarized in Tables A.1 and A.2 at the end of this Appendix. Those tables are based on two different databases that I created, which I call the "phase one" and "phase two" databases. This Appendix explains how I created the databases.

Tables A.1 and A.2 are updated versions of tables originally published in an article in Washington & Lee Law Review in 2014.[1] The data in those tables ended in 2005 at the end of the Rehnquist Court. The data in Tables A.1 and A.2 includes cases decided by the Roberts Court through June 2023. The Roberts Court data is based on data from the Supreme Court Database, as described more fully later.[2] The following explanation of database creation is mostly copied from the *Washington & Lee Law Review*, with some modifications to account for recent updating.

Creation of the databases proceeded in two phases. In phase one, I segregated public law cases from other cases so that phase two analysis could focus exclusively on public law cases. Phase one applied a simple, quick, objective method to review approximately 27,000 Supreme Court cases and identify the public law cases within the larger universe.[3]

In phase one, classification was based strictly on the identity of the parties. If all parties to the litigation are private actors, the case is classified as PP (private law). If a private actor is adverse to a government actor, the case is classified as PG (public law).[4] The PG classification provided an excellent proxy for identifying true "public law cases." "Public law cases" are litigated cases involving a dispute between a private party and a government actor in which the private party alleges that the government actor committed, or threatened to commit, a violation of some established legal norm.[5] Phase two of the analysis (for the original article) confirmed that approximately 98 percent of the cases classified as PG in phase one are "public law cases" as defined previously.[6]

The original phase one database divided Supreme Court history into eight time periods; the final period was from 1972 to 2005.[7] For this book, to conform Table A.1 to the periodization in Table 1.2, I divided the last fifty-one years into two separate periods: 1972 to 1994, and 1995 to 2023. Table A.1 shows that there are 3,367 cases

TABLE A.1 *Data Supporting Figure 2.1*

Period	Chief Justices	Years	Total # Cases in Phase One Database	PG (Public Law)	PP (Private Law)	Other
1	Marshall	1801–1835	1,219	449 (36.8%)	742 (60.9%)	28 (2.3%)
2	Taney	1836–1864	1,597	467 (29.2%)	1,109 (69.4%)	21 (1.3%)
3	Chase, Waite	1865–1888	4,537	1,726 (38.0%)	2,740 (60.4%)	71 (1.6%)
4	Fuller	1888–1910	4,918	2,178 (44.3%)	2,576 (52.4%)	164 (3.3%)
5	White, Taft, Hughes	1910–1936	5,670	3,070 (54.1%)	2,158 (38.1%)	442 (7.8%)
6	Hughes, Stone, Vinson	1936–1954	2,345	1,649 (70.3%)	580 (24.7%)	116 (4.9%)
7	Warren, Burger	1954–1972	2,329	1,689 (72.5%)	487 (20.9%)	153 (6.6%)
8	Burger, Rehnquist	1972–1994	3,367	2,348 (69.7%)	666 (19.8%)	353 (10.5%)
9	Rehnquist, Roberts	1995–2023	2,311	1,546 (66.9%)	584 (25.3%)	181 (7.8%)

in the phase one database for the period 1972 to 1994. Those 3,367 cases are all the cases from period 8 in the original database with a decision date before January 1995. Table A.1 shows that there are 2,311 cases in the phase one database for the period from 1995 to 2023. Those 2,311 cases include all cases in the Supreme Court Database with a date of decision between January 1995 and June 2023. For the most recent period, I relied on variables 13–16 in the Supreme Court Database to classify cases as PG, PP, or other.[8] Table A.1 presents the results of phase one analysis. The data is presented graphically in Figure 2.1.

Whereas phase one involved "quick and dirty" analysis of more than 28,000 Supreme Court decisions, phase two entailed more detailed analysis of about 1,300 cases from periods 1, 2, 3, 6, 7, 8, and 9. (See Table A.2.) I excluded periods 4 and 5 from the phase two database because the original empirical project examined the contrast between nineteenth century public law litigation and modern public law litigation.

For phase two, I selected a random sample of PG cases from each of the seven periods identified in the preceding paragraph. Research assistants and I analyzed the Supreme Court decisions, the lower court decisions (when available), and the parties' arguments. We recorded information about the type of law invoked by lawyers, lower court judges, and Supreme Court Justices – including common law, state law,

TABLE A.2 *Data Supporting Figures 2.2 and 2.3*

	Period One (1801–1835)	Period Two (1836–1864)	Period Three (1865–1888)	Period Six (1936–1954)	Period Seven (1954–1972)	Period Eight (1972–1994)	Period Nine (1995–2023)
Private Party Raised Int'l Law Claim (1)	41.9% [34.1, 49.7] (N = 155)	41.7% [34.1, 49.3] (N = 163)	15.6% [10.3, 20.9] (N = 179)	4.7% [1.5, 7.9] (N = 169)	.9% [0, 2.2] (N = 215)	2.6% [0.7, 4.5] (N = 265)	n.a
Private Party Raised Con Law Claim (2)	8.4% [4.0, 12.8] (N = 155)	18.4% [12.4, 24.4] (N = 163)	18.4% [12.7, 24.1] (N = 179)	50.9% [43.3, 58.5] (N = 169)	63.3% [56.8, 69.8] (N = 215)	73.6% [68.3, 78.9] (N = 265)	n.a
Court Below Applied Int'l Law to Decide Merits (3)	44.1% [35.4, 52.8] (N = 127)	46.9% [38.7, 55.1] (N = 143)	15.7% [10.0, 21.4] (N = 159)	3.2% [0.4, 6.0] (N = 157)	1.0% [0, 2.4] (N = 196)	2.1% [0.2, 4.0] (N = 234)	n.a
Court Below Applied Con Law to Decide Merits (4)	6.3% [2.1, 10.5] (N = 127)	15.4% [9.5, 21.3] (N = 143)	16.4% [10.6, 22.2] (N = 159]	49.0% [41.2, 56.8] (N = 157)	61.7% [54.9, 68.5] (N = 196)	67.9% [61.9, 73.9] (N = 234)	n.a
Supreme Court Applied Int'l Law to Decide Merits (5)	42.5% [34.1, 50.9] (N = 134)	41.8% [33.4, 50.2] (N = 134)	15.4% [9.7, 21.1] (N = 156)	4.1% [0.9, 7.3] (N = 148)	1.1% [0, 2.6] (N = 187)	3.2% [1.3, 5.1] (N = 216)	0.6% [0, 1.7] (N = 168)
Supreme Court Applied Con Law to Decide Merits (6)	9.0% [4.1, 13.9] (N = 134)	16.4% [10.1, 22.7] (N = 134)	21.2% [14.8, 27.6] (N = 156)	47.3% [39.2, 55.4] (N = 148)	58.3% [51.2, 65.4] (N = 187)	67.6% [61.3, 73.9] (N = 216)	54.2% [46.6, 61.8] (N = 168)
Supreme Court Applied Neither Int'l Law nor Con Law (7)	52.2% [43.7, 60.7] (N = 134)	45.5% [37.0, 54.0] (N = 134)	64.1% [56.5, 71.7] (N = 156)	50.7% [42.6, 58.8] (N = 148)	41.2% [34.1, 48.3] (N = 187)	29.2% [23.1, 35.3] (N = 216)	45.2% [37.7, 52.7] (N = 168)

For all cells, N is the number of cases in the sample on which the estimate is based. Numbers in brackets show the 95 percent confidence interval for the estimate.

For rows 1 and 2, N is the total number of cases in the phase two database for each period, after eliminating: (1) cases that were not "public law" cases; and (2) cases for which there was insufficient information.

For rows 3 and 4, N is the subset of those cases for each period that yielded a decision on the merits in the court below. The "court below" is the last court that addressed the case before it reached the Supreme Court.

For rows 5–7, N is the subset of those cases for each period that yielded a decision on the merits in the Supreme Court.

federal statutes, treaties, customary international law, and federal constitutional law.[9] We documented the frequency with which lawyers and judges invoked and applied different types of law in different time periods. Wc also recorded a large volume of other information for every case in the phase two database. The phase two database enables one to derive a quantitative measurement of constitutionalization – that is, the extent to which constitutional law has displaced other sources of law as the dominant discourse in public law cases.

The preceding paragraph describes construction of the phase two database for the purpose of the article published in 2014. All of the data in Table A.2 for periods 1, 2, 3, 6, and 7 replicates data from the original article. To complete Table A.2, I excluded from Period Eight all cases in the initial phase two data decided after 1994 and recalculated figures for Period Eight based on that truncated data set. For Period Nine, I selected a random sample of 200 PG cases from the 1,546 PG cases included in the phase one database for that period. I reviewed all 200 cases on Westlaw. I did not examine private party arguments or lower court decisions. Accordingly, for period nine, the entry for those rows is "n.a." Preliminary analysis indicated that the Supreme Court reached a decision on the merits in 168 of those 200 cases. Analysis of those 168 decisions showed that the Court applied constitutional law in 91 cases; it applied statutes in 68 cases; it applied a treaty in 1 case; and I classified 8 cases as "other." (If the Court applied both constitutional law and a statute, I classified it as a case where the Court applied constitutional law.) The results of phase two analysis are presented in Table A.2 and in Figures 2.2 and 2.3.

Notes

INTRODUCTION

1. Ronald Reagan, Farewell Address to the Nation (Jan. 11, 1989), available at www.reaganlibrary.gov/archives/speech/farewell-address-nation.
2. *See* Cook Political Report, 2024 CPR House Race Ratings (Feb. 29, 2024), www.cookpolitical.com/ratings/house-race-ratings.
3. McDonald v. City of Chicago, 561 U.S. 742 (2010).
4. Obergefell v. Hodges, 576 U.S. 644 (2015).
5. Abraham Lincoln, First Inaugural Address (March 4, 1861) (quoted in FRIEDMAN (2009), at 6).
6. *See* Thayer (1893)
7. *See, e.g.*, O'Donnell (2016)
8. The V-Dem database is available at https://v-dem.net/data/the-v-dem-dataset/. The numbers in the text are taken from version 12 of the dataset, published in 2022. The codebook that accompanies the dataset explains the different variables. *See* Michael Coppedge et al., V-Dem Codebook, v12 (March 2022), available at www.v-dem.net/static/website/img/refs/codebookv12.pdf. Both the liberal democracy index and the participatory democracy index build on the electoral democracy index. The electoral democracy index measures the degree to which there is "electoral competition for the electorate's approval under circumstances when suffrage is extensive; political and civil society organizations can operate freely; [and] elections are clean and not marred by fraud or systematic irregularities." *Id.*, at 43. The liberal democracy index also incorporates variables to measure the degree to which law protects "individual and minority rights against the tyranny of the state and the tyranny of the majority." *Id.* at 44. The participatory index incorporates variables to measure the level of "active participation by citizens in all political processes, electoral and non-electoral." *Id.*
9. Repucci & Slipowitz (2021), at 10.
10. *Democracy Index 2016: Revenge of the "Deplorables,"* THE ECONOMIST, 2017, at 37, 44.
11. Pew Research Center, Public Trust in Government: 1958–2023, available at www.pewresearch.org/politics/2023/09/19/public-trust-in-government-1958-2023/.
12. *See id.*
13. *See* Jeffrey B. Lewis et al., *Voteview: Congressional Roll-Call Votes Database* (2024), https://voteview.com/.
14. Data in Table 0.1 is taken from the Voteview database, https://voteview.com/.
15. *See generally* BROWNSTEIN (2007).

16. Larry Kramer argues that the Court's 1958 decision in Cooper v. Aaron, 358 U.S. 1 (1958), solidified the principle of judicial supremacy, which establishes the Supreme Court as the dominant player in our constitutional system. *See* KRAMER, (2004). The Court went even further in City of Boerne v. Flores, 521 U.S. 507 (1997), claiming for itself an effective monopoly on the power of constitutional interpretation. *See* Chapter 1, pp. 19–23 for further elaboration of this point.
17. Reynolds v. Sims, 377 U.S. 533, 565 (1964).
18. *See* U.S. Const., Preamble (stating that "We the People … do ordain and establish this Constitution" in order to "promote the general Welfare, and secure the Blessings of Liberty to ourselves and our Posterity"). *See also* RAKOVE (1996), at 18 (noting that "the theory of popular sovereignty … was itself one of the great rallying points of the Federalist argument in 1787 and 1788").
19. This book does not address constitutional issues related to the division of power between Congress and the executive branch. That will be the subject of a subsequent volume.
20. V-Dem Institute, Democracy Report 2022: Autocratization Changing Nature?, available at https://v-dem.net/publications/democracy-reports/.
21. Ronald Reagan, Farewell Address to the Nation (Jan. 11, 1989).
22. Brown v. Bd. of Education, 347 U.S. 483 (1954) (Nos. 1, 2, 3, 4, 5), Brief for United States as Amicus Curiae, pp. 6–8, available at 1952 WL 82045.
23. KLARMAN (2004), at, 299. Justice Reed, who was probably the last Justice to agree to support Chief Justice Warren's opinion in *Brown* was also probably swayed by foreign policy considerations. *See* Barrett (2004), at 547.
24. *See* President Biden, National Security Strategy 8–9 (Oct. 2022).

1 A POLITICAL PROCESS THEORY FOR THE TWENTY-FIRST CENTURY

1. ELY (1980).
2. United States v. Carolene Products Co., 304 U.S. 144 (1938).
3. *See id.*, at 152, n.4.
4. ELY (1980), at 102.
5. *See id.*, Chapter 3.
6. *Id.*, at 87.
7. *Id.*, at 103.
8. *Id.*
9. *Id.*
10. *Carolene Products*, 304 U.S. at 152, n.4.
11. ELY (1980), at 12–13.
12. *Id.*, at 103.
13. BICKEL (1986).
14. Professor Friedman's comprehensive history of the counter-majoritarian difficulty highlights Bickel's influence on the subsequent development of constitutional theory. *See* Friedman (2002b); Friedman (1998).
15. BICKEL (1986), at 16–17.
16. FRIEDMAN (2009), at 9.
17. *Id.*, at 11.
18. *Id.*, at 9.
19. *See* Joseph Copeland, Favorable Views of Supreme Court Remain Near Historic Low (Aug. 8, 2024), www.pewresearch.org/short-reads/2024/08/08/favorable-views-of-supreme-court-remain-near-historic-low/.

20. Ely (1980), at 183.
21. *See generally* Waldron (2006).
22. *See*, e.g., The Federalist, No. 10 (James Madison).
23. There are currently twenty-five states that allow citizens to engage in direct democracy through some type of voter initiative or popular referendum. *See* National Conference of State Legislatures, Initiative and Referendum States, www.ncsl.org/elections-and-campaigns/initiative-and-referendum-states (last visited Sept. 14, 2024).
24. U.S. Const., art. I, sec. 2, cl. 1.
25. U.S. Const., art. II, sec. 1, cl. 1.
26. U.S. Const., art. I, sec. 3, cl. 1; amend. XVII.
27. *See*, e.g., Balkin & Siegel (2006).
28. *See* U.S. Const., amend I. *See also* Bhagwat (2020).
29. *See generally* Rakove (1996), at 203–43.
30. *Id.*, at 203 (quoting John Adams, *Thoughts on Government*).
31. *Id.*, at 205.
32. *See* Purcell (2000) (presenting a detailed defense of legislative primacy as a core constitutional principle).
33. Wilson (1885), at 11.
34. Roper v. Simmons, 543 U.S. 551, 616 (2005) (Scalia, J., dissenting) (internal quotations omitted).
35. Hurtado v. California, 110 U.S. 516, 535 (1884).
36. Bickel (1986), at 25.
37. Barnett (2011), at 66.] *See also* Solum (2013), at, 457; Whittington (1999).
38. *See* Solum (2013), at 499–524.
39. U.S. Const., art. II, sec. 1, cl. 5 (emphasis added).
40. Elliott v. Cruz, 137 A.3d 646 (Comm. Ct. Pa. 2016).
41. *Id.*, at 658.
42. Solum (2013), at 471.
43. *Id.*, at 472.
44. *See* Balkin (2011), at, 6–7, 349–52
45. *Id.*, at 6.
46. Professor Balkin says that when "standards apply to a situation, they are normally conclusive in deciding a legal question.... Principles, by contrast, are norms that, when relevant, are not conclusive but must be considered in reaching a decision." *Id.*, at 349.
47. *Id.*, at 28.
48. *Id.*, at 7.
49. Solum (2013), at 459.
50. *Id.*, at 460. *See also* Whittington (2013), at, 377–78
51. *See* Balkin (2011), at 41–49.
52. 554 U.S. 570 (2008).
53. Balkin (2011), at 349.
54. *Heller*, 554 U.S. at 599.
55. *Id.*, at 637 (Stevens, J., dissenting).
56. Whittington (2013), at 380.
57. *Heller*'s supporters contend that the Second Amendment protects a prepolitical, natural right. I agree that the right of self-defense is a natural right. However, governments have regulated the right of self-defense for as long as criminal law has existed. Nothing in the text of the Second Amendment suggests that it was designed to restrict the preexisting power of governments to regulate the right of self-defense.

58. *Heller*, 554 U.S. at 636.
59. *See generally* BARNETT (2016)
60. In some cases, the originalist effort to limit judicial discretion in the construction zone by applying the fixation thesis and the constraint principle to vague standards may encourage judges to hide their normative preferences behind a veil of historical analysis. In *Heller*, Justice Scalia cherry-picked historical materials that supported his normative policy preferences. His commitment to an originalist methodology led him to hide his normative preferences behind a pseudo-objective historical analysis.
61. *See* Solum (2024), at, 955–67
62. Marbury v. Madison, 5 U.S. 137 (1803). Although *Marbury* is often said to be the first case of judicial review, Professor Whittington has identified two earlier cases. *See* Keith E. Whittington, The Judicial Review of Congress Database, 1789–2022 (July 2022) (available at https://scholar.princeton.edu/kewhitt/judicial-review-congress-database).
63. Ware v. Hylton, 3 U.S. 199 (1796).
64. Professor Mark Tushnet is credited with coining the term "weak judicial review." *See* Tushnet (2003).
65. *See, e.g.*, GARDBAUM (2013), at, 25–36 DIXON (2023), at, 205–16
66. GARDBAUM (2013), at 26–27. *See also* Tushnet (2003), at 2786 ("[T]he mark of weak-form review is that ordinary legislative majorities can displace judicial interpretations of the constitution in the relatively short run.").
67. *See* Waldron (2006). As discussed previously, if the constitutional text is unambiguous, strong judicial review is not problematic. However, in litigated constitutional cases, the text is rarely unambiguous.
68. U.S. CONST., art. VI.
69. *See, e.g.*, Breard v. Greene, 523 U.S. 371, 376 (1998) (noting that when a federal "statute which is subsequent in time is inconsistent with a treaty, the statute to the extent of conflict renders the treaty null.").
70. Ware v. Hylton, 3 U.S. 199 (1796).
71. U.S. CONST. art. II, sec. 3.
72. *See* Swaine (2008) (discussing the President's constitutional duty to take care that treaties are faithfully executed).
73. *See generally* INTERNATIONAL LAW IN THE U.S. SUPREME COURT: CONTINUITY AND CHANGE (David L. Sloss, Michael D. Ramsey, and William S. Dodge eds., 2011).
74. United States v. Schooner Peggy, 5 U.S. 103 (1801).
75. *See, e.g.*, Hamdan v. Rumsfeld, 548 U.S. 557, 625–35 (2006) (applying the Geneva Conventions as an aid to interpreting a federal statute, and invalidating federal executive action that was inconsistent with the Geneva Conventions).
76. A different approach that has some of the virtues of weak judicial review is for the Court to decide the constitutional issue presented on the narrowest possible ground. *See, e.g.*, Dames & Moore v. Regan, 453 U.S. 654, 660 (1981) (referring to the "necessity to rest decision on the narrowest possible ground capable of deciding the case").
77. Ashwander v. Tennessee Valley Authority, 297 U.S. 288, 348 (1936) (Brandeis, J., concurring).
78. ELY (1980), at 76.
79. Landau & Dixon (2020), at 1317.
80. *Id.*, at 1325.
81. *See id.*, at 1363–70 (analyzing abusive judicial review in Venezuela).
82. 139 S. Ct. 2484 (2019).
83. Even Chief Justice Roberts, who wrote the majority opinion in *Rucho*, conceded that extreme partisan gerrymandering is "incompatible with democratic principles." *Rucho*, 139 S. Ct., at 2506.

84. Landau and Dixon (2020), at 1349.
85. 424 U.S. 1 (1976).
86. 570 U.S. 529 (2013).
87. *See id.*, at 560–66 (Ginsburg, J., dissenting).
88. *See, e.g.*, ATTANASIO (2018)
89. Professor Karlan makes a similar point. *See* Karlan (2012).
90. Solum (2024), at 917.
91. Lemley (2022).
92. *See generally* KRAMER (2004); TUSHNET (1999), at, 26–30
93. *See* KRAMER (2004).
94. *See id.* at 220–21 (discussing Cooper v. Aaron, 358 U.S. 1 (1958)). Professor Friedman contends that judicial supremacy had become accepted as a "cultural norm" by the late nineteenth century. *See* Friedman (2002a), at, 48–51. As explained in Chapter 2, I think the New Deal Court's commitment to deferential judicial review supports Professor Kramer's claim that judicial supremacy did not become fully entrenched until the 1950s.
95. *Cooper*, 358 U.S. at 4.
96. *See* James Madison, The Report of 1800 (Jan. 7, 1800) (contending that state governments have an independent duty to interpret the Constitution for themselves, and that states are bound only by the Constitution, not by [incorrect] federal interpretations of the Constitution).
97. *Cooper*, 358 U.S. at 18.
98. U.S. Const. art VI.
99. *See* KRAMER (2004), at 220–25.
100. *See* Chapter 2.
101. Lemley (2022), at 97 (emphasis in original).
102. 521 U.S. 507 (1997).
103. 494 U.S. 872 (1990).
104. 374 U.S. 398 (1963).
105. 406 U.S. 205 (1972).
106. *See Smith*, 494 U.S. at 907–921 (Blackmun, J., dissenting).
107. *Smith*, 494 U.S. 872 (1990). The Court later carved out an exception for laws that purposefully discriminate against a particular religious group. *See* Church of the Lukumi Babalu Aye v. City of Hialeah, 508 U.S. 520 (1993).
108. *See Smith*, 494 U.S. at 892–903 (O'Connor, J., concurring); *id.* at 907–09 (Blackmun, J., dissenting).
109. 384 U.S. 641 (1966).
110. 17 U.S. 316 (1819).
111. *Katzenbach*, 384 U.S. at 650 (quoting *McCulloch*, 17 U.S. at 421).
112. See generally Post and Siegel (2003); Tushnet (2009).
113. *See Boerne*, 521 U.S. at 529–36.
114. *See* Cox (1966).
115. *See Katzenbach*, 384 U.S. at 651 n.10 (arguing that Section 5 grants Congress authority to strengthen protection for Fourteenth Amendment rights, but not to "dilute equal protection and due process decisions of this Court").
116. *See* Post and Siegel (2003), at 1955–59.
117. *See Boerne*, 521 U.S. at 524 ("The power to interpret the Constitution … remains in the Judiciary.").
118. U.S. Const., amend XIV, sec. 5.
119. Frantz (1964), at, 1356

120. McConnell (1997), at 182
121. *Id.* (quoting Senator Oliver Morton, Cong. Globe, 42d Cong., 2d Sess. 525 (1872)).
122. *Boerne*, 521 U.S. at 529.
123. *Id.*
124. *See* Meese (1987) (defending a departmentalist approach to constitutional interpretation).
125. *See* Tushnet (2003), at 2782–83 (explaining why *Marbury* is best understood as a departmentalist decision).
126. In light of the modern Court's tendency to act in ways that are precisely the opposite of what Justice Stone recommended in *Carolene Products*, one scholar has called the Court the "Anti-*Carolene* Court." Stephanopoulos (2019).
127. *See, e.g.*, The Federalist, No. 15 (Alexander Hamilton).
128. The Court defended *Boerne* on federalism grounds. For reasons explained in Chapter 7, the federalism justification for *Boerne* is entirely unconvincing.
129. For a similar critique of a contemporaneous decision that also advanced judicial imperialism, see Fitzgerald (1999).
130. *See* Alexander & Schauer (1997); Alexander & Schauer (2000).
131. *See* TUSHNET (1999), at 26–30.
132. *See* CUSHMAN (1998).
133. 134 U.S. 1 (1890).
134. 298 U.S. 238 (1936) (applying strong judicial review to invalidate a federal statute on the grounds that it exceeded Congress's power under the Commerce Clause).
135. 298 U.S. 587 (1936) (applying the *Lochner* era doctrine of substantive due process to invalidate a state minimum wage law).
136. 300 U.S. 379 (1937) (upholding a state minimum wage law and expressly overruling two *Lochner* era decisions, including Morehead v. Tipaldo).
137. 301 U.S. 1 (1937) (upholding the National Labor Relations Act as a valid exercise of Congress's Commerce Power).
138. 347 U.S. 483 (1954).
139. 514 U.S. 549 (1995).
140. The Court arguably revived strong judicial review to enforce federalism-based limits on Congress three years earlier in New York v. United States, 505 U.S. 144 (1992).
141. As noted previously, I plan to write a second volume that will focus on the division of power between Congress and the executive branch.
142. DECLARATION OF INDEPENDENCE (U.S. 1776); *see also* Tsesis (2012).
143. *See* Introduction.
144. *See* Introduction.
145. U.S. Const., amend IX.
146. U.S. Const., amend X.
147. U.S. Const., art. IV, sec. 4. The Supreme Court has historically treated the Republican Form Clause as a nonjusticiable constitutional provision. *See, e.g.*, Colegrove v. Green, 328 U.S. 549, 556 (1946). Professor Ely argued persuasively that the Court's refusal to enforce that clause is rooted in a category mistake. *See* ELY (1980), at 118–19.
148. 424 U.S. 1 (1976).
149. 570 U.S. 529 (2013).
150. 139 S. Ct. 2484 (2019).
151. 377 U.S. 533 (1964).
152. *See, e.g.*, Shanor (2016).
153. *See* BENKLER, FARIS, AND ROBERTS (2018).
154. Red Lion Broadcasting Co. v. Federal Communications Comm'n, 395 U.S. 367 (1969).

155. In re Complaint of Syracuse Peace Council, 2 F.C.C.Rcd. 5043 (1987).
156. *See* Syracuse Peace Council v. F.C.C., 867 F.2d 654 (D.C. Cir. 1989) (affirming FCC decision); Syracuse Peace Council v. F.C.C., 493 U.S. 1019 (1990) (denying cert.).
157. *See* Leiter (2022); SUNSTEIN (1995), at, 53–92
158. 567 U.S. 709 (2012).
159. *See* Sloss (2021a).
160. *See* SUNSTEIN (1995), at xvi–xx (discussing the Madisonian First Amendment); *see also* SLOSS (2022), at 218–22 (comparing Madisonian and libertarian theories).
161. *See* Sloss (2014), at 1785–92.
162. *See* ELY (1980), at 135–79.
163. 570 U.S. 529 (2013) (weakening statutory protection for minority voting rights under the 1965 Voting Rights Act).
164. 551 U.S. 701 (2007) (invalidating local ordinance designed to reduce racial segregation in public school education).
165. 521 U.S. 507 (1997) (invalidating federal legislation designed to protect religious minorities).
166. *See* Chapter 6.
167. International Convention on the Elimination of All Forms of Racial Discrimination, *opened for signature* Dec. 21, 1965, S. EXEC. DOC. C, 95–2 (1978), 660 U.N.T.S. 195 (entered into force Jan. 4, 1969).
168. International Covenant on Civil and Political Rights, *opened for signature* Dec. 16, 1966, S. EXEC DOC. E, 95–2 (1978), 999 U.N.T.S. 171 (entered into force March 23, 1976).
169. *See* ELY (1980), at 43–72.
170. United States v. Carolene Products Co., 304 U.S. 144, 152 n.4 (1938).
171. The Senate consented to ratification of the ICCPR on April 2, 1992. 138 Cong. Rec. S4781–84 (1992).
172. *See* ICCPR, art. 17 (right to privacy); art. 23 (right to marry).
173. U.S. Const. art. VI, cl. 2.
174. *See generally* Sloss (1999).
175. *See* Chapter 5.
176. *See, e.g.*, Breard v. Greene, 523 U.S. 371, 376 (1998).
177. Wechsler (1954).
178. *See id.*
179. *See generally* FELDMAN & SULLIVAN (2019), at 135–40. *But see* Nat'l League of Cities v. Usery, 426 U.S. 833 (1976) (invalidating portions of the Fair Labor Standards Act on Tenth Amendment grounds) (*overruled by* Garcia v. San Antonio Metropolitan Transit Auth., 469 U.S. 528 (1985)).
180. To the best of my knowledge, Ely did not actually cite Wechsler's political safeguards article in any of his published writing, but there is little doubt that Ely approved of Wechsler's theory.
181. 514 U.S. 549 (1995).
182. *Id.*; United States v. Morrison, 529 U.S. 598 (2000).
183. *Morrison*, 529 U.S. 598; City of Boerne v. Flores, 521 U.S. 507 (1997).
184. Printz v. United States, 521 U.S. 898 (1997); New York v. United States, 505 U.S. 144 (1992).
185. Alden v. Maine, 527 U.S. 706 (1999); Seminole Tribe v. Florida, 517 U.S. 44 (1996).
186. The Federalist No. 48, at 309 (James Madison).
187. *See* Lemley (2022); Olson (2004).

188. Justice Souter made this point forcefully in his dissenting opinion in *Lopez*. *See* United States v. Lopez, 514 U.S. 549, 603–15 (1995) (Souter, J., dissenting).
189. *See* Sloss (2024).
190. *See* Fairman (1949).
191. *See, e.g.*, Benton v. Maryland, 395 U.S. 784, 807–09 (1969) (Harlan, J., dissenting); Duncan v. Louisiana, 391 U.S. 145, 171–83 (1968) (Harlan, J., dissenting); Malloy v. Hogan, 378 U.S. 1, 27–33 (1964) (Harlan, J., dissenting); Mapp v. Ohio, 367 U.S. 643, 678–86 (1961) (Harlan, J., dissenting).
192. *See* Ramos v. Louisiana, 140 S. Ct. 1390 (2020); Timbs v. Indiana, 139 S. Ct. 682 (2019); McDonald v. City of Chicago, 561 U.S. 742 (2010).
193. *See* Table 6.1, p. 146.
194. *See* Tables 6.1 and 7.2.
195. *See* Ackerman (2014), Ackerman (1998).
196. For a detailed statutory proposal along these lines, see the "Supreme Court Biennial Appointments and Term Limits Act of 2023," S.3096 (118th Cong.).

2 FOUR REVOLUTIONS IN CONSTITUTIONAL LAW

1. Much of the data in Figures 2.1 to 2.3 is taken from Sloss (2014). However, the data analysis in that article stopped at the end of the Rehnquist Court. For the purpose of this project, I relied on the Supreme Court database to update the analysis through the end of the October 2022 Supreme Court term. *See* Harold J. Spaeth, Lee Epstein, et al. 2023 Supreme Court Database, Version 2023 Release 1, http://supremecourtdatabase.org. Additional details related to data collection and data analysis are included in the Appendix.
2. Sloss (2014), at 1760.
3. For a comprehensive account of international law in the Supreme Court from the Founding until the early twenty-first century, see Sloss, Ramsey, and Dodge (2011).
4. Ely (1980), at 76.
5. 95 U.S. 714 (1878).
6. 95 U.S. 714 (1878).
7. *Id.* at 719–20.
8. *Id.* at 734.
9. *Id.* at 722.
10. *Id.*
11. *Id.* at 730 (quoting D'Arcy v. Ketchum, 52 U.S. 165, 176 (1851)).
12. *See* Sloss (2014), at 1762, n.17.
13. Scholars have argued that nineteenth-century courts applied customary international law as general common law, not federal common law. *See, e.g.*, Bradley & Goldsmith (1997). However, under the system derived from Swift v. Tyson, 41 U.S. 1 (1842), courts could not apply general common law to invalidate a state statute. In *Pennoyer*, Justice Field strongly implied that a state statute purporting to authorize jurisdiction in excess of territorial limits derived from international law would be invalid. Hence, Justice Field may have conceived of those territorial limits as something like federal common law, which does preempt conflicting state law. For further elaboration of this point, *see* Sloss (2014), at 1763, n. 18.
14. *See Pennoyer*, 95 U.S. at 716.
15. *See, e.g.*, Scott v. McNeal, 154 U.S. 34, 46 (1894). *See also* Lee & Sloss (2011), at 124, 151–52.
16. *See generally* Strauss (2010).

17. WILSON (1885), at 11.
18. 109 U.S. 3 (1883).
19. *See* Slaughter-House Cases, 83 U.S. 36 (1873); Barron v. Baltimore, 32 U.S. 243 (1833).
20. *See generally* SHUGERMAN (2012), at 123–43
21. Professor Keith Whittington has compiled a comprehensive database of cases where the Supreme Court exercised its power of judicial review to assess the constitutionality of federal statutes. *See* Keith E. Whittington, The Judicial Review of Congress Database, 1789–2022 (July 2022) (available at https://scholar.princeton.edu/kewhitt/judicial-review-congress-database). That database identifies only fifteen Supreme Court decisions before 1890 where the Court applied a provision in the Bill of Rights to invalidate a federal statute. Table A.1, in the Appendix, shows that the Court decided more than 7,000 cases before 1890.
22. *Id.* at 1760.
23. Under the "later-in-time rule," Congress has the power to enact statutes to override treaties as a matter of domestic law, even though the United States cannot unilaterally alter the content of international law. For a discussion of the evolution of the later-in-time rule in the nineteenth century, see Hollis (2011), at 73–76.
24. *See generally* Sloss (2014).
25. *See* Hulsebosch (2009).
26. *See* JAMES KENT, COMMENTARIES ON AMERICAN LAW (11th ed. 1867) (George Comstock ed.). Part I, on the law of nations, comprises about 200 pages in a 650-page treatise.
27. WHITTINGTON (2019).
28. *See* Whittington, The Judicial Review of Congress Database, 1789–2022 (July 2022)
29. 4 U.S. 12 (1800).
30. *See* WHITTINGTON (2019), at 73–74.
31. *Mossman*, 4 U.S. at 13.
32. *Id.*, at 14.
33. Mossman was one of numerous cases litigated during this period in which British creditors sued American debtors to recover debts incurred before the Revolutionary War. Repayment of those debts was generally suspended during the War. *See* GOEBEL (1971), at 741–56.
34. 110 U.S. 516 (1884).
35. *Id.* at 535.
36. Congressional Research Service, Table of Laws Held Unconstitutional in Whole or in Part by the Supreme Court. Professor Whittington's database does not include decisions invalidating state and local laws.
37. *See id.* This figure includes one case involving the Dormant Foreign Commerce Clause. Brown v. Maryland, 25 U.S. 419 (1827).
38. *See* CHEMERINSKY (2015), at 473–74
39. *See id.*, at 657–62.
40. WHITTINGTON (2019), at 62 (referring to the pre-Civil War period).
41. The Court decided several cases after World War I that effectively transferred foreign affairs powers from Congress to the President. *See* White (1999).
42. CHEMERINSKY (2015), at 255.
43. *See generally* BERNSTEIN (2012) (presenting a sympathetic account of *Lochner* jurisprudence).
44. *See* PURCELL (2000), at 46–51
45. *See generally* Johnson, Benjamin (2022).

46. Judiciary Act of 1925, Pub. L. No. 68–415, 43 Stat. 936.
47. *See* Johnson, Benjamin (2022).
48. *Id.* at 836 (emphasis added).
49. *See generally* SEGALL (2012).
50. PURCELL (2000), at 12.
51. *See, e.g.*, Hoke v. United States, 227 U.S. 308 (1913) (upholding the Mann Act); Champion v. Ames, 188 U.S. 321 (1903) (upholding a federal law that prohibited lotteries). *See also* Table 2.1.
52. *See, e.g.*, Carter v. Carter Coal Co., 298 U.S. 238 (1936) (invalidating portions of the Bituminous Coal Conservation Act of 1935); Schechter Poultry Corp. v. United States, 295 U.S. 495 (1935) (invalidating part of the National Industrial Recovery Act); United States v. E.C. Knight Co., 156 U.S. 1 (1895) (invalidating part of the Sherman Antitrust Act).
53. *See, e.g.*, Hammer v. Dagenhart, 247 U.S. 251 (1918) (holding that a federal tax on companies that shipped goods made by child labor was unconstitutional).
54. *See* United States v. Butler, 297 U.S. 1 (1936) (holding that subsidies for farmers in the Agricultural Adjustment Act of 1933 were unconstitutional); Bailey v. Drexel Furniture Co., 259 U.S. 20 (1922) (holding that a federal tax on goods produced by child labor was unconstitutional).
55. PURCELL (2000), at 12.
56. Slaughter-House Cases, 83 U.S. 36 (1873).
57. CHEMERINSKY (2015), at 644 (citing WRIGHT (1942), at 154).
58. 198 U.S. 45 (1905).
59. *See* Morehead v. New York ex rel. Tipaldo, 298 U.S. 587 (1936); Adkins v. Children's Hospital, 261 U.S. 525 (1923).
60. *See, e.g.*, Coppage v. Kansas, 236 U.S. 1 (1915).
61. *See* GRABER (2023), at xxx–xxxiv.
62. *Id.*, at xxxii–xxxiii.
63. U.S. Const., amend XIV.
64. Leading scholars have done extensive historical research to help clarify the original public meaning of the Fourteenth Amendment Privileges and Immunities Clause. *See, e.g.*, GREEN (2015); LASH (2014). Their accounts provide important insights, but they do not present evidence to contradict Professor Graber's claim that the authors of the Fourteenth Amendment expected that Congress, not the courts, would have primary responsibility for interpreting and implementing the Amendment. *See also* Ex parte Virginia, 100 U.S. 339, 345 (1879) (noting that the Civil War Amendments "were intended to be … enlargements of the power of Congress.… It is the power of Congress which has been enlarged.")
65. *See, e.g.*, Karlan (2012).
66. 300 U.S. 379 (1937).
67. 261 U.S. 525 (1923).
68. 301 U.S. 1 (1937).
69. 301 U.S. 548 (1937).
70. 301 U.S. 619 (1937).
71. *See* CUSHMAN (1998). Professor Cushman argues that the 1937 decisions upholding the validity of federal statutes were more evolutionary than revolutionary.
72. *See* PURCELL (2000), at 165–77 (discussing Justice Brandeis' concept of legislative primacy).
73. United States v. Carolene Products, 304 U.S. 144, 152 (1938).

74. Professor Whittington's database identifies three cases decided during this period where he claims that the Court invalidated statutes on federalism grounds. *See* United States v. Five Gambling Devices, 346 U.S. 441 (1953); Collins v. Handyman, 341 U.S. 651 (1951); Tenney v. Brandhove, 341 U.S. 367 (1951). I respectfully disagree. In all three cases, the Court practiced constitutional avoidance and decided the cases on statutory grounds. In *Five Gambling Devices*, the Court stated explicitly: "We do not intimate any ultimate answer to the appellees' constitutional questions." 346 U.S. at 446. *See also* Collins v. Hardyman, 341 U.S. at 662 ("We say nothing of the power of Congress to authorize such civil actions.... We think that Congress has not, in the narrow class of conspiracies defined by this statute, included the conspiracy charged here. We therefore reach no constitutional questions."); Tenney v. Brandhove, 341 U.S. at 372 ("We do not have to wrestle with far-reaching questions of constitutionality.... We think it is clear that the legislation on which this action is founded does not impose liability on the facts before us.")
75. Adamson v. California, 332 U.S. 46 (1947).
76. *See* Betts v. Brady, 316 U.S. 455 (1942) (Sixth Amendment right to state-funded counsel does not bind states); Palko v. Connecticut, 302 U.S. 319 (1937) (Fifth Amendment Double Jeopardy Clause does not bind states).
77. *See* Chicago, B & Q. R. Co. v. Chicago, 166 U.S. 226 (1897) (holding that the Takings Clause binds state governments); Gitlow v. New York, 268 U.S. 652 (1925) (holding that the Free Speech Clause binds state governments); Near v. Minnesota, 283 U.S. 697 (1931) (holding that freedom of the press binds the states); Powell v. Alabama, 287 U.S. 45 (1932) (holding that the Sixth Amendment right to counsel binds the states).
78. De Jonge v. Oregon, 299 U.S. 353 (1937).
79. Cantwell v. Connecticut, 310 U.S. 296 (1940).
80. Everson v. Bd. of Educ., 330 U.S. 1 (1947).
81. Wolf v. Colorado, 338 U.S. 25 (1949).
82. In re Oliver, 333 U.S. 257 (1948).
83. 316 U.S. 535 (1942) (protecting the right to procreate).
84. 319 U.S. 624 (1943) (protecting freedom of opinion). The Court treated *Barnette* as a First Amendment case, but the First Amendment does not explicitly mention freedom of thought or freedom of opinion. Professors Feldman and Sullivan treat *Barnette* as an example of the right not to speak, which they acknowledge is not separately enumerated in the First Amendment. *See* FELDMAN AND SULLIVAN (2019), at 1390–93. International human rights law treats freedom of opinion as a distinct right, separate from both free speech and freedom of religion. *See* Sloss & Sandholtz (2019), at 1215.
85. Griswold v. Connecticut, 381 U.S. 479 (1965), is generally cited as the foundation of modern substantive due process doctrine. In his opinion for the Court in *Griswold*, Justice Douglas cited both *Barnette* and *Skinner* as key precedents. *See Griswold*, 381 U.S. at 483, 485.
86. *See* Sloss and Sandholtz (2019), at 1214–20. *Everson* held that the Establishment Clause binds the states. That Clause does not qualify as a fundamental human right because the UDHR does not include any provision that is analogous to the Establishment Clause. *See* Chapter 7.
87. *See id.* at 1189–90 (explaining how we constructed the list of rights).
88. *See id.* at 1205 (Fig. 9). *See also id.* at 1211–32 (presenting a more detailed explanation). We classified rights in four categories: exclusive state control, state primacy, federal primacy, and exclusive federal control. *See id.* at 1205. Clearly, the distinction between "state primacy" and "federal primacy," both of which involve overlapping state and federal regulatory authority, involves some judgment calls. We explain and defend our judgment calls in the article.

89. *See id.*, at 1211–14.
90. Pub. L. No. 74–721, 49 Stat. 620 (Aug. 14, 1935).
91. Pub. L. No. 74–198, 49 Stat. 449 (July 5, 1935).
92. Pub. L. No. 75–412, 50 Stat. 888 (Sept. 1, 1937).
93. Pub. L. No. 75–718, 52 Stat. 1060 (June 25, 1938).
94. *See* Sloss and Sandholtz (2019), at 1211–14.
95. *See* United States v. Darby, 312 U.S. 100 (1941) (upholding the validity of the FLSA); NLRB v. Jones & Laughlin Steel Corp., 301 U.S. 1 (1937) (upholding the validity of the NLRA); Steward Machine Co. v. Davis, 301 U.S. 548 (1937) (upholding the validity of Title IX of the Social Security Act); Helvering v. Davis, 301 U.S. 619 (1937) (upholding the validity of Titles II and VIII of the Social Security Act).
96. 109 U.S. 3 (1883) (adopting a narrow construction of the scope of Congress's power under Section 5 of the Fourteenth Amendment).
97. During this period, the Court generally construed the Fourteenth Amendment to protect a narrow class of fundamental rights – those for which it could be said that "neither liberty nor justice would exist if they were sacrificed." Palko v. Connecticut, 302 U.S. 319, 326 (1937). Several of the rights protected under the NLRA and the FLSA arguably meet this standard because they are included in Articles 23 and 24 of the UDHR.
98. *See, e.g.*, Post & Siegel (2003). *See also* Chapter 1.
99. 304 U.S. 64 (1938).
100. *See* PURCELL (2000), at 3 ("Brandeis wrote *Erie* not only to terminate the 'federal general common law' but also to cabin more generally the lawmaking powers of the national courts").
101. Monaghan (1975).
102. Reynolds v. Sims, 377 U.S. 533, 565 (1964).
103. *See* ELY (1980), at 116–25.
104. 424 U.S. 1 (1976).
105. 358 U.S. 1 (1958).
106. *See* Chapter 1.
107. *See* Wechsler (1954).
108. In Oregon v. Mitchell, 400 U.S. 112 (1970), the Court invalidated an amendment to the Voting Rights Act that granted eighteen-year-olds a right to vote in state and local elections. Article I, sec. 4 of the Constitution empowers Congress to make laws governing elections for Congress, but the Court said that Congress exceeded its power by prescribing a minimum voting age for state and local elections. The Twenty-Sixth Amendment, ratified in 1971, reversed the result of Oregon v. Mitchell by establishing that eighteen-year-olds have a constitutional right to vote.
109. *See, e.g.*, Loving v. Virginia, 388 U.S. 1 (1967) (invalidating state law that prohibited interracial marriage); Brown v. Bd. of Education, 347 U.S. 483 (1954) (invalidating state laws that called for racial segregation in public schools); Bolling v. Sharpe, 347 U.S. 497 (1954) (invalidating D.C. law on racial segregation in public schools).
110. *See, e.g.*, Brandenburg v. Ohio, 395 U.S. 444 (1969).
111. Griswold v. Connecticut, 381 U.S. 479 (1965).
112. *See, e.g.*, Miranda v. Arizona, 384 U.S. 436 (1966) (strengthening the Fifth Amendment privilege against self-incrimination); Gideon v. Wainwright, 372 U.S. 335 (1963) (guaranteeing the right to appointed counsel for indigent defendants under the Sixth Amendment); Mapp v. Ohio, 367 U.S. 643 (1961) (holding that the Fourth Amendment exclusionary rule binds the states).

113. *See* Ackerman (2018).
114. *See* Cox (1966).
115. *See* Sloss (2016), at 240–45
116. *See id.* at 245–48 (explaining why the Court chose not to cite international human rights law explicitly in *Brown* and *Bolling*).
117. *But see* Kennedy v. Mendoza-Martinez, 372 U.S. 144, 161 n.16 (1963) (citing the UDHR in an opinion holding that federal statutes that deprived Americans of US citizenship were unconstitutional).
118. Sloss and Sandholtz (2019), at 1185–86.
119. *See id.* at 1234–36.
120. Dobbs v. Jackson Women's Health Org., 142 S. Ct. 2228 (2022).
121. Many people believe that a woman's right to choose to have an abortion is a fundamental human right. Whether that right is protected under international human rights law is debatable. *See* Sloss (2024), at 148–51. Regardless, the right to have an abortion is not one of the sixty-eight rights included in our analysis because it is not listed explicitly in the UDHR. In contrast, the right to privacy is specifically enumerated in the UDHR.
122. *See* Tushnet (2009), at 498–99; *see also* Cox (1966), at 94–108.
123. Pub. L. No. 89–110, 79 Stat. 437 (Aug. 6, 1965).
124. Pub. L. No. 88–352, 78 Stat. 243 (July 2, 1964).
125. Pub. L. No. 90–284, 82 Stat. 81 (Apr. 11, 1968).
126. Pub. L. No. 84–880, 70 Stat. 815 (Aug. 1, 1956).
127. Pub. L. No. 89–97, 79 Stat. 286 (July 30, 1965).
128. Pub. L. No. 91–596, 84 Stat. 1590 (Dec. 29, 1970).
129. *See* Sloss and Sandholtz (2019), at 1224–28.
130. *See* Dean (2001), at 1–12; Hodder-Williams (1980), at 33–45
131. Martin-Quinn scores for Justices are available at http://mqscores.wustl.edu/measures.php. They provide a mean score for every term for every Justice. For example, Justice Byron White served for thirty-two years. He is assigned thirty-two separate scores, one for each term. I computed lifetime scores for individual Justices by using the mean of that Justice's scores for each term. A higher positive score is more conservative. A higher negative score is more liberal. Three liberals left the Court in Nixon's first term: Earl Warren (-1.26), Hugo Black (-1.76), and Abe Fortas (-1.32). President Nixon replaced them with three conservatives: Warren Burger (1.89), William Rehnquist (4.17) (as Associate Justice), and Lewis Powell (0.97). He also replaced John Marshall Harlan (1.62) with Harry Blackmun (-0.03), which moved the Court slightly in the other direction, but the overall trend was quite conservative.
132. *See* Wechsler (1954).
133. National League of Cities v. Usery, 426 U.S. 833 (1976).
134. 469 U.S. 528 (1985).
135. Benton v. Maryland, 395 U.S. 784 (1969).
136. Schilb v. Kuebel, 404 U.S. 357 (1971).
137. 561 U.S. 742 (2010) (incorporating the second Amendment).
138. *See* Frontiero v. Richardson, 411 U.S. 677 (1973) and Reed v. Reed, 404 U.S. 71 (1971) (establishing heightened scrutiny for Equal Protection claims under the Fourteenth Amendment). *See also* Title IX of the Education Amendments Act of 1972, Pub L. No. 92–318, 86 Stat. 235, 373 (June 23, 1972) (prohibiting discrimination against women in federally funded higher education programs). Although the Court decided Roe v. Wade under the Due Process Clause, that decision also made a significant contribution to gender equality.

139. Education for All Handicapped Children Act of 1975, Pub. L. No. 94–142, 89 Stat. 773 (Nov. 29, 1975) (providing federal protection for the right to free elementary education, which is protected under Article 26 of the UDHR).
140. *See* Sloss & Sandholtz (2019), at 1234–36.
141. Immigration and Naturalization Service v. Chadha, 462 U.S. 919 (1983).
142. *Id.*, at 1002 (White, J., dissenting).
143. *See* Monroe v. Pape, 365 U.S. 167 (1961) (opening the door for civil plaintiffs to bring claims against state and local government officers under section 1983); Brown v. Allen, 344 U.S. 443 (1953) (expanding opportunities for state prisoners to bring federal habeas claims to challenge their convictions and/or sentences).
144. *See generally* HUQ (2021).
145. *See* Anderson v. Creighton, 483 U.S. 635 (1987); Harlow v. Fitzgerald, 457 U.S. 800 (1982); Butz v. Economou, 438 U.S. 478 (1978); Scheur v. Rhodes, 416 U.S. 232 (1974). *See also* FALLON ET AL. (2015), at 1030–54
146. 428 U.S. 465 (1976) (holding that an unlawful search that violated the Fourth Amendment does not provide grounds for a state prisoner to obtain federal habeas relief).
147. 433 U.S. 72 (1977) (establishing a "cause and prejudice" standard to avoid procedural default for claims that were not adequately raised in state court proceedings).
148. 489 U.S. 288 (1989) (holding that new constitutional rules do not apply retroactively on collateral review).
149. 367 U.S. 643 (1961).
150. 468 U.S. 897 (1984).
151. *See* LAFAVE ET AL. (2009), §3.1(c)
152. 384 U.S. 436 (1966).
153. 470 U.S. 298 (1985).
154. HUQ (2021), at 118. *See also* LAFAVE ET AL. (2009), §9.5(a).
155. *See* Chapter 1 for an explanation of the term "antidemocratic judicial review."
156. 424 U.S. 1 (1976).
157. *See id.* at 48–49 (stating that "the concept that government may restrict the speech of some elements of our society in order to enhance the relative voice of others is wholly foreign to the First Amendment").
158. In re Complaint of Syracuse Peace Council, 2 F.C.C.Rcd. 5043 (1987).
159. Red Lion Broadcasting Co. v. Federal Communications Comm'n, 395 U.S. 367 (1969).
160. *See* Syracuse Peace Council v. FCC, 867 F.2d 654 (D.C. Cir. 1989) (affirming FCC decision); Syracuse Peace Council v. F.C.C., 493 U.S. 1019 (1990) (denying cert.).
161. *See* McGinnis (2009), at 411–12.
162. Jeffrey Rosen, *Packing the Courts* (New York Times, May 10, 2013) (quoting AVERY AND MCLAUGHLIN (2013).
163. NOAH FELDMAN, TAKEOVER: HOW A CONSERVATIVE STUDENT CLUB CAPTURED THE SUPREME COURT (audiobook).
164. 514 U.S. 549 (1995).
165. 505 U.S. 144 (1992).
166. United States v. Morrison, 529 U.S. 598 (2000); *Lopez*, 514 U.S. 549.
167. *Morrison*, 529 U.S. 598; City of Boerne v. Flores, 521 U.S. 507 (1997).
168. Printz v. United States, 521 U.S. 898 (1997).
169. *See* Alden v. Maine, 527 U.S. 706 (1999); Seminole Tribe v. Florida, 517 U.S. 44 (1996).
170. New York State Rifle and Pistol Ass'n. v. Bruen, 142 S. Ct. 2111 (2022); McDonald v. City of Chicago, 561 U.S. 742 (2010).

171. Obergefell v. Hodges, 576 U.S. 644 (2015).
172. Parents Involved in Community Schools v. Seattle School Dist., 551 U.S. 701 (2007).
173. Landau & Dixon (2020), at 1325.
174. 530 U.S. 567 (2000).
175. 570 U.S. 529 (2013).
176. 139 S. Ct. 2484 (2019).
177. 558 U.S. 310 (2010).
178. Hasen (2025), at 1698.
179. *See, e.g.*, MEIKLEJOHN (1948).
180. *See, e.g.*, Shanor (2016).
181. 567 U.S. 709 (2012).
182. *See generally*, HOWARD (2020).
183. National Federation of Independent Business v. Sebelius, 567 U.S. 519 (2012).
184. West Virginia v. Environmental Protection Agency, 597 U.S. 697 (2022).
185. The Federalist No. 48, at 309 (James Madison). Madison made this claim about legislatures, but it applies today to the Supreme Court.
186. Lemley (2022), at 97.
187. 144 S. Ct. 2312 (2024).
188. *See* Just Security Podcast, Presidential Immunity after Trump v. United States (July 3, 2024).
189. *See* Historians' Amicus Brief in Trump v. United States.
190. Trump v. Anderson, 601 U.S. 100 (2024).
191. *See* Trump v. Anderson, No. 23–719, Brief of Constitutional Law Professor Mark A. Graber as Amicus Curiae in Support of Respondent, 2024 WL 513704.
192. Johnson v. Louisiana, 406 U.S. 399, 400 (1972) (Marshall, J., dissenting).

3 ELECTIONS

1. Issacharoff & Pildes (1998), at 646.
2. *See* Atkinson & Ganz (2024).
3. *Id.*, at 107.
4. *Id.*, at 116.
5. *See* Kleinfeld (2023), at 1.
6. *See id.*, at 19–22.
7. *Id.*, at 3.
8. Jeffrey M. Jones, Independent Party ID Tied for High, Democratic ID at New Low (Jan. 12, 2024).
9. *See* Foley (2024).
10. *See* Kleinfeld (2023), at 1–3, 40–43.
11. Atkinson & Ganz (2024), at 121.
12. *See id.*, at 120. *See also* Kleinfeld (2023), at 17 ("Polarization among the American public was occurring, but it was largely among the politically engaged public, which was not the majority.").
13. Atkinson and Ganz (2024), at 112 (quoting Pew Research report).
14. John Adams, *Thoughts on Government* (quoted in RAKOVE (1996), at 203). As noted in Chapter 1, this quotation is associated with the democratic concept of representation, as opposed to the republican concept.
15. Atkinson and Ganz (2024), at 125.

16. *See generally* Brownstein (2007).
17. Colegrove v. Green, 328 U.S. 549 (1946).
18. Baker v. Carr, 369 U.S. 186 (1962).
19. McKay (1963), at 706–10.
20. Wesberry v. Sanders, 376 U.S. 1 (1964).
21. Reynolds v. Sims, 377 U.S. 533 (1964).
22. U.S. Const. art. I, sec. 2, cl. 1.
23. *Wesberry*, 376 U.S. at 14 (emphasis added).
24. *Id.* at 18.
25. *See* Karlan (2005), at 1338.
26. Sims v. Frink, 208 F. Supp. 431 (M.D. Ala. 1962).
27. Reynolds v. Sims, 377 U.S. 533, 545 (1964).
28. *Id.* at 560 (quoting *Wesberry*).
29. *Id.* at 568.
30. *Id.*, at 577.
31. *Id.*, at 565 (emphasis added).
32. *See* Sunstein (1995), at 94–101.
33. *See* Charles (2005), at 1113–30.
34. *Id.*, at 1121.
35. The Federalist No. 10, at 122–28 (James Madison).
36. *Id.*, at 123.
37. *Reynolds*, at 558 (quoting Gray v. Sanders, 372 U.S. 368, 379–80 (1963)).
38. *Id.* at 564 n. 41 (quoting MacDougall v. Green, 335 U.S. at 281, 288, 290 (1948)).
39. U.S. Const., amend XV.
40. U.S. Const., amend XIX.
41. U.S. Const., amend XXIII.
42. U.S. Const., amend XXVI.
43. U.S. Const., amend XXIV.
44. U.S. Const., amend XVII.
45. 424 U.S. 1 (1976).
46. 530 U.S. 567 (2000).
47. 570 U.S. 529 (2013).
48. 139 S. Ct. 2484 (2019).
49. Federal Election Campaign Act Amendments of 1974, Pub. L. No. 93–443, 88 Stat. 1263 (Oct. 15, 1974).
50. *See* Issacharoff et al. (2016), at 383–85
51. 424 U.S. 1 (1976).
52. *Id.*, at 39–51.
53. *Id.*, at 51–54.
54. *Id.*, at 54–59.
55. *Id.*, at 25–26.
56. *Id.*, at 25–26.
57. *Id.*, at 48–49.
58. *Reynolds*, 377 U.S. at 565.
59. *Buckley*, 424 U.S. at 48–49.
60. *See id.*, at 257–66 (White, J., concurring in part and dissenting in part).
61. Justice White noted in passing that the limit on expenditure of personal or family wealth "tends to equalize access to the political arena." *Id.*, at 266. Justice Marshall, who was not on the Court when *Reynolds* was decided, sounded a similar theme regarding personal

and family wealth. *See id.*, at 286–90 (Marshall, J., concurring in part and dissenting in part). However, Marshall agreed with the majority that the other expenditure restrictions were unconstitutional. He dissented only with respect to the family wealth restriction.

62. *See* Karlan (2012), at 18–25.
63. 383 U.S. 301 (1966).
64. 384 U.S. 641 (1966).
65. *See* Karlan (2012), at 22–25; *see also* Cox (1966).
66. *Buckley*, 424 U.S. at 15.
67. *Id.*, at 39.
68. *Id.*, at 262 (White, J.).
69. *See id.*, at 16 (stating that "the dependence of a communication on the expenditure of money" does not "introduce a nonspeech element or … reduce the exacting scrutiny required by the First Amendment").
70. *See* Southworth (2023), at 4 (noting that "under the leadership of Chief Justice John Roberts, the Court has invalidated or severely limited nearly every campaign finance restriction it has considered").
71. National Conference of State Legislatures, State Primary Election Types.
72. California Democratic Party v. Jones, 530 U.S. 567, 570 (2000).
73. Pildes (2004), at 103.
74. 530 U.S. 567 (2000).
75. Pildes (2004), at 103, n.304.
76. *Jones*, 530 U.S. at 586.
77. *See* The Federalist No. 10, at 122–28 (James Madison).
78. *Jones*, 530 U.S. at 582.
79. Pildes (2004), at 103, n.306.
80. *Jones*, 530 U.S. at 582.
81. The First Amendment protects "the right of the people peaceably to assemble." Freedom of assembly is a distinct right that involves physical gatherings. The Court did not recognize a First Amendment right to freedom of association until 1958, when it decided NAACP v. Alabama, 357 U.S. 449 (1958).
82. *See* Ely (1980), at 77–88.
83. Pildes (2004), at 101–02.
84. *Id.*, at 44.
85. *See generally* Rosenbluth & Shapiro (2018).
86. Pildes (2004), at 44.
87. *See* Pildes (2011).
88. 552 U.S. 442 (2008).
89. *See id.*, at 447–48.
90. *Id.*, at 444.
91. 570 U.S. 529 (2013).
92. 42 U.S.C. § 1973(a). This particular language results from the 1982 amendment to the Act.
93. South Carolina v. Katzenbach, 383 U.S. 301, 318–19 (1966).
94. *Shelby County*, 570 U.S. at 538.
95. The John R. Lewis Voting Rights Advancement Act of 2023 would establish a detailed coverage formula to determine which states and political subdivisions are subject to pre-clearance, but the bill has not made it out of the House Judiciary Committee. *See* Chapter 8.
96. *Katzenbach*, 383 U.S. 301 (1966).
97. *Id.*, at 326 (quoting McCulloch v. Maryland, 17 U.S. 316, 421 (1819)).

98. *Id.*, at 324.
99. *See, e.g.*, City of Rome v. United States, 446 U.S. 156 (1980); Lopez v. Monterey County, 525 U.S. 266 (1999).
100. Fannie Lou Hamer, Rosa Parks, and Coretta Scott King Voting Rights Act Reauthorization and Amendments Act of 2006, Pub. L. No. 109–246, 120 Stat. 577 (July 27, 2006).
101. *Shelby County*, 570 U.S. at 555.
102. *Id.*, at 542.
103. *Katzenbach*, 383 U.S. at 328–29.
104. *See* Northwest Austin Municipal Util. Dist. No. One v. Holder, 557 U.S. 193 (2009). *See also Shelby County*, 570 U.S. at 588 (Ginsburg, J., dissenting). ("In today's decision, the Court ratchets up what was pure dictum in *Northwest Austin*, attributing breadth to the equal sovereignty principle in flat contradiction of *Katzenbach*.")
105. U.S. Const., amend XV.
106. McConnell (1997).
107. City of Boerne v. Flores, 521 U.S. 507 (1997).
108. *See* McConnell (1997), at 169–83; GRABER (2023), at xlvi-xlvii. *See also* Chapter 1, (discussing *Boerne*).
109. *Shelby County*, 570 U.S. at 587 (Ginsburg, J., dissenting).
110. *Id.*, at 553 (majority opinion).
111. Pub. L. No. 109–246, sec. 2(b)(5), 120 Stat. 578.
112. *Id.*, sec. 2(b)(7).
113. *Shelby County*, 570 U.S. at 550–55.
114. Persily (2007), at 192–93.
115. *See id.*, at 193–94.
116. *Id.*, at 195.
117. Kevin Morris and Coryn Grange, Growing Racial Disparities in Voter Turnout, 2008–2022, p. 17 (Brennan Center for Justice, March 2024).
118. *Id.*, at 17.
119. *Id.*, at 21.
120. Rucho v. Common Cause, 139 S. Ct. 2484 (2019).
121. 478 U.S. 109 (1986).
122. *Id.*, at 144 (O'Connor, J., concurring in the judgment).
123. 541 U.S. 287 (2004).
124. *See id.*, at 277–91 (Scalia, J., plurality opinion).
125. Common Cause v. Rucho, 318 F.Supp.3d 777, 803–08 (MD NC 2018).
126. *Id.* at 808.
127. *Id.* at 810.
128. Rucho v. Common Cause, 139 S. Ct. at 2518 (Kagan, J., dissenting).
129. *See* KEENA ET AL. (2021), at 20–43.
130. Data about the actual number of votes cast for Democratic and Republican candidates in each district is taken from Ballotpedia, https://ballotpedia.org/United_States_House_of_Representatives_elections_in_North_Carolina,_2016. The numbers in the text are my calculations based on that data.
131. Wesberry v. Sanders, 376 U.S. 1, 10 (1964).
132. *Rucho*, 139 S. Ct., at 2502–03.
133. Federalist No. 10 (Madison).
134. *Id.*
135. Kang (2017), at 354.

136. *Rucho*, 139 S. Ct. at 2511 (Kagan, J., dissenting) (quoting James Madison, 4 Annals of Cong. 934 (1794)).
137. Arizona State Legislature v. Arizona Independent Redistricting Comm'n, 576 U.S. 787, 824 (2015).
138. U.S. Const. art. I, sec. 4, cl. 1.
139. *Rucho*, 139 S. Ct. at 2497.
140. *See id.*, at 2494–96.
141. Reynolds v. Sims, 377 U.S. 533 (1964).
142. *Rucho*, 139 S. Ct. at 2512–13 (Kagan, J., dissenting).
143. *Id.* at 2513 (Kagan, J., dissenting).
144. *Id.* at 2498 (majority opinion).
145. *See id.*, at 2498–2502.
146. *See, e.g., Rucho*, 139 S. Ct. at 2516 (Kagan, J., dissenting) (advocating a three-part test that combines intent and effects); Davis v. Bandemer, 478 U.S. 109, 127 (1986) (White, J.) (saying that plaintiffs must "prove both intentional discrimination … and an actual discriminatory effect"); *id.*, at 161 (Powell, J., concurring and dissenting) (same).
147. *See, e.g.*, League of United Latin American Citizens v. Perry, 548 U.S. 399, 410–13 (2006) (describing the Republican effort to undo a pro-Democratic bias that was created when the Democratic Party controlled both Houses of the Texas legislature and the governorship).
148. *See* HASEN (2020), at 136–37.
149. *See* Johnson, Kevin (2022), at 3 ("The U.S. is the only country in the world that elects its election officials, and one of very few to allow high-ranking party members to lead election administration.").
150. Ben Kamisar, Almost a Third of Americans Still Believe the 2020 Election Result was Fraudulent (June 20, 2023).
151. Johnson, Kevin (2022), at 19.
152. ELY (1980), at 183.
153. The proposal for a national popular vote compact is a potentially promising idea for reforming Presidential elections that is broadly compatible with the main arguments in this book. *See* KOZA ET AL. (2024).
154. *See especially* Foley (2024) and Pildes (2024).
155. See Ballotpedia, States with Initiative or Referendum, https://ballotpedia.org/States_with_initiative_or_referendum.
156. ELY (1980), at 76.
157. *See* Foley (2018), at 1139–50.
158. *See id. See also* Chapter 8.
159. Pildes (2024), at 168.
160. *See* Cook Political Report, 2024 CPR House Race Ratings (June 14, 2024).
161. For comparison, Michigan has a total of thirteen House seats. It uses an independent commission for redistricting, which tends to maximize the number of competitive seats. Cook Political Report includes four Michigan House seats in its list of competitive races, including two "tossups," one that "leans Republican," and one that is "likely Democrat." *See id.*
162. Pildes (2024), at 167.
163. *Id.*
164. Brennan Center for Justice, Who Controlled Redistricting in Every State? (Oct. 5, 2022).
165. Cook Political Report (June 14, 2024). For Table 3.1, I counted a seat as "competitive" if Cook says that it "leans" Republican or Democratic, but not if Cook classifies it as "likely Republican" or "likely Democrat."

166. *See* Brennan Center Report, *supra* note 165 (identifying Arizona, California, Colorado, and Michigan as states with independent commissions, and identifying Hawaii, Idaho, Montana, New Jersey, and Washington as states with political commissions).
167. *See* Common Cause, Charge Report: Community Redistricting Report Card (Oct. 13, 2023).
168. The six states with only one Representative in the House are Alaska, Delaware, North Dakota, South Dakota, Vermont, and Wyoming. Of those six, Alaska is the only one with a competitive seat because Alaska uses an all-candidate primary followed by instant runoff voting.
169. Reynolds v. Sims, 377 U.S. 533, 565 (1964).
170. As of this writing, there is significant conservative opposition to RCV. In the first half of 2024, five Republican-dominated states banned RCV. *See* https://pluribusnews.com/news-and-events/ranked-choice-voting-suffers-red-state-backlash/. Since RCV empowers voters, and reduces the power of political parties, the opposition to RCV is best understood as an effort by political parties to maintain their power over the electoral process.
171. *See* Foley (2024), at 1767–70.
172. *See id*; *see also* Atkinson and Ganz (2024), at 137–41.
173. *See* Nonpartisan Top Four Primary Election, www.elections.alaska.gov/election-information/#RankedChoice.
174. *See* Atkinson, Foley & Ganz (2024), at 1659–62 (explaining instant runoff voting).
175. *See* RCV Detailed Report, available at www.elections.alaska.gov/results/22GENR/US%20SEN.pdf.
176. See Atkinson, Foley, & Ganz (2024), at 1673–77.
177. *See* National Conference of State Legislatures, State Primary Election Types.
178. The results of the Wyoming election are available at https://sos.wyo.gov/Elections/Docs/2022/2022PrimaryResults.aspx. Harriet Hageman received more votes in the Republican primary (113,000) than the combined total of Cheney votes in the primary (49,000) and Democratic votes in the general election (47,000). Given these figures, if Wyoming used IRV, Hageman might well have won in the first round of IRV with a majority of all votes cast.
179. *See* Pildes (2024), at 175–76.
180. Some variants of RCV are better than others in terms of promoting the election of candidates whose views align with the median voter. For more on this point, *see* pp. 85–86.
181. *See* National Conference of State Legislatures, State Primary Election Types.
182. *See id.*
183. Pildes (2024), at 174.
184. One could reasonably argue that the rule should also be extended to elections for local offices, but I will not address that issue here.
185. Pildes (2024), at 177.
186. Washington Post Editorial Board, Put Ranked-Choice Voting at the Top of Your List (Oct. 3, 2024).
187. Atkinson, Foley, & Ganz (2024), at 1658.
188. *Id.* at 1655.
189. Foley (2024), at 1788.
190. *Id.*, at 1788–95.
191. *See id.*
192. 384 U.S. 436 (1966).
193. *See* U.S. Const., art. I, sec. 4, cl. 1.
194. Foley (2024).

4 ELECTION-RELATED MISINFORMATION

1. LEVITSKY and ZIBLATT (2018), at 9. *See also* GINSBURG and HUQ (2018).
2. *See* LEVITSKY & ZIBLATT (2018), at 60–67.
3. *See* Final Report: Select Committee to Investigate the January 6th Attack on the United States Capitol, Dec. 22, 2022 (117th Cong., Second Sess., H. Rep. 117–663) [hereinafter, "Jan. 6 Report"].
4. *See id.*, at 195–233.
5. Hasen (2025), at 1711.
6. Jennifer Agiesta and Ariel Edwards-Levy, CNN Poll: Percentage of Republicans Who Think Biden's 2020 Win was Illegitimate Ticks Back Up Near 70% (Aug. 3, 2023).
7. Torres-Spelliscy (2022), at 1733.
8. *See* https://coalitionfornationalfactchecking.org/#draft.
9. *See* FELDMAN AND SULLIVAN (2019), at 935–38.
10. See Jankowicz (2024); Norden, Panditharatne, & Harris (2024).
11. *See, e.g.*, Adams et al. (2022).
12. *See* BENKLER, FARIS, & ROBERTS (2018).
13. *See* Miller (2021).
14. *See* Pearlstein (2023).
15. *See* Norton (2023).
16. *See* SLOSS (2022), at 218–22.
17. *See, e.g.*, SCHAUER (1982).
18. *See* Netanel (2023), at 541–46.
19. *Id.*, at 546.
20. Arendt (1967).
21. The term is taken from BENKLER ET AL. (2018).
22. International Covenant on Civil and Political Rights, art. 19, *adopted* Dec. 19, 1966, 999 U.N.T.S. 171 (entered into force Mar. 23, 1976) [hereinafter, ICCPR].
23. Pub. L. No. 73–416, 48 Stat. 1064 (June 19, 1934).
24. Witt (2023), at 718.
25. *Id.* at 725.
26. 47 U.S.C. Sec. 309(a).
27. Bhagwat (2023), at 43.
28. *Id.*, at 44.
29. *See* Leiter (2022), at 908–10.
30. *Id.*, at 910 (citing 29 Fed. Reg. 10426 (1964)).
31. Sigma Delta Chi's New Code of Ethics, SOC'Y PROF. JOURNALISTS (quoted in Bhagwat (2023), at 46).
32. *See* Bhagwat (2023), at 42–48.
33. *See* BROWNELL (2023).
34. *Id.*, at 184.
35. *Id.*, at 199–200.
36. *See id.*, at 305–07.
37. Red Lion Broadcasting Co. v. Federal Communications Comm'n, 395 U.S. 367 (1969).
38. *Id.*, at 371.
39. *Id.*, at 373.
40. *Id.*, at 386.
41. *Id.*
42. *Id.*, at 390.

43. *Id.*
44. *Id.*, at 375.
45. Miami Herald Pub. Co. v. Tornillo, 418 U.S. 241 (1974).
46. *Id.*, at 258, n.24.
47. *Id.*, at 261 (White, J., concurring).
48. *Red Lion*, 395 U.S. at 376.
49. MINOW (2021), at 2–3.
50. FCC v. Pacifica Foundation, 438 U.S. 726 (1978).
51. *Id.*, at 729.
52. *Id.*, at 732.
53. *Red Lion*, 395 U.S. at 386.
54. *Pacifica*, 438 U.S. at 748–49.
55. Syracuse Peace Council v. FCC, 867 F.2d 654, 656 (D.C. Cir. 1989).
56. *Id.*, at 656.
57. Syracuse Peace Council v. Television Station WTVH Syracuse, New York, 99 FCC 2d 1389 (1984).
58. Meredith Corp. v. FCC, 809 F.2d 863, 868 (D.C. Cir. 1987).
59. *Id.*, at 865.
60. See FCC, Commissioners from 1934 to Present, at www.fcc.gov/commissioners-1934-present.
61. Inquiry Into Section 73.1910 of the Commission's Rules and Regulations Concerning Alternatives to the General Fairness Doctrine Obligations of Broadcast Licensees in Gen. Docket No. 84–282, 102 FCC 2d 143 (1985) [hereinafter, 1985 Fairness Report].
62. In re Complaint of Syracuse Peace Council, 2 F.C.C.Rcd. 5043 (1987).
63. *Id.*, para. 19.
64. *Id.*, para. 36.
65. *Id.*, para. 38.
66. *Id.*, paras. 42–43.
67. *Id.*, para. 37. *See also* para. 62 (stating that *Red Lion* was expressly premised on the scarcity of broadcast frequencies).
68. *Id.*, para. 55.
69. In re Complaint of Syracuse Peace Council, para. 65.
70. *Id.*, para. 85.
71. *Id.*, para. 74.
72. Syracuse Peace Council v. F.C.C., 867 F.2d 654, 656 (D.C. Cir. 1987).
73. In re Complaint of Syracuse Peace Council, para. 19.
74. Syracuse Peace Council v. F.C.C., 493 U.S. 1019 (1990).
75. *See* BROWNELL (2023), at 256.
76. BENKLER et al. (2018).
77. *Id.*, at 73–74.
78. *See id.*, at 46–65.
79. *Id.*, at 74.
80. *Id.*, at 76.
81. *Id.*, at 77.
82. *Id.*, at 74.
83. *Id.*
84. Center for Countering Digital Hate, Musk Misleading Election Claims Viewed 1.2 BN Times on X With no Fact Checks (Aug. 8, 2024).
85. Kevin M. Kruse and Julian Zelizer, How Policy Decisions Spawned Today's Hyperpolarized Media (Wash. Post, Jan. 17, 2019).

86. *Id.*
87. Leiter (2022), at 908.
88. *Id.*, at 911.
89. *Id.*
90. *See id.*, at 906–18.
91. *Id.*, at 906.
92. Taylor Orth & Carl Bialik, YouGov, Trust in Media 2024: Which news sources Americans trust – and which they think lean left or right (May 30, 2024).
93. In fact, the UK's Office of Communications found that two major Fox News programs "breached rules regarding adequate representations of alternative views, due impartiality on major political matters, and inclusion of an appropriately wide range of significant views when covering major political matters. This was equivalent to saying that Fox violated the old U.S. Fairness Doctrine." Leiter (2022), at 916.
94. *See* Agiesta & Edwards-Levy (2023).
95. Abrams v. United States, 250 U.S. 616, 630 (1919) (Holmes, J., dissenting).
96. *See, e.g.*, Metzger, Hartsell & Flanagin (2020).
97. Some companies do a much better job than other companies in restricting the use of their platforms to disseminate misinformation. Nevertheless, "the deliberate spread of false or misleading information … has ballooned in recent years." Jankowicz (2024). *See also* Jim Rutenberg and Steven Lee Myers, Trump Allies are Winning War over Disinformation (New York Times, March 17, 2024).
98. The statute is the "National Endowment for Fact-Checking Act." *See* https://coalitionfornationalfactchecking.org/#draft.
99. *See* Jan. 6 Report, *supra* note 3, at 213–31.
100. *See* 52 USC § 30104(f)(3) (defining the term "electioneering communication").
101. *See* Sloss (2021a); Sloss (2021b); The National Endowment for Fact-Checking Act, https://coalitionfornationalfactchecking.org/#overview.
102. The Supreme Court's recent decision in Murthy v. Missouri, 144 S. Ct. 1972 (2024), makes clear that government "jawboning" does not violate the First Amendment, provided that government pressure does not cross the line from persuasion to coercion.
103. *See* DiResta (2018).
104. *See* Pearlstein (2023).
105. *See* Jessica McDonald, Vance Wrong on Child Tax Credit, Harris' Remarks about Climate Change and Having Kids (Aug. 2, 2024).
106. *See* "About the National Endowment for Democracy," www.ned.org/about/ (last visited Aug. 3, 2024).
107. *See* Text of Proposed Legislation, at https://coalitionfornationalfactchecking.org/#draft.
108. *See* IFCN Code of Principles, at www.ifcncodeofprinciples.poynter.org/.
109. For a more detailed presentation of this argument, see "Constitutional Analysis of Proposed Legislation," https://coalitionfornationalfactchecking.org/#FirstDraft.
110. Alexandra Steigrad, Fox News Earns its Highest July Ratings Ever to Blow Away Cable Rivals CNN, MSNBC (New York Post, July 31, 2024).
111. *See* Madison Czopek, Trump Trial Judge Didn't Overrule All Defense Objections and Sustain All Prosecution Objections (Politifact, May 31, 2024).
112. *See* Netanel (2023).
113. Sullivan (1992).
114. *See id.*, at 59–62.
115. *See* Tsesis (2020).
116. *See* Greene (2021).

117. *See, e.g.*, Reed v. Town of Gilbert, 576 U.S. 155, 175–79 (2015) (Breyer, J., concurring); United States v. Alvarez, 567 U.S. 709, 730 (2012) (Breyer, J., concurring).
118. *See* Sullivan (1992), at 96–112.
119. Reed v. Town of Gilbert, 576 U.S. 155, 159 (2015).
120. *Id.*, at 159.
121. *Id.*
122. *Id.*, at 182 (Kagan, J., concurring).
123. *Id.*, at 183.
124. *Id.*, at 185.
125. *Id.*
126. Gunther (1972), at 8. Since John Roberts became Chief Justice, the Court has decided only two cases where it upheld laws that were subject to strict scrutiny under the First Amendment: Williams-Yulee v. Florida Bar, 575 U.S. 433 (2015), and Holder v. Humanitarian Law Project, 561 U.S. 1 (2010).
127. *Accord*, Norton (2023).
128. See Brandenburg v. Ohio, 395 U.S. 444 (1969).
129. See Chaplinsky v. New Hampshire, 315 U.S. 568 (1942).
130. See Virginia Bd. of Pharmacy v. Virginia Citizens Consumer Council, Inc., 425 U.S. 748 (1976).
131. See New York Times v. Sullivan, 376 U.S. 254 (1964); Beauharnais v. Illinois, 343 U.S. 250 (1952).
132. See Miller v. California, 413 U.S. 15 (1973); Roth v. United States, 354 U.S. 476 (1957).
133. See New York v. Ferber, 458 U.S. 747 (1982).
134. The Court's pronouncements have not been entirely consistent. At times, the Court suggests that speech in these categories is wholly unprotected by the First Amendment. At other times, the Court says that speech in these categories deserves lesser protection. For present purposes, that distinction is immaterial.
135. *See* Pearlstein (2023).
136. *See* Miller (2021).
137. 559 U.S. 460 (2010).
138. *Id.*, at 464–65.
139. *Id.*, at 465.
140. *Id.*, at 466.
141. *Id.*, at 468.
142. *See id.*, at 491–99 (Alito, J., dissenting).
143. *Id.*, at 472.
144. *Id.*
145. *Id.*, at 468.
146. Pub. L. No. 73-416, 48 Stat. 1064.
147. *Id.*, at 472.
148. United States v. Alvarez, 567 U.S. 709 (2012).
149. *Id.*, at 715.
150. *Id.*, at 717.
151. *Id.*, at 716–17.
152. *Id.*, at 717.
153. *Id.*, at 718.
154. *Id.*, at 720–21.
155. *Id.*, at 726.
156. *Id.*, at 730 (Breyer, J., concurring).
157. *Id.*, at 730.

158. *Id.*, at 737.
159. Reed v. Town of Gilbert, 576 U.S. 155, 176 (2015) (Breyer, J., concurring).
160. *Alvarez*, 567 U.S., at 739 (Alito, J., dissenting).
161. *Id.*, at 747.
162. *See id.*, at 747–49.
163. *Id.*, at 748–49.
164. *Id.*, at 717.
165. Gunther (1972), at 8.
166. As discussed in the next section, Justice Kagan's majority opinion in Moody v. NetChoice, 144 S. Ct. 2383 (2024), suggests that she might be reluctant to uphold a law targeting election-related misinformation on social media.
167. *Alvarez*, 567 U.S., at 748–49 (Alito, J., dissenting).
168. *See* IFCN Code of Principles, at www.ifcncodeofprinciples.poynter.org/.
169. 144 S. Ct. 2383 (2024).
170. *Id.*, at 2394.
171. *Id.*, at 2397.
172. *Id.*, at 2409 (Barrett, J., concurring).
173. *Id.*, at 2403.
174. *Id.*, at 2407.
175. *Id.*, at 2403.
176. *See id.*, at 2399–2403.
177. *Id.*, at 2411 (Jackson, J., concurring) (quoting *Red Lion*, 395 U.S. at 386).
178. *Id.*, at 2403 (quoting Brown v. Entertainment Merchants Ass'n, 564 U.S. 786, 790 (2011)).
179. *Red Lion*, 395 U.S. at 390.
180. *Moody*, 144 S. Ct. at 2407.
181. *Id.*
182. Reed v. Town of Gilbert, 576 U.S. 155, 176 (2015) (Breyer, J., concurring).
183. *See* Tsesis (2020), at 40–51.
184. *See* Moody v. NetChoice, 144 S.Ct. 2383, 2409–11 (Barrett, J., concurring).
185. *Reed*, 576 U.S. at 182 (Kagan, J., concurring).
186. *See* FCC v. Pacifica Foundation, 438 U.S. 726, 748–49 (1978) (comparing a radio broadcast to an assault).
187. *Red Lion*, 395 U.S. at 390.

5 INDIVIDUAL RIGHTS UNDER INTERNATIONAL LAW

1. Ware v. Hylton, 3 U.S. 199 (1796).
2. I coined this term in my book on the death of treaty supremacy. *See* Sloss (2016).
3. Treaty for the Cession of Louisiana, U.S.-Fr., Apr. 30, 1803, 8 Stat. 200.
4. Treaty for the Cession of Louisiana, U.S.-Fr., Apr. 30, 1803, 8 Stat. 200, art. 3; Treaty of Amity, Settlement and Limits, U.S.-Spain, Feb. 22, 1819, 8 Stat. 252, art. 8.
5. United States v. Percheman, 32 U.S. 51, 87 (1833).
6. *Id.*
7. *See* Cummings & McFarland (1937), at 124–25.
8. *See, e.g.*, An Act for Ascertaining and Adjusting the Titles and Claims to Land, within the Territory of Orleans, and the District of Louisiana, 1805, ch. 26, sec. 5, 2 Stat. 324, 327–28; An Act for Ascertaining Claims and Titles to Land within the Territory of Florida, 1822, ch. 129, 3 Stat. 709. *See also* An Act for Ascertaining and Adjusting the Titles and Claims to Land, within the Territory of Orleans, and the District of Louisiana, 1805, ch.

26, 2 Stat. 324–25 n.(a) (summarizing legislation between 1804 and 1844 relating to land claims in Louisiana and Florida).

9. *See, e.g.*, An Act Confirming the Titles to Lots in the Town of Mobile, and in the Former Province of West Florida, Which Claims Have Been Favorably Reported on by the Commissioners Appointed by the United States, 1822, ch. 122, 3 Stat. 699, 699–700.
10. *See* Coles (1956), at 41.
11. *See* Sloss (2012), at 150–51.
12. *See, e.g.*, Menard's Heirs v. Massey, 49 U.S. 293, 306–07 (1850) ("Boards of Commissioners were created, with liberal powers … and by this means many claims were confirmed, the legal title added, and incipient concessions completed into perfect and conclusive titles against the government.").
13. *See* Swisher (1974), at 747.
14. Cummings & McFarland (1937), at 120. There are no reliable estimates of the number of claims under the Florida treaty, but that treaty probably gave rise to a comparable number of claims.
15. *Id.* at 120.
16. Swisher (1974), at 747–48.
17. *Id.* at 747.
18. In a few cases, the Court determined that a Spanish grant was invalid because Spain purported to grant land to someone after the United States had acquired sovereignty. *See, e.g.*, Garcia v. Lee, 37 U.S. 511, 521 (1838). In such cases, the initial grant was invalid not because of Spanish law, but because Spain did not have sovereignty over the property it purported to grant.
19. *See, e.g.*, United States v. Wiggins, 39 U.S. 334, 350 (1840) ("[T]he United States were bound, after the cession of the country, to the same extent that Spain had been bound before the ratification of the treaty….").
20. 31 U.S. 691 (1832).
21. Cummings & McFarland (1937), at 126.
22. *Id.* at 127.
23. *Id.*
24. *Id.*
25. *Id.*
26. United States v. Wiggins, 39 U.S. 334, 350 (1840).
27. *See* Dibble (2003), at 173–81.
28. *Id.* at 134, 173–81.
29. *See* 42 U.S.C. sec. 1381a ("Every aged, blind, or disabled individual who is determined under part A to be eligible on the basis of his income and resources shall, in accordance with and subject to the provisions of this subchapter, be paid benefits by the Commissioner of Social Security.")
30. *See* Cummings & McFarland (1937), at 123–24 (noting that Attorney General John Crittenden, during his tenure as Attorney General, succeeded in "saving nearly two million acres for the public domain").
31. *See* Swisher (1974), at 748.
32. Dibble (2003), at 173–81.
33. *See* Baxter (1966), at 143–45.
34. White and Webster served as cocounsel in both Mitchel v. United States, 34 U.S. 711 (1835) and United States v. Arredondo, 31 U.S. 691 (1832). *Mitchel* was significant because the Court granted about 1.2 million acres of land to private claimants, the largest single victory (in terms of acreage) for private claimants in any of the Louisiana-Florida land cases.

35. DIBBLE (2003), at 159.
36. BAXTER (1966), at 142.
37. *See generally* HAMILTON (2007), at 1–4.
38. This section is largely copied from Sloss (2014), pp. 1814–25.
39. This section focuses solely on "exclusion" cases, where the government sought to prevent Chinese persons from entering the country. It does not address "deportation" cases, where the government sought to remove someone who had entered previously.
40. *See generally* SALYER (1995).
41. The Court did invalidate some state laws that discriminated against Chinese residents. *See, e.g.*, Yick Wo v. Hopkins, 118 U.S. 356 (1886). Also, in Wong Wing v. United States, the Court invalidated a federal statute subjecting Chinese persons to criminal penalties without granting them Fifth or Sixth Amendment jury rights. 163 U.S. 228 (1896).
42. Burlingame Treaty, U.S.-China, July 28, 1868, 16 Stat. 739.
43. *Id.*, art. V.
44. SALYER (1995), at 7–8.
45. *Id.*, at 12–14.
46. Treaty Concerning Immigration, U.S.-China, art. I, Nov. 17, 1880, 22 Stat. 826.
47. *Id.*
48. *Id.*, art. II.
49. Burlingame Treaty, *supra* note 42, art. V.
50. Act of May 6, 1882, 22 Stat. 58.
51. *Id.*, sec. 9.
52. SALYER (1995), at 18.
53. *Id.* at 19.
54. *See, e.g.*, In re Chin A On, 18 F. 506, 507 (D.C. Cal. 1883); Case of the Chinese Merchant, 13 F. 605, 608 (C.C. Cal. 1882).
55. Act of July 5, 1884, 23 Stat. 115.
56. *See* SALYER (1995), at 76.
57. Act of May 6, 1882, 22 Stat. 58, sec. 4.
58. Act of July 5, 1884, 23 Stat. 115, sec. 4 (emphasis added).
59. 112 U.S. 536 (1884).
60. *Id.* at 549.
61. 124 U.S. 621 (1888).
62. *See* SALYER (1995), at 18–19.
63. *Id.* at 20.
64. Scott Act, Oct. 1, 1888, 25 Stat. 504.
65. *Id.*, sec. 1.
66. *Id.*, sec. 2.
67. 130 U.S. 581 (1889).
68. *Id.* at 589.
69. *Id.* at 600.
70. *See, e.g.*, Lau Ow Bew v. United States, 144 U.S. 47 (1892).
71. *See, e.g.*, United States v. Wong Kim Ark, 169 U.S. 649 (1898).
72. *See, e.g.*, United States v. Gue Lim, 176 U.S. 459 (1900).
73. *Chinese Immigration: Hearing before the House Select Comm. On Immigration and Naturalization*, 51st Cong. 272–73 (1890) (statement of S.J. Ruddell, customs inspector in San Francisco).
74. SALYER (1995), at 33.
75. Act of March 3, 1891, 26 Stat. 1084.

76. *See generally* Nishimura Ekiu v. United States, 142 U.S. 651 (1892).
77. *See* Salyer (1995), at 26–32.
78. *Id.* These figures apply only to exclusion cases, not deportation cases.
79. 144 U.S. 47 (1892).
80. *Id.* at 48.
81. Act of July 5, 1884, sec. 6, 23 Stat. 115, 116.
82. *Lau Ow Bew*, 144 U.S. at 59.
83. *Id.* at 59–62.
84. *Id.* at 62 (quoting *Chew Heong*, 112 U.S. at 549).
85. Non-Chinese immigrants did not fare as well because the 1891 Act barred judicial review of administrative decisions in those cases.
86. Convention on Immigration, U.S.-China, art. I, March 17, 1894, 28 Stat. 1210.
87. *Id.*, art. III.
88. *See* Salyer (1995), at 96–97.
89. Act of August 18, 1894, 28 Stat. 390.
90. 158 U.S. 538 (1895).
91. *Id.* at 540.
92. Nishimura Ekiu v. United States, 142 U.S. 651 (1892).
93. *Lem Moon Sing*, 158 U.S. at 541–47.
94. *Nishimura Ekiu*, 142 U.S. at 656.
95. *Lem Moon Sing*, 158 U.S. at 541–47.
96. The Court's opinion in *Lem Moon Sing* presents the issues as if there is a stark choice between *de novo* review or zero review, with no possible middle ground. *Id.* at 546–47. In this respect, the Court's opinion is at odds with modern administrative law, which recognizes various circumstances where deferential judicial review is appropriate.
97. 169 U.S. 649, 653 (1898).
98. Act of August 18, 1894, 28 Stat. 390 (emphasis added).
99. Salyer (1995), at 80, Table 3.
100. 198 U.S. 253 (1905). The Court left an opening for petitioners who alleged abuse of authority by administrative officers.
101. *See* Van Alstine (2011).
102. 175 U.S. 677, 700 (1900).
103. Ramsey (2011), at 225.
104. *See id.*, at 234–38.
105. UN Charter, arts. 55, 56.
106. UDHR, Preamble.
107. *See* Chapter 2, *see also* Sloss & Sandholtz (2019).
108. *See* Sloss, Treaty Supremacy (2016), at 181–290 (presenting a detailed account of the de facto Bricker Amendment).
109. This section is largely copied from Sloss (2016b).
110. California Supreme Court Archives, 2nd Civ. No. 17309, L.A. 21149, Fujii v. California [hereinafter, Fujii Case File].
111. The Alien Land Law permitted noncitizens to own land if the right to own land was specifically protected by a bilateral treaty. However, as of 1950, the United States was not party to any bilateral treaty with Japan that protected the right of Japanese nationals to own land in the United States.
112. Fujii Case File, Respondent's Brief, pp. 24–43 (Feb. 20, 1950).
113. Fujii Case File, Appellant's Opening Brief, p. 100 (Nov. 15, 1949).
114. United Nations Charter, arts. 55, 56.

115. U.S. Const. art. VI, cl. 2.
116. Fujii v. California, 217 P.2d 481 (Cal.App.2nd 1950).
117. *Id.* at 484.
118. *Id.* at 484–88.
119. "Ruling Holds Alien Land Law Invalid," Los Angeles Times, April 25, 1950 (A1).
120. "Charter of United Nations Held to Invalidate California Alien Land Act," Los Angeles Daily Journal, April 25, 1950 (*reprinted in* 96 Cong. Rec. 5993, 6000).
121. *See* 96 Cong. Rec. 5993–6000 (April 28, 1950). The Congressional Record does not record the time spent on a subject. The one-hour estimate is based on the length of printed material.
122. *Id.* at 5998.
123. *Id.* at 5996.
124. Missouri v. Holland, 252 U.S. 416 (1920).
125. 96 Cong. Rec., at 5997.
126. *Id.* at 5998.
127. *Id.* at 5998–99.
128. United Nations Charter, art. 55.
129. Fujii Case File, Petition for Rehearing (May 9, 1950).
130. Brief of American Civil Liberties Union, Southern California Branch, and American Jewish Congress, Amici Curiae in Support of Appellant in Opposition to Petition for Rehearing (Fujii Case File).
131. Fujii Case File, Application for Leave to Join with Brief Amici Curiae (May 16, 1950).
132. *See* Lockwood (1984).
133. Fujii v. State, 218 P.2d 595 (Cal.App.2nd 1950).
134. This section borrows liberally from Sloss (2016), at 173–79.
135. *See* Golove & Hulsebosch (2010).
136. *See* Morris (1984), at 194–219.
137. U.S. Const., art. VI, cl. 2.
138. *See generally* Sloss (2016).
139. Even in the nineteenth century, there were different variants of NSE doctrine, at least one of which focused more on judicial enforcement of treaties by courts. *See id.*, at 107–152.
140. *See id.*, at 85–105.
141. American Law Institute, Restatement (Second) of the Foreign Relations Law of the United States (1965).
142. *See id.*, section 141.
143. *See* Sloss (2016), at 276–82.
144. *See id.*, at 187–98, 225–29, 240–48.
145. *See id.*, at 198–200, 219–23.
146. *See id.*, at 223–25, 248–56.
147. *See generally* Tananbaum (1988); Kaufman (1990).
148. *See* 1 Foreign Relations of the United States, 1952–1954, at 1768–856 (William Z. Slany et al. eds., 1983) (compiling executive branch materials related to the Bricker Amendment).
149. *See* Sloss (2016), at 220–23, 253–56.
150. Fujii v. State, 242 P.2d 617 (CA 1952).
151. *See* Sloss (2016), at 231–40.
152. *See id.*, at 250–53.
153. *See id.*, at 257–63.

154. *See id.*, at 276–84.
155. See Siegel (2006); Dorf (2002), at 984–85; Strauss (2001), at 1476–78.
156. Fujii v. State, 218 P.2d 595 (Cal.App.2nd 1950).
157. Fairman (1952), at 689.
158. *See* TANANBAUM (1988), at 175–90. For a fascinating account of Lyndon Johnson's behind-the-scenes role as Senate minority leader, see CARO (2002), at 519–41.
159. 347 U.S. 483 (1954).
160. 347 U.S. 497 (1954).
161. *See* Bolling v. Sharpe, 347 U.S. 497 (1954) (No. 8), Brief for Petitioners, *available at* 1952 WL 47257; *see also* SLOSS (2016), at 241–48.
162. *See* DUDZIAK (2000).
163. *See* Brown v. Bd. of Educ., 347 U.S. 483 (1954) (Nos. 1, 2, 3, 4, 5), Brief for United States as Amicus Curiae, *available at* 1952 WL 82045.
164. *See* Chapter 2. *See also* Sloss & Sandholtz (2019), at 1216–32.
165. ICCPR, *opened for signature*, Dec. 16, 1966, 999 U.N.T.S. 171 (entered into force Mar. 23, 1976).
166. ICESCR, *opened for signature*, Dec. 16, 1966, 999 U.N.T.S. 3 (entered into force Jan. 3, 1976).
167. International Convention on the Elimination of All Forms of Racial Discrimination, *opened for signature*, Dec. 21, 1965, 660 U.N.T.S. 195 (entered into force Jan. 4, 1969).
168. Convention on the Elimination of All Forms of Discrimination against Women, *opened for signature*, Dec. 18, 1979, 1249 U.N.T.S. 13 (entered into force Sept. 3, 1981).
169. Convention against Torture, *opened for signature*, Dec. 10, 1984, 1465 U.N.T.S. 85 (entered into force June 26, 1987).
170. Convention on the Rights of the Child, *opened for signature*, Nov. 20, 1989, 1577 U.N.T.S. 3 (entered into force Sept. 2, 1990).
171. American Convention on Human Rights, Nov. 22, 1969, O.A.S.T.S. No. 36 (entered into force July 18, 1978).
172. *See Treaties and Executive Agreements: Hearings before a Subcomm. Of the Senate Judiciary Comm. On S.J. Res. 1 and S.J. Res.* 43, at 824 (83rd Cong. 1953).
173. *See* Sloss (1999), at 173–75.
174. Message from the President of the United States Transmitting Four Treaties Pertaining to Human Rights, S. EXEC. DOCS. C, D, E and F, 95–2 (1978).
175. Senate Comm. on Foreign Relations, International Covenant on Civil and Political Rights, S. EXEC. REP. NO. 102–23, at 2 (1992).
176. *See* Senate Comm. on Foreign Relations, Report on Convention against Torture and Other Cruel, Inhuman or Degrading Treatment or Punishment, S. EXEC. REP. NO. 101–30, at 2 (1990).
177. *See* Sloss (1999), at 139–42.
178. *See id.*, at 139–42, 175–78.
179. *See* SLOSS (2016), at 303–310; Sloss (1999), at 152–71.
180. *See* U.S. Const., art VI.
181. *See, e.g.*, Bradley (2008).
182. *See* SLOSS (2016), at 291–93.
183. *See id.*, at 303–310.
184. Message from the President of the United States Transmitting Four Treaties Pertaining to Human Rights, S. EXEC. DOCS. C, D, E and F, 95–2 (1978).
185. *International Covenant on Civil and Political Rights: Hearing before the S. Comm. on Foreign Relations*, at 15 (102nd Cong. 1992) (statement of Richard Schifter).

186. Senate Comm. on Foreign Relations, International Covenant on Civil and Political Rights, S. EXEC. REP. NO. 102–23, at 3 (1992) (emphasis added). *See also International Human Rights Treaties: Hearings before the S. Comm. on Foreign Relations*, at 29 (prepared statement of Roberts B. Owen) (96th Cong. 1979) (stating that the purpose of the reservations was to ensure that "further changes in our [domestic] laws will be brought about only through the normal legislative process").
187. *See* SLOSS (2016), at 15–57.
188. ICCPR, art. 6, para. 5.
189. *See* Stanford v. Kentucky, 492 U.S. 361 (1989) (holding that the Constitution does not bar application of the death penalty to sixteen and seventeen year olds); Thompson v. Oklahoma, 487 U.S. 815 (1988) (holding that the Constitution bars application of the death penalty to fifteen year olds).
190. Roper v. Simmons, 543 U.S. 551 (2005).
191. Senate Comm. on Foreign Relations, International Covenant on Civil and Political Rights, S. EXEC. REP. NO. 102–23, at 3 (1992).
192. *See* Henkin (1995).

6 WEAK REVIEW, STRONG RIGHTS

1. The chapter title is adapted from TUSHNET (2008).
2. *See* ELY (1980), at 135–79.
3. *See id.*, at 43–72.
4. International Covenant on Civil and Political Rights, adopted Dec. 19, 1966, 999 U.N.T.S. 171 (entered into force Mar. 23, 1976) [hereinafter, ICCPR].
5. *See infra* notes 65–66 and accompanying text.
6. *See generally* GARDBAUM (2013). According to Professor Gardbaum, the "new Commonwealth model" includes both weak judicial review and "pre-enactment political rights review." *See id.*, at 25–30. The proposal developed in this chapter focuses on weak judicial review; it does not address the separate issue of pre-enactment political review.
7. *See* Chapter 2.
8. *See* Table 6.3.
9. *See* Sloss (2024), at 135–39.
10. Twining v. New Jersey, 211 U.S. 78, 102 (1908).
11. *See* Universal Declaration of Human Rights, G.A. Res. 217 (III)(A) (Dec. 10, 1948), art. 17(2) ("No one shall be arbitrarily deprived of his property.") [hereinafter UDHR].
12. ICESCR, *opened for signature* Dec. 16, 1966, 999 U.N.T.S. 3 (entered into force Jan. 3, 1976). On the drafting history, see Pechota (1981).
13. Of course, governments may take private property only for a "public use," but the public use requirement imposes at best a very weak constraint on government action. *See* Kelo v. City of New London, 545 U.S. 469 (2005).
14. *See, e.g.*, Swann v. Charlotte-Mecklenburg Bd. of Ed., 402 U.S. 1 (1971); Loving v. Virginia, 388 U.S. 1 (1967); Brown v. Bd. of Educ., 347 U.S. 483 (1954).
15. The two most prominent counterexamples involve women's rights and gay rights. On women's rights, see Siegel (2006). On gay rights, see Obergefell v. Hodges, 576 U.S. 644 (2015); Lawrence v. Texas, 539 U.S. 558 (2003); Romer v. Evans, 517 U.S. 620 (1996).
16. 521 U.S. 507 (1997).
17. *See* Chapter 1 (discussing *Boerne*).

18. 570 U.S. 529 (2013).
19. *See* Chapter 3 (discussing *Shelby County*).
20. 438 U.S. 265 (1978).
21. *See, e.g.*, Strauder v. West Virginia, 100 U.S. 303, 306 (1880) (noting that the Fourteenth Amendment "is one of a series of constitutional provisions having a common purpose; namely, securing to a race recently emancipated … all the civil rights that the superior race enjoy").
22. There are, of course, counterexamples. For example, California passed a ballot initiative in 1996 that banned affirmative action in higher education, among other things. See Proposition 209, Prohibition Against Discrimination or Preferential Treatment by State and Other Public Entities (Nov. 1996), at https://lao.ca.gov/ballot/1996/prop209_11_1996.html.
23. *See* Driver (2024), at 652–56.
24. *Id.*, at 654.
25. *Id.*
26. *See, e.g.*, Students for Fair Admissions v. Harvard, 600 U.S. 181, 232–52 (2023) (Thomas, J., concurring) (providing "an originalist defense of the colorblind Constitution").
27. *See* Finkelman (2003), at 685–90.
28. *See id.*, at 681–85.
29. 438 U.S. 265 (1978).
30. *See id.*, at 408–21 (Stevens, J., concurring in the judgment in part and dissenting in part).
31. *See id.*, at 359 (opinion of Justices Brennan, White, Marshall, and Blackmun, concurring in the judgment in part and dissenting in part).
32. *See id.*, at 324–79.
33. *See id.*, at 287–91 (Powell, J.).
34. *See id.*, at 305–20.
35. *Id.*, at 320.
36. 515 U.S. 200 (1995).
37. *Id.*, at 227.
38. *Id.*, at 237 (internal citations and quotations omitted).
39. 539 U.S. 244 (2003).
40. 539 U.S. 306 (2003).
41. 579 U.S. 365 (2016).
42. 600 U.S. 181 (2023).
43. International Convention on the Elimination of All Forms of Racial Discrimination, *opened for signature* Dec. 21, 1965, 660 U.N.T.S. 195 (entered into force Jan. 4, 1969), art. 1, para. 1 [hereinafter, CERD].
44. *Id.*, art. 1, para. 4.
45. *Id.*
46. Grutter v. Bollinger, 539 U.S. 306, 342 (2003).
47. CERD, art. 1, para. 4.
48. Parents Involved v. Seattle School Dist., 551 U.S. 701 (2007).
49. *See id.*, at 711–18. For a very different version of the facts, *see id.*, at 804–19 (Breyer, J. dissenting).
50. United States v. Lopez, 514 U.S. 549, 557 (1995).
51. *See Parents Involved*, 551 U.S. at 720–35.
52. *Id.*, at 787 (Kennedy, J., concurring).
53. *Id.*, at 803 (Breyer, J., dissenting) (emphasis in original).
54. *Id.*, at 837.
55. *See id.*, at 838–55 (concluding that the plans were narrowly tailored to serve a compelling interest).

56. *See id.*, at 720–25 (plurality opinion).
57. 402 U.S. 1 (1971).
58. *Parents Involved*, 551 U.S. at 804–05 (quoting *Swann*, 402 U.S. at 16).
59. *See Parents Involved*, at 737 (plurality opinion).
60. *See id.*, at 823–31 (Breyer, J., dissenting).
61. *Id.*, at 736 (plurality opinion).
62. ROTHSTEIN (2017), at xii.
63. *Id.*, at xiv.
64. See Chapter 5.
65. 252 U.S. 416 (1920).
66. The Court's decision in Missouri v. Holland, 252 U.S. 416 (1920), supports this conclusion. In Bond v. United States, 572 U.S. 844 (2014), three Justices challenged the continued vitality of *Holland*, but it remains controlling precedent. For analysis of *Bond*, see Sloss (2015).
67. U.S. Const., art. I, sec. 9, cl. 3.
68. U.S. Const., art. I, sec. 10, cl. 1.
69. ICCPR, art. 15, para. 1 ("No one shall be guilty of any criminal offence on account of any act or omission which did not constitute a criminal offence … at the time when it was committed. Nor shall a heavier penalty be imposed than the one that was applicable at the time when the criminal offence was committed.")
70. *Id.*, art. 14, para. 1.
71. U.S. Const., art. I, sec. 9, cl. 2.
72. ICCPR, art. 9, para. 4.
73. *But see* Boumediene v. Bush, 553 U.S. 723 (2008) (holding that Congress violated the Suspension Clause).
74. U.S. Const., art. I, sec. 10, cl. 1.
75. CHEMERINSKY (2015), at 490.
76. As noted in Chapter 2, the Contracts Clause was heavily litigated in the nineteenth century. However, it was mostly supplanted by the Takings Clause in the twentieth century. *See generally* CHEMERINSKY (2015), at 662–69.
77. The Sixth Amendment includes a right for criminal defendants "to be informed of the nature and cause of the accusation." Art. 14(3)(a) is substantially identical. The Supreme Court has never explicitly held that this clause is "incorporated" against the states, but the right is included in the Due Process Clause as a matter of procedural due process.
78. Elsewhere, I have provided a side-by-side comparison of the key textual provisions. *See* Sloss (2024), at 153–57.
79. ICCPR, art. 9, para. 3.
80. In Ramos v. Louisiana, 590 U.S. 83 (2020), the Supreme Court held that the Sixth Amendment right to a unanimous jury verdict binds the states under incorporation doctrine. In fact, the Sixth Amendment does not mention a right to a unanimous jury verdict; it is arguably an unenumerated right. Regardless, for purposes of Table 6.1, I classify the right in *Ramos* as part of the Sixth Amendment right to a jury trial.
81. *See* Chapter 7.
82. *See* Fed Rule Crim Pro, Rule 7; *see also* LAFAVE ET AL. (2009), at 770–87.
83. *See* FRIEDENTHAL, KANE & MILLER (2015), at 493–99.
84. ICCPR, art. 8.
85. Saenz v. Roe, 526 U.S. 489 (1999). Under current Supreme Court doctrine, the right to interstate travel is the only right protected under the Fourteenth Amendment Privileges and Immunities Clause.
86. ICCPR, art. 12, para. 1.

87. CERD, art. 5.
88. They are: the right to appeal a criminal conviction, the right to state-appointed counsel, and the right to be presumed innocent. *See* Table 6.3 and accompanying text.
89. *See* Mullane v. Central Hanover Bank & Trust Co., 339 U.S. 306 (1950).
90. *See* Goldberg v. Kelly, 397 U.S. 254 (1970).
91. *See* Caperton v. A.T. Massey Coal Co., 556 U.S. 868 (2009).
92. ICCPR, art. 14, para. 1.
93. One could quibble about whether personal jurisdiction doctrine is properly classified as "procedural" or "substantive" due process. Either way, the ICCPR does not provide an analogue to personal jurisdiction doctrine. As discussed in Chapter 2, the Supreme Court constitutionalized personal jurisdiction by borrowing concepts from international law and incorporating those concepts into the Due Process Clause. If the Court wants to make a serious effort to restore legislative primacy, it should repudiate personal jurisdiction doctrine in its entirety and replace that doctrine with common law *forum non conveniens*, a doctrine that is substantively similar but is subject to legislative override.
94. *See generally* CHEMERINKSY (2015), at 719–823.
95. ICCPR, art. 26.
96. *Id.*, art. 2.
97. CERD, art. 5.
98. If one thinks that affirmative action programs are a form of discrimination, then the statement in the text is not true with respect to such programs. However, for the reasons explained earlier in this chapter, I do not believe that affirmative action programs are discriminatory.
99. *See* Sloss (2024), at 106–07.
100. 597 U.S. 215 (2022).
101. *See* Sloss (2024), at 148–51.
102. As a policy matter, I would support federal legislation that prohibits state interference with a woman's right to choose during the first trimester and that imposes some restrictions on state regulation during the second trimester. However, as a constitutional matter, the principle of legislative primacy means that this is a question for legislatures, not courts.
103. 397 U.S. 358 (1970).
104. 372 U.S. 335 (1963).
105. 351 U.S. 12 (1956) (holding that the Fourteenth Amendment precludes states from charging a fee to an indigent defendant to obtain the transcript needed to appeal his conviction).
106. 319 U.S. 624, 642 (1943) ("If there is any fixed star in our constitutional constellation, it is that no official, high or petty, can prescribe what shall be orthodox in … matters of opinion.").
107. 357 U.S. 449 (1958) (holding that a court order requiring disclosure of membership in the NAACP violated the members' rights to freedom of association).
108. 262 U.S. 390 (1923).
109. 268 U.S. 510 (1925).
110. 431 U.S. 494 (1977).
111. 316 U.S. 535 (1942).
112. 381 U.S. 479 (1965).
113. 388 U.S. 1 (1967).
114. *See, e.g.*, Toonen v. Australia, Comm'n No. 488/1992, U.N. Doc. CCPR/C/50/D/488/1992 (Nov. 5, 1992) (concluding that a Tasmanian state law that criminalized homosexual sodomy violated the ICCPR). *See also* Zong et al. (2024).

115. 576 U.S. 644 (2015).
116. 539 U.S. 558 (2003).
117. 5 U.S.C. § 702.
118. *See* 28 U.S.C. §§ 2241, 2254, and 2255.
119. 28 U.S.C. §§ 2201–02.
120. Unlike 42 U.S.C. § 1983 – which covers both damages and injunctive relief against state officers – the APA allows only injunctive relief against federal officers. The Federal Tort Claims Act allows suits for money damages against federal officers, but it is of limited utility in this context. *See* Sloss (2000), at 1130–51. If Congress chooses to permit suits for money damages against federal officers, a special statutory provision would be needed.
121. Article 2(1)(d) of the Race Convention obligates states to "bring to an end, by all appropriate means," racial discrimination by private parties. The United States adopted a reservation specifying that "the United States does not accept any obligation under this Convention to enact legislation or take other measures … with respect to private conduct except as mandated by the Constitution and laws of the United States." 140 Cong. Rec. 14, 326–27 (1994).
122. ICCPR, art. 14, para. 3(f).
123. *See* Sloss & Sandholtz (2019), at 1223.
124. CERD, art. 1, para. 1.
125. *See* Washington v. Davis, 426 U.S. 229 (1976).
126. CERD, art. 5(a).
127. *Id.*, art. 5(b).
128. *Id.*, art. 5(c).
129. *Id.*, art. 5(d).
130. *Id.*, art. 5(e).
131. Ashwander v. Tennessee Valley Authority, 297 U.S. 338, 347 (1936) (Brandeis, J., concurring). For an insightful analysis of the canon, see Schauer (1995).
132. *See* Sloss (2006), at 38–58.
133. *See* CERD, art. 4(a); ICCPR, art. 20(2).
134. *See* R.A.V. v. City of St. Paul, 505 U.S. 377 (1992).
135. *See* 140 Cong. Rec. 14326–27 (1994) (CERD); 138 Cong. Rec. 8070–71 (1992) (ICCPR).
136. 536 U.S. 304, 348 (2002) (Scalia, J., dissenting).
137. *See* Yoo (1999).
138. *See* McGinnis (2009).
139. The ICCPR establishes a body of experts, the Human Rights Committee, which has some authority to oversee treaty implementation. *See* ICCPR, arts. 28–45. However, the Committee has no authority to issue legally binding decisions.
140. *See* 140 Cong. Rec. 14326–27 (1994).
141. Even Justice Scalia acknowledged that the views of international and foreign tribunals merit consideration when U.S. courts are interpreting multilateral treaties. *See* Scalia (2004).
142. *See* Chapter 5.
143. *See* Chapter 2, Figures 2.2 and 2.3; *see also* Appendix, Table A.2.
144. *See* Chapter 5.
145. *See* Kaufman (1990), at 94–116.
146. *See* Chapter 2. *See also* Sloss and Sandholtz (2019), at 1216–34.
147. *See* Chapter 7.
148. *See* Chapter 5, *see also* Sloss (1999), at 138–44.
149. Senate Comm. on Foreign Relations, International Covenant on Civil and Political Rights, S. Exec. Rep. No. 102-23, at 3 (1992).

150. *See* Table 6.3 and accompanying text.
151. *See* Chapter 1.
152. John Adams, *Thoughts on Government* (quoted in Rakove (1996), at 203).
153. *See generally* Gardbaum (2013).
154. The V-Dem database is available at https://v-dem.net/data/the-v-dem-dataset/. The numbers in Table 6.4 are taken from version 12 of the dataset, published in 2022.
155. If one conceptualizes the strong/weak distinction as a continuum with shades of gray, Canada comes closer to a system of strong review than any of the other non-U.S. countries in Table 6.4. *See* Gardbaum (2013), at 229–31. Notably, Canada had the second-lowest score on the liberal democracy index in 2021, only slightly higher than the United States.
156. Freedom House data is available for download at https://freedomhouse.org/report/freedom-world (last visited Sept. 12, 2024).
157. Gardbaum (2013), at 25.
158. *Id.*
159. 521 U.S. 507 (1997).
160. 570 U.S. 529 (2013).
161. 551 U.S. 701 (2007).

7 FEDERALISM

1. *See* the final section of this chapter for further elaboration of this point.
2. 505 U.S. 144 (1992).
3. One could add a separate category for limits on Congress's power under the Spending Clause, as applied by the Court in Nat'l Federation of Independent Business v. Sebelius, 567 U.S. 519 (2012). However, the key Spending Clause limit in *Sebelius* is best understood as a special application of the anti-commandeering doctrine. *See* the section on anti-commandeering later in this chapter.
4. *See, e.g.*, Barnett (2016), at 167–202.
5. U.S. Const. art. I, § 8, cl. 3.
6. *See* Heart of Atlanta Motel v. United States, 379 U.S. 241 (1964); Katzenbach v. McClung, 379 U.S. 294 (1964).
7. 514 U.S. 549 (1995).
8. *Id.*, at 551 (citing 18 U.S.C. § 922(q)).
9. *Id.*, at 558.
10. *Id.*, at 563.
11. *Id.*, at 564.
12. *Id.*, at 567–68.
13. 18 U.S.C. § 922(q)(2)(A) (emphasis added).
14. *Lopez*, 514 U.S. at 558.
15. *See* United States v. Dorsey, 418 F.3d 1038, 1045–46 (9th Cir. 2005); United States v. Danks, 221 F.3d 1037, 1038–39 (8th Cir. 1999).
16. Gonzalez v. Raich, 545 U.S. 1, 46 (2005) (O'Connor, J., dissenting).
17. *See* Pub. L. No. 104-208, Div. A, Title I, § 101(f), 110 Stat. 3009–369, 3009–372 (1996).
18. *Lopez*, at 564.
19. The Supreme Court has not ruled on the constitutionality of the amended statute, but two federal appellate courts have upheld its validity, and there does not appear to be any contrary authority. *See Dorsey*, 418 F.3d at 1045–46 (9th Cir. 2005); *Danks*, 221 F.3d at 1038–39 (8th Cir. 1999).

20. *See, e.g.*, Wickard v. Filburn, 317 U.S. 111 (1942); United States v. Darby, 312 U.S. 100 (1941); NLRB v. Jones & Laughlin Steel Corp., 301 U.S. 1 (1937).
21. *Wickard*, 317 U.S. at 120 (citing Chief Justice Marshall's opinion in *Gibbons v. Ogden*, 22 U.S. 1 (1824)).
22. *See id.*, at 127–28.
23. *Lopez*, at 567–68.
24. *Id.*, at 564.
25. U.S. Const., art. I, § 7.
26. *See, e.g.*, Andrew Solender, Capitol Hill Stunner: 2023 Led to Fewest Laws in Decades (Dec. 18, 2023); Chris Cillizza, The Least Productive Congress Ever (July 17, 2023).
27. U.S. Const., art. I, § 2, cl. 1.
28. U.S. Const., art. I, § 3, cl. 1.
29. Defenders of the *Lopez* decision argue that the constitutional text I am citing involves only procedural limits on Congress's legislative power, not substantive limits. That is true, but that argument merely reinforces the point that the Constitution's Framers made a deliberate choice to rely on procedural mechanisms to constrain Congress. The fact that the Framers did not include substantive limits on the Commerce Power in Article I reflects that deliberate choice; it should not be construed as an invitation for the Supreme Court to create its own limits by engaging in judicial lawmaking.
30. 545 U.S. 1 (2005).
31. Nat'l Federation of Independent Business v. Sebelius, 567 U.S. 519 (2012).
32. 529 U.S. 598 (2000).
33. *Id.*, at 613.
34. Gonzales v. Raich, 545 U.S. 1, 5 (2005).
35. *Id.*, at 7.
36. *Id.*, at 24.
37. *Sebelius*, 567 U.S. at 539.
38. *Id.*, at 549.
39. *See* Resnik (2001), at 630–42.
40. *Wickard*, 317 U.S. at 120 (citing Gibbons v. Ogden, 22 U.S. 1 (1824)).
41. U.S. Const., amend XIV, sec. 5.
42. *See* U.S. Const., amend XIII, sec. 2 ("Congress shall have power to enforce this article by appropriate legislation."); U.S. Const., amend XV, sec. 2 ("The Congress shall have power to enforce this article by appropriate legislation.").
43. Graber (2023), at xxxii–xxxiii. *See* Chapter 2.
44. Cong. Globe, 42nd Cong., 2nd Sess. 525 (1872) (statement of Senator Oliver Morton) (quoted in McConnell (1997), at 182).
45. 521 U.S. 507 (1997). *See* Chapter 1, for analysis of *Boerne*.
46. 570 U.S. 529 (2013). *See* Chapter 3, for analysis of *Shelby County*.
47. *See* Katzenbach v. Morgan, 384 U.S. 641 (1966) (Fourteenth Amendment); South Carolina v. Katzenbach, 383 U.S. 301 (1966) (Fifteenth Amendment); Wickard v. Filburn, 317 U.S. 111 (1942) (Commerce Power).
48. *See* Chapter 1, (discussing *Boerne*); Chapter 3, (discussing *Shelby County*); Chapter 7, (discussing *Lopez*).
49. Voting Rights Act of 1965, Pub. L. No. 89-110, 79 Stat. 437. House Democrats voted 217 to 54 in favor of the legislation. House Republicans voted 111 to 20 in favor. Senate Democrats voted 49 to 17 in favor. Senate Republicans voted 30 to 1 in favor. *See* 89th Cong., Cong. Index (CCH) 9, 146 (Aug. 3, 1965) (providing the House of Representatives voting record); 89th Cong., Cong. Index (CCH) 9, 147–48 (Aug. 4, 1965) (providing the Senate voting record).

50. The Gun Free School Zones Act of 1990, enacted as part of the Crime Control Act of 1990, Pub. L. No. 101-647, 104 Stat. 4789 (1990). The Act passed in the House by a vote of 313–1, with 118 Members not voting. Democrats voted in favor 178–0. Republicans voted in favor 135–1. https://clerk.house.gov/Votes/1990534. It passed in the Senate by unanimous voice vote. www.congress.gov/bill/101st-congress/senate-bill/3266/all-actions.
51. The Religious Freedom Restoration Act of 1993, Pub. L. No. 103-141, 107 Stat. 1488 (1993). The Act passed in the House by unanimous voice vote. www.congress.gov/bill/103rd-congress/house-bill/1308/all-actions. It passed the Senate by a vote of 97–3. Democrats voted 54–2. Republicans voted 43–1. www.senate.gov/legislative/LIS/roll_call_votes/vote1031/vote_103_1_00331.htm.
52. *See* Chapter 1 (discussing rules, standards, and principles).
53. The evidence shows that there was contemporaneous majority support for both the Gun Free School Zones Act and RFRA because Congress responded to *Lopez* and *Boerne*, respectively, by amending 18 U.S.C. § 922(q) to reverse the outcome in *Lopez* (*see* note 17 and accompanying text), and by enacting the Religious Land Use and Institutionalized Persons Act (RLUIPA) to partially reverse the outcome in *Boerne*. One could argue that evidence of *contemporaneous* majority support for the Voting Rights Act is lacking, but Congress reauthorized the Voting Rights Act in 1970, 1975, 1982, and 2006.
54. Pub. L. No. 106-274, 114 Stat. 803 (2000). Both Houses of Congress approved RLUIPA by unanimous voice vote. www.congress.gov/bill/106th-congress/senate-bill/2869/all-actions.
55. *See* Burwell v. Hobby Lobby Stores, Inc., 573 U.S. 682, 695 (2014) (noting that RLUIPA "imposes the same general test as RFRA but on a more limited category of governmental actions").
56. Cutter v. Wilkinson, 544 U.S. 709 (2005).
57. *See, e.g.*, Midrash Sephardi, Inc. v. Town of Surfside, 366 F.3d 1214 (11th Cir. 2004); Charles v. Verhagen, 348 F.3d 601 (7th Cir. 2003); Mayweathers v. Newland, 314 F.3d 1062 (9th Cir. 2002).
58. Morris and Grange (2024), at 21.
59. *See* Chapter 3.
60. Congress.Gov, Bill Summary, www.congress.gov/bill/117th-congress/house-bill/4.
61. *See* Congress.Gov, www.congress.gov/bill/117th-congress/senate-bill/4/all-actions.
62. Roper Center, Public Opinion on the Voting Rights Act (Aug. 6, 2015), https://ropercenter.cornell.edu/blog/public-opinion-voting-rights-act.
63. U.S. Const., amend XI.
64. Seminole Tribe of Florida v. Florida, 517 U.S. 44 (1996). For an insightful analysis of the Court's sovereign immunity doctrine, written shortly after the decision in *Seminole Tribe*, see (1997).
65. Alden v. Maine, 527 U.S. 706, 713 (1999).
66. *Id.*
67. The Court decided all three cases by the same 5–4 vote, with Chief Justice Rehnquist, and Justices O'Connor, Scalia, Kennedy, and Thomas in the majority. Justices Stevens, Souter, Ginsburg, and Breyer dissented in all three cases.
68. Jeffries (1998), at 49.
69. *See* CHEMERINSKY (2012), at 441.
70. *See* Monell v. Dept. of Social Services, 436 U.S. 658 (1978); Home Tel. and Tel. Co. v. City of Los Angeles, 227 U.S. 278 (1913).
71. 209 U.S. 123 (1908).

72. *Seminole Tribe*, 517 U.S. at 174 (Souter, J., dissenting).
73. *See* Edelman v. Jordan, 415 U.S. 651 (1974).
74. Jeffries (1998), at 62.
75. 502 U.S. 21, 27 (1991).
76. *See* Jeffries (1998), at 63–68.
77. *Edelman*, 415 U.S. at 663.
78. Jeffries (1998), at 60.
79. *Edelman*, 415 U.S. at 663.
80. Atascadero State Hosp. v. Scanlon, 473 U.S. 234, 238 (1985).
81. *Seminole Tribe*, 517 U.S. 44 (1996).
82. Fitzpatrick v. Bitzer, 427 U.S. 445 (1976).
83. *See* FALLON ET AL. (2015), at 958–62.
84. Florida Prepaid Postsecondary Education Expense Board v. College Savings Bank, 527 U.S. 627 (1999) (invalidating provisions of the Patent Remedy Act that authorized suits against states for patent infringement).
85. Kimel v. Fla. Bd. of Regents, 528 U.S. 62 (2000) (invalidating a provision of the Age Discrimination in Employment Act that authorized suits against states).
86. Univ. of Ala. v. Garrett, 531 U.S. 356 (2001) (invalidating a provision of the Americans with Disabilities Act that authorized individuals with disabilities to sue states for employment discrimination).
87. Nevada Dept. of Human Resources v. Hibbs, 538 U.S. 721 (2003) (upholding statutory abrogation of sovereign immunity in the Family and Medical Leave Act as a remedy for gender discrimination).
88. Tennessee v. Lane, 541 U.S. 509 (2004) (in a claim under the Americans with Disabilities Act, upholding congressional power to abrogate sovereign immunity to enforce the constitutional right of access to courts).
89. Ex parte Virginia, 100 U.S. 339, 345 (1879). *See also* GRABER (2023), at xxxii–xxxiii (noting that the Fourteenth Amendment's authors regarded "Congress as the institution primarily responsible for interpreting and implementing the post-Civil War amendments.")
90. New York v. United States, 505 U.S. 144, 157 (1992).
91. *Id.*, at 161.
92. 521 U.S. 898 (1997).
93. *Id.*, at 935.
94. Nat'l Federation of Independent Business v. Sebelius, 567 U.S. 519, 579 (2012) (quoting *New York*, 505 U.S. at 175).
95. *See, e.g.*, South Dakota v. Dole, 483 U.S. 203 (1987) (upholding a federal law that directed the Secretary of Transportation to withhold federal highway funds from states that did not raise their drinking age to 21).
96. *See* CHEMERINSKY (2015), at 422–31.
97. Pub. L. No. 106-229, 114 Stat. 464 (2000).
98. *See* Uniform Law Commission, Electronic Transactions Act, www.uniformlaws.org/committees/community-home?communitykey=2c04b76c-2b7d-4399–977e-d5876ba7e034.
99. *See Sebelius*, 567 U.S. at 575–85.
100. Justice Ginsburg argued in dissent that the majority's distinction between "old" and "new" Medicaid was not an accurate description of the ACA, but she lost 7–2 on the anti-commandeering issue.
101. *See id.*, at 579–80 ("Instead of simply refusing to grant the new funds to States that will not accept the new conditions, Congress has also threatened to withhold those States' existing Medicaid funds.").

102. *Id.*, at 581.
103. *Id.*, at 579 (quoting New York v. United States, 505 U.S. at 175).
104. As of May 2024, forty states had adopted the Medicaid expansion program. Ten states continued to opt out. *See* KFF, Status of State Medicaid Expansion Decisions: Interactive Map (May 8, 2024).
105. New York v. United States, 505 U.S. at 168.
106. *Id.*, at 169.
107. *See id.*, at 189–94 (White, J., concurring in part and dissenting in part).
108. *Id.*, at 194.
109. *Printz*, 521 U.S. 898 (1997). *Accord*, Jackson (1998).
110. *See Printz*, 521 U.S. at 966 (Stevens, J., dissenting) ("The burden on state officials that we approved in FERC was far more extensive than the minimal, temporary imposition posed by the Brady Act.").
111. *Printz*, 521 U.S. at 925.
112. 384 U.S. 436 (1966).
113. 378 U.S. 108 (1964).
114. *See* note 134 and accompanying text (this chapter).
115. Sloss (2024), at 114.
116. *Id.*, at 115.
117. 561 U.S. 742 (2010).
118. *Id.*, at 767 (quoting Washington v. Glucksberg, 521 U.S. 702, 721 (1997)).
119. Malloy v. Hogan, 378 U.S. 1, 16 (1964) (Harlan, J., dissenting) (arguing that the rule of "compelled uniformity" adopted by the majority in that case "is inconsistent with the purpose of our federal system").
120. 332 U.S. 46 (1947).
121. *Id.*, at 74 (Black, J., dissenting).
122. *See id.*, at 71–75 (Black, J. dissenting).
123. Fairman (1949).
124. Professor Akhil Amar defends a variant of incorporation doctrine that he calls "refined incorporation." *See* AMAR (1998), at 163–230. If implemented, his approach would yield results similar to total incorporation.
125. *See* Chapter 1 and Chapter 2.
126. *See McDonald*, 561 U.S. at 761–63.
127. *See* Sloss (2024), at 97–98.
128. Palko v. Connecticut, 302 U.S. 319, 326 (1937).
129. Twining v. New Jersey, 211 U.S. 78, 102 (1908).
130. Timbs v. Indiana, 586 U.S. 146, 150 (2019) ("deeply rooted in this Nation's history and tradition"); McDonald v. City of Chicago, 561 U.S. 742, 767 (2010) ("deeply rooted in this Nation's history and tradition"); Benton v. Maryland, 395 U.S. 784, 796 (1969) ("deeply ingrained in … the Anglo-American system of jurisprudence"); Duncan v. Louisiana, 391 U.S. 145, 148–54 (1968) (providing detailed historical analysis); Klopfer v. North Carolina, 386 U.S. 213, 223 (1967) ("right has its roots at the very foundation of our English law heritage").
131. Adamson v. California, 332 U.S. 46, 54 (1947) ("implicit in the concept of ordered liberty"); Palko v. Connecticut, 302 U.S. 319, 326 (1937) ("neither liberty nor justice would exist if they were sacrificed"); De Jonge v. Oregon, 299 U.S. 353, 364 (1937) ("fundamental principles of liberty and justice which lie at the base of all civil and political institutions"); Twining v. New Jersey, 211 U.S. 78, 102 (1908) ("immutable principles of justice"); Chicago, B & Q. R. Co. v. Chicago, 166 U.S. 226, 236 (1897) ("founded in natural equity, and … laid down as a principle of universal law").

132. Apodaca v. Oregon, 406 U.S. 404 (1972); Washington v. Texas, 388 U.S. 14, 17–18 (1967) ("essential to a fair trial"); Pointer v. Texas, 380 U.S. 400, 403 (1965) ("essential to a fair trial"); Irvin v. Dowd, 366 U.S. 717, 722 (1961) ("fair trial by a panel of impartial, indifferent jurors"); In re Oliver, 333 U.S. 257, 266–73 (1948); Betts v. Brady, 316 U.S. 455, 462 (1942) ("fundamental fairness"); West v. Louisiana, 194 U.S. 258, 261–65 (1904).
133. Gideon v. Wainwright, 372 U.S. 335, 340–44 (1963); Mapp v. Ohio, 367 U.S. 643, 650–56 (1961); Wolf v. Colorado, 338 U.S. 25, 26–29 (1949); Powell v. Alabama, 287 U.S. 45, 60–68 (1932).
134. Schilb v. Kuebel, 404 U.S. 357 (1971) (Eighth Am. Excessive Bail Clause); Aguilar v. Texas, 378 U.S. 108 (1964) (Fourth Am. warrant requirement); Malloy v. Hogan. 378 U.S. 1 (1964) (Fifth Am. Self-Incrimination Clause); Edwards v. South Carolina, 372 U.S. 229 (1963) (First Am. right to petition government); Robinson v. California, 370 U.S. 660 (1962) (Cruel and Unusual Punishments Clause); Everson v. Board of Ed., 330 U.S. 1 (1947) (Establishment Clause); Cantwell v. Connecticut, 310 U.S. 296 (1940) (Free Exercise Clause); Near v. Minnesota, 283 U.S. 697 (1931) (Free Press Clause); Gitlow v. New York, 268 U.S. 652 (1925) (Free Speech Clause).
135. Duncan v. Louisiana, 391 U.S. 145, 180–81 (1968) (Harlan, J., dissenting).
136. I have argued elsewhere that the natural law test offered a theoretically coherent rationale for transferring decision-making authority from the states to the federal courts. *See* Sloss (2024), at 123–26 (defending a natural law approach). I stand by that argument. However, for the reasons explained in Chapter 6, it is better for federal courts to enforce fundamental human rights against the states by applying treaties under the Supremacy Clause, rather than applying the Bill of Rights under the Fourteenth Amendment.
137. 514 U.S. 549 (1995).
138. *See* National Conference of State Legislatures, School Safety: Guns in Schools (updated June 20, 2023). ("The vast majority of states generally prohibit firearms in K-12 schools; however, almost all make some exception to their laws.")
139. As a practical matter, if a defendant is subject to prosecution under both state and federal laws, state and federal prosecutors consult with each other to determine who will take the lead. In cases where federal prosecutors "bully" their state counterparts, the blame for federal interference with state autonomy is properly placed on prosecutors, not Congress.
140. 561 U.S. 742 (2010).
141. The Supreme Court decided three cases in the late nineteenth century in which it explicitly rejected claims that the Second Amendment binds the states. *See* Miller v. Texas, 153 U.S. 535 (1894); Presser v. Illinois, 116 U.S. 252 (1886); United States v. Cruikshank, 92 U.S. 542 (1876). Since adoption of the Fourteenth Amendment, state firearms laws are subject to restrictions based on the Equal Protection Clause. *See, e.g.*, Chan v. City of Troy, 559 N.W.2d 374 (Mich. Ct. App. 1997) (invalidating a state firearms law that discriminated between citizens and non-citizens as a violation of the Equal Protection Clause).
142. *Lopez*, 514 U.S., at 564.
143. 142 S. Ct. 2111 (2022).
144. *See* Charles (2023) (noting that *Bruen* "invalidated New York's law and the similar statutory framework then existing in about six states, including California").
145. *See, e.g.*, Arizona Free Enterprise Club's Freedom Club PAC v. Bennett, 564 U.S. 721 (2011) (applying the First Amendment via the Fourteenth Amendment and invalidating an Arizona law that provided for public funding of elections for state offices).
146. *See, e.g.*, *Bruen*, 142 S. Ct. 2111 (2022) (Second Amendment, as applied to states under Fourteenth Amendment, limits power of states to impose restrictions on individuals who seek a license to carry a firearm outside the home).

147. *See, e.g.*, Roper v. Simmons, 543 U.S. 551 (2005) (Eighth Amendment, as applied to states under Fourteenth Amendment, bars states from imposing capital punishment on an individual who was less than eighteen-years-old when he committed the crime).
148. Palko v. Connecticut, 302 U.S. 319, 326 (1937).
149. Twining v. New Jersey, 211 U.S. 78, 102 (1908).
150. Universal Declaration of Human Rights, G.A. Res. 217A, U.N. Doc. A/810 (Dec. 10, 1948) [hereinafter UDHR].
151. Sloss (2024), at 128.
152. *See* Glendon (2001), at 21–51.
153. Perry (2017).
154. *See, e.g.*, Elkins et al. (2013); Beck et al. (2019).
155. *See* Sloss (2024), Table Three, pp. 136–37.
156. The database is available for download at https://comparativeconstitutionsproject.org/. The figures in Table 7.2 are derived from 2021 data. The database includes data for 197 "states." Four of those "states" are not U.N. member states: Abkhazia, Kosovo, South Ossetia, and Taiwan. The database has blank entries for 2021 for all the individual rights provisions for 14 of the 197 states (including Abkhazia and South Ossetia). I excluded those fourteen states from the denominator used to calculate the percentages in the right-hand column. That left a denominator of 183 states, including Kosovo and Taiwan.
157. Timbs v. Indiana, 586 U.S. 146 (2019).
158. McDonald v. City of Chicago, 561 U.S. 742 (2010).
159. Duncan v. Louisiana, 391 U.S. 145 (1968).
160. Mapp v. Ohio, 367 U.S. 643 (1961).
161. Everson v. Board of Ed., 330 U.S. 1 (1947).
162. The Court applied an historical test in *Timbs, McDonald*, and *Duncan*. *See* Table 7.1 and note 130. It applied a combined historical/natural law test in *Mapp*. *See supra* note 133 and accompanying text. It decided *Everson* by pure judicial fiat. *See supra* note 134 and accompanying text.
163. Nat'l Federation of Independent Business v. Sebelius, 567 U.S. 519 (2012).

8 A ROADMAP FOR REVOLUTIONARY CHANGE

1. *See* Ackerman (1991); Ackerman (1998); Ackerman (2014).
2. U.S. Const., art. V.
3. U.S. Const., amend XVII (restricting pay raises for Senators and Representatives).
4. In a thoughtful and important book, Professor Levinson called for a constitutional convention to fix the problems with our broken Constitution. *See* Levinson (2006). Although Prof. Levinson presents an insightful analysis of what is broken, I am doubtful that a constitutional convention is the best way to fix those problems.
5. *See* Ackerman (2014), at 43–47, 64–78.
6. *See* Ackerman (1998), at 306–375.
7. Ackerman (2014), at 76–78.
8. *See id.*, at 44–47.
9. *See, e.g.*, Siegel (2006).
10. Although the Court decided Roe v. Wade under the Due Process Clause, not the Equal Protection Clause, *Roe* is properly described as a central component of the de facto ERA. Other leading gender discrimination cases decided in the same time frame include Craig v. Boren, 429 U.S. 190 (1976), Weinberger v. Wiesenfeld, 420 U.S. 636 (1975), Frontiero v. Richardson, 411 U.S. 677 (1973), and Reed v. Reed, 404 U.S. 71 (1971).

11. Title IX of the 1972 Education Amendments prohibits gender-based discrimination in federally funded higher education programs. Pub. L. No. 92-318, 86 Stat. 235, 373 (June 23, 1972).
12. *See* Siegel (2006).
13. *See, e.g.*, Balkin & Siegel (2006); Siegel (2006); Siegel (2001).
14. *See* SLOSS (2016), at 319–29.
15. ACKERMAN (1998), at 11.
16. *Id.*
17. *See* Fishkin & Pozen (2018); Balkin (2008); Tushnet (2004).
18. Professor Aaron Belkin has made a similar argument. *See* Belkin (2019).
19. *See* ACKERMAN (2014), at 41–47.
20. From 1960 to 1983, the top 10 percent of households earned between 33 and 36 percent of national income. That share began increasing in about 1984. As of 2022, the top 10 percent earned about 48 percent of national income. In contrast, from 1960 to 1983, the bottom 50 percent of households earned between 18 and 21 percent of national income. That share began decreasing in 1983–84. As of 2022, the bottom 50 percent earned about 10 percent of national income. All data is taken from The World Inequality Database, *See* https://wid.world/data/.
21. Abortion rights activists are divided among themselves as to whether it makes sense to codify Roe v. Wade in federal legislation, or take a different approach. I express no position on that question. To qualify as a genuine landmark statute, though, abortion rights legislation must have sufficient popular support to withstand a repeal effort by the next Republican President.
22. E.O. 14023, 86 Fed. Reg. 19569 (Apr. 9, 2021).
23. Presidential Commission on the Supreme Court of the United States, Final Report (Dec. 2021) [hereinafter, "Final Report"].
24. Supreme Court Biennial Appointments and Term Limits Act of 2023, S.3096 [Whitehouse Bill]. The title of the legislation is misleading; it does not actually impose term limits on Supreme Court Justices. Legislation to impose term limits would likely be unconstitutional. *See* Final Report, at 130–40.
25. Judicial Modernization and Transparency Act, S.5229 [Wyden Bill].
26. *See id.*
27. *See* Whitehouse Bill, p. 3; Wyden Bill, p. 2. Under Wyden's proposal, appointments would continue until the Court hits a ceiling of fifteen Justices. The Whitehouse bill, in a rather indirect manner, sets a ceiling of eighteen Justices.
28. *See* Final Report, at 67–74.
29. Wyden Bill, p. 3. The bill includes provisions on recusal that might reduce the number of "voting Justices" in some cases. *See id.*, p. 4.
30. U.S. Const., art. III, sec. 2, cl. 2.
31. U.S. Const., art. I, sec. 8, cl. 18.
32. *See* Final Report, at 169–81.
33. *Id.*, at 181.
34. Whitehouse Bill, p. 2.
35. U.S. Const., art. III, sec. 2, cl. 2.
36. Final Report, at 136.
37. *See id.*, at 130–40, especially 136–38.
38. *See id.*, at 155.
39. *See id.*, at 154–69.
40. Assume that Congress enacts something like the Whitehouse bill with the addition of my proposed hardball provision. When a case challenging the constitutionality of the

legislation comes to the Supreme Court, the Court would first have to decide whether to sit as a body of nine Justices or eleven Justices to adjudicate the merits of the constitutional claim. I would like to be a fly on the wall to hear the Justices debate that question among themselves.

41. *See* Juliet Eilperin and Mike DeBonis, President Obama Nominates Merrick Garland to the Supreme Court, WASH. POST (March 16, 2016).
42. Wyden Bill, p. 3.
43. Tushnet (2009), at 498–99.
44. 570 U.S. 529 (2013).
45. *See* Chapter 3.
46. H.R. 14 (118th Cong., 1st Sess.).
47. *See id.*, secs. 5 and 6.
48. 424 U.S. 1 (1976).
49. *See* Chapter 3.
50. 558 U.S. 310 (2010).
51. *See id.*
52. H.R. 11, Freedom to Vote Act (118th Cong., 1st Sess., July 18, 2023).
53. Sections 6003 to 6007 deal with expenditures by foreign nationals. The Court has previously upheld statutory restrictions on campaign expenditures by foreign nationals. Bluman v. Fed'l Election Comm'n, 565 U.S. 1104 (Mem. 2012) (summarily affirming a lower court decision holding that statutory restrictions on foreign nationals did not violate the First Amendment).
54. *See. e.g.*, Nunziato (2019), at 1554–57 (contending that the Honest Ads Act, which is incorporated as a central element of Title VI of the Freedom to Vote Act, is probably constitutional under current First Amendment doctrine).
55. The bill passed the House by a vote of 240 to 189, with 198 Democrats, 41 Republicans, and one Independent voting in favor. https://clerk.house.gov/Votes/200234. It passed the Senate by a vote of 60–40, with forty-eight Democrats, eleven Republicans, and one Independent voting in favor. www.senate.gov/legislative/LIS/roll_call_votes/vote1072/vote_107_2_00054.htm.
56. *See* Marian Currinder, Michael Beckel, and Amisa Ratliff, Why We Left Congress: How the Legislative Branch Is Broken and What We Can Do about It (Dec. 6, 2018), at 10 (quoting former Rep. Zach Wamp).
57. *See id.*, at 8–9.
58. *See* Chapter 3.
59. U.S. Const., art. IV, sec. 4. ("The United States shall guarantee to every State in this Union a Republican Form of Government.")
60. See H.R. 11, *supra* note 52, sections 5001 to 5008.
61. *Id.*, sec. 5007.
62. *See* MCGANN ET AL. (2016), at 58–67, 78–81.
63. *See id.*, at 1–14; *see also* Li & Miller (2024).
64. *See* H.R. 11, *supra* note 52, sections 5001 to 5008.
65. *See id.*, sec. 5003(b) (establishing ranked criteria for redistricting); *see also* 52 USC 10301 et seq.
66. *See* H.R. 11, sec. 5001 (noting sources of Congress's constitutional authority).
67. *See* Foley (2018), at 1139–50.
68. *See generally* CHEMERINSKY (2015), at 443–54.
69. U.S. Const., art. I, sec. 4.
70. *See* Foley (2018).

71. ELY (1980), at 183.
72. There are situations where the Voting Rights Act requires whoever is in charge of redistricting to create "safe seats" for minority representatives. *See, e.g.*, Allen v. Milligan, 599 U.S. 1 (2023).
73. 377 U.S. 533, 565 (1964) (emphasis added).
74. *See* Chapter 3.
75. *See* Chapter 6.
76. *See* Chapter 7.
77. *See* Chapter 6.
78. *See* Chapter 4.
79. Red Lion Broadcasting Co. v. FCC, 395 U.S. 367, 390 (1969).
80. *See* Chapter 4.
81. 304 U.S. 64 (1938).
82. Hannah Arendt, "Truth and Politics," THE NEW YORKER (Feb. 17, 1967).
83. *See* Chapter 4.
84. *See* Chapter 5.
85. *See* Chapter 6.
86. *See* Chapter 6.
87. *See* Final Report, *supra* note 23, at 183–202.
88. *Id.*, at 189.
89. *Id.*

APPENDIX

1. *See* Sloss (2014), at 1845–48.
2. Harold J. Spaeth, Lee Epstein, et al. 2023 Supreme Court Database, Version 2023 Release 1, http://supremecourtdatabase.org.
3. With the addition of cases from the Roberts Court, phase one data includes a total of 28,293 cases – every Supreme Court decision from the Marshall Court through June 2023.
4. The phase one database includes three types of cases that are neither PP nor PG. If one of the parties is a foreign state, the case is classified as FS. FS cases are not "public law" because they do not involve a dispute between a private party and a domestic government actor. Suits between domestic government actors, such as a suit between the United States and New York, are classified as GG. GG cases do not qualify as "public law" because they do not involve a dispute between a private party and a government actor. Mixed party cases, in which a government actor and a private party are co-parties, are classified as MP.
5. *See* Sloss (2014), at 1767–68.
6. In phase one, student research assistants reviewed every Supreme Court decision from John Marshall's first term as Chief Justice until William Rehnquist's last term. Students classified every case as PP, PG, FS, GG, or MP. To facilitate timely completion, I instructed students to spend no more than five minutes per case and to resolve doubts in favor of a PG classification. The latter instruction yielded an overestimate of the number of PG cases in phase one; that was a deliberate attempt to ensure that no PG cases were excluded from the universe from which I drew a random sample in phase two.
7. *See id.*, at 1777–78.
8. In a total of forty-one cases where the entries in the Supreme Court Database were unclear, I checked on Westlaw to confirm the identity of the parties for the purpose of phase one classification.

9. For periods 6 to 8, two students reviewed every sample case and entered information into an Excel file in accordance with my detailed instructions. Students compared their entries to each others' and referred disagreements to me. I reviewed the Excel files for consistency and accuracy. For periods 1 to 3, I reviewed the cases myself and entered data into Excel files. The nineteenth-century jurisprudence is sufficiently unfamiliar to most law students that I could not rely on student research assistants to enter accurate information about nineteenth-century cases.

Bibliography

BOOKS, ARTICLES, REPORTS, ETC.

ACKERMAN, BRUCE, WE THE PEOPLE, VOLUME I: FOUNDATIONS (1991).

ACKERMAN, BRUCE, WE THE PEOPLE, VOLUME 2: TRANSFORMATIONS (1998).

ACKERMAN, BRUCE, WE THE PEOPLE, VOLUME 3: THE CIVIL RIGHTS REVOLUTION (2014).

Adams, Katherine et al., *Report of the Commission*, in SOCIAL MEDIA, FREEDOM OF SPEECH, AND THE FUTURE OF OUR DEMOCRACY (Lee C. Bollinger & Geoffrey R. Stone, eds. 2022).

Agiesta, Jennifer and Ariel Edwards-Levy, CNN Poll: Percentage of Republicans Who Think Biden's 2020 Win was Illegitimate Ticks Back Up Near 70% (Aug. 3, 2023), www.cnn.com/2023/08/03/politics/cnn-poll-republicans-think-2020-election-illegitimate/index.html.

Alexander, Larry and Frederick Schauer, *On Extrajudicial Constitutional Interpretation*, 110 HARV. L. REV. 1359 (1997).

Alexander, Larry and Frederick Schauer, *Defending Judicial Supremacy: A Reply*, 17 CONST'L COMMENTARY 455 (2000).

AMAR, AKHIL REED, THE BILL OF RIGHTS: CREATION AND RECONSTRUCTION (1998).

AMERICAN LAW INSTITUTE, RESTATEMENT (SECOND) OF THE FOREIGN RELATIONS LAW OF THE UNITED STATES (1965).

Arendt, Hannah, *Truth and Politics*, THE NEW YORKER, Feb. 17, 1967.

Atkinson, Nathan, Edward Foley, and Scott C. Ganz, *Beyond the Spoiler Effect: Can Ranked-Choice Voting Solve the Problem of Political Polarization* 2024 UNIV. ILL. L. REV. 1655 (2024).

Atkinson, Nathan and Scott C. Ganz, *Robust Electoral Competition: Rethinking Electoral Systems to Encourage Representative Outcomes*, 84 MD. L. REV. 102 (2024).

ATTANASIO, JOHN, POLITICS AND CAPITAL: AUCTIONING THE AMERICAN DREAM (2018).

AVERY, MICHAEL AND DANIELLE MCLAUGHLIN, THE FEDERALIST SOCIETY: HOW CONSERVATIVES TOOK THE LAW BACK FROM LIBERALS (2013).

BALKIN, JACK M., LIVING ORIGINALISM (2011).

Balkin, Jack M. and Reva D. Siegel, *Principles, Practices and Social Movements*, 154 U. PENN. L. REV. 927 (2006).

Balkin, Jack M., *Constitutional Hardball and Constitutional Crises*, 26 QUINNIPIAC L. REV. 579 (2008).

Barnett, Randy E., *Interpretation and Construction*, 34 HARV. J. L. & PUB. POL'Y 65 (2011).

BARNETT, RANDY E., OUR REPUBLICAN CONSTITUTION: SECURING THE LIBERTY AND SOVEREIGNTY OF WE THE PEOPLE (2016).

Barrett, John Q., *Supreme Court Law Clerks' Recollections of Brown v. Board of Education*, 78 ST. JOHN'S L. REV. 515 (2004).

BAXTER, MAURICE G., DANIEL WEBSTER AND THE SUPREME COURT (1966).

Beck, Colin J. et al., *Constitutions in World Society: A New Measure of Human Rights*, in CONSTITUTION-MAKING AND TRANSNATIONAL LEGAL ORDER (Tom Ginsburg, Terence C. Halliday & Gregory Shaffer eds., 2019).

Belkin, Aaron, *Court Expansion and the Restoration of Democracy: The Case for Constitutional Hardball*, 2019 PEPP. L. REV. 19 (2019).

BENKLER, YOCHAI, ROBERT FARIS, and HAL ROBERTS, NETWORK PROPAGANDA: MANIPULATION, DISINFORMATION, AND RADICALIZATION IN AMERICAN POLITICS (2018).

BERNSTEIN, DAVID E., REHABILITATING LOCHNER: DEFENDING INDIVIDUAL RIGHTS AGAINST PROGRESSIVE REFORM (2012).

BHAGWAT, ASHUTOSH, OUR DEMOCRATIC FIRST AMENDMENT (2020).

Bhagwat, Ashutosh, *The New Gatekeepers?: Social Media and the Search for Truth*, 3 J. FREE SPEECH L. 41 (2023).

BICKEL, ALEXANDER M., THE LEAST DANGEROUS BRANCH: THE SUPREME COURT AT THE BAR OF POLITICS (2nd ed. 1986) (first published in 1962).

Bradley, Curtis A., *Self-Execution and Treaty Duality*, 2008 SUPREME CT. REV. 131 (2008).

Bradley, Curtis A. and Jack L. Goldsmith, *Customary International Law as Federal Law: A Critique of the Modern Position*, 110 HARV. L. REV. 815 (1997).

Brennan Center for Justice, Who Controlled Redistricting in Every State? (Oct. 5, 2022), available at www.brennancenter.org/our-work/research-reports/who-controlled-redistricting-every-state.

Brief for Petitioners, Bolling v. Sharpe, 347 U.S. 497 (1954) (No. 8), available at 1952 WL 47257.

BROWNELL, KATHRYN CRAMER, 24/7 POLITICS: CABLE TELEVISION AND THE FRAGMENTING OF AMERICA FROM WATERGATE TO FOX NEWS (2023).

BROWNSTEIN, RONALD, THE SECOND CIVIL WAR: HOW EXTREME PARTISANSHIP HAS PARALYZED WASHINGTON AND POLARIZED AMERICA (2007).

CARO, ROBERT A., THE YEARS OF LYNDON JOHNSON: MASTER OF THE SENATE (2002).

Center for Countering Digital Hate, Musk Misleading Election Claims Viewed 1.2 BN Times on X With no Fact Checks (Aug. 8, 2024), https://counterhate.com/research/musk-misleading-election-claims-viewed-1-2bn-times-on-x-with-no-fact-checks/.

Charles, Guy-Uriel, *Judging the Law of Politics*, 103 MICH. L. REV. 1099 (2005).

Charles, Jacob D., *Will Bruen Imperil California Gun Laws?* 45 LOS ANGELES LAWYER 16 (2023).

CHEMERINSKY, ERWIN, FEDERAL JURISDICTION (6th ed. 2012).

CHEMERINSKY, ERWIN, CONSTITUTIONAL LAW: PRINCIPLES AND POLICIES (5th ed. 2015).

Cillizza, Chris, The Least Productive Congress Ever (July 17, 2023), www.washingtonpost.com/news/the-fix/wp/2013/07/17/the-least-productive-congress-ever/.

Coles, Harry L., Jr., *Applicability of the Public Land System to Louisiana*, 43 MISS. VALLEY HIST. REV. 39 (1956).

Common Cause, Charge Report: Community Redistricting Report Card (Oct. 13, 2023), available at www.commoncause.org/wp-content/uploads/2023/11/CommunityRedistricting ReportCard_Digital_REV3.pdf.

Congressional Research Service, Table of Laws Held Unconstitutional in Whole or in Part by the Supreme Court, available at https://constitution.congress.gov/resources/unconstitutional-laws/.

Cook Political Report, 2024 CPR House Race Ratings (Feb. 29, 2024), www.cookpolitical.com/ratings/house-race-ratings.

Cook Political Report, 2024 CPR House Race Ratings (June 14, 2024), www.cookpolitical.com/ratings/house-race-ratings.

Copeland, Joseph, Favorable Views of Supreme Court Remain Near Historic Low (Aug. 8, 2024), www.pewresearch.org/short-reads/2024/08/08/favorable-views-of-supreme-court-remain-near-historic-low/.

Coppedge, Michael, et al., V-Dem Codebook, v12 (Mar. 2022), available at www.v-dem.net/static/website/img/refs/codebookv12.pdf.

Cox, Archibald, *Foreword: Constitutional Adjudication and the Promotion of Human Rights*, 80 HARV. L. REV. 91 (1966).

CUMMINGS, HOMER and CARL MCFARLAND, FEDERAL JUSTICE: CHAPTERS IN THE HISTORY OF JUSTICE AND THE FEDERAL EXECUTIVE (1937).

Currinder, Marian, Michael Beckel, and Amisa Ratliff, Why We Left Congress: How the Legislative Branch Is Broken and What We Can Do about It (Dec. 6, 2018), available at www.rstreet.org/research/why-we-left-congress-how-the-legislative-branch-is-broken-and-what-we-can-do-about-it-2/.

CUSHMAN, BARRY, RETHINKING THE NEW DEAL COURT: THE STRUCTURE OF A CONSTITUTIONAL REVOLUTION (1998).

Czopek, Madison, Trump Trial Judge Didn't Overrule All Defense Objections and Sustain All Prosecution Objections (Politifact, May 31, 2024), www.politifact.com/factchecks/2024/may/31/jesse-watters/trump-trial-judge-didnt-overrule-all-defense-objec/.

DEAN, JOHN W., THE REHNQUIST CHOICE: THE UNTOLD STORY OF THE NIXON APPOINTMENT THAT REDEFINED THE SUPREME COURT (2001).

DIBBLE, ERNEST F., JOSEPH MILLS WHITE: ANTI-JACKSONIAN FLORIDIAN (2003).

DiResta, Renee, *Free Speech Is Not the Same as Free Reach*, WIRED, Aug. 30, 2018, www.wired.com/story/free-speech-is-not-the-same-as-free-reach/.

DIXON, ROSALIND, RESPONSIVE JUDICIAL REVIEW, DEMOCRACY AND DYSFUNCTION IN THE MODERN AGE (2023).

Dorf, Michael C., *Equal Protection Incorporation*, 88 VA. L. REV. 951 (2002).

Driver, Justin, *The Strange Career of Antisubordination*, 91 U. CHICAGO L. REV. 651 (2024).

DUDZIAK, MARY L., COLD WAR CIVIL RIGHTS: RACE AND THE IMAGE OF AMERICAN DEMOCRACY (2000).

ECONOMIST, THE, DEMOCRACY INDEX 2016: REVENGE OF THE "DEPLORABLES" (2017).

Eilperin, Juliet and Mike DeBonis, *President Obama Nominates Merrick Garland to the Supreme Court*, WASH. POST, Mar. 16, 2016.

Elkins, Zachary et al., *Getting to Rights: Treaty Ratification, Constitutional Convergence, and Human Rights Practice*, 54 HARV. INT'L L.J. 61 (2013).

ELY, JOHN HART, DEMOCRACY AND DISTRUST: A THEORY OF JUDICIAL REVIEW (1980).

Fairman, Charles, *Does the Fourteenth Amendment Incorporate the Bill of Rights?, The Original Understanding*, 2 STAN. L. REV. 5 (1949).

Fairman, Charles, *Editorial Comment: Finis to Fujii*, 46 AM. J. INT'L L. 682 (1952).

FALLON, RICHARD H., JR. ET AL., HART & WECHSLER'S THE FEDERAL COURTS AND THE FEDERAL SYSTEM (7th ed. 2015).

THE FEDERALIST PAPERS (Isaac Kramnick, ed. 1987).

FELDMAN, NOAH R. and KATHLEEN SULLIVAN, CONSTITUTIONAL LAW (20th ed. 2019).

Feldman, Noah, Takeover: How a Conservative Student Club Captured the Supreme Court (audiobook).

Finkelman, Paul, *John Bingham and the Background to the Fourteenth Amendment*, 36 AKRON L. REV. 671 (2003).

Fishkin, Joseph and David E. Pozen, *Asymmetric Constitutional Hardball*, 118 COLUM. L. REV. 915 (2018).

Fitzgerald, Laura S., *Beyond Marbury: Jurisdictional Self-Dealing in Seminole Tribe*, 52 VAND. L. REV. 407 (1999).

Foley, Edward B., *Constitutional Preservation and the Judicial Review of Partisan Gerrymanders*, 52 GEORGIA L. REV. 1105 (2018).

Foley, Edward B., *Maximum Convergence Voting: Madisonian Constitutional Theory and Electoral System Design*, 76 FLA. L. REV. 1751 (2024).

Frantz, Laurent B., *Congressional Power to Enforce the Fourteenth Amendment against Private Acts*, 73 YALE L. J. 1353 (1964).

FRIEDENTHAL, JACK H., MARY KAY KANE & ARTHUR R. MILLER, CIVIL PROCEDURE (5th ed. 2015).

Friedman, Barry, *The History of the Countermajoritarian Difficulty, Part One: The Road to Judicial Supremacy*, 73 N.YU. L. REV. 333 (1998).

Friedman, Barry, *The History of the Countermajoritarian Difficulty, Part Two: Reconstruction's Political Court*, 91 GEO. L. J. 1 (2002) [2002a].

Friedman, Barry, *The Birth of an Academic Obsession: The History of the Countermajoritarian Difficulty, Part Five*, 112 YALE L. J. 153 (2002) [2002b].

FRIEDMAN, BARRY, THE WILL OF THE PEOPLE: HOW PUBLIC OPINION HAS INFLUENCED THE SUPREME COURT AND SHAPED THE MEANING OF THE CONSTITUTION (2009).

GARDBAUM, STEPHEN, THE NEW COMMONWEALTH MODEL OF CONSTITUTIONALISM (2013).

GINSBURG, TOM and AZIZ Z. HUQ, HOW TO SAVE A CONSTITUTIONAL DEMOCRACY (2018).

GLENDON, MARY ANN, A WORLD MADE NEW: ELEANOR ROOSEVELT AND THE UNIVERSAL DECLARATION OF HUMAN RIGHTS (2001).

GOEBEL, JULIUS JR., ANTECEDENTS AND BEGINNINGS TO 1801 (1971) (The Oliver Wendell Holmes Devise History of the Supreme Court, Vol. I).

Golove, David M. and Daniel J. Hulsebosch, *A Civilized Nation: The Early American Constitution, The Law of Nations, and the Pursuit of International Recognition*, 85 N.Y.U. L. REV. 932 (2010).

GRABER, MARK A., PUNISH TREASON, REWARD LOYALTY: THE FORGOTTEN GOALS OF CONSTITUTIONAL REFORM AFTER THE CIVIL WAR (2023).

GREEN, CHRISTOPHER R., EQUAL CITIZENSHIP, CIVIL RIGHTS, AND THE CONSTITUTION: THE ORIGINAL SENSE OF THE PRIVILEGES AND IMMUNITIES CLAUSE (2015).

GREENE, JAMAL, HOW RIGHTS WENT WRONG: WHY OUR OBSESSION WITH RIGHTS IS TEARING AMERICA APART (2021).

Gunther, Gerald, *Foreword: In Search of Evolving Doctrine on a Changing Court: A Model for a Newer Equal Protection*, 86 HARV. L. REV. 1 (1972).

HAMILTON, DANIEL W., THE LIMITS OF SOVEREIGNTY: PROPERTY CONFISCATION IN THE UNION AND THE CONFEDERACY DURING THE CIVIL WAR (2007).

HASEN, RICHARD L., ELECTION MELTDOWN: DIRTY TRICKS, DISTRUST, AND THE THREAT TO AMERICAN DEMOCRACY (2020).

Hasen, Richard L., *The Stagnation, Retrogression, and Potential Pro-Voter Transformation of U.S. Election Law*, 134 YALE L. J. 1673 (2025).

Henkin, Louis, *U.S. Ratification of Human Rights Conventions: The Ghost of Senator Bricker*, 89 AM. J. INT'L L. 341 (1995).

Historians' Amicus Brief in Trump v. United States, available at www.brennancenter.org/our-work/research-reports/historians-amicus-brief-trump-v-united-states.

HODDER-WILLIAMS, RICHARD, THE POLITICS OF THE U.S. SUPREME COURT (1980).

Hollis, Duncan B., *Treaties in the Supreme Court, 1861–1900*, in SLOSS, RAMSEY & DODGE (2011).

HOWARD, PHILIP N., LIE MACHINES: HOW TO SAVE DEMOCRACY FROM TROLL ARMIES, DECEITFUL ROBOTS, JUNK NEWS OPERATIONS, AND POLITICAL OPERATIVES (2020).

Hulsebosch, Daniel J., *An Empire of Law: Chancellor Kent and the Revolution in Books in the Early Republic*, 60 ALABAMA L. REV. 377 (2009).

HUQ, AZIZ Z., THE COLLAPSE OF CONSTITUTIONAL REMEDIES (2021).

Issacharoff, Samuel and Richard H. Pildes, *Politics as Markets: Partisan Lockups of the Democratic Process*, 50 STAN. L. REV. 643 (1998).

ISSACHAROFF, SAMUEL ET AL., THE LAW OF DEMOCRACY: LEGAL STRUCTURE OF THE POLITICAL PROCESS (5th ed. 2016).

Jackson, Vicki C., *Federalism and the Uses and Limits of Law: Printz and Principle*, 111 HARV. L. REV. 2180 (1998).

Jankowicz, Nina, *The Coming Flood of Disinformation: How Washington Gave Up on the Fight Against Falsehoods* (FOREIGN AFFAIRS, Feb. 7, 2024).

Jeffries, John C., Jr., *In Praise of the Eleventh Amendment and Section 1983*, 84 VA. L. REV. 47 (1998).

Johnson, Kevin, New Models for Keeping Partisans Out of Election Administration (Jan. 31, 2022), available at www.cartercenter.org/resources/pdfs/news/peace_publications/democracy/new-models-keeping-partisans-out-election-admin-013122.pdf.

Johnson, Benjamin B., *The Origins of Supreme Court Question Selection*, 122 COLUM. L. REV. 793 (2022).

Jones, Jeffrey M., Independent Party ID Tied for High, Democratic ID at New Low (Jan. 12, 2024), available at https://news.gallup.com/poll/548459/independent-party-tied-high-democratic-new-low.aspx#:~:text=U.S.%20adults'%20political%20party%20identification,Republicans%20and%2027%25%20as%20Democrats.

Just Security Podcast, Presidential Immunity after Trump v. United States (July 3, 2024), available at www.justsecurity.org/97447/podcast-trump-v-united-states/.

Kamisar, Ben, Almost a Third of Americans Still Believe the 2020 Election Result Was Fraudulent (June 20, 2023), www.nbcnews.com/meet-the-press/meetthepressblog/almost-third-americans-still-believe-2020-election-result-was-fraudule-rcna90145.

Kang, Michael S., *Gerrymandering and the Constitutional Norm against Government Partisanship*, 116 MICH. L. REV. 351 (2017).

Karlan, Pamela S., *John Hart Ely and the Problem of Gerrymandering: The Lion in Winter*, 114 YALE L. J. 1329 (2005).

Karlan, Pamela S., *Foreword: Democracy and Disdain*, 126 HARV. L. REV. 1 (2012).

KFF, Status of State Medicaid Expansion Decisions: Interactive Map (May 8, 2024), www.kff.org/affordable-care-act/issue-brief/status-of-state-medicaid-expansion-decisions-interactive-map/.

KAUFMAN, NATALIE HEVENER, HUMAN RIGHTS TREATIES AND THE SENATE: A HISTORY OF OPPOSITION (1990).

Keena, Alex et al., Gerrymandering the States: Partisanship, Race, and the Transformation of American Federalism (2021).

Kent, James, Commentaries on American Law (11th ed. 1867) (George Comstock ed.).

Klarman, Michael J., From Jim Crow to Civil Rights: The Supreme Court and the Struggle for Racial Equality (2004).

Kleinfeld, Rachel, Polarization, Democracy, and Political Violence in the United States: What the Research Says (Carnegie Endowment for International Peace, Sept. 2023).

Koza, John R. et al., Every Vote Equal: A State-Based Plan for Electing the President by National Popular Vote (5th ed. 2024).

Kramer, Larry D., The People Themselves: Popular Constitutionalism and Judicial Review (2004).

Kruse, Kevin M. and Julian Zelizer, How Policy Decisions Spawned Today's Hyperpolarized Media, Wash. Post, Jan. 17, 2019.

LaFave, Wayne R. et al., Criminal Procedure (5th ed. 2009).

Landau, David and Rosalind Dixon, *Abusive Judicial Review: Courts against Democracy*, 53 U.C. Davis L. Rev. 1313 (2020).

Lash, Kurt T., The Fourteenth Amendment and the Privileges and Immunities of American Citizenship (2014).

Lee, Thomas H. and David L. Sloss, *International Law as an Interpretive Tool in the Supreme Court: 1861–1900*, in Sloss, Ramsey & Dodge (2011).

Leiter, Brian, *The Epistemology of the Internet and the Regulation of Speech in America*, 20 Geo. J. L. & Pub. Pol. 903 (2022).

Lemley, Mark A., *The Imperial Supreme Court*, 136 Harv. L. Rev. F. 97 (2022).

Levinson, Sanford, Our Undemocratic Constitution: Where the Constitution Goes Wrong (and How We the People Can Correct It) (2006).

Levitsky, Steven and Daniel Ziblatt, How Democracies Die (2018).

Lewis, Jeffrey B., et al., *Voteview: Congressional Roll-Call Votes Database* (2024), https://voteview.com/.

Li, Michael and Peter Miller, How Gerrymandering Tilts the 2024 Race for the House (Sept. 24, 2024), www.brennancenter.org/our-work/research-reports/how-gerrymandering-tilts-2024-race-house.

Lockwoood, Bert B., Jr., *The United Nations Charter and United States Civil Rights Litigation: 1946–1955*, 69 Iowa L. Rev. 901 (1984).

Los Angeles Daily Journal, Charter of United Nations Held to Invalidate California Alien Land Act, April 25, 1950 (*reprinted in* 96 Cong. Rec. 5993, 6000).

Los Angeles Times, Ruling Holds Alien Land Law Invalid, April 25, 1950 (A1).

Madison, James, The Report of 1800 (Jan. 7, 1800), available at https://founders.archives.gov/documents/Madison/01–17–02-0202.

McConnell, Michael W., *Institutions and Interpretation: A Critique of City of Boerne v. Flores*, 111 Harv. L. Rev. 153 (1997).

McDonald, Jessica, Vance Wrong on Child Tax Credit, Harris' Remarks about Climate Change and Having Kids (Aug. 2, 2024), www.factcheck.org/2024/08/vance-wrong-on-child-tax-credit-harris-remarks-about-climate-change-and-having-kids/.

McGann, Anthony J. et al., Gerrymandering in America: The House of Representatives, the Supreme Court, and the Future of Popular Sovereignty (2016).

McGinnis, John O., *An Opinionated History of the Federalist Society*, 7 Geo. J. L. & Pub. Pol'y 403 (2009) [2009a].

McGinnis, John O., *Medellin and the Future of International Delegation*, 118 YALE L. J. 1712 (2009) [2009b].

McKay, Robert B., *Political Thickets and Crazy Quilts: Reapportionment and Equal Protection*, 61 MICH. L. REV. 645 (1963).

Meese, Edwin III, *The Law of the Constitution*, 61 TULANE L. REV. 979 (1987).

MEIKLEJOHN, ALEXANDER, FREE SPEECH AND ITS RELATION TO SELF-GOVERNMENT (1948).

Metzger, Miriam J., Ethan H. Hartsell, and Andrew J. Flanagin, *Cognitive Dissonance or Credibility? A Comparison of Two Theoretical Explanations for Selective Exposure to Partisan News*, 47(1) COMMUNICATIONS RESEARCH (2020).

Miller, Erin L. *Amplified Speech*, 43 CARDOZO L. REV. 1 (2021).

MINOW, MARTHA, SAVING THE NEWS: WHY THE CONSTITUTION CALLS FOR GOVERNMENT ACTION TO PRESERVE FREEDOM OF SPEECH (2021).

Monaghan, Henry P., *Foreword: Constitutional Common Law*, 89 HARV. L. REV. 1 (1975).

MORRIS, RICHARD, THE FORGING OF THE UNION (1984).

Morris, Kevin and Coryn Grange, Growing Racial Disparities in Voter Turnout, 2008–2022, (Brennan Center for Justice, Mar. 2024), available at www.brennancenter.org/our-work/research-reports/growing-racial-disparities-voter-turnout-2008-2022.

Netanel, Neil, *Applying Militant Democracy to Defend against Social Media Harms*, 45 CARDOZO L. REV. 489 (2023).

Norden, Lawrence, Mekela Panditharatne, and David Harris, Multiple Threats Converge to Heighten Disinformation Risks to This Year's US Elections (Just Security, Feb. 16, 2024).

Norton, Helen, *Distrust, Negative First Amendment Theory, and the Regulation of Lies*, 4 J. FREE SPEECH L. 595 (2023).

Nunziato, Dawn Carla, *The Marketplace of Ideas Online*, 94 NOTRE DAME L. REV. 1519 (2019).

O'Donnell, Norah, Are Members of Congress Becoming Telemarketers?, CBS NEWS (Apr. 24, 2016), www.cbsnews.com/news/60-minutes-are-members-of-congress-becoming-telemarketers/.

Olson, Theodore B., *Tex Lazar Memorial Lecture*, 9 TEX. REV. L. & POL. 1 (2004).

Orth, Taylor and Carl Bialik, YouGov, Trust in Media 2024: Which news sources Americans trust—and which they think lean left or right (May 30, 2024), https://today.yougov.com/politics/articles/49552-trust-in-media-2024-which-news-outlets-americans-trust.

Pearlstein, Deborah, *Democracy Harms and the First Amendment*, 4 J. FREE SPEECH L. 617 (2023).

Pechota, Vratislav, *The Development of the Covenant on Civil and Political Rights*, in THE INTERNATIONAL BILL OF RIGHTS: THE COVENANT ON CIVIL AND POLITICAL RIGHTS (Louis Henkin, ed. 1981).

PERRY, MICHAEL J., A GLOBAL POLITICAL MORALITY: HUMAN RIGHTS, DEMOCRACY, AND CONSTITUTIONALISM (2017).

Persily, Nathaniel, *The Promise and Pitfalls of the New Voting Rights Act*, 117 YALE L. J. 174 (2007).

Pew Research Center, Public Trust in Government: 1958–2023, available at www.pewresearch.org/politics/2023/09/19/public-trust-in-government-1958-2023/.

Pildes, Richard H., *The Supreme Court, 2003 Term—Foreword: The Constitutionalization of Democratic Politics*, 118 HARV. L. REV. 29 (2004).

Pildes, Richard H., *Why the Center Does Not Hold: The Causes of Hyperpolarized Democracy in America*, 99 CAL. L. REV. 273 (2011).

Pildes, Richard H., *Political Reforms to Combat Extremism*, in OUR NATION AT RISK, ELECTION INTEGRITY AS A NATIONAL SECURITY ISSUE 163–88 (Julian E. Zelizer and Karen J. Greenberg eds., 2024).

Post, Robert C. and Reva B. Siegel, *Legislative Constitutionalism and Section Five Power: Policentric Interpretation of the Family and Medical Leave Act*, 112 YALE L. J. 1943 (2003).

PURCELL, EDWARD A., BRANDEIS AND THE PROGRESSIVE CONSTITUTION (2000).

RAKOVE, JACK, ORIGINAL MEANINGS: POLITICS AND IDEAS IN THE MAKING OF THE CONSTITUTION (1996).

Ramsey, Michael D., *Customary International Law in the Supreme Court, 1901–1945*, in SLOSS, RAMSEY, DODGE (2011).

Repucci, Sarah and Amy Slipowitz, Freedom House, Freedom in the World 2021: Democracy Under Siege (2021).

Resnik, Judith, *Categorical Federalism: Jurisdiction, Gender, and the Globe*, 111 YALE L. J. 619 (2001).

Roper Center, Public Opinion on the Voting Rights Act (Aug. 6, 2015), https://ropercenter.cornell.edu/blog/public-opinion-voting-rights-act.

Rosen, Jeffrey, *Packing the Courts*, NEW YORK TIMES, May 10, 2013.

ROSENBLUTH, FRANCES MCCALL and IAN SHAPIRO, RESPONSIBLE PARTIES: SAVING DEMOCRACY FROM ITSELF (2018).

ROTHSTEIN, RICHARD, THE COLOR OF LAW (2017).

Rutenberg, Jim and Steven Lee Myers, Trump Allies are Winning War Over Disinformation, NEW YORK TIMES, Mar. 17, 2024.

SALYER, LUCY E., LAWS HARSH AS TIGERS: CHINESE IMMIGRANTS AND THE SHAPING OF MODERN IMMIGRATION LAW (1995).

Scalia, Antonin, *Keynote Address: Foreign Legal Authority in the Federal Courts*, 98 AM. SOC'Y INT'L L. PROC. 305 (2004).

SCHAUER, FREDERICK, FREE SPEECH: A PHILOSOPHICAL ENQUIRY (1982).

Schauer, Frederick, *Ashwander Revisited*, 1995 SUP. CT. REV. 71 (1995).

SEGALL, ERIC J., SUPREME MYTHS: WHY THE SUPREME COURT IS NOT A COURT AND ITS JUSTICES ARE NOT JUDGES (2012).

Shanor, Amanda, *The New Lochner*, 2016 WIS. L. REV. 133 (2016).

SHUGERMAN, JED HANDELSMAN, THE PEOPLE'S COURTS: PURSUING JUDICIAL INDEPENDENCE IN AMERICA (2012).

Siegel, Reva B., *Text in Contest: Gender and the Constitution from a Social Movement Perspective*, 150 U. PA. L. REV. 297 (2001).

Siegel, Reva B., *Constitutional Culture, Social Movement Conflict and Constitutional Change: The Case of the de Facto ERA*, 94 CAL. L. REV. 1323 (2006).

Sloss, David L., *The Domestication of International Human Rights: Non-Self-Executing Declarations and Human Rights Treaties*, 24 YALE J. INT'L L. 129 (1999).

Sloss, David L., *Ex parte Young and Federal Remedies for Human Rights Treaty Violations*, 75 WASH. L. REV. 1103 (2000).

Sloss, David L., *Using International Law to Enhance Democracy*, 47 VA. J. INT'L L. 1 (2006).

SLOSS, DAVID L., MICHAEL D. RAMSEY and WILLIAM S. DODGE (eds.), INTERNATIONAL LAW IN THE U.S. SUPREME COURT: CONTINUITY AND CHANGE (2011).

Sloss, David L., *Executing Foster v. Neilson: The Two-Step Approach to Analyzing Self-Executing Treaties*, 53 HARV. INT'L L.J. 135 (2012).

Sloss, David L., *Polymorphous Public Law Litigation: The Forgotten History of Nineteenth Century Public Law Litigation*, 71 WASH. & LEE L. REV. 1757 (2014).

Sloss, David L., *Bond v. United States: Choosing the Lesser of Two Evils*, 90 NOTRE DAME L. REV. 1583 (2015).

Sloss, David L., The Death of Treaty Supremacy: An Invisible Constitutional Change (2016) [2016a].

Sloss, David L., *How International Human Rights Transformed the U.S. Constitution*, 38 Human Rights Quarterly 426 (2016) [2016b].

Sloss, David L. and Wayne Sandholtz, *Universal Human Rights and Constitutional Change*, 27 Wm. & Mary Bill of Rights J. 1183 (2019).

Sloss, David L., *Stop Electronic Amplification of Lies*, 66 St. Louis Univ. L.J. 129 (2021) [2021a].

Sloss, David L., Enhance Fact-Checking to Protect Democracy (Dec. 6, 2021), [2021b] www.acslaw.org/expertforum/enhance-fact-checking-to-protect-democracy/.

Sloss, David L., Tyrants on Twitter: Protecting Democracies from Information Warfare (2022).

Sloss, David L., *Guns, Abortion and Courts*, 64 Santa Clara L. Rev. 83 (2024).

Solender, Andrew, Capitol Hill Stunner: 2023 Led to Fewest Laws in Decades (Dec. 18, 2023), www.axios.com/2023/12/19/118-congress-bills-least-unproductive-chart.

Solum, Lawrence B., *Originalism and Constitutional Construction*, 82 Fordham L. Rev. 453 (2013).

Solum, Lawrence B., *Outcome Reasons and Process Reasons in Normative Constitutional Theory*, 172 U. Pa. L. Rev. 913 (2024).

Southworth, Ann, Big Money Unleashed: The Campaign to Deregulate Election Spending (2023).

Spaeth, Harold J., Lee Epstein, et al., 2023 Supreme Court Database, Version 2023 Release 1, http://supremecourtdatabase.org.

Steigrad, Alexandra, Fox News Earns its Highest July Ratings Ever to Blow Away Cable Rivals CNN, MSNBC, New York Post, July 31, 2024, https://nypost.com/2024/07/31/media/fox-news-has-its-highest-july-ratings-ever-to-beat-cnn-msnbc/.

Stephanopoulos, Nicholas O., *The Anti-Carolene Court*, 2019 Sup. Ct. Rev. 111 (2019).

Strauss, David A., *The Irrelevance of Constitutional Amendments*, 114 Harv. L. Rev. 1457 (2001).

Strauss, David A., The Living Constitution (2010).

Sullivan, Kathleen M., *The Supreme Court 1991 Term, Foreword: The Justices of Rules and Standards*, 106 Harv. L. Rev. 22 (1992).

Sunstein, Cass R., Democracy and the Problem of Free Speech (1995).

Swaine, Edward T., *Taking Care of Treaties*, 108 Colum. L. Rev. 331 (2008).

Swisher, Carl B., History of the Supreme Court of the United States: The Taney Period: 1836–1864 (1974).

Tananbaum, Duane, The Bricker Amendment Controversy: A Test of Eisenhower's Political Leadership (1988).

Thayer, James B., *The Origin and Scope of the American Doctrine of Constitutional Law*, 7 Harv. L. Rev. 17 (1893).

Torres-Spelliscy, Ciara, *The Political Branding of the Big Lie*, 2022 U. Ill. L. Rev. 1711, 1733 (2022).

Trump v. Anderson, No. 23–719, Brief of Constitutional Law Professor Mark A. Graber as Amicus Curiae in Support of Respondent, 2024 WL 513704.

Tsesis, Alexander, *Self-Government and the Declaration of Independence*, 97 Cornell L. Rev. 693 (2012).

Tsesis, Alexander, Free Speech in the Balance (2020).

Tushnet, Mark, Taking the Constitution Away from the Courts (1999).

Tushnet, Mark, *Alternative Forms of Judicial Review*, 101 Mich. L. Rev. 2781 (2003).

Tushnet, Mark, *Constitutional Hardball*, 37 J. Marshall L. Rev. 523 (2004).

TUSHNET, MARK, WEAK COURTS, STRONG RIGHTS (2008).
Tushnet, Mark, *The Story of City of Boerne v. Flores, Federalism, Rights, and Judicial Supremacy, in Constitutional Law Stories* (Michael C. Dorf, 2nd ed. 2009).
V-Dem Institute, Democracy Report 2022: Autocratization Changing Nature?, available at https://v-dem.net/publications/democracy-reports/.
Van Alstine, Michael P., *Treaties in the Supreme Court, 1901–1945*, in SLOSS, RAMSEY, DODGE (2011).
Vazquez, Carlos Manuel, *What Is Eleventh Amendment Immunity?*, 106 YALE L. J. 1683 (1997).
Waldron, Jeremy, *The Core of the Case against Judicial Review*, 115 YALE L. J. 1346 (2006).
Washington Post Editorial Board, Put Ranked-Choice Voting at the Top of Your List (Oct. 3, 2024).
Wechsler, Herbert, *The Political Safeguards of Federalism, the Role of the States in the Composition and Selection of the National Government*, 54 COLUM. L. REV. 543 (1954).
White, G. Edward, *The Transformation of the Constitutional Regime of Foreign Relations*, 85 VA. L. REV. 1 (1999).
Whittington, Keith E., CONSTITUTIONAL INTERPRETATION: TEXTUAL MEANING, ORIGINAL INTENT, AND JUDICIAL REVIEW (1999).
Whittington, Keith E., *Originalism: A Critical Introduction*, 82 FORDHAM L. REV. 375 (2013).
WHITTINGTON, KEITH E., REPUGNANT LAWS: JUDICIAL REVIEW OF ACTS OF CONGRESS FROM THE FOUNDING TO THE PRESENT (2019).
Whittington, Keith E., The Judicial Review of Congress Database, 1789–2022 (July 2022), available at https://scholar.princeton.edu/kewhitt/judicial-review-congress-database.
Witt, John Fabian, *Weaponized from the Beginning*, 4 J. FREE SPEECH L. 715 (2023).
WILSON, WOODROW, CONGRESSIONAL GOVERNMENT (1885).
World Inequality Database, https://wid.world/data/.
WRIGHT, BENJAMIN, THE GROWTH OF AMERICAN CONSTITUTIONAL LAW (1942).
Yoo, John C., *Globalism and the Constitution: Treaties, Non-Self-Execution, and the Original Understanding*, 99 COLUM. L. REV. 1955 (1999).
Zong, Lauren et al., *International Regulation of Sexual Orientation, Gender Identity, and Sexual Anatomy*, 25 GEO. J. GENDER & L. 627 (2024).

FEDERAL STATUTES

Act of May 6, 1882, 22 Stat. 58.
Act of July 5, 1884, 23 Stat. 115.
Act of March 3, 1891, 26 Stat. 1084.
Act of August 18, 1894, 28 Stat. 390.
An Act for Ascertaining and Adjusting the Titles and Claims to Land, Within the Territory of Orleans, and the District of Louisiana, 1805, ch. 26, Sec. 5, 2 Stat. 324.
An Act Confirming the Titles to Lots in the Town of Mobile, and in the Former Province of West Florida, Which Claims Have Been Favorably Reported on by the Commissioners Appointed by the United States, 1822, ch. 122, 3 Stat. 699.
An Act for Ascertaining Claims and Titles to Land Within the Territory of Florida, 1822, ch. 129, 3 Stat. 709.
Communications Act of 1934, Pub. L. No. 73-416, 48 Stat. 1064 (June 19, 1934).
Crime Control Act of 1990, Pub. L. No. 101-647, 104 Stat. 4789 (1990).

Education for All Handicapped Children Act of 1975, Pub. L. No. 94-142, 89 Stat. 773 (Nov. 29, 1975).
Electronic Signatures in Global and National Commerce Act, Pub. L. No. 106-229, 114 Stat. 464 (2000).
Fair Labor Standards Act, Pub. L. No. 75-718, 52 Stat. 1060 (June 25, 1938).
Fannie Lou Hamer, Rosa Parks, and Coretta Scott King Voting Rights Act Reauthorization and Amendments Act of 2006, Pub. L. No. 109-246, 120 Stat. 577 (July 27, 2006).
Federal Election Campaign Act Amendments of 1974, Pub. L. No. 93-443, 88 Stat. 1263 (Oct. 15, 1974).
Housing Act of 1937, Pub. L. No. 75-412, 50 Stat. 888 (Sept. 1, 1937).
Judiciary Act of 1925, Pub. L. No. 68-415, 43 Stat. 936 (1925).
National Labor Relations Act, Pub. L. No. 74-198, 49 Stat. 449 (July 5, 1935).
Religious Freedom Restoration Act of 1993, Pub. L. No. 103-141, 107 Stat. 1488 (1993).
Religious Land Use and Institutionalized Persons Act of 2000, Pub. L. No. 106-274, 114 Stat. 803 (2000).
Scott Act, Oct. 1, 1888, 25 Stat. 504.
Social Security Act, Pub. L. No. 74-721, 49 Stat. 620 (Aug. 14, 1935).
Title IX of the Education Amendments Act of 1972, Pub L. No. 92-318, 86 Stat. 235, 373 (June 23, 1972).
Voting Rights Act of 1965, Pub. L. No. 89-110, 79 Stat. 437 (1965).

OTHER GOVERNMENT DOCUMENTS

Alaska Division of Elections, Nonpartisan Top Four Primary Election, www.elections.alaska.gov/election-information/#RankedChoice
Alaska Division of Elections, RCV Detailed Report, available at www.elections.alaska.gov/results/22GENR/US%20SEN.pdf
Brief for United States as Amicus Curiae, Brown v. Bd. of Education, 347 U.S. 483 (1954) (Nos. 1, 2, 3, 4, 5), available at 1952 WL 82045.
California Supreme Court Archives, 2nd Civ. No. 17309, L.A. 21149, Fujii v. California [Fujii Case File].
Chinese Immigration: Hearing Before the House Select Comm. On Immigration and Naturalization, 51st Cong. (1890).
Executive Order, E.O. 14023, 86 Fed. Reg. 19569 (Apr. 9, 2021).
Final Report: Select Committee to Investigate the January 6th Attack on the United States Capitol, Dec. 22, 2022 (117th Cong., Second Sess., H. Rep. 117-663) ["Jan. 6 Report"].
1 Foreign Relations of the United States, 1952–1954 (William Z. Slany et al. eds., 1983).
Freedom to Vote Act, H.R. 11 (118th Cong., 1st Sess., July 18, 2023), www.congress.gov/bill/118th-congress/house-bill/11
Inquiry into Section 73.1910 of the Commission's Rules and Regulations Concerning Alternatives to the General Fairness Doctrine Obligations of Broadcast Licensees in Gen. Docket No. 84-282, 102 FCC 2d 143 (1985) [1985 Fairness Report].
International Covenant on Civil and Political Rights: Hearing Before the S. Comm. on Foreign Relations (102nd Cong., 1992).
International Human Rights Treaties: Hearings Before the S. Comm. on Foreign Relations (96th Cong., 1979).
John R. Lewis Voting Rights Advancement Act of 2023, H.R. 14 (118th Cong., 1st Sess.), available at www.congress.gov/bill/118th-congress/house-bill/14/text

Judicial Modernization and Transparency Act, S.5229, www.congress.gov/bill/118th-congress/senate-bill/5229

Message from the President of the United States Transmitting Four Treaties Pertaining to Human Rights, S. Exec. Docs. C, D, E and F, 95-2 (1978).

National Conference of State Legislatures, Initiative and Referendum States, www.ncsl.org/elections-and-campaigns/initiative-and-referendum-states (last visited Sept. 14, 2024).

National Conference of State Legislatures, School Safety: Guns in Schools (updated June 20, 2023) www.ncsl.org/education/school-safety-guns-in-schools

National Conference of State Legislatures, State Primary Election Types, available at www.ncsl.org/elections-and-campaigns/state-primary-election-types

National Endowment for Democracy, About the National Endowment for Democracy, www.ned.org/about/ (last visited Aug. 3, 2024).

Presidential Commission on the Supreme Court of the United States, Final Report (Dec. 2021).

Proposition 209, Prohibition against Discrimination or Preferential Treatment by State and Other Public Entities (Nov. 1996), at https://lao.ca.gov/ballot/1996/prop209_11_1996.html

Senate Comm. on Foreign Relations, Report on Convention against Torture and Other Cruel, Inhuman or Degrading Treatment or Punishment, S. Exec. Rep. No. 101-30 (1990).

Senate Comm. on Foreign Relations, International Covenant on Civil and Political Rights, S. Exec. Rep. No. 102-23 (1992).

Supreme Court Biennial Appointments and Term Limits Act of 2023, S.3096, www.congress.gov/bill/118th-congress/senate-bill/3096.

Treaties and Executive Agreements: Hearings Before a Subcomm. of the Senate Judiciary Comm. on S.J. Res. 1 and S.J. Res. 43 (83rd Cong., 1953).

TREATIES AND OTHER INTERNATIONAL DOCUMENTS

Treaty for the Cession of Louisiana, U.S.-Fr., Apr. 30, 1803, 8 Stat. 200.

Treaty of Amity, Settlement and Limits, U.S.-Spain, Feb. 22, 1819, 8 Stat. 252.

Burlingame Treaty, U.S.-China, July 28, 1868, 16 Stat. 739.

Treaty Concerning Immigration, U.S.-China, Nov. 17, 1880, 22 Stat. 826.

Convention on Immigration, U.S.-China, Mar. 17, 1894, 28 Stat. 1210.

Charter of the United Nations, Oct. 24, 1945, 1 UNTS 16.

Universal Declaration of Human Rights, G.A. Res. 217 (III)(A) (Dec. 10, 1948).

International Convention on the Elimination of All Forms of Racial Discrimination, *opened for signature* Dec. 21, 1965, 660 U.N.T.S. 195 (entered into force Jan. 4, 1969).

International Covenant on Economic, Social, and Cultural Rights, *opened for signature* Dec. 16, 1966, 999 U.N.T.S. 3 (entered into force Jan. 3, 1976).

International Covenant on Civil and Political Rights, *opened for signature* Dec. 16, 1966, 999 U.N.T.S. 171 (entered into force Mar. 23, 1976).

American Convention on Human Rights, Nov. 22, 1969, O.A.S.T.S. No. 36 (entered into force July 18, 1978).

Convention on the Elimination of All Forms of Discrimination Against Women, *opened for signature* Dec. 18, 1979, 1249 U.N.T.S. 13 (entered into force Sept. 3, 1981).

Convention Against Torture, *opened for signature* Dec. 10, 1984, 1465 U.N.T.S. 85 (entered into force June 26, 1987).

Convention on the Rights of the Child, *opened for signature* Nov. 20, 1989, 1577 U.N.T.S. 3 (entered into force Sept. 2, 1990).

Toonen v. Australia, Comm'n No. 488/1992, U.N. Doc. CCPR/C/50/D/488/1992 (Nov. 5, 1992).

International Fact-Checking Network, IFCN Code of Principles, at www.ifcncodeofprinciples.poynter.org/

Office of the High Commissioner of Human Rights, Status of Ratification: Interactive Dashboard, available at https://indicators.ohchr.org/ (last visited Aug. 13, 2024).

Index

Printed by Integrated Books International,
United States of America